A TEXT BOOK OF

LINEAR INTEGRATED CIRCUITS

FOR
SEMESTER – II

S.E. DEGREE COURSE IN ELECTORNICS/ELECTRONICS & COMMUNICATION/
ELECTRONICS AND TELECOMMUNICATION/INDUSTRIAL ELECTRONICS ENGINEERING

As Per New Revised Syllabus of North Maharashtra University, Jalgaon

Mrs. DEEPA S. PANDIT
B.E. (E & TC), M. Tech (Embedded Systems)
Assistant Professor, Electronics and Telecommunication Dept.
IOK, College of Engineering,
Pimple Jagtap, Pune.

LINEAR INTEGRATED CIRCUITS (S.E. : E & TC NMU) **ISBN 978-93-83971-51-0**

First Edition : **January 2014**

© : **Authors**

The text of this publication, or any part thereof, should not be reproduced or transmitted in any form or stored in any computer storage system or device for distribution including photocopy, recording, taping or information retrieval system or reproduced on any disc, tape, perforated media or other information storage device etc., without the written permission of Authors with whom the rights are reserved. Breach of this condition is liable for legal action.

Every effort has been made to avoid errors or omissions in this publication. In spite of this, errors may have crept in. Any mistake, error or discrepancy so noted and shall be brought to our notice shall be taken care of in the next edition. It is notified that neither the publisher nor the authors or seller shall be responsible for any damage or loss of action to any one, of any kind, in any manner, therefrom.

Published By : **NIRALI PRAKASHAN** Abhyudaya Pragati, 1312, Shivaji Nagar, Off J.M. Road, PUNE – 411005 Tel - (020) 25512336/37/39, Fax - (020) 25511379 Email : niralipune@pragationline.com	**Printed at** **Repro Knowledgecast Limited** **India**

DISTRIBUTION CENTRES
PUNE

Nirali Prakashan
119, Budhwar Peth, Jogeshwari Mandir Lane
Pune 411002, Maharashtra
Tel : (020) 2445 2044, 66022708, Fax : (020) 2445 1538
Email : bookorder@pragationline.com

Nirali Prakashan
S. No. 28/25, Dhyari,
Near Pari Company, Pune 411041
Tel : (020) 24690204 Fax : (020) 24690316
Email : dhyari@pragationline.com
       bookorder@pragationline.com

MUMBAI
Nirali Prakashan
385, S.V.P. Road, Rasdhara Co-op. Hsg. Society Ltd.,
Girgaum, Mumbai 400004, Maharashtra
Tel : (022) 2385 6339 / 2386 9976, Fax : (022) 2386 9976
Email : niralimumbai@pragationline.com

DISTRIBUTION BRANCHES

NAGPUR
Pratibha Book Distributors
Above Maratha Mandir, Shop No. 3, First Floor,
Rani Jhansi Square, Sitabuldi, Nagpur 440012,
Maharashtra, Tel : (0712) 254 7129

BENGALURU
Pragati Book House
House No. 1, Sanjeevappa Lane, Avenue Road Cross,
Opp. Rice Church, Bengaluru – 560002.
Tel : (080) 64513344, 64513355,
Mob : 9880582331, 9845021552
Email:bharatsavla@yahoo.com

JALGAON
Nirali Prakashan
34, V. V. Golani Market, Navi Peth, Jalgaon 425001,
Maharashtra, Tel : (0257) 222 0395
Mob : 94234 91860

KOLHAPUR
Nirali Prakashan
New Mahadvar Road,
Kedar Plaza, 1st Floor Opp. IDBI Bank
Kolhapur 416 012, Maharashtra. Mob : 9855046155

CHENNAI
Pragati Books
9/1, Montieth Road, Behind Taas Mahal, Egmore,
Chennai 600008 Tamil Nadu, Tel : (044) 6518 3535,
Mob : 94440 01782 / 98450 21552 / 98805 82331, Email : bharatsavla@yahoo.com

RETAIL OUTLETS
PUNE

Pragati Book Centre
157, Budhwar Peth, Opp. Ratan Talkies,
Pune 411002, Maharashtra
Tel : (020) 2445 8887 / 6602 2707, Fax : (020) 2445 8887

Pragati Book Centre
Amber Chamber, 28/A, Budhwar Peth,
Appa Balwant Chowk, Pune : 411002, Maharashtra,
Tel : (020) 20240335 / 66281669
Email : pbcpune@pragationline.com

Pragati Book Centre
676/B, Budhwar Peth, Opp. Jogeshwari Mandir,
Pune 411002, Maharashtra
Tel : (020) 6601 7784 / 6602 0855

PBC Book Sellers & Stationers
152, Budhwar Peth, Pune 411002, Maharashtra
Tel : (020) 2445 2254 / 6609 2463

MUMBAI
Pragati Book Corner
Indira Niwas, 111 - A, Bhavani Shankar Road, Dadar (W), Mumbai 400028, Maharashtra
Tel : (022) 2422 3526 / 6662 5254, Email : pbcmumbai@pragationline.com

www.pragationline.com   info@pragationline.com

✹ करवीर निवासिनी श्री. महालक्ष्मी देवी, कोल्हापूर
✹
यांचे चरणी अर्पण

PREFACE

It gives me an immense pleasure to present this text Book of **"Linear Integrated Circuits"** for Second Year Degree Course in Electronics Group of Engineering students. The object of this book is to present the subject matter in the most precise, compact and in a lucid manner.

The book is written mainly for the second year students of Electronics/Electronics and Communication, Electronics and Telecommunication/ Industrial Electronics Engineering sources of North Maharashtra University for the subject "Linear Integrated Circuits".

I hereby, welcome the positive changes made in this present revision of syllabus, Operational Amplifier, Op-Amp Application, Active Filter and Voltage Regulator, Comparators and Waveform Generation, A/D Interfacing Circuits and PLL.

I have tried to introduce the subject to the average students, with a large number of **Solved Examples**. The subject matter has been developed in a logical and coherent manner with neat illustrations along with a fairly large number of **Exercises**.

The main objectives of this text are :

- **To cover the basic principles of linear integrated circuits.**
- **To develop a very good understanding of the subject matter.**

My spcial thanks goes to my husband **Mr. Sheetal S. Pandit** for his constant support and help and my daughter **Akshata** for her patience.

I am very much thankful to Shri. Dineshbhai Furia and Shri. Jignesh Furia of M/s Nirali Prakashan, Pune for giving a platform to provide good inputs the students community. I am grateful to Mr. Mallikarjun Munde, a Senior Manager for his endless efforts to make this book as best as it can be. I am also thankful to Mr. Santosh Bare, Mrs. Anjali Muley, Mrs. Prajakta Shrimandilkar & Mrs. Sonal Pokharkar for their co-operation throughout the work.

I also thankful to **Mr. Pruthviraj M. More**, Branch Manager, Jalgaon office for his valuable help and efforts for promotion of my books.

Although every care has been taken to check mistakes, and errors, yet it is difficult to claim perfection. Any errors, mistakes and suggestions for the improvement of this book, brought to our notice will be thankfully acknowledged and incorporated in the next edition.

January 2014   **Authors**
Pune

SYLLABUS

UNIT I : OPERATIONAL AMPLIFIER (9 Lectures, 16 Marks)

(a) Ideal op-amp characteristics, schematic development stages of op-amp.

(b) Current sources and active loads.

(c) Difference, intermediate and output stages including Miller capacitors for frequency computation.

(d) Internal circuit of op-amp IC µA741, operational amplifier parameters, offset null techniques of op-amp features.

(e) Data sheet interpretation and data sheet study of op-amp IC 741.

(f) Measurement of op-amp parameters, effects of real operational amplifier parameters on circuit performance.

(g) Frequency response and stability, frequency and phase compensation techniques.

UNIT II : OP-AMP APPLICATIONS (9 Lectures, 16 Marks)

(a) Non-inverting amplifier and voltage follower, inverting amplifier.

(b) Peak amplifier, a.c. amplifier, AF amplifier IC LM 380.

(c) Analog adder, averaging amplifier, integrator, differentiator.

(d) Analog computation, basic building blocks, basic linear differential equation.

(e) Differential and instrumentation amplifiers using one, two and three op-amps, instrumentation amplifier IC µA 725, bridge amplifier.

(f) Voltage-to-current and current-to-voltage converters, analog multipliers, dividers.

(g) Log/antilog amplifiers.

UNIT III : ACTIVE FILTER AND VOLTAGE REGULATORS (8 Lectures, 16 Marks)

(a) Active filters : types and response.

(b) Analysis and synthesis of first, second and higher order active filters.

(c) Butterworth filters all pass filter.

(d) Voltage regulators : Series op-amp regulator, IC voltage regulator.

(e) Voltage regulator IC µA 723 and its applications as positive/negative and fixed/adjustable voltage regulators.

(f) Three terminal voltage regulators : positive/negative and fixed/adjustable voltage regulators.

(g) Dual tracking regulators, switching regulator : concept and schematic, IC MC 1723 and its application.

UNIT IV : COMPARATORS AND WAVEFORM GENERATION (8 Lectures, 16 Marks)

(a) Comparators : introduction, parameters; op-amp as comparator, comparator IC 710, peak detectors.

(b) Waveform generation : Schmitt's trigger, square-triangle wave oscillators, relaxation oscillators and pulse generators.

(c) Timer IC 555 and its use as timer circuit and multi-vibrators.

(d) Analysis and design of R-C (phase shift, wien bridge) oscillators.

(e) Voltage controlled oscillator IC SE/NE 566, function generator IC LM 8038.

(f) Clippers and clampers; precision rectifiers.

UNIT V : A/D INTERFACE CIRCUITS AND PLL (8 Lectures, 16 Marks)

(a) A/D interface circuits : Analog to digital (A/D) and digital to analog (D/A) converters.

(b) Sample and hold circuits analog multiplexers.

(c) Phase lock loop (PLL) : operating principles, lock and capture range.

(d) PLL as amplitude and frequency modulation detection, frequency shift keying (FSK) decoder, frequency synthesiser.

(e) PLL IC SE/NE 565.

❑❑❑

CONTENTS

UNIT - I
1. OPERATIONAL AMPLIFIER — 1.1 – 1.88

UNIT - II
2. OP-AMP APPLICATIONS — 2.1 – 2.108

UNIT - III
3. ACTIVE FILTER AND VOLTAGE REGULATORS — 3.1 – 3.48

UNIT - IV
4. COMPARATORS AND WAVEFORMS GENERATION — 4.1 – 4.58

UNIT - V
5. A/D INTERFACE CIRCUITS AND PLL — 5.1 – 5.28

❐❐❐

Unit I

OPERATIONAL AMPLIFIER

1.1 INTRODUCTION

The term operational amplifier or op-amp was first used by John R. Ragazzini in 1947. The op-amp is a multistage amplifier which has number of amplifier stages interconnected to each other. The first operational amplifier or op-amp was introduced in the market by Fairchild company as µA 741, which became popular within a short span of years. The op-amp is used in number of applications.

1.2 BLOCK DIAGRAM OF AN OPERATIONAL AMPLIFIER

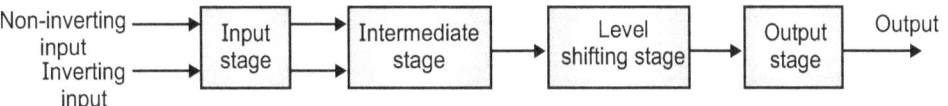

Fig. 1.1 : Block diagram of an operational amplifier

Input stage : Dual input balanced output differential amplifier.

Intermediate stage : Dual input unbalanced output differential amplifier.

Level shifting stage : Emitter follower using constant current source.

Output stage : Complementary symmetry push-pull amplifier.

An operational amplifier is a direct coupled, high gain amplifier which consists of one or more differential amplifiers and a level translator and an output stage. The output stage is a push-pull or push-pull complementary symmetry pair.

The operational amplifier is a versatile device that can be used to amplify DC as well as AC input signals. It was originally designed for computing mathematical functions as addition, subtraction, multiplication and integration.

If the suitable feedback components are added, the modern day op-amp can be used for a variety of applications such as AC and DC signal amplification, active filters, oscillators, comparators, regulators and others.

The input stage is the dual input balanced output differential amplifier. This stage provides most of the gain of the amplifier and also sets the input resistance of the op-amp. The second stage is the intermediate stage i.e. another differential amplifier which is driven by the output of the first stage. In most amplifiers second stage is dual input - unbalanced output. Due to direct coupling between all the stages, the DC voltage at the output of intermediate stage goes above the ground level. To shift that DC level back to the ground, a level shifting or level translator circuit is used.

The final stage is the output stage. The output stage is usually a push-pull complementary amplifier. The output stage increases the output voltage swing and raises the current supplying capability of the op-amp. Output stage also provides low output resistance.

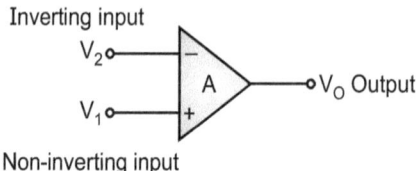

Fig. 1.2 : Symbol for op-amp

In figure, V_1 = Voltage at the non-inverting input (volts)

V_2 = Voltage at the inverting input (volts)

V_O = Output voltage (volts)

A = Large signal voltage gain

1.3 DIFFERENTIAL AMPLIFIER AND ITS ANALYSIS

Differential amplifier is the basic building block of the operational amplifiers. The differential amplifier amplifies the difference between the two input signals V_{in_1} and V_{in_2}.

Let us consider, the two identical emitter biased circuits in which transistor Q_1 has the same characteristics as transistor Q_2.

$R_{E_1} = R_{E_2}$, $R_{C_1} = R_{C_2}$ and the magnitude of $+V_{CC}$ is equal to the magnitude of $-V_{EE}$.

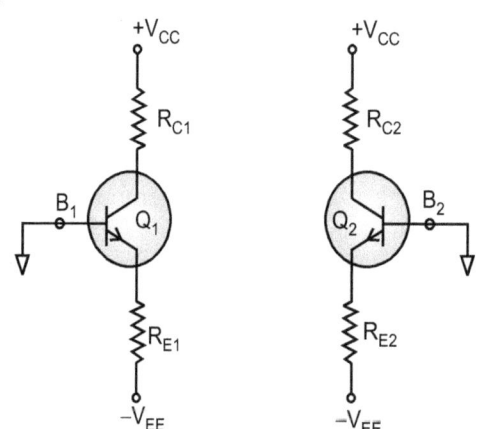

Fig. 1.3 : Two identical emitter-biased circuits

To obtain a single circuit, one must reconnect these two circuit as follows :

1. Reconnect $+V_{CC}$ supply voltages of the two circuits as the voltages are of the same polarity and amplitude. Similarly reconnect $-V_{EE}$ supply voltages.

2. Reconnect the emitter E_1 of transistor Q_1 to the emitter E_2 of transistor Q_2.
3. Show input signal V_{in_1} applied to the base B_1 and V_{in_2} applied to the base B_2 of the transistor Q_2.

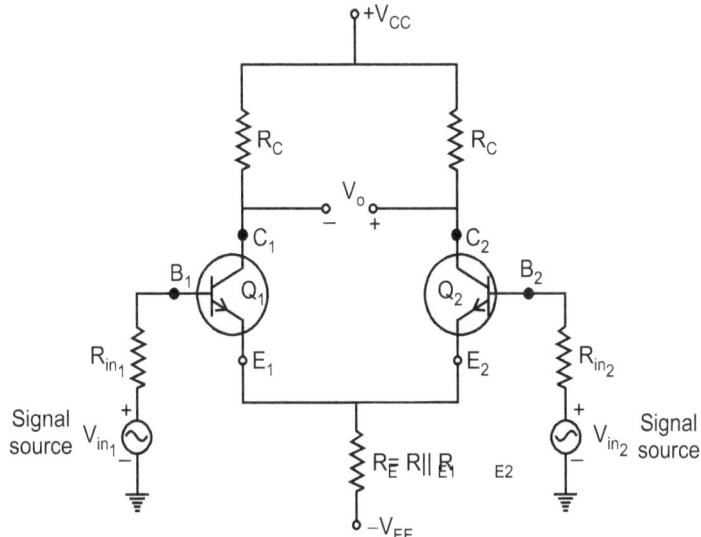

Fig. 1.4 : Dual input balanced output differential amplifier

1.3.1 Operation of Differential Amplifier

The basic operation of differential amplifier is divided into two parts:
1. Operation in differential mode.
2. Operation in common mode.

Operation in differential mode:

To understand the operation in differential mode, the two inputs V_{in1} and V_{in_2} are applied with the same magnitude but opposite phase i.e. $V_{in_1} = -V_{in_2}$. To obtain these signals center tap transformer is used.

During the positive half cycle of V_s, the input to the transistor Q_1 is positive sinusoidal signal and input to the transistor Q_2 is negative sinusoidal signal because of the center tapped transformer. At the output of the two collectors, we get 180° out of phase signals with respect to their input signals as shown in Fig. 1.5. The output voltage is the difference between the outputs of the two collectors. Therefore, the amplitude of the output V_o is doubled. Similarly, the equal and opposite signal voltages appear across R_E and cancels each other. Therefore, the signal current flowing through R_E is equal to zero. Thus, R_E does not introduce negative feedback in differential mode.

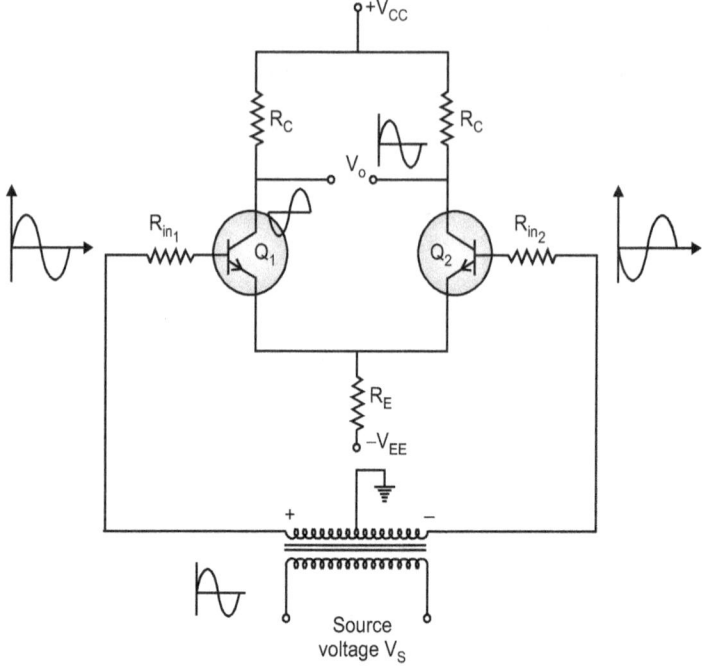

Fig. 1.5 : Operation in differential mode

Common Mode Operation :

To understand the operation of differential amplifier in common mode, the signal with same magnitude and phase is applied to both the transistors. Therefore $V_{in_1} = V_{in_2} = V_S$.

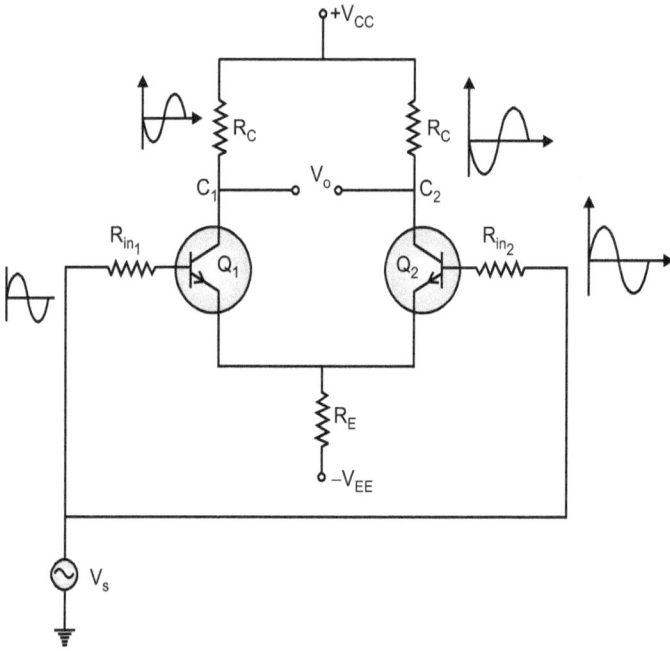

Fig. 1.6 : Common mode operation

As the same input is applied, we get same output at both the collectors. Therefore, the net output between the two collectors is zero. Practically, small output voltage appears due to inequalities or mismatching of the transistors.

Since the two inputs to the transistors are same the voltage across R_E will be added which introduces a negative feedback.

1.4 DIFFERENTIAL AMPLIFIER CONFIGURATIONS

There are four differential amplifier configurations :

1. Dual input balanced output differential amplifier,
2. Dual input unbalanced output differential amplifier,
3. Single input balanced output differential amplifier,
4. Single input unbalanced output differential amplifier.

A multistage amplifier with a desired voltage gain can be designed by using a direct connection between successive stages of differential amplifiers. Direct connection between stages removes the lower cut off frequency. Therefore, the differential amplifiers are capable of amplifying DC as well as AC input signals.

1.4.1 Dual Input Balanced Output Differential Amplifier

Fig. 1.4 shows the dual input balanced output differential amplifier. Here V_{in_1} and V_{in_2} acts as input to the bases B_1 and B_2 of transistors Q_1 and Q_2 respectively. The output V_O is measured between two collectors C_1 and C_2 which are at the same DC potential. Since, the output is at the same DC potential with respect to ground, it is called as balanced output.

1.4.1.1 DC Analysis

DC analysis means operating point calculation for the differential amplifier i.e. I_{CQ} and V_{CEQ}. To calculate the operating point values obtain the DC equivalent circuit of differential amplifier by reducing V_{in_1} and V_{in_2} = 0.

Fig. 1.7 shows the DC equivalent circuit for the dual input balanced output differential amplifier. Internal resistances of the input signals are denoted by R_{in} because $R_{in_1} = R_{in_2}$ since both emitter-biased sections are symmetrical.

Here both sections are identical, so to calculate I_{CQ} and V_{CEQ} apply KVL to the base-emitter loop of the transistor Q_1.

$$- R_{in} I_B - V_{BE} - 2 I_E R_E + V_{EE} = 0$$

$$I_B = \frac{I_E}{\beta_{dc}} \quad \text{since} \quad I_C = I_E$$

$$\frac{R_{in}I_E}{\beta_{dc}} + V_{BE} + 2I_ER_E = V_{EE}$$

$$\frac{R_{in}I_E}{\beta_{dc}} + 2I_ER_E = V_{EE} - V_{BE}$$

$$\left[\frac{R_{in}}{\beta_{dc}} + 2R_E\right]I_E = V_{EE} - V_{BE}$$

$$I_E = \frac{V_{EE} - V_{BE}}{\frac{R_{in}}{\beta_{dc}} + 2R_E}$$

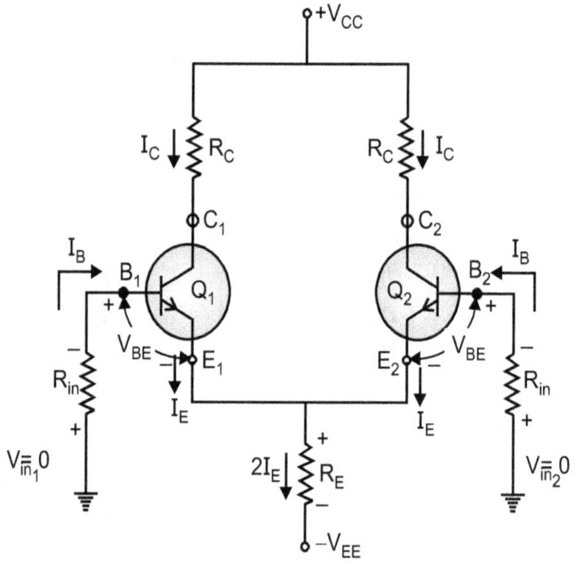

Fig. 1.7 : DC equivalent circuit for dual input balanced output differential amplifier

Generally, R_E is chosen such that

$$\frac{R_{in}}{\beta_{dc}} << 2R_E$$

$$I_E = \frac{V_{EE} - V_{BE}}{2R_E}$$

∴
$$\boxed{I_{CQ} = \frac{V_{EE} - V_{BE}}{2R_E}}$$

From the above equation by selecting the proper value of R_E, we can obtain a desired value of emitter current. Emitter current is independent of the collector resistance R_C.

The voltage at the collector V_C is

$$V_C = V_{CC} - I_C R_C$$

∴ Collector to emitter voltage V_{CE} is

$$V_{CE} = V_C - V_E$$
$$= V_{CC} - I_C R_C - (-V_{BE})$$
$$\boxed{V_{CEQ} = V_{CC} - I_C R_C + V_{BE}}$$

1.4.1.2 AC Analysis

AC analysis means calculation of voltage gain and input resistance R_i of the differential amplifiers. To obtain the AC equivalent circuit of the differential amplifier,

1. Set the DC voltage $+V_{CC}$ and $-V_{EE}$ at zero.
2. Substitute the small signal T-equivalent models.

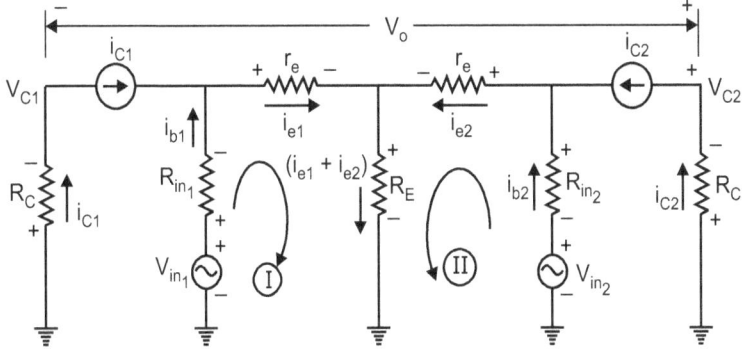

(a) AC equivalent circuit

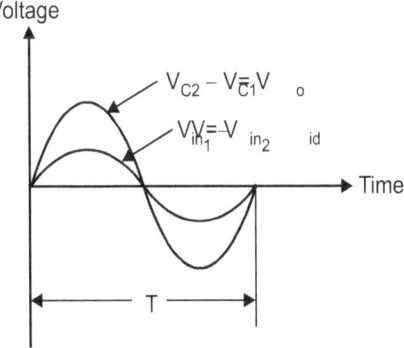

(b) Input and output waveforms

Fig. 1.8 : Dual input balanced output differential amplifier

1. **Differential Gain (A_d) :**

   Here $I_{E_1} = I_{E_2}$ ∴ $r_{e_1} = r_{e_2}$

   The AC emitter resistance of transistor Q_1 and Q_2 is simply denoted by r_e.

The voltage across each collector resistor is shown out of phase by 180° with respect to the input voltages V_{in_1} and V_{in_2}. This polarity assignment is in accordance with the common emitter configuration.

Apply KVL for loop I and II.

$$-V_{in_1} + R_{in_1} \cdot i_{b_1} + r_e \cdot i_{e_1} + (i_{e_1} + i_{e_2}) R_E = 0$$

$$V_{in_1} - R_{in_1} \cdot i_{b_1} - r_e \cdot i_{e_1} - (i_{e_1} + i_{e_2}) R_E = 0 \qquad \ldots (1.1)$$

$$-V_{in_2} + R_{in_2} \cdot i_{b_2} + r_e \cdot i_{e_2} + (i_{e_1} + i_{e_2}) R_E = 0$$

$$V_{in_2} - R_{in_2} \cdot i_{b_2} - r_e \cdot i_{e_2} - (i_{e_1} + i_{e_2}) R_E = 0 \qquad \ldots (1.2)$$

$$i_{b_1} = \frac{i_{e_1}}{\beta_{ac}} \qquad\qquad i_{b_2} = \frac{i_{e_2}}{\beta_{ac}}$$

$$V_{in_1} - \frac{R_{in_1}}{\beta_{ac}} \cdot i_{e_1} - r_e \cdot i_{e_1} - (i_{e_1} + i_{e_2}) R_E = 0$$

$$V_{in_2} - \frac{R_{in_2}}{\beta_{ac}} \cdot i_{e_2} - r_e \cdot i_{e_2} - (i_{e_1} + i_{e_2}) R_E = 0$$

$$\frac{R_{in_1}}{\beta_{ac}} \cdot i_{e_1} + r_e \cdot i_{e_1} + (i_{e_1} + i_{e_2}) R_E = V_{in_1}$$

$$\frac{R_{in_2}}{\beta_{ac}} \cdot i_{e_2} + r_e \cdot i_{e_2} + (i_{e_1} + i_{e_2}) R_E = V_{in_2}$$

$\frac{R_{in_1}}{\beta_{ac}}$ and $\frac{R_{in_2}}{\beta_{ac}}$ values are very small. So these values can be neglected for simplicity.

$$(r_e + R_E) i_{e_1} + (R_E) \cdot i_{e_2} = V_{in_1} \qquad \ldots (1.3)$$

$$(R_E) \cdot i_{e_1} + (r_e + R_E) \cdot i_{e_2} = V_{in_2} \qquad \ldots (1.4)$$

Equations (1.3) and (1.4) can be solved simultaneously for i_{e_1} and i_{e_2} by using Crammer's rule.

$$\Delta = \begin{vmatrix} r_e + R_E & R_E \\ R_E & r_e + R_E \end{vmatrix}$$

$$= (r_e + R_E)^2 - R_E^2$$

$$i_{e_1} = \frac{\begin{vmatrix} V_{in_1} & R_E \\ V_{in_2} & r_e + R_E \end{vmatrix}}{\Delta}$$

$$i_{e_1} = \frac{V_{in_1}(r_e + R_E) - (R_E) V_{in_2}}{(r_e + R_E)^2 - R_E^2}$$

$$i_{e_2} = \frac{\begin{vmatrix} r_e + R_E & V_{in_1} \\ R_E & V_{in_2} \end{vmatrix}}{\Delta}$$

$$= \frac{(r_e + R_E) V_{in_2} - (R_E) V_{in_1}}{\Delta}$$

$$= \frac{(r_e + R_E) V_{in_2} - (R_E) V_{in_1}}{(r_e + R_E)^2 - (R_E)^2}$$

The output voltage is $V_o = V_{C_2} - V_{C_1}$

$$V_o = -R_C i_{c_2} - (-R_C i_{c_1}) = R_C i_{c_1} - R_C i_{c_2}$$

$$= R_C \left(i_{c_1} - i_{c_2} \right)$$

$$= R_C \left(i_{e_1} - i_{e_2} \right)$$

Substitute the values of i_{e_1} and i_{e_2}.

$$V_o = R_C \left[\frac{(r_e + R_E) V_{in_1} - (R_E) V_{in_2}}{(r_e + R_E)^2 - (R_E)^2} - \frac{(r_e + R_E) V_{in_2} - (R_E) V_{in_1}}{(r_e + R_E)^2 - (R_E)^2} \right]$$

$$V_o = R_C \left[\frac{(r_e + R_E)(V_{in_1} - V_{in_2}) + R_E (V_{in_1} - V_{in_2})}{(r_e + R_E)^2 - (R_E)^2} \right]$$

$$V_o = R_C \left[\frac{(r_e + 2R_E)(V_{in_1} - V_{in_2})}{r_e^2 + 2r_e R_E + R_E^2 - R_E^2} \right] = R_C \left[\frac{(r_e + 2R_E)(V_{in_1} - V_{in_2})}{r_e^2 + 2r_e R_E} \right]$$

$$= R_C \left[\frac{(r_e + 2R_E)(V_{in_1} - V_{in_2})}{r_e (r_e + 2R_E)} \right] = R_C \cdot \frac{(V_{in_1} - V_{in_2})}{r_e}$$

$$= \frac{R_C}{r_e} (V_{in_1} - V_{in_2})$$

$$V_O = \frac{R_C}{r_e} \cdot V_{id}$$

$$\boxed{A_d = \frac{V_O}{V_{id}} = \frac{R_C}{r_e}}$$

2. Differential Input Resistance (R_i):

Differential input resistance is defined as the equivalent resistance that would be measured at input terminal with the other terminal grounded. To determine input resistance R_{i_1}, make the signal source V_{in_2} at zero. Similarly to determine the R_{i_2}, set the V_{in_1} at zero. Usually, R_{in_1} and R_{in_2} are very small and hence will be ignored in the derivation.

$$R_{i_1} = \left. \left| \frac{V_{in_1}}{i_{b_1}} \right| \right|_{V_{in_2} = 0}$$

$$= \left. \left| \frac{V_{in_1}}{i_{e_1}/\beta_{ac}} \right| \right|_{V_{in_2} = 0}$$

Substitute the value of i_{e_1},

$$= \frac{V_{in_1} \beta_{ac}}{\dfrac{(r_e + R_E) V_{in_1} - (R_E) V_{in_2}}{(r_e + R_E)^2 - (R_E)^2}}$$

$$= \frac{\beta_{ac} V_{in_1}}{\dfrac{(r_e + R_E) V_{in_1} - (R_E) V_{in_2}}{r_e (r_e + 2R_E)}}$$

$$R_{i_1} = \frac{\beta_{ac} V_{in_1}}{\dfrac{(r_e + R_E) V_{in_1} - 0}{r_e (r_e + 2R_E)}}$$

$$= \frac{\beta_{ac} V_{in_1} \left(r_e^2 + 2R_E \, r_e \right)}{(r_e + R_E) V_{in_1}}$$

$$= \frac{\beta_{ac} \, r_e (r_e + 2R_E)}{(r_e + R_E)}$$

Generally $R_E \gg r_e$ ∴ $(r_e + 2R_E) = 2R_E$ and $(r_e + R_E) = R_E$

∴ $$R_{i_1} = \frac{\beta_{ac} r_e \times 2R_E}{R_E}$$

∴ $$\boxed{R_{i_1} = 2\beta_{ac} r_e}$$

Similarly,

$$R_{i_2} = \left|\frac{V_{in_2}}{i_{b_2}}\right|_{V_{in_1} = 0}$$

$$= \left|\frac{V_{in_2}}{i_{e_2}/\beta_{ac}}\right|_{V_{in_1} = 0}$$

$$= \frac{\beta_{ac} V_{in_2}}{\dfrac{(r_e + R_E) V_{in_2} - R_E(0)}{(r_e + R_E)^2 - (R_E)^2}}$$

$$= \frac{\beta_{ac} V_{in_2} (r_e^2 + 2R_E r_e)}{(r_e + R_E) V_{in_2}}$$

$$= \frac{\beta_{ac} r_e (r_e + 2R_E)}{r_e + R_E}$$

$$= \frac{\beta_{ac} r_e \, 2R_E}{R_E}$$

∴ $$\boxed{R_{i_2} = 2\beta_{ac} r_e}$$

3. Output Resistance (R_o):

Output resistance is defined as the equivalent resistance that would be measured at either output terminals w.r.t. ground. Therefore, the output resistance R_o, measured between collector C_1 and ground is equal to that of the collector resistor R_C. Similarly, R_{o_2} measured at collector C_2 w.r.t. ground is equal to that of the collector resistor R_C. Thus,

$$R_{o_1} = R_{o_2} = R_C$$

The current gain of the differential amplifier is undefined. Therefore, common emitter differential amplifier is a small signal amplifier used as a voltage amplifier not as a current or power amplifier.

1.4.1.3 AC Analysis using h-parameters

For AC analysis the two input signals should be equal in magnitude and 180° out of phase w.r.t. each other.

Hence, $V_{in_1} = V_{in_2} = \dfrac{V_{in}}{2}$

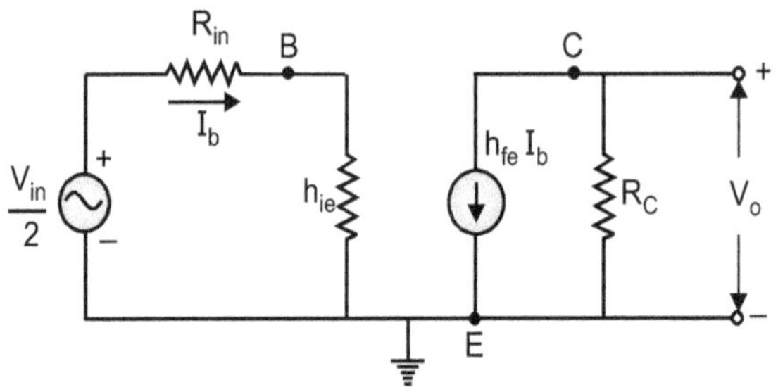

Fig. 1.9 : h-parameter equivalent circuit

Apply KVL to the input side, we get,

$$\dfrac{V_{in}}{2} = I_b R_{in} + h_{ie} I_b$$

∴ $I_b = \dfrac{V_{in}}{2(R_{in} + h_{ie})}$

Apply KVL to the output side, we get,

$$V_o = -h_{fe} I_b R_C$$

Substitute the value for I_b into this equation.

$$V_o = \dfrac{-h_{fe} R_C V_{in}}{2(R_{in} + h_{ie})}$$

$$\dfrac{V_o}{V_{in}} = \dfrac{-h_{fe} R_C}{2(R_{in} + h_{ie})}$$

The negtive sign indicates the phase relationship between input V_{in} and output V_o. i.e. 180° out of phase.

1. **Differential Gain (A_d) :**

   Differential input voltage V_{id} is given by

   $$V_{id} = V_1 - V_2$$

   $$= \dfrac{V_{in}}{2} - \left(-\dfrac{V_{in}}{2}\right)$$

   $$= V_{in}$$

$$A_d = \frac{V_o}{V_{id}} = \frac{V_o}{V_{in}}$$

$$\boxed{A_d = \frac{-h_{fe} R_C}{2(R_{in} + h_{ie})}}$$

2. Common Mode Gain (A_c):

For common mode connection,

$$V_{in_1} = V_{in_2} = V_{in}$$

So common mode input signal is the average of two input signals.

∴
$$V_c = \frac{V_{in_1} + V_{in_2}}{2}$$

$$= \frac{V_{in} + V_{in}}{2} = V_{in}$$

The h-parameter AC equivalent circuit for common mode operation is shown in Fig. 1.10.

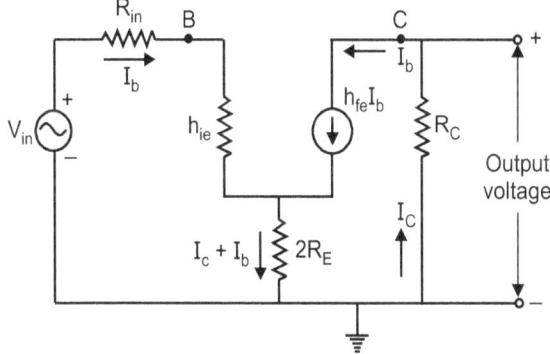

Fig. 1.10 : AC equivalent circuit using h-parameter for common mode operation

Apply KVL to the input side, we get,

$$V_{in} = I_b R_{in} + I_b h_{ie} + 2R_E (I_c + I_b)$$

But
$$I_c = h_{fe} I_b$$

∴
$$V_{in} = I_b R_{in} + I_b h_{ie} + 2R_E (1 + h_{fe}) I_b$$

$$= I_b \left[R_{in} + h_{ie} + (1 + h_{fe}) 2R_E \right]$$

∴
$$I_b = \frac{V_{in}}{\left[R_{in} + h_{ie} + (1 + h_{fe}) 2R_E \right]}$$

The output voltage V_o is given by

$$V_o = -I_C R_C = -h_{fe} I_b R_C$$

$$V_o = \frac{-h_{fe} \times V_{in} \times R_C}{(R_{in} + h_{ie}) + (1 + h_{fe}) 2R_E}$$

$$V_o = \frac{-h_{fe} V_{in} R_C}{(R_{in} + h_{ie}) + [(1 + h_{fe}) 2R_E]}$$

$$\boxed{A_C = \frac{V_o}{V_{in}} = \frac{-h_{fe} R_C}{(R_{in} + h_{ie}) + [(1 + h_{fe}) 2R_E]}}$$

3. **Differential Input Resistance (R_i) :**

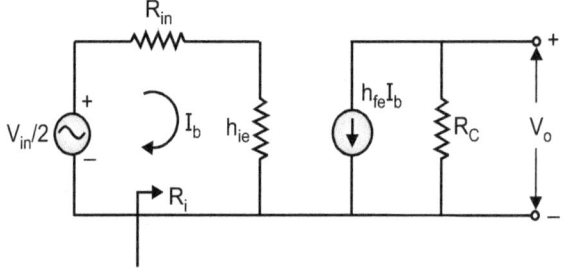

Fig. 1.11 : h-parameter equivalent circuit for differential input resistance

Apply KVL to the input side,

$$\frac{V_{in}}{2} = I_b R_{in} + I_b h_{ie}$$

$$= I_b (R_{in} + h_{ie})$$

$$\frac{V_{in}}{I_b} = 2 (R_{in} + h_{ie})$$

∴ $\boxed{R_i = 2 (R_{in} + h_{ie})}$

4. **Output Resistance (R_o) :**

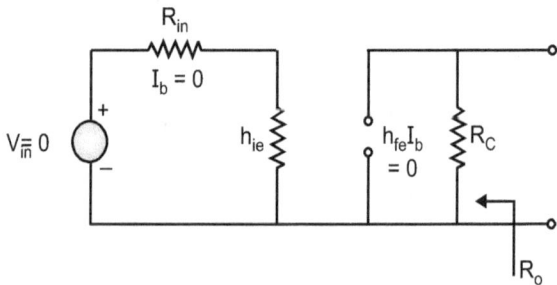

Fig. 1.12 : h-parameter equivalent circuit for differential output resistance

Here V_{in} = 0, I_b = 0, therefore, $h_{fe} I_b$ = 0 therefore the current source acts as a open circuit.

For the circuit shown above,

$$R_o = R_C$$

1.4.2 Dual Input Unbalanced Output Differential Amplifier

In this configuration, two input signals are used but the output is measured at only one of the collector w.r.t. ground. Therefore, the output is called unbalanced. The output is unbalanced because the collector at which the output voltage is measured at some finite DC potential w.r.t. ground means there is some DC voltage at the output terminal without any input signal applied.

1.4.2.1 DC Analysis

DC analysis is same as that of the dual input balanced output differential amplifier because biasing arrangements are same for both configurations.

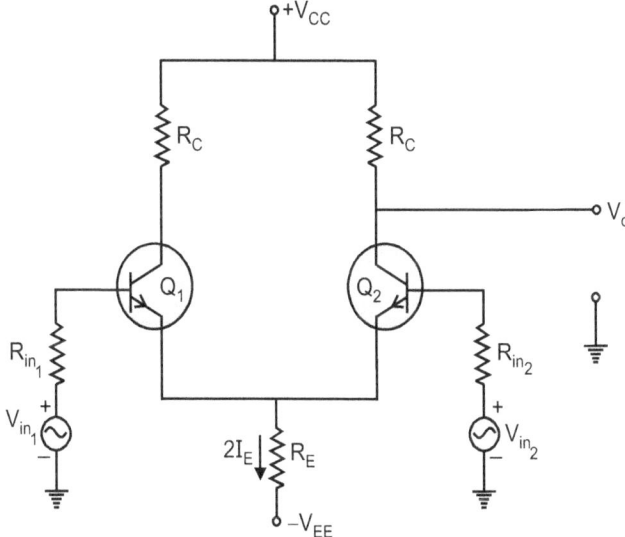

Fig. 1.13 : Dual input unbalanced output differential amplifier

$$I_E = I_{CQ} = \frac{V_{EE} - V_{BE}}{2R_E}$$

$$V_{CEQ} = V_{CC} + V_{BE} - R_C I_{CQ}$$

1.4.2.2 AC Analysis

Apply KVL for loop 1 and loop 2.

$$V_{in_1} - R_{in_1} \cdot i_{b_1} - r_e \cdot i_{e_1} - R_E \left(i_{e_1} + i_{e_2} \right) = 0$$

$$V_{in_2} - R_{in_2} \cdot i_{b_2} - r_e \cdot i_{e_2} - R_E (i_{e_1} + i_{e_2}) = 0$$

$$i_{e_1} = \frac{(r_e + R_E) V_{in_1} - (R_E) V_{in_2}}{(r_e + R_E)^2 - (R_E)^2}$$

$$i_{e_2} = \frac{(r_e + R_E) V_{in_2} - (R_E) V_{in_1}}{(r_e + R_E)^2 - (R_E)^2}$$

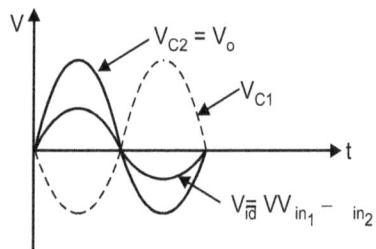

(a) AC equivalent circuit

(b) Input and output waveforms

Fig. 1.14 : Dual input unbalanced output differential amplifier

The output voltage is

$$V_o = V_{C_2} = -R_C i_{c_2} \quad \text{since } i_c \approx i_e$$

$$V_o = -R_C \frac{(r_e + R_E) V_{in_2} - (R_E) V_{in_1}}{r_e^2 + 2 r_e R_E}$$

Generally, $R_E \gg r_e$; here $(r_e + R_E) \approx R_E$ and $(r_e + 2R_E) \approx 2R_E$.

$$\therefore \quad V_o = R_C \frac{(R_E) V_{in_1} - (R_E) V_{in_2}}{2 r_e R_E} = R_C \frac{R_E (V_{in_1} - V_{in_2})}{2 r_e R_E}$$

$$= \frac{R_C}{2 r_e} (V_{in_1} - V_{in_2})$$

$$V_o = \frac{R_C}{2r_e} V_{id}$$

$$\boxed{A_d = \frac{V_o}{V_{id}} = \frac{R_C}{2r_e}}$$

The voltage gain of dual input unbalanced output differential amplifier is half of the gain of the dual input balanced output differential amplifier.

In dual input unbalanced output differential amplifier the DC voltage at the output terminal is the error voltage in the desired output signal. Therefore, to reduce the undesired DC voltage to zero, this configuration is generally followed by a level translator circuit.

1.4.2.3 AC Analysis using h-parameters

1. Differential gain, $A_d = \dfrac{h_{fe} R_C}{2(R_{in} + h_{ie})}$

2. Input resistance, $R_i = 2(R_s + h_{ie})$

3. Output resistance, $R_o = R_C$

The input and output resistance R_i and R_o have remain unchanged.

1.4.3 Single Input Balanced Output Differential Amplifier

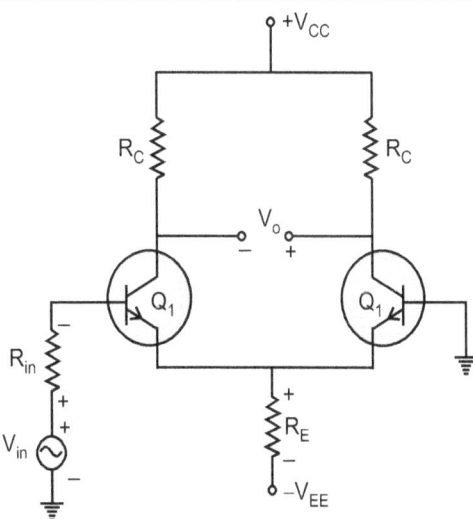

Fig. 1.15 : Single input balanced output differential amplifier

Fig. 1.15 shows the single input balanced output differential amplifier. Here the input is applied to the base of transistor Q_1, and the output is measured between the two collectors, which are at the same potential.

1.4.3.1 DC Analysis

DC analysis procedure and bias equations are same to those of the previous two configurations.

$$I_E = I_{CQ} = \frac{V_{EE} - V_{BE}}{2R_E + R_{in}/\beta_{dc}}$$

$$V_{CE} = V_{CEQ} = V_{CC} + V_{BE} - R_C I_{CQ}$$

1.4.3.2 AC Analysis

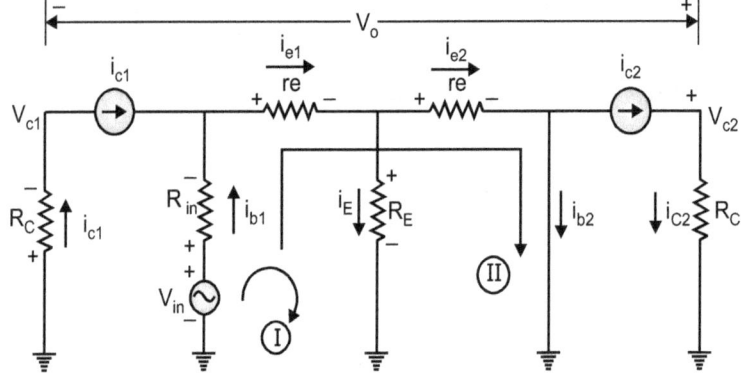

(a) AC equivalent circuit

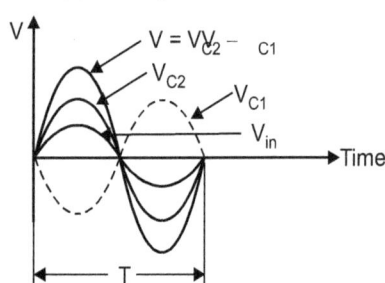

(b) Input - output waveforms

Fig. 1.16 : Single input balanced output differential amplifier

1. **Differential Gain (A_d) :**

   Apply KVL to loop I and II,

   $$V_{in} - R_{in} i_{b_1} - r_e i_{e_1} - R_E I_E = 0 \qquad \text{... (1.5)}$$

   $$V_{in} - R_{in} i_{b_1} - r_e i_{e_1} - r_e i_{e_2} = 0 \qquad \text{... (1.6)}$$

   $$I_E = (i_{e_1} - i_{e_2}), \quad i_{b_1} = \frac{i_{e_1}}{\beta_{ac}} \quad \text{and} \quad i_{b_2} = \frac{i_{e_2}}{\beta_{ac}}$$

$$V_{in} - \frac{R_{in}}{\beta_{ac}} i_{e_1} - r_e i_{e_1} - (R_E)(i_{e_1} - i_{e_2}) = 0$$

$$V_{in} - \left(\frac{R_{in}}{\beta_{AC}} + r_e + R_E\right) i_{e_1} - R_E i_{e_2} = 0$$

$$(r_e + R_E) i_{e_1} - R_E i_{e_2} = V_{in} \qquad \ldots (1.7)$$

Since $\frac{R_{in}}{\beta_{ac}}$ is small

$$V_{in} - \frac{R_{in}}{\beta_{ac}} i_{e_1} - r_e i_{e_1} - r_e i_{e_2} = 0$$

$$V_{in} - \left(\frac{R_{in}}{\beta_{ac}} + r_e\right) i_{e_1} - r_e i_{e_2} = 0$$

$$V_{in} - r_e i_{e_1} - r_e i_{e_2} = 0$$

$$r_e i_{e_1} + r_e i_{e_2} = V_{in} \qquad \ldots (1.8)$$

$$i_{e_1} = \frac{\begin{vmatrix} V_{in} & -R_E \\ V_{in} & r_e \end{vmatrix}}{\begin{vmatrix} r_e + R_E & -R_E \\ r_e & r_e \end{vmatrix}}$$

$$= \frac{r_e V_{in} + R_E V_{in}}{r_e(r_e + R_E) + R_E r_e}$$

$$= \frac{(r_e + R_E) V_{in}}{r_e^2 + r_e R_E + R_E r_e}$$

$$= \frac{(r_e + R_E) V_{in}}{r_e^2 + 2 r_e R_E}$$

$$= \frac{(r_e + R_E) V_{in}}{r_e (r_e + 2R_E)}$$

$$i_{e_2} = \frac{\begin{vmatrix} r_e + R_E & V_{in} \\ r_e & V_{in} \end{vmatrix}}{\begin{vmatrix} r_e + R_E & -R_E \\ r_e & r_e \end{vmatrix}}$$

$$= \frac{(r_e + R_E) V_{in} - r_e V_{in}}{r_e(r_e + R_E) + r_e R_E}$$

$$= \frac{R_E V_{in}}{r_e^2 + 2 r_e R_E}$$

$$= \frac{R_E V_{in}}{r_e (r_e + 2R_E)}$$

$$\begin{aligned} V_o &= V_{C_2} - V_{C_1} \\ &= R_C i_{c_2} - (-R_C i_{c_1}) \\ &= R_C i_{c_2} + R_C i_{c_1} \\ &= R_C (i_{c_2} + i_{c_1}) \end{aligned}$$

$$\therefore i_{c_1} \approx i_{e_1}, \quad i_{c_2} \approx i_{e_2}$$

$$V_o = R_C \left[\frac{(r_e + R_E) V_{in}}{r_e (r_e + 2R_E)} + \frac{R_E V_{in}}{r_e (r_e + 2R_E)} \right]$$

$$= R_C \left[\frac{r_e V_{in} + R_E V_{in} + R_E V_{in}}{r_e (r_e + 2R_E)} \right]$$

$$= R_C \frac{(r_e + 2R_E) V_{in}}{r_e (r_e + 2R_E)}$$

$$V_o = \frac{R_C}{r_e} V_{in}$$

$$\therefore \boxed{A_d = \frac{V_o}{V_{in}} = \frac{R_C}{r_e}}$$

2. **Differential Input Resistance (R_i) :**

$$R_i = 2\beta_{ac} r_e$$

3. **Output Resistance (R_o) :**

$$R_{o_1} = R_{o_2} = R_C$$

1.4.4 Single Input Unbalanced Output Differential Amplifier

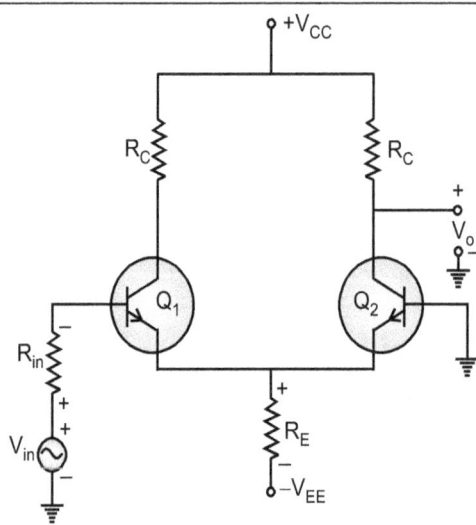

Fig. 1.17 : Single input unbalanced output differential amplifier

This differential amplifier configuration is not used commonly because this configuration requires more components as well as gives less voltage gain. There is a DC output voltage without any input signal applied.

1.4.4.1 DC Analysis

The DC analysis is same as the previous one.

$$I_E = I_{CQ} = \frac{V_{EE} - V_{BE}}{2R_E + R_{in}/\beta_{dc}}$$

$$V_{CE} = V_{CEQ} = V_{CC} + V_{BE} - R_C I_{CQ}$$

1.4.4.2 AC Analysis

The output voltage is $\quad V_o = V_{C_2} = R_C i_{C_2} = R_C i_{e_2}$

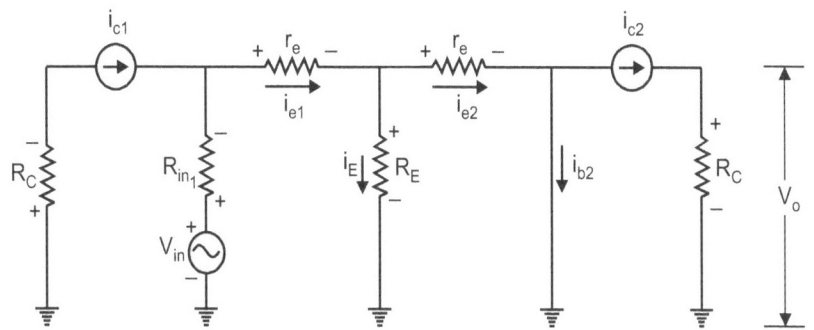

(a) AC equivalent circuit

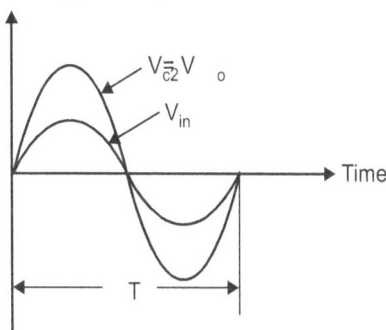

(b) Input - output waveforms

Fig. 1.18

1. **Differential Gain (A_d) :**

$$V_o = R_C \frac{(R_E) V_{in}}{r_e (r_e + 2R_E)} = R_C \frac{R_E V_{in}}{r_e (2R_E)} \quad \text{if } R_E \gg r_e$$

$$= \frac{R_C}{2r_e} \cdot V_{in}$$

$$\therefore \quad \boxed{A_d = \frac{V_o}{V_{in}} = \frac{R_C}{2r_e}}$$

2. **Differential Input Resistance (R_i):**

$$R_i = 2\beta_{ac} r_e \text{ if } R_E \gg r_e$$

3. **Output Resistance R_o:**

$$R_o = R_C$$

1.5 SUMMARY OF ALL THE FOUR CONFIGURATIONS USING r PARAMETERS

Configuration	Differential gain (A_d)	Input resistance (R_i)	Output resistance (R_o)
Dual input balanced output differential amplifier	$\dfrac{R_C}{r_e}$	$2\beta_{ac} r_e$	R_C
Dual input unbalanced output differential amplifier	$\dfrac{R_C}{2r_e}$	$2\beta_{ac} r_e$	R_C
Single input balanced output differential amplifier	$\dfrac{R_C}{r_e}$	$2\beta_{ac} r_e$	R_C
Single input unbalanced output differential amplifier	$\dfrac{R_C}{2r_e}$	$2\beta_{ac} r_e$	R_C

1.5.1 Summary of Configurations using h-Parameters

1. Dual input balanced output differential amplifier.
2. Single input balanced output differential amplifier.

$$\text{Differential gain } (A_d) = \frac{h_{fe} R_C}{(R_{in} + h_{ie})}$$

$$\text{Differential input resistance } (R_i) = 2(R_{in} + h_{ie})$$

$$\text{Output resistance } (R_o) = R_C$$

3. Dual input unbalanced output differential amplifier.
4. Single input unbalanced output differential amplifier.

$$\text{Differential gain } (A_d) = \frac{h_{fe} R_C}{2(R_{in} + h_{ie})}$$

$$\text{Differential input resistance } (R_i) = 2(R_{in} + h_{ie})$$

$$\text{Output resistance } (R_o) = R_C$$

Example 1.1 :

The following specifications are given for the dual input balanced output differential amplifier :

$R_C = 2.2\ k\Omega$, $R_E = 4.7\ k\Omega$, $R_{in_1} = R_{in_2} = 50\ \Omega$, $+V_{CC} = 10\ V$, $-V_{EE} = -10\ V$ and the transistor is the CA 3086 with $\beta_{ac} = \beta_{dc} = 100$ and $V_{BE} = 0.715\ V$.

Determine :

1. I_{CQ} and V_{CEQ} values,
2. The voltage gain,
3. Input resistance and output resistance.

Solution :

$$I_{CQ} = I_E = \frac{V_{EE} - V_{BE}}{\frac{R_{in}}{\beta_{dc}} + 2R_E}$$

$$= \frac{10 - 0.715}{\frac{50}{100} + 9400}$$

$$= 0.988\ mA$$

$$V_{CEQ} = V_{CC} + V_{BE} - R_C I_{CQ}$$

$$= 10 + 0.715 - (2200 \times 0.988 \times 10^{-3})$$

$$= 8.54\ V$$

The AC emitter resistance,

$$r_e = \frac{26\ mV}{I_E}$$

$$= \frac{26\ mV}{0.988\ mA} = 25.3\ \Omega$$

$$A_d = \frac{V_o}{V_{id}} = \frac{R_C}{r_e} = \frac{2200}{25.3} = 86.96$$

$$R_i = 2\beta_{ac} r_e = 2 \times 100 \times 25.3 = 5.06\ k\Omega$$

$$R_{o_1} = R_{o_2} = R_o = R_C = 2.2\ k\Omega$$

Example 1.2 :

Calculate the values of I_{CQ} and V_{CEQ} for the circuit shown in Fig. 1.19.

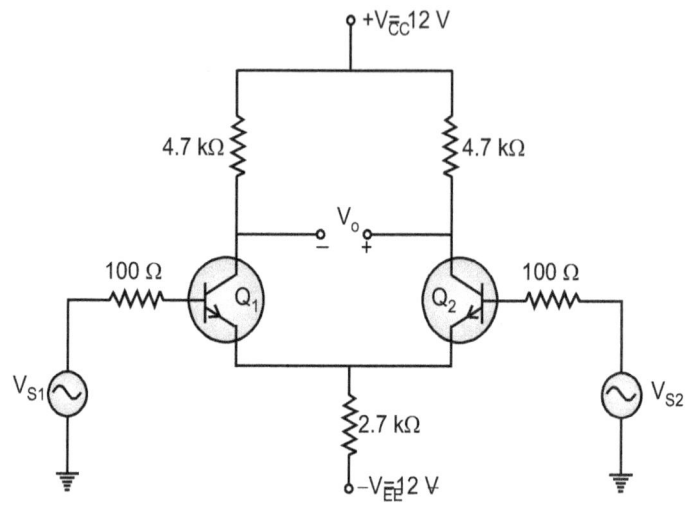

Fig. 1.19

Solution :

Given data : R_C = 4.7 kΩ, R_E = 2.7 kΩ, V_{CC} = +12 V

$$I_E = \frac{V_{EE} - V_{BE}}{2R_E}$$

Assume V_{BE} = 0.7

$$I_E = \frac{12 - 0.7}{2 \times 2.7 \times 10^3}$$

$$= 2.09 \text{ mA}$$

∴ $I_{CQ} = I_E$ = 2.09 mA

$V_{CEQ} = V_{CC} + V_{BE} - I_C R_C$

∴ V_{CEQ} = 12 + 0.7 − (2.09 × 4.7) = 2.86 V

Example 1.3 :

For the same differential amplifier shown in above example, calculate the values of A_d, A_c, CMRR, R_{in} and R_o. Assume that both the transistors are identical with h_{fe} = 100 and h_{ie} = 1 kΩ.

Solution :

Given data : $R_{in_1} = R_{in_2} = 100\ \Omega$, $R_E = 2.7\ k\Omega$, $R_C = 4.7\ k\Omega$, $h_{fe} = 100$, $h_{ie} = 1\ k\Omega$

1. Differential gain,

$$A_d = \frac{h_{fe} R_C}{(R_{in} + h_{ie})}$$

$$= \frac{100 \times 4.7 \times 10^3}{(100 + 1 \times 10^3)}$$

$$= 427.27$$

2. Common mode gain,

$$A_c = \frac{-h_{fe} R_C}{2R_E (1 + h_{fe}) + R_{in} + h_{ie}}$$

$$= \frac{100 \times 4.7 \times 10^3}{2 \times 2.7 \times 10^3 (101) + 100 + (1 \times 10^3)} = 0.86$$

3.
$$CMRR = \frac{A_d}{A_c} = \frac{427.27}{0.86} = 496.81$$

$$= 20 \log 496.81 = 53.92\ dB$$

4. Input resistance, $R_{in} = 2(R_{in} + h_{ie})$

$$= 2(100 + 1000)$$

$$= 2.2\ k\Omega$$

5. Output resistance, $R_o = R_C = 4.7\ k\Omega$

1.6 DIFFERENTIAL AMPLIFIER WITH SWAMPING RESISTORS

The dependence of voltage gain of the differential amplifiers on variations in r_e can be reduced by using external resistors R_E' in series with each emitter. R_E' also increases linearity of the differential amplifiers. The value of R_E' is large enough to swamp the effect of r_e. Therefore, R_E' sometimes called as swamping resistor.

The emitter current can be calculated by using KVL around base-emitter loop of transistor Q_1 with $V_{in_1} = V_{in_2} = 0\ V$.

$$-R_{in} I_B - V_{BE} - R_E' I_E - R_E (2I_E) + V_{EE} = 0$$

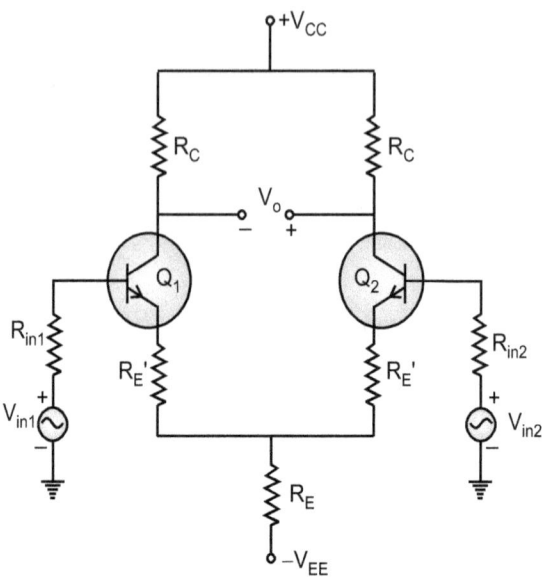

Fig. 1.20 : Dual input balanced output differential amplifier with emitter resistors R_E'

Substitute $I_B \approx I_E / \beta_{dc}$ and simplify, we get,

$$I_E = \frac{V_{EE} - V_{BE}}{2R_E + R_E' + R_{in} / \beta_{dc}}$$

$$V_{CE} = V_{CC} + V_{BE} - R_C I_C$$

When external resistors R_E' are added to each emitter lead, the new voltage gain and new input resistance can be obtained for any configuration simply by replacing r_e by $(r_e + R_E')$.

$$A_d = \frac{V_o}{V_{id}} = \frac{R_C}{r_e + R_E'}$$

and the new input resistance becomes

$$R_{i_1} = R_{i_2} = 2\beta_{ac} (r_e + R_E')$$

The output resistance remains the same.

$$R_{o_1} = R_{o_2} = R_C$$

Thus, the use of R_E' reduces the voltage gain but increases the input resistance.

1.7 COMMON MODE REJECTION RATIO (CMRR)

When the same voltage is applied to both the inputs, the differential amplifier is said to be operated in a common mode configuration. Many disturbance signals, noise signals appear as a common input signal to both the input terminals of the differential amplifiers. Such a common signal should be rejected by the differential amplifier.

The ability of a differential amplifier to reject a common mode signal is expressed by a ratio called common mode rejection ratio denoted by CMRR.

$$CMRR = \frac{A_d}{A_c}$$

Ideally $A_c = 0$. Hence, the ideal value of CMRR is infinite.

$$CMRR \text{ in dB} = 20 \log \left(\frac{A_d}{A_c}\right) \text{ dB}$$

The output voltage can be expressed in terms of CMRR.

$$\therefore \quad V_o = A_d V_d + A_c V_c$$

$$= A_d V_d \left[1 + \frac{A_c V_c}{A_d V_d}\right] = A_d V_d \left[1 + \frac{A_c}{A_d} \cdot \frac{V_c}{V_d}\right]$$

$$V_o = A_d V_d \left[1 + \frac{1}{CMRR} \cdot \frac{V_c}{V_d}\right]$$

Example 1.4 :

Determine the output voltage of a differential amplifier for the input voltages of 300 µV and 240 µV. The differential gain of the amplifier is 5000 and the value of the CMRR is (i) 100, (ii) 10^5.

Solution :

$$V_d = V_1 - V_2 = 300 - 240 = 60 \text{ µV}$$

$$V_c = \frac{V_1 + V_2}{2} = \frac{300 + 240}{2} = 270 \text{ µV}$$

(i) CMRR = 100

$$CMRR = \frac{5000}{A_c}$$

$$100 = \frac{5000}{A_c}$$

$$A_c = 50$$

$$\therefore \quad V_o = A_d V_d + A_c V_c$$
$$= 5000 \times 60 \times 10^{-6} + 50 \times 270 \times 10^{-6}$$
$$= 313.5 \text{ mV}$$

(ii) CMRR = 10^5

$$\therefore \quad A_c = \frac{A_d}{\text{CMRR}}$$
$$= \frac{5000}{10^5} = 0.05$$

$$\therefore \quad V_d = A_d V_d + A_c V_c$$
$$= 5000 \times 60 \times 10^{-6} + 0.05 \times 270 \times 10^{-6} \text{ V}$$
$$= 300.0135 \text{ mV}$$

Example 1.5 :

An op-amp has a differential gain of 80 dB and CMRR of 95 dB. If $V_1 = 2$ µV and $V_2 = 1.6$ µV, then calculate the differential and common mode output values.

Solution :

Given data : $A_d = 80$ dB and CMRR = 95 dB

$$80 = 20 \log A_d$$
$$A_d = 1 \times 10^4$$
$$95 = 20 \log \text{CMRR}$$
$$\text{CMRR} = 5.6234 \times 10^4$$

Differential output can be calculated as

$$V_d = A_d (V_1 - V_2)$$
$$= 1 \times 10^4 (2 - 1.6) \times 10^{-6}$$
$$= 4 \text{ mV}$$

$$V_c = A_d \left(\frac{V_1 + V_2}{2}\right)$$

$$\text{CMRR} = \frac{A_d}{A_c}$$

$$A_c = \frac{1 \times 10^4}{5.6234 \times 10^4} = 0.1778$$

$$V_c = 0.1778 \times \frac{(2 + 1.6)}{2} \times 10^{-6}$$
$$= 0.32 \text{ µV}$$

Example 1.6 :

The common mode input to a differential amplifier, having differential gain of 125 is $4 \sin 200 \pi t$. Determine the common mode output if CMRR is 60 dB.

Solution :

The CMRR in dB is

$$60 = 20 \log \text{CMRR}$$

$$\log\left(\frac{A_d}{A_c}\right) = 3$$

$$\therefore \quad \frac{A_d}{A_c} = 1000$$

Now,

$$A_d = 125$$

$$\therefore \quad \frac{125}{1000} = A_c = 0.125$$

Hence, the common mode output is

$$= A_c V_c$$
$$= 0.125 \times 4 \sin 200 \pi t$$
$$= 0.5 \sin (200 \pi t) \text{ V}$$

1.8 METHODS OF IMPROVING CMRR

To obtain the better performance of differential amplifier the common mode rejection ratio must be high.

$$\text{CMRR} = \frac{A_d}{A_c}$$

where, A_d = Differential gain

A_c = Common mode gain

To improve CMRR the common mode gain A_c must be reduced. The value of common mode gain can be obtained zero when R_E tends to infinity. Due to increase in value of R_E, R_E introduces a negative feedback in common mode operation. But in practice to select the large value of R_E is not possible because the large value of R_E needs large biasing voltage as well as it increases the size of the chip.

So to improve CMRR two methods are used :

(1) Using constant current source.
(2) Using current mirror circuit.

1.8.1 Constant Current Source

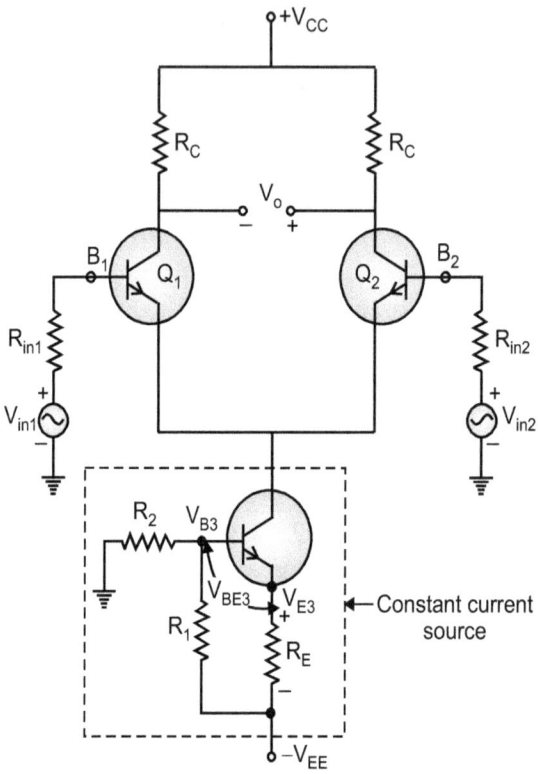

Fig. 1.21 : Dual input balanced output differential amplifier using constant current bias

In differential amplifier, the combination of R_E and V_{EE} is used to set up the DC emitter current. We can also use the constant current bias circuit to set up the DC emitter current if desired.

The constant current bias is required to provide current stabilization and assures a stable operating point. The DC collector current in transistor Q_3 is established by resistors R_1, R_2 and R_E.

Apply voltage divider rule, the voltage at the base of the transistor Q_3 is

$$V_{B_3} = \frac{-R_2 V_{EE}}{R_1 + R_2}$$

$$V_{E_3} = V_{B_3} - V_{BE_3}$$

$$= \frac{-R_2 V_{EE}}{R_1 + R_2} - V_{BE_3}$$

$$\therefore \quad I_{E_3} = I_{C_3} = \frac{V_{E_3} - (-V_{EE})}{R_E}$$

$$I_{C_3} = \frac{V_{EE} - [R_2 V_{EE}/(R_1 + R_2)] - V_{BE_3}}{R_E}$$

$$I_{E_1} = I_{E_2} = \frac{I_{C_3}}{2}$$

$$= \frac{V_{EE} - [R_2 V_{EE}/R_1 + R_2]}{2R_E} - V_{BE_3}$$

The collector circuit is fixed because no signal is injected into either the emitter or the base of Q_3.

As internal resistance of constant current source is very high, it acts as a very high R_E and improves the CMRR of a differential amplifier by reducing common mode gain A_C. Here V_{EE}, R_1, R_2, R_E and V_{BE} are constant. Therefore, transistor Q_3 acts as a constant current source.

For thermal compensation constant current transistor Q_3, resistor R_1 is replaced by diodes D_1 and D_2 to the junctions of Q_1 and Q_2.

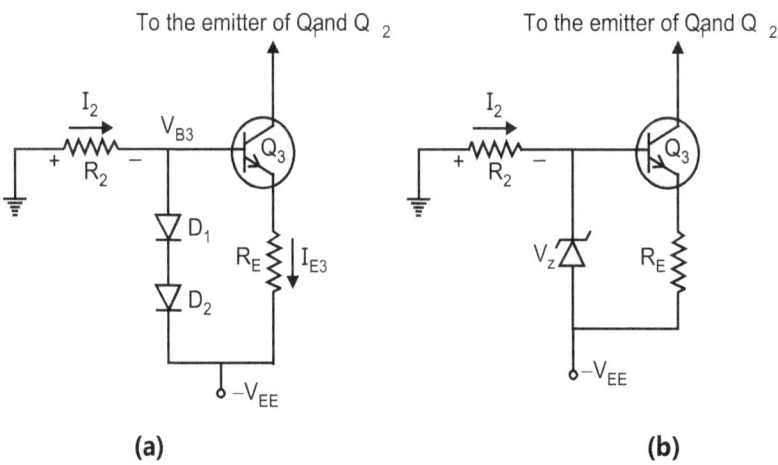

Fig. 1.22 : Constant current source with diode compensation

Assume that the voltage drop across the diode is same as V_D.

$$V_{B_3} = -V_{EE} + 2V_D$$

$$V_{E_3} = V_{B_3} - V_{BE}$$

$$V_{E_3} = -V_{EE} + 2V_D - V_{BE}$$

$$I_{E_3} = \frac{V_{E_3} - (-V_{EE})}{R_E}$$

$$= \frac{-V_{EE} + 2V_D - V_{BE} + V_{EE}}{R_E}$$

$$\boxed{I_{E_3} = \frac{2V_D - V_{BE}}{R_E}}$$

Therefore the emitter current I_{E_3} depends on the voltage drop across diodes.

Similarly, the zener diode can be used in place of two diodes for temperature compensation constant current bias circuit using zener diode is as shown in Fig. 1.22 (b).

The voltage at the base of transistor Q_3 is

$$V_{B_3} = -V_{EE} + V_Z$$

$$V_{E_3} = V_{B_3} - V_{BE}$$

$$V_{E_3} = -V_{EE} + V_Z - V_{BE}$$

and
$$I_{E_3} = \frac{V_{E_3} - (-V_{EE})}{R_E}$$

$$I_{E_3} = \frac{-V_{EE} + V_Z - V_{BE} + V_{EE}}{R_E}$$

$$\boxed{I_{E_3} = \frac{V_Z - V_{BE}}{R_E}}$$

Example 1.7 :

Calculate the constant current I in the circuit shown in Fig. 1.23.

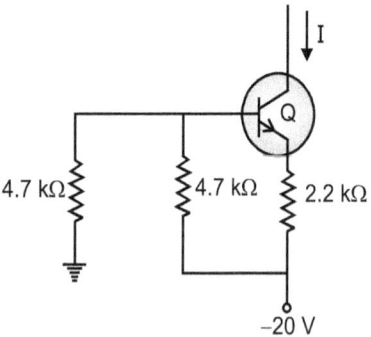

Fig. 1.23

Solution :

$$V_{B_3} = \frac{-V_{EE} R_1}{R_1 + R_2} = \frac{-20 \times 4.7 \times 10^3}{(4.7 + 4.7)}$$

$$= -10 \text{ V}$$

$$V_{E_3} = V_{B_3} - V_{BE}$$

$$= -10 - 0.7$$

$$= -10.7 \text{ V}$$

$$I_E = \frac{V_E - (-V_{EE})}{R_E}$$

$$= \frac{-10.7 + 20}{2.2 \times 10^3} = 4.22 \text{ mA}$$

Example 1.8 :

For the constant current source circuit shown in Fig. 1.24, find the current I_{CC} if zener voltage is 5 V.

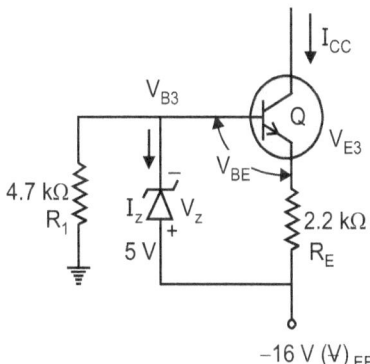

Fig. 1.24

Solution :

$$V_{BE_3} = -V_{EE} + V_Z$$

$$= -16 + 5 = -11 \text{ V}$$

$$V_{E_3} = V_{B_3} - V_{BE}$$

$$= -11 - 0.7 = -11.7 \text{ V}$$

$$I_{E_3} = \frac{V_E - (-V_{EE})}{R_E}$$

$$= \frac{-11.7 + 16}{2.2} = 1.9545 \text{ mA}$$

Example 1.9 :

Design a dual-input balanced-output differential amplifier with a constant current bias using diodes to satisfy the following requirements :

(1) Differential voltage gain $A_d = 45 \pm 5$.

(2) Current supplied by the constant current bias circuit = 4.5 mA.

(3) Supply voltage $|V_{CC}| = |-V_{EE}| = 10$ V.

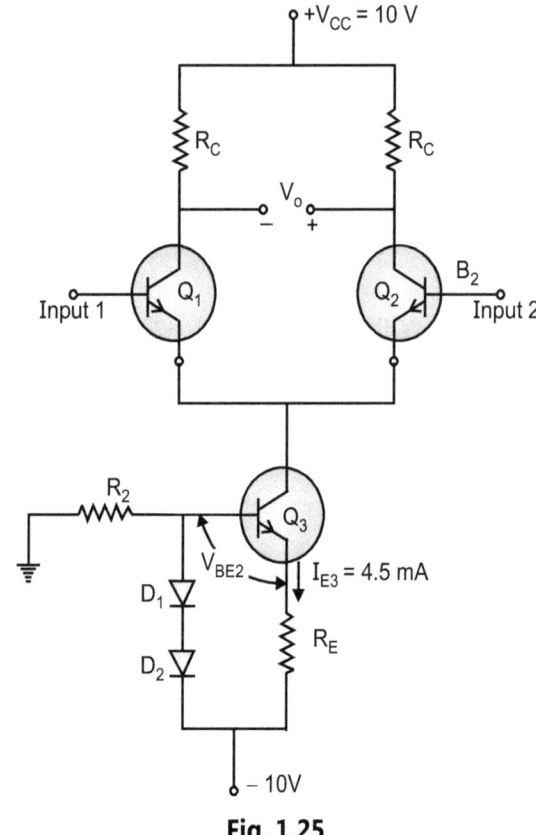

Fig. 1.25

Solution :

(a) **Design the constant current source :** Assume the two diodes are identical and $V_{D_1} = V_{D_2} = 0.7$.

The desired value of emitter current is $I_{E_3} = 4.5$ mA.

Applying KVL to the base of the transistor Q_3.

$$V_{D_1} + V_{D_2} = V_{BE_3} + V_{RE}$$

$$2V_D = V_D + I_E R_E \qquad \text{Assuming } V_D = V_{BE_3}$$

$$I_E = \frac{V_D}{R_E}$$

$$R_E = \frac{V_D}{I_E} = \frac{0.7}{4.5 \times 10^{-3}} = 155.55 \, \Omega$$

$$\therefore \quad R_E = 150 \, \Omega$$

To calculate R_2, we can write

$$V_{R_2} = V_{EE} + V_{D_2} + V_{D_1}$$
$$= -10 + 0.7 + 0.7$$
$$V_{R_2} = -8.6 \, V$$

In constant current source $I_{E_3} = I_2$.

$$\therefore \quad R_2 = \frac{V_{R_2}}{I_{E_3}}$$

$$= \frac{8.6}{4.5 \times 10^{-3}} = 1.91 \, k\Omega$$

$$\therefore \quad R_2 \approx 2 \, k\Omega$$

To determine the collector resistors assume $h_{fe} = 100$ and $h_{ie} = 1.1 \, k\Omega$.

The expression for voltage gain A_d is,

$$A_d = \frac{h_{fe} \, R_C}{(R_s + h_{ie})}$$

Assume $R_s = 0$.

$$A_d = \frac{100 \times R_C}{0 + 1.1 \, k\Omega}$$

$$\therefore \quad R_C = \frac{45 \times 1.1 \times 10^3}{100}$$

$$R_C = 495 \, \Omega$$

The standard value is 470 Ω.

$$\therefore \quad R_C = 470 \, \Omega.$$

1.8.2 Current Mirror

The circuit where the output current is forced to equal the input current is called as current mirror circuit. Thus, in a current mirror, the output current is a mirror image of the input current. It is a special case of constant current bias and therefore used as a constant current source in differential amplifiers. Current mirror circuit requires less components than the constant current bias.

Because of its simplicity and ease of fabrication, the current mirror circuit is used in integrated amplifiers such as differential and operational amplifiers.

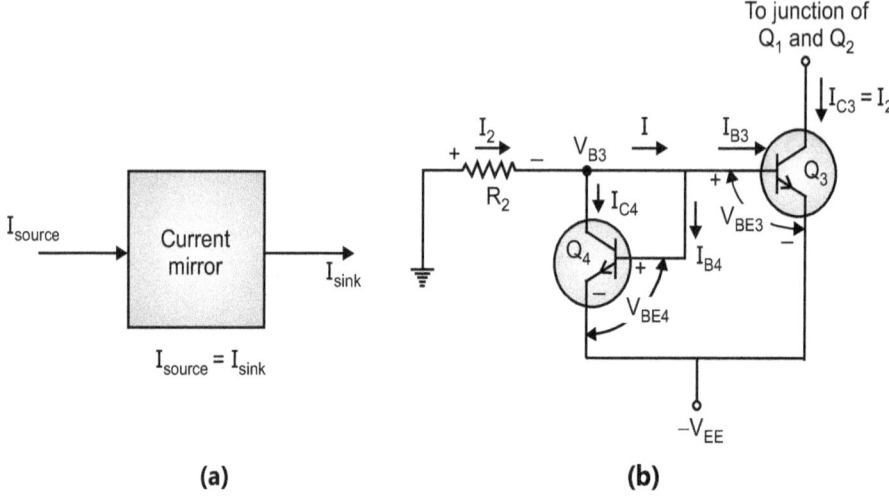

(a)   (b)

Fig. 1.26 : Current mirror circuit

Remember that for the proper operation of the circuit it is necessary to construct a current mirror circuit using a transistor array such as the CA3086 in which a needed diode is formed by using an adjacent transistor. The transistor array helps to achieve the required collector current thermal stability in a current mirror circuit. Since Q_3 and Q_4 are identical transistors, their base-emitter voltages must be the same and their base and collector current must also be equal.

$$\therefore \quad V_{BE_3} = V_{BE_4}$$

$$I_{C_3} = I_{C_4}$$

$$I_{B_3} = I_{B_4}$$

Summing currents at node V_{B_3}, we obtain

$$I_2 = I_{C_4} + I$$

$$= I_{C_4} + 2I_{B_4}$$

$$= I_{C_3} + 2I_{B_3}$$

$$= I_{C_3} + 2\left(\frac{I_{C_3}}{\beta_{dc}}\right)$$

$$I_2 = I_{C_3}\left(1 + \frac{2}{\beta_{dc}}\right)$$

Generally, β_{dc} is large enough so that $\dfrac{2}{\beta_{dc}}$ is negligibly small.

∴ $\quad I_2 = I_{C_3}$

The current I_2 is obtained by applying KVL to the base-emitter loop of transistor Q_3.

$$-R_2 I_2 - V_{BE_3} + V_{EE} = 0$$

$$I_2 = \dfrac{V_{EE} - V_{BE_3}}{R_2}$$

Thus, an appropriate value of R_2 can be chosen to set a desired value of collector current in a current mirror circuit.

Example 1.10 :

For the current mirror circuit shown in Fig. 1.27, find a suitable value for R_2 so that the circuit delivers a constant biasing current of 2 mA to the transistors of the differential amplifier.

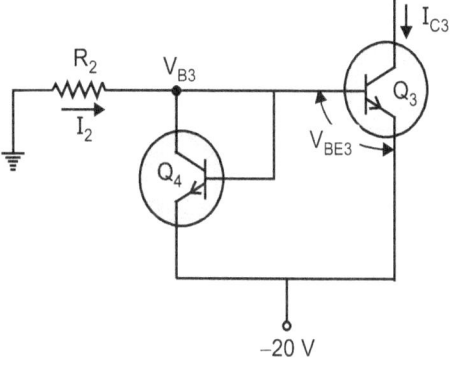

Fig. 1.27

Solution :

Given data : $-V_{EE} = -20$ V

$\qquad\qquad I_{C_3} = 2$ mA

$\qquad\qquad I_2 = \dfrac{V_{EE} - V_{BE_3}}{R_2}$

$\qquad\qquad V_{BE_3} = 0.7$ V

∴ $\qquad 2 \times 10^{-3} = \dfrac{20 - 0.7}{R_2}$

$\qquad\qquad R_2 = \dfrac{19.3}{2 \times 10^{-3}}$

$\qquad\qquad R_2 = 9.65$ kΩ

1.8.3 Wilson Current Source

This is the another type of current source used in practice.

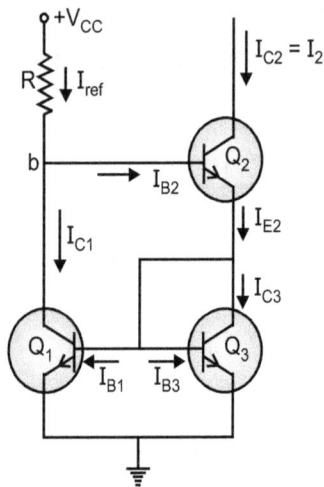

Fig. 1.28 : Wilson current source

Features :

(1) High output resistance.

(2) Low sensitivity to the transistor base current.

High output resistance is the feature due to negative feedback through Q_3.

Analysis :

Apply KCL at node b.

$$I_{ref} = I_{B_2} + I_{C_1} \quad \ldots (1.9)$$

and
$$I_{E_2} = I_{C_3} + I_{B_1} + I_{B_3} \quad \ldots (1.10)$$

Q_1, Q_2 and Q_3 are identical so $V_{BE_1} = V_{BE_2} = V_{BE_3}$

$$I_{B_1} = I_{B_2} = I_{B_3} = I_B$$

$$I_{E_2} = I_{C_3} + 2I_B \quad \ldots (1.11)$$

$$I_{E_2} = I_{B_2} + I_{C_2} \quad \ldots (1.12)$$

$$I_{E_2} = I_B + I_{C_2}$$

Now,
$$I_{C_2} = I_{E_2} - I_B$$

$$= I_{C_3} + 2I_B - I_B$$

$$= I_{C_3} + I_B \quad \ldots (1.13)$$

Since
$$I_{C_3} = I_{C_1} \quad I_{C_2} = I_{C_1} + I_B$$

Compare equations (1.9) and (1.13),

$$I_2 = I_{C_2} = I_{ref}$$

Use equation (1.10).

Now, $\quad I_{E_2} = I_{C_3} + 2I_B$

But $\quad I_B = \dfrac{I_{C_3}}{\beta}$

$$I_{E_2} = I_{C_3} + \dfrac{2I_{C_3}}{\beta}$$

$$I_{E_2} = I_{C_3}\left[1 + \dfrac{2}{\beta}\right] \quad \ldots (1.14)$$

$$I_{C_2} = I_{E_2}\left[\dfrac{\beta}{1 + \beta}\right] \quad \ldots (1.15)$$

$$I_{C_2} = I_{C_3}\left[1 + \dfrac{2}{\beta}\right]\left[\dfrac{\beta}{1 + \beta}\right] \quad \ldots (1.16)$$

$$I_{C_3} = I_{C_2}\dfrac{1}{\left[1 + \dfrac{2}{\beta}\right]\left[\dfrac{\beta}{1 + \beta}\right]} \quad \ldots (1.17)$$

From equation (1.9) we can write

$$I_{ref} = I_{C_1} + I_{B_2}$$

$$I_{C_1} = I_{ref} - I_{B_2}$$

$$I_{C_1} = I_{ref} - \dfrac{I_{C_2}}{\beta} \quad \ldots (1.18)$$

Since the two transistors are identical

$$I_{C_3} = I_{C_1}$$

From equation (1.17) and (1.18)

$$I_{C_2}\dfrac{1}{\left[1 + \dfrac{2}{\beta}\right]\left[\dfrac{\beta}{1 + \beta}\right]} = I_{ref} - \dfrac{I_{C_2}}{\beta}$$

$$I_{C_2}\left[\dfrac{(1 + \beta)\beta}{\beta(2 + \beta)} + \dfrac{1}{\beta}\right] = I_{ref}$$

$$I_{C_2}\left[\frac{\beta^2 + \beta + 2 + \beta}{\beta(2+\beta)}\right] = I_{ref}$$

$$I_{C_2}\left[\frac{\beta^2 + 2\beta + 2}{\beta(2+\beta)}\right] = I_{ref}$$

$$I_{C_2} = I_{ref}\left[\frac{\beta(2+\beta)}{\beta^2 + 2\beta + 2}\right]$$

$$I_{C_2} = I_{ref}\left[\frac{\beta^2 + 2\beta + 2 - 2}{\beta^2 + 2\beta + 2}\right]$$

$$I_{C_2} = I_{ref}\left[1 - \frac{2}{\beta^2 + 2\beta + 2}\right]$$

1.8.4 Widlar Current Source

Widlar current source is used when lower input currents are required.

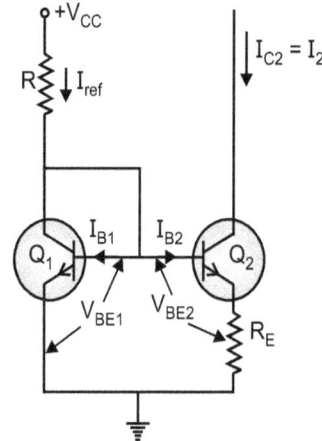

Fig. 1.29 : Widlar current source

In Fig. 1.29. Two transistors are identical but due to R_E, V_{BE_1} and V_{BE_2} are different.

$$V_{BE_2} < V_{BE_1}$$

$$I_{C_2} < I_{C_1}$$

Circuit is called as lens instead of mirror.

Apply KVL to base-emitter loop.

$$V_{BE_1} = V_{BE_2} + (I_{B_2} + I_{C_2}) R_E$$

$$V_{BE_1} - V_{BE_2} = (I_{B_2} + I_{C_2}) R_E$$

For a transistor,
$$I_{C_1} = I_S e^{V_{BE_1}/V_T}$$

$$I_{C_2} = I_S e^{V_{BE_2}/V_T}$$

Eber's Moll equations.

$$\frac{I_{C_1}}{I_{C_2}} = e^{(V_{BE_1} - V_{BE_2})/V_T}$$

Take $\ln$ to both sides,

$$\ln\left[\frac{I_{C_1}}{I_{C_2}}\right] = \frac{V_{BE_1} - V_{BE_2}}{V_T}$$

$$V_{BE_1} - V_{BE_2} = V_T \ln\left[\frac{I_{C_1}}{I_{C_2}}\right]$$

$$(I_{B_2} + I_{C_2}) R_E = V_T \ln\left[\frac{I_{C_1}}{I_{C_2}}\right]$$

Neglect I_{B_2} for large value of β,

$$I_{C_2} R_E = V_T \ln\left[\frac{I_{C_1}}{I_{C_2}}\right]$$

Transcendental equation and must be solved by trial and error method.

To design the source I_{C_1} and I_{C_2} are usually known and to calculate R_E above equation is used.

1.8.5 Use of Active Load to Improve CMRR

To improve CMRR, differential gain A_d must be increased where

$$A_d = \frac{R_C}{r_e}$$

To increase A_d, R_C must be high.

But the physical value of R_C cannot be increased beyond a limit because

(i) it needs large biasing voltages to maintain quiescent collector current.

(ii) increase in R_C increases the chip area.

The current mirror has very low d.c. resistance and high a.c. resistance. The requirement of increased gain is satisfied without disturbing the d.c. conditions while providing large a.c. resistance. Therefore, current mirror can be used as a collector load by replacing R_C. Such a load is called an active load. Basically it acts as a current source providing a.c. resistance. Such type of active load is shown in Fig. 1.30.

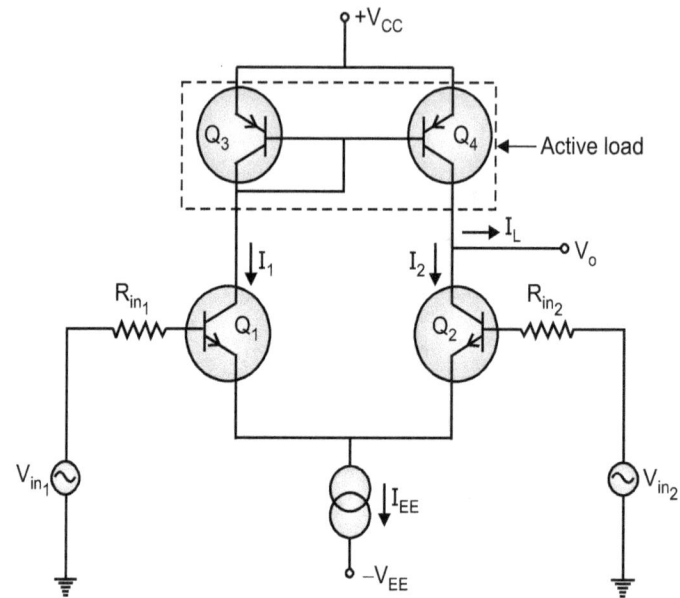

Fig. 1.30

Under the d.c. conditions $V_{in_1} = V_{in_2} = 0$.

Therefore, $I_1 = I_2 = \dfrac{I_{EE}}{2}$

The transistors Q_3 and Q_4 form a current mirror circuit.

Therefore, $I = I_1 = I_2$

∴ $I_L = I - I_2 = 0$

But when V_{in_1} increases than V_{in_2}, the current I_1 increases and I_2 decreases because $I_1 + I_2 = I_{EE}$ constant. Therefore, the current I always remains equal to I_1 due to current mirror action.

1.9 LEVEL SHIFTER

As there are no coupling capacitors between the intermediate stage and the input stage, there is a significant DC component at the output along with AC output.

Due to this DC component at the output, the output gets distorted as well as it limits the maximum output voltage swing.

The main purpose of the level shifting stage is to shift the output dc level towards the ground.

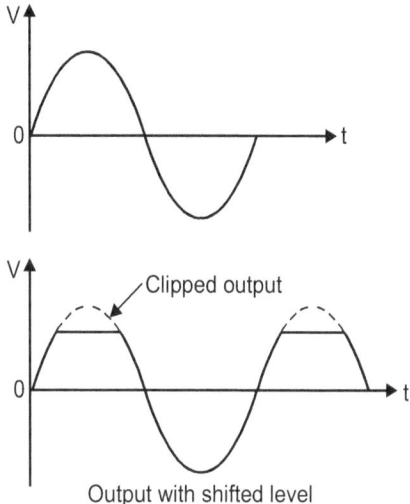

Fig. 1.31

1.9.1 Circuits used for Level Shifting

1. Basic emitter follower used as level shifting circuit :

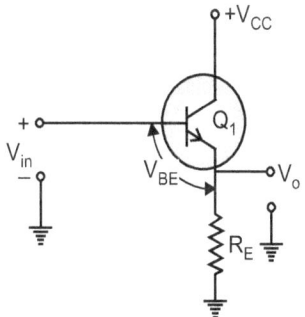

Fig. 1.32 (a) : Basic emitter follower used as level shifting circuit

It is basically an emitter follower circuit. In this circuit, the amount of shift obtained is equal to V_{BE} which is almost 0.7 V. If V_{in} is the increased level signal and V_o is the output with reduced level. Therefore, the output voltage we can write as

$$V_o = V_{in} - V_{BE}$$

2. Voltage divider network as a level shifting circuit :

Generally, a shift of 0.7 V is not sufficient. Hence, the circuit is modified with the help of two resistances R_1 and R_2.

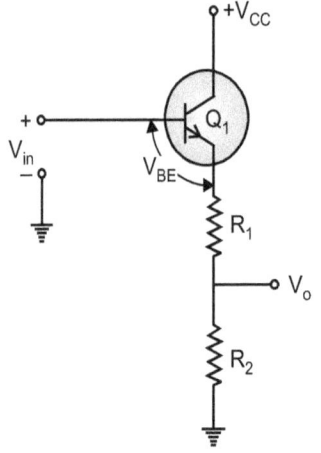

To find the level shift, consider current I flowing through the emitter of the transistor Q_1.

Applying KVL to base emitter loop, we get

$$V_{in} - V_{BE} - I(R_1 + R_2) = 0$$

$$I = \frac{V_{in} - V_{BE}}{R_1 + R_2}$$

$$V_o = IR_2$$

$$V_o = \frac{(V_{in} - V_{BE})R_2}{R_1 + R_2}$$

Fig. 1.32 (b) : Voltage divided network as a level shifting circuit

By proper selection of R_1 and R_2 level at V_o can be controlled. The main drawback of this circuit is that the signal voltage also gets attenuated by the factor $R_2/(R_1 + R_2)$. As R_2 is decreased to improve the DC level shift, the AC gain starts decreasing. Another disadvantage of the circuit is that its output impedance is also high.

3. Level shifting with constant current bias :

Another improved circuit with constant current bias circuit can be used as a level shifting network. The constant current bias is provided with the help of the transistor Q_2.

$$V_o = V_{in} - V_{BE} - I_1 R_1$$

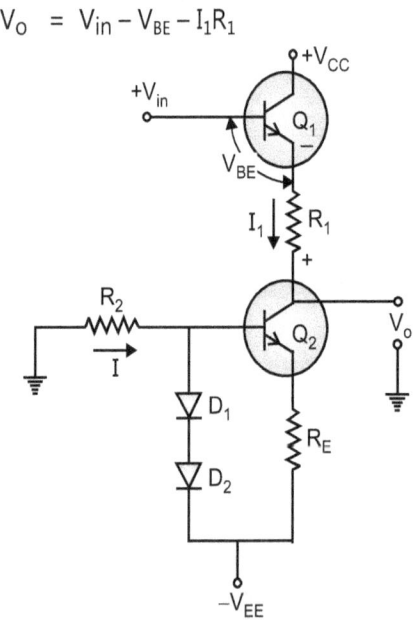

Fig. 1.33 : Constant current bias used as a level shifter

Choosing I_1 and R_1, V_o can be obtained as zero.

4. Level shifting network with current mirror :

Another level shifting circuit uses a current mirror circuit with basic emitter follower circuit. Because of current mirror action,

$$I_1 = I$$

Now,
$$I_1 = I = \frac{V_{EE} - V_{BE}}{R_2}$$

while
$$V_o = V_{in} - V_{BE} - I_1 R_1$$

Choosing proper values of I and R_1, the output V_o can be brought to zero level.

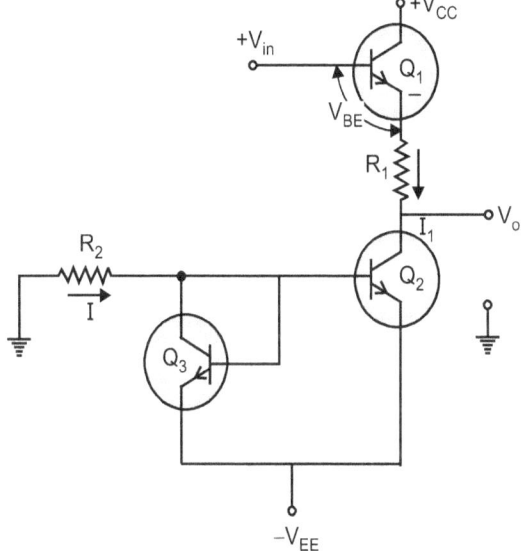

Fig. 1.34 : Level shifter with current mirror

Example 1.11 :

Fig. 1.35 shows a typical level shifting network. If input DC level is 6.84 V and R_2 is 270 Ω, design the value of R_1 if output voltage level required is zero volts.

Solution :

Applying KVL to base-emitter loop,
$$V_{in} - V_{BE} - I(R_1 + R_2) = 0$$

$$I = \frac{V_{in} - V_{BE}}{R_1 + R_2}$$

while
$$V_o = IR_2 = \frac{(V_{in} - V_{BE}) R_2}{R_1 + R_2}$$

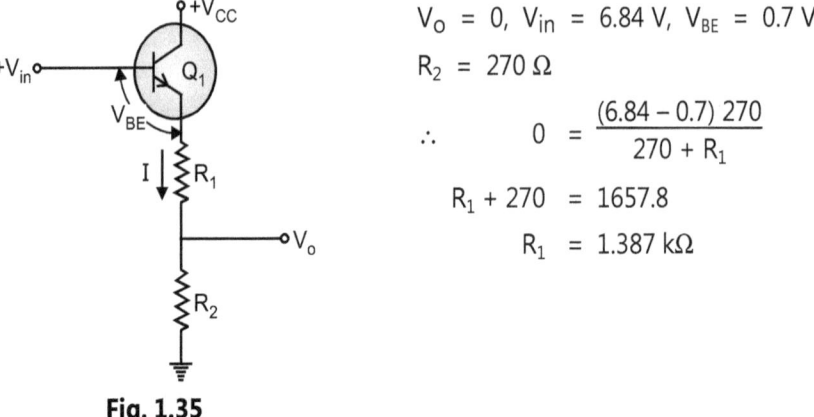

$V_O = 0$, $V_{in} = 6.84$ V, $V_{BE} = 0.7$ V,
$R_2 = 270$ Ω

$$\therefore \quad 0 = \frac{(6.84 - 0.7)\,270}{270 + R_1}$$

$R_1 + 270 = 1657.8$

$R_1 = 1.387$ kΩ

Fig. 1.35

This is the required value of R_1 to get 0 V output level.

1.10 OUTPUT STAGE

The output stage is the last stage of the op-amp. Generally, complementary symmetry push-pull amplifier is used to provide the low output resistance.

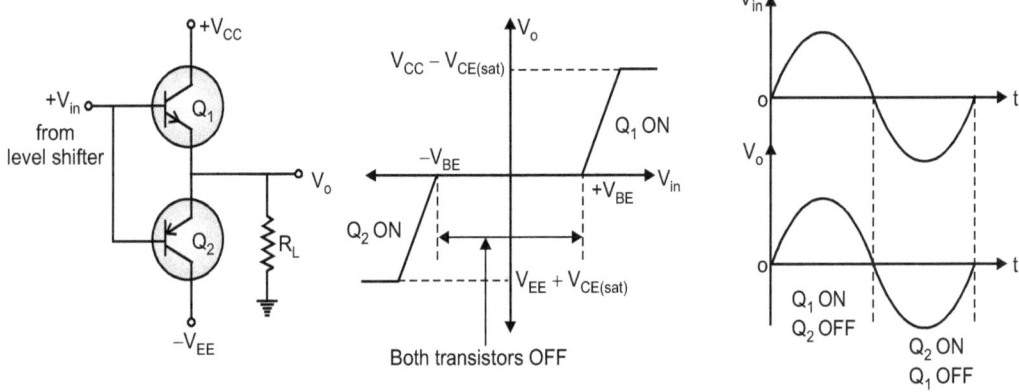

(a) Output stage (b) Transfer characteristics of complementary output stage
(c) Input and output waveforms
Fig. 1.36

1.10.1 Operation of the Output Stage

During the positive half cycle transistor Q_1 turns ON and transistor Q_2 remains OFF, therefore, the output is due to Q_1 alone. During the –ve half cycle, the transistor Q_1 remains OFF and Q_2 becomes ON. When the $V_{in} \leq V_{BE(ON)}$, output remains zero.

Therefore, dead band occurs as shown in Fig. 1.37. This introduces the crossover distortion in the output of the op-amp.

This type of distortion can be reduced with the help of a bias voltage. This can be achieved by connecting two silicon diodes between the bases of Q_1 and Q_2 as shown in Fig. 1.37.

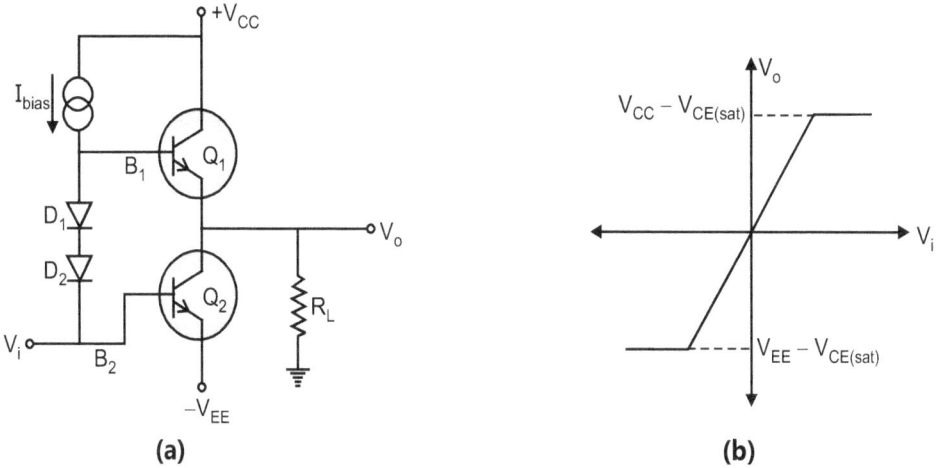

(a) **(b)**

Fig. 1.37 : Complementary push-pull amplifier with diodes D_1 and D_2

1.11 INTERNAL SCHEMATIC DIAGRAM OF IC 741

Fig. 1.38 shows the internal schematic of the IC 741 op-amp which becomes an industry standard. The diagram consists of all the internal stages along with their capabilities and limitations. All the models of IC 741 has the same internal schematic diagram. Data sheet consists of all electrical specifications absolute maximum ratings, performance curves and typical applications.

The first stage is the input stage which is a dual input balanced output differential amplifier stage consisting of Q_1 and Q_2 transistors to which the inputs are applied. To increase the maximum signal input capacity transistors Q_3 and Q_4 are used.

The constant current source consisting of transistors Q_9 and Q_{10} supplies the base current for Q_3 and Q_4. This constant current helps to establish a operating point for the input stage. The diode connected to transistors Q_8 and Q_{11}, gives the base potential of transistors Q_9 and Q_{10} respectively. The resistances R_1, R_2 and R_3 with Q_5 and Q_6 forms a controlled current source. The 10 kΩ potentiometer is connected between offset null terminals and the wiper is connected to the negative supply. This helps to control the emitter currents of transistors Q_5 and Q_6, which minimizes offset voltage and currents. Transistor Q_7 supplies the base currents to transistors Q_5 and Q_6. For Q_5 and Q_6, the base currents and collector currents are equal since transistors are identical.

Transistors Q_4 and Q_6 forms complementary symmetry amplifier. The output of differential stage is applied to the common collector amplifier formed by Q_{16} and resistance R_9. The output of common collector drives the common emitter amplifier, which provides bias for transistors Q_{18} and Q_{19}. The transistor Q_{17} and resistance R_8 and transistor Q_{13} forms the common emitter amplifier. Transistors Q_{12} and Q_{13} form a current mirror.

Transistors Q_{14} and Q_{20} along with R_6 and R_7 forms the output stage. The output is measured at the junction of R_6 and R_7, which are in the emitter circuit of Q_{14} and Q_{20} respectively.

Transistors Q_{22} acts a a buffer between Q_{17} and Q_{20} and also provides the negative feedback to Q_{16}. The transistors Q_{15}, Q_{21} and Q_{23} provides the current limiting for the output complementary symmetry stage.

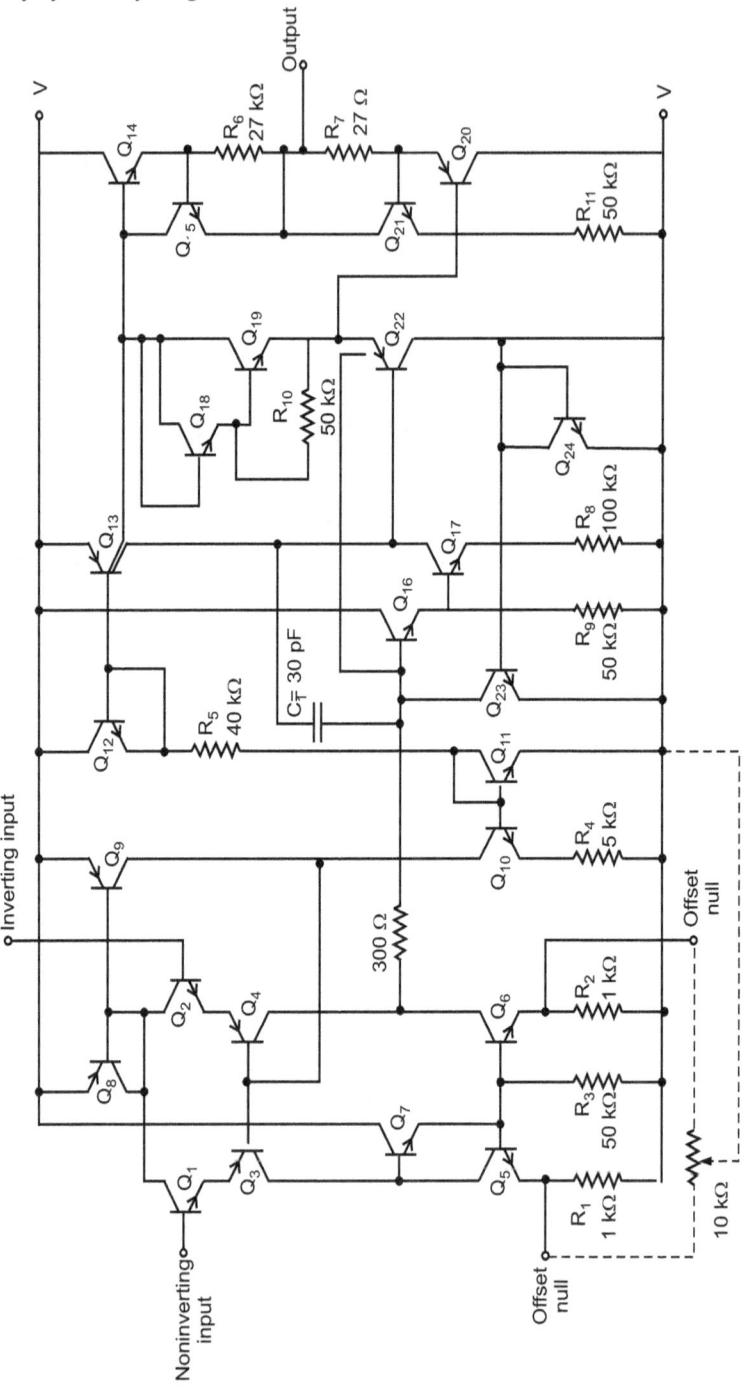

Fig. 1.38 : Internal schematic of IC 741

1.12 OP-AMP CONFIGURATION

1.12.1 Open Loop Configuration of Op-Amp

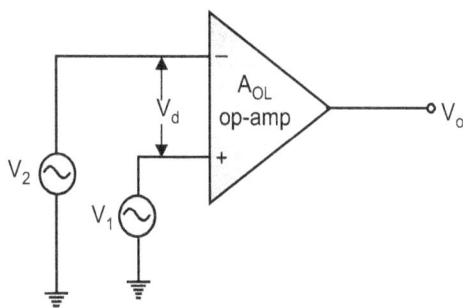

Fig. 1.39 : Open loop configuration of op-amp

The simple way to use an op-amp is in the open-loop mode. The output voltage of op-amp varies linearly only between the two supply voltages applied to the op-amp that is V_{CC} and $-V_{EE}$.

Due to the very large gain in open-loop condition, the output voltage is either at $+V_{sat}$ and $-V_{sat}$ as $V_1 > V_2$ or $V_2 > V_1$ respectively. Therefore, very small noise voltage present at the input also gets amplified due to its high open-loop gain and op-amp operates in saturation.

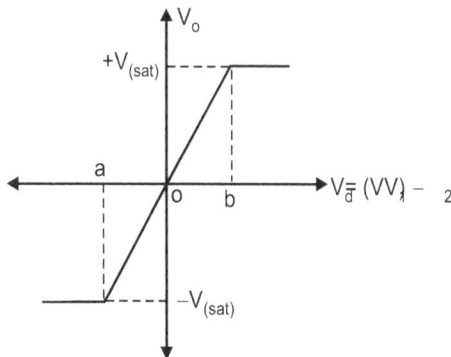

Fig. 1.40 : Transfer characteristics of open-loop op-amp

Fig. 1.40 shows the transfer characteristics of open-loop op-amp. From Fig. 1.40 it is clear that output is linear only for a small range of input i.e. from point a to b. This range is very small. This indicates the inability of op-amp to work as a linear small signal amplifier in the open-loop mode. Therefore, op-amp is generally not used in open-loop configuration.

1.12.2 Closed Loop Operation of Op-amp

As seen earlier, the op-amp cannot operate linearly in open-loop mode. But the utility of an op-amp can be increased by operating it in closed loop mode. The closed loop operation of an op-amp is possible with the help of feedback. The feedback allows to feed some part of the output back to input terminals. In the linear applications, the op-amp is always used with negative feedback. The negative feedback helps to control gain of the op-amp. The –ve feedback is possible by adding a resistor in feedback path as shown in Fig. 1.41.

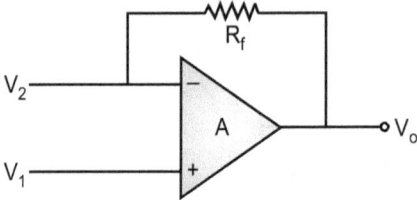

Fig. 1.41 : Closed loop configuration of op-amp

The gain resulting with feedback is called closed loop gain of the op-amp. Due to feedback resistance, there is a reduction in the gain. The closed loop gain is much less than the open-loop gain.

Most of the linear circuits use op-amp in a closed loop mode with negative feedback with R_f. This is because due to reduction in gain, the output is not driven into the saturation and the circuit behaves in a linear manner.

The advantages of negative feedback are :

1. It reduces the gain and makes it controllable.
2. It reduces the possibility of distortion.
3. It increases the bandwidth i.e. frequency range.
4. It increases the input resistance of the op-amp.
5. It decreases the output resistance of the op-amp.
6. It reduces the effect of temperature, power supply on the gain of the circuit.

1.13 VOLTAGE TRANSFER CURVE OF OP-AMP

Ideal voltage transfer curve : Ideally open loop gain of op-amp is ∞.

$$A_{OL} = \frac{V_o}{V_d} = \infty$$

$$V_d = \frac{V_o}{\infty} = 0$$

$$V_o = A_{OL} V_d$$

Due to infinite gain, the output of op-amp is always at the saturation level $\pm V_{sat}$ for zero input. Thus, voltage transfer curve is a vertical line.

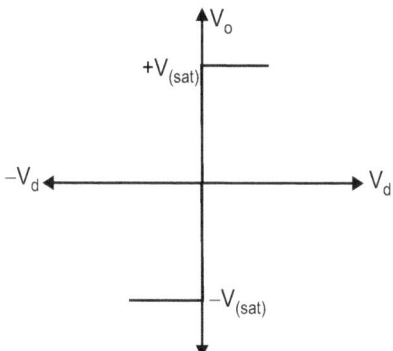

Fig. 1.42 : Ideal voltage transfer curve

Practical voltage transfer curve : Practically A_{OL} is finite for the op-amp. For op-amp, IC 741C, it is 2×10^5.

$$V_o = A_{OL} V_d$$
$$\pm V_{sat} = 2 \times 10^5 V_d$$

The saturation voltages are almost ± 15 V.

$$V_d = \frac{\pm 15}{2 \times 10^5} = \pm 75 \, \mu V$$

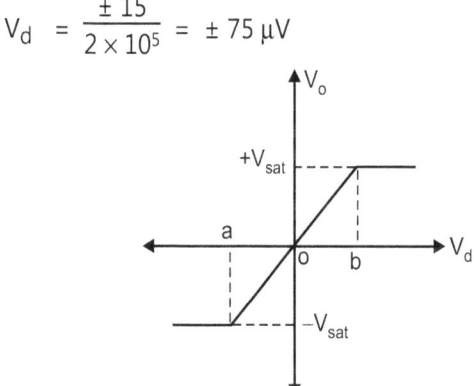

Fig. 1.43 : Practical voltage transfer curve

Hence, practically till V_d is between −75 µV and +75 µV, the output will vary linearly with input. But once V_d exceeds ± 75 µV, the output is saturated.

1.14 THE IDEAL OP-AMP ANALYSIS

An ideal op-amp has the following characteristics :
1. Infinite voltage gain.
2. Infinite input resistance R_i so that any signal can drive the op-amp and there will not be any loading effect on the preceding stages.
3. Zero output resistance R_o so that output can drive an infinite number of other devices.
4. Zero output voltage for zero input voltage.

5. Infinite bandwidth so that any signal from 0 to ∞ Hz can be amplified.
6. Infinite common mode rejection ratio so that output common mode noise is zero.
7. Infinite slew rate so that when the input voltage changes simultaneous changes occurs in output voltage.

1.15 EQUIVALENT CIRCUIT OF AN OP-AMP

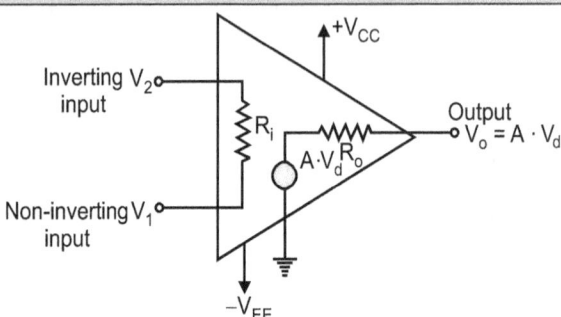

Fig. 1.44 : Equivalent circuit of an op-amp

Fig. 1.44 shows the equivalent circuit of an op-amp. The equivalent circuit is useful in analyzing the basic operating principles of op-amps as well as to observe the effects of feedback arrangement. For the circuit shown above, the output voltage is

$$V_o = AV_d = A(V_1 - V_2)$$

where,
- A = Large signal voltage gain
- V_d = Difference input voltage
- V_1 = Voltage at the inverting input terminal
- V_2 = Voltage at the non-inverting input terminal.

1.16 AC AND DC CHARACTERISTICS OF OP-AMP

The op-amp characteristics are mainly used to compare the performance of various op-amp ICs and to select the best op-amp for the required application.

The op-amp characteristics are divided into two categories : AC characteristics and DC characteristics.

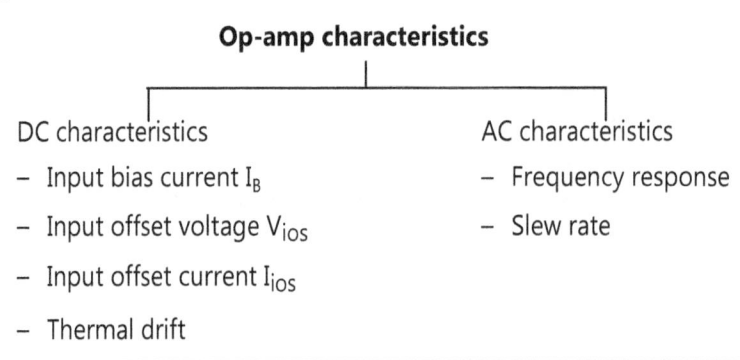

1.16.1 DC Characteristics

1. **Input offset voltage (V_{io}) :**

   It is the voltage that must be applied between the two input terminals of an op-amp to null the output.

   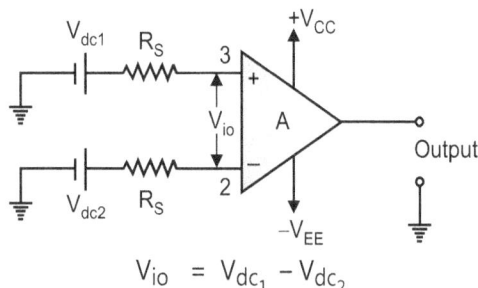

   $$V_{io} = V_{dc_1} - V_{dc_2}$$

   Fig. 1.45 : Input offset voltage measurement

2. **Input offset current (I_{io}) :**

   The algebraic difference between the currents into the inverting and non-inverting terminals is referred to as input offset voltage I_{ios}.

   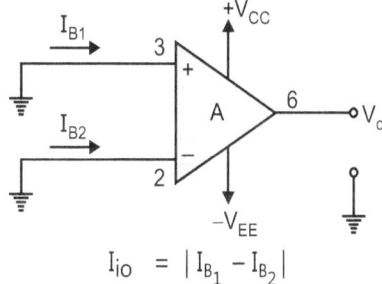

   $$I_{io} = |I_{B_1} - I_{B_2}|$$

   Fig. 1.46 : Input offset current measurement

3. **Differential input resistance (R_i) :**

   It is the equivalent resistance that can be measured at either the inverting or non-inverting input terminal with the other terminal grounded.

4. **Common Mode Rejection Ratio (CMRR) :**

   It is defined as the ratio of the differential voltage gain A_d to the common mode gain A_c.

   i.e. $$\text{CMRR} = \frac{A_d}{A_c}$$

   Generally, A_c is very small and A_d is very large. Therefore, CMRR is very large.

5. **Supply Voltage Rejection Ratio (SVRR) or Power Supply Rejection Ratio (PSRR) :**

   It is defined as the change in op-amp's input offset voltage V_{io} caused by variations in supply voltages. It is also known as power supply rejection ratio.

   $$\text{SVRR or PSRR} = \frac{\Delta V_{ios}}{\Delta V_{CC}}$$

6. Output resistance (R_o) :

Output resistance R_o is the equivalent resistance that can be measured between the output terminals of the op-amp and the ground.

7. Supply current (I_s) :

It is the current drawn by the op-amp from the power supply.

8. Input capacitance (C_i) :

It is the equivalent capacitance that can be measured at either the inverting or non-inverting input terminal with the other input terminal grounded.

9. Power consumption (P_c) :

It is the amount of power consumption by an op-amp with zero input voltage, for the proper functioning. It is denoted as P_c.

10. Output offset voltage (V_{oo}) :

The output offset voltage is the voltage present at the output terminals when both the input terminal are grounded.

11. Gain-bandwidth product :

The gain-bandwidth product is the bandwidth of the op-amp corresponding to unity gain.

12. Thermal drift :

The op-amp parameter changes with temperature, supply voltage changes and time. The effect of change in temperature on the parameter is most severe.

Thermal voltage drift :

It is also called as input offset voltage drift. It is defined as average rate of change of input offset voltage per unit change in temperature. Mathematically, it is given by

$$\text{Input offset voltage drift} = \frac{\Delta V_{io}}{\Delta T}$$

It is expressed in $\mu V/°C$. The drift is not constant and it is non-uniform over specified operating temperature range. The value of the input offset voltage may increase or decrease with the increasing temperature.

$$\text{Input bias current drift} = \frac{\Delta I_b}{\Delta T}$$

$$\text{Input offset current drift} = \frac{\Delta I_{io}}{\Delta T}$$

13. Offset voltage adjustment range :

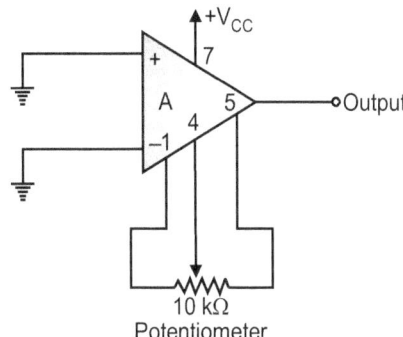

Fig. 1.47 : Offset voltage adjustment

The pins 1 and 5 are offset null pins for op-amp 741. A 10 kΩ potentiometer can be connected between the pins 1 and 5. The variable end of the potentiometer is connected to $-V_{EE}$. By varying potentiometer, the output can be adjusted to zero.

The range for which input offset voltage can be adjusted using the potentiometer so as to reduce output to zero, is called as offset voltage adjustment range.

For op-amp 741, it is ± 15 mV.

14. Transient response rise time :

When the output of the op-amp suddenly changes like pulse type, then the rise time of the response depends on the cut-off frequency f_H of the op-amp. Such a rise time is called as cut-off frequency, limited rise time or transient response rise time. It is inversely proportional to the cut-off frequency and is given by

$$t_r = \frac{0.35}{f_H}$$

1.16.2 AC Characteristics

The important AC characteristics of op-amp are :

(i) Slew Rate,

(ii) Frequency response.

1. Slew Rate :

It is defined as the maximum rate of change of output voltage per unit of time and is expressed in volts per microseconds.

$$SR = \left.\frac{dV_o}{dt}\right|_{max} \text{ V/μs}$$

Consider unity gain op-amp circuit with purely sinusoidal input. Output must be same as input.

$$V_s = V_m \sin \omega t$$
$$V_o = V_m \sin \omega t$$
$$\therefore \quad \frac{dV_o}{dt} = V_m (\omega \cos \omega t)$$

But
$$SR = \left.\frac{dV_o}{dt}\right|_{max}$$

The above equation has maximum output when $\cos \omega t = 1$.

$$\therefore \quad S = V_m \omega = 2\pi f V_m$$

$$\boxed{S = 2\pi f V_m} \; V/m$$

$$\boxed{f_m = \frac{S}{2\pi V_m}}$$

V_m is the peak of output waveform.

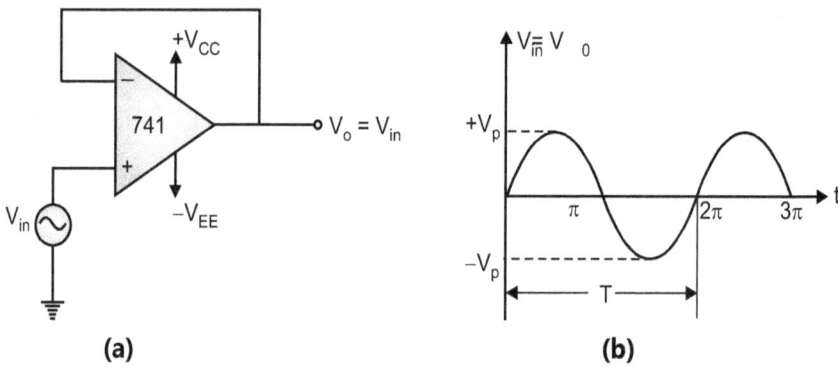

(a)   (b)

Fig. 1.48 : Unity gain amplifier with sinusoidal input

Example 1.12 :

An op-amp operates as a unity gain buffer with 3 V (peak to peak) square wave input. If op-amp is ideal with slew rate 0.5 V/μsec, find the maximum frequency of operation.

Solution :

Peak to peak voltage of square wave = 3 V

$$V_m = \frac{V_{P-P}}{2} = \frac{3}{2} = 1.5 \; V$$

$$f_m = \frac{S}{2\pi V_m} = \frac{\left(\frac{0.5}{10^{-6}}\right)}{2\pi \times 1.5} = 53.051 \; kHz$$

Example 1.13 :

For a typical op-amp, I_{CQ} = 15 μA and C = 35 pF. The peak value of input is 12 V. Determine slew rate and maximum possible frequency of input voltage that can be applied to get undistorted output.

Solution :

$I_{max} = I_{CQ}$ = 15 μA, C = 35 pF, V_m = 12 V

$$\therefore \quad S = \frac{I_{max}}{C} = \frac{15 \times 10^{-6}}{35 \times 10^{-12}} = 0.4285 \times 10^6 \text{ V/sec}$$

and

$$f_m = \frac{S}{2\pi V_m} = \frac{0.4285 \times 10^6}{2 \times \pi \times 12} = 5.684 \text{ kHz}$$

Upto this frequency, output will be undistorted.

Example 1.14 :

An op-amp has 7 kHz sine wave input signal. Find the largest amplitude that the output of the amplifier can have without distortion with I_{CQ} of 8 μA and C_C of 27 pF.

Solution :

$$S = \frac{I}{C} = \frac{8 \times 10^{-6}}{27 \times 10^{-12}} = 0.2962 \text{ V/μsec}$$

$$f_m = \frac{S}{2\pi V_m} = 7 \text{ kHz}$$

$$V_m = \frac{S}{2\pi f_m} = \frac{\frac{0.2962}{10^{-6}}}{2\pi \times 7 \times 10^{-3}} = 6.736 \text{ volts}$$

Example 1.15 :

The parameters of an IC 741 op-amp are I_{CQ} = 10 μA and C_C = 33 pF. The input voltage has an amplitude of 15 V. What is the slew rate ? Also calculate the maximum possible frequency of the input signal. Which gives undistorted output.

Solution :

$$S = \left.\frac{dV_o}{dt}\right|_{max} \quad \text{- Rate of charging of the internal capacitor}$$

$$= \frac{dV_C}{dt} \quad \text{where, } V_C = \text{capacitor voltage}$$

or

$$\left.\frac{dV_o}{dt}\right|_{max} = \frac{d}{dt}\left[\frac{Q}{C_C}\right]$$

Since charge $Q = C_c \cdot V_c$

$$\frac{1}{C_c}\left[\frac{dQ}{dt}\right] = \frac{I_{max}}{C_c}$$

$$S = \frac{I_{max}}{C_c}$$

$$S = \frac{10 \times 10^{-6}}{33 \times 10^{-12}} = 0.303 \text{ V/}\mu s$$

$$V_m = 15 \text{ V}$$

$$\therefore f_{max} = \frac{0.303/10^{-6}}{2\pi \times 15}$$

$$= 3.215 \text{ kHz}$$

Example 1.16 :

An op-amp has a slew rate of 0.5 V/μs. If the input signal varies by 0.25 V in 10 μs. Find the maximum voltage gain.

Solution :

$$S = 0.5 \text{ V/}\mu s$$

$$\frac{dV_i}{dt} = \left(\frac{0.25}{10}\right) \text{V/}\mu s = 0.025 \text{ V/}\mu s$$

$$A = \frac{V_o}{V_i}$$

$$V_o = AV_i$$

$$\frac{dV_o}{dt} = A\frac{dV_i}{dt}$$

$$\left.\frac{dV_o}{dt}\right|_{max} = SR$$

$$A_{max} = \frac{\left.\frac{dV_o}{dt}\right|_{max}}{\frac{dV_i}{dt}} = \frac{SR}{(dV_i/dt)}$$

$$= \frac{0.5/10^{-6}}{0.025 \times 10^{-6}} = 20$$

$$\therefore A_{max} = 20$$

Example 1.17 :

For an op-amp, PSRR = 70 dB (min), CMRR = 10^5 and differential mode gain $A_d = 10^5$. The output voltage changes by 20 V in 4 μsec.

Calculate :

(i) Numerical value of PSRR,

(ii) Common mode gain,

(iii) Slew rate.

Solution :

Note that PSRR must be as small as possible and given 70 dB indicates the amount by which change in supply voltage is rejected. Ideally, it should be zero.

Hence, while calculating numerical value, given PSRR must be treated negative i.e. -70 dB.

(i)
$$\text{PSRR in dB} = 20 \log_{10} \text{PSRR}$$
$$-70 = 20 \log_{10} \text{PSRR}$$
$$\text{PSRR} = \text{Antilog}(-3.5)$$
$$= 3.1622 \times 10^{-4} \text{ V/V}$$

(ii)
$$\text{CMRR} = \frac{A_d}{A_c}$$
$$A_c = \frac{10^5}{10^5}$$
$$A_c = 1$$

(iii) ΔV_o = 20 V and Δt = 4 μsec

$$S = \left.\frac{\Delta V_o}{\Delta t}\right|_{max}$$
$$= \frac{20}{4 \times 10^{-6}} = 5 \times 10^6 \text{ V/sec}$$

2. Full Power Response

Full power bandwidth is obtain when the frequency of operation is maximum.

The maximum frequency of operation at which the output can be obtained without distortion.

Maximum power bandwidth can be obtained as follows :

Consider the input signal,

$$V_{in} = V_m \sin \omega t$$
$$= V_m \sin (2\pi f t)$$

For the unity gain amplifier.

$$V_o = V_{in}$$
$$\frac{dV_o}{dt} = V_m (\omega \cos \omega t)$$

But

$$S = \left.\frac{dV_o}{dt}\right|_{max}$$

The above equation has maximum output when

$$\cos \omega t = 1$$
$$S = V_m \omega$$
$$S = 2\pi f V_m$$

$$\boxed{f_{max} = \frac{S}{2\pi V_m}}$$

3. Frequency Response :

Ideally, op-amp should have an infinite bandwidth. This means the gain of op-amp must remain same for all frequencies from zero to infinite. Uptill now we have assumed gain of the op-amp as constant, but practically op-amp gain decreases as the frequency increases. Such a gain reduction with respect to frequency is called as roll off. This happens because gain of the op-amp depends on the frequency and hence mathematically it is a complex number. It is magnitude and phase angle changes with the frequency.

The plot showing the variations in magnitude and phase angle of the gain due to the change in frequency is called frequency of response of the op-amp.

As the frequency increases, the two effects become more evident :

1. The gain (magnitude) of the amplifier decreases.
2. The phase shift between the output and input signals increases.

In op-amp, the changes in gain and phase shift as a function of frequency is attributed to the internally integrated capacitors as well as stray capacitors. These capacitors are due to semiconductor devices such as BJTs and FETs as well as the internal construction of the op-amp.

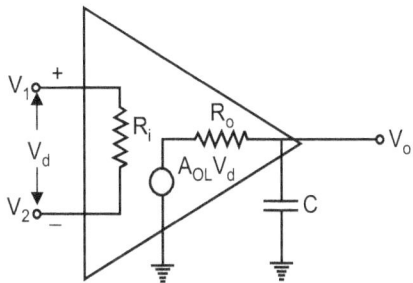

Fig. 1.49 : High frequency model of op-amp

Let $-jX_C$ be the capacitive reactance due to capacitor C. Using voltage divider rule,

$$V_o = -jX_C \left[\frac{A_{OL} V_d}{R_o - jX_C}\right]$$

$$-j = \frac{1}{j} \quad \text{and} \quad X_C = \frac{1}{2\pi f C}$$

$$V_o = \frac{\frac{1}{j2\pi f C}}{R_o + \frac{1}{j2\pi f C}} (A_{OL} V_d)$$

$$V_o = \frac{A_{OL} V_d}{1 + j2\pi f C R_o}$$

Hence, the open loop voltage gain as a function of frequency is

$$A_{OL}(f) = \frac{V_o}{V_d}$$

$$A_{OL}(f) = \frac{A_{OL}}{1 + j2\pi f C R_o}$$

$$f_o = \frac{1}{2\pi R_o C}$$

$$A_{OL}(f) = \frac{A_{OL}}{1 + j(f/f_o)}$$

where, $A_{OL}(f)$ = Open loop voltage gain as a function of frequency

A_{OL} = Gain of op-amp at zero Hz

f = Operating frequency

f_o = Break frequency or cut-off frequency of op-amp

The break frequency f_o depends on the value of C and on output resistance R_o. Therefore, f_o is fixed for a given op-amp. The above equation can be written in the polar form as :

$$|A_{OL}(f)| = \frac{A_{OL}}{\sqrt{1 + (f/f_o)^2}}$$

$$A_{OL}(f) = \phi(f) = -\tan^{-1}\left(\frac{f}{f_o}\right)$$

At 0 Hz, the denominator is 1, the open-loop gain $A_{OL}(f)$ is equal to A_{OL} and $\phi(f) = 0°$.

As the frequency increases till f_o, the gain is almost constant but after f_o, the gain reduces with a rate of – 20 dB/decade. The maximum possible phase shift is – 90°.

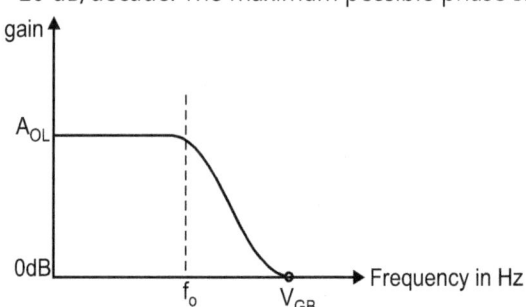

Fig. 1.50 : Frequency response of an op-amp with a single break frequency

(i) From 0 Hz to the break frequency f_o, the open loop gain remains constant.

(ii) At $f = f_o$, the gain is 3 dB down from its value at 0 Hz. Hence, the frequency f_o is called – 3 dB frequency. It is called as corner frequency.

(iii) After $f = f_o$, the gain $A_{OL}(f)$ decreases at a rate of 20 dB/decade or 6 dB/octave. A decade is 10 times change in frequency while octave is 2 times change in frequency. As gain decreases, the slope of the magnitude plot is – 20 dB/decade.

(iv) At a certain frequency, the gain reduces to 0 dB. This means 20 log $|A_{OL}(f)|$ is 0 dB. i.e. $|A_{OL}(f)| = 1$. Such a frequency is called gain crossover frequency or unity gain bandwidth (V_{GB}). It is also called as closed loop bandwidth.

$$V_{GB} = A_{OL} \cdot f_o$$

1.17 COMPARISON OF IDEAL VERSUS PRACTICAL CHARACTERISTICS OF IC 741C

Parameter	Symbol	Ideal	Typical for IC 741C
Open loop voltage gain	A_{OL}	∞	2×10^5
Input offset voltage	V_{io}	0	6 mV
Input offset current	I_{io}	0	20 nA
Input bias current	I_B	0	80 nA
Input impedance	R_i	∞	2 MΩ
Output resistance	R_o	0	75 Ω
Power Supply Rejection Ratio	PSRR	0	30 µV/V
Common Mode Rejection Ratio	CMRR	∞	90 dB
Bandwidth	BW	∞	1 MHz
Slew Rate	SR	∞	0.5 V/µs
Power consumption	P_C	0	50 mw

1.18 OP-AMP TECHNOLOGIES

Various technologies are used for the op-amps with the help of

1. Bipolar technology,
2. MOSFET technology,
3. BiCMOS technology,
4. JFET technology.

1. Bipolar op-amps :

In a bipolar op-amp, all the stages are designed with the help of bipolar transistors. Bipolar op-amps are used for the applications when there is a requirement of large output currents. Bipolar op-amps can sink and source very large currents. Bipolar op-amps produce less noise. It has very large unity gain bandwidth.

Features of bipolar op-amps :

- Provides high voltage gain.
- Can sink and source large currents.
- Have very large unity gain bandwidth.
- Low output resistance.
- High input resistance.
- Produces less noise.

2. **MOSFET op-amps :**

It uses only MOSFETs without any BJT using complementary MOS technology. MOSFETs are mainly used in applications where there is a requirement to drive large capacitive loads. CMOS op-amps have high output resistance. The overall voltage gain of CMOS op-amp is lower than that of the bipolar op-amps.

Features of CMOS op-amps :
- Uses only MOSFETs.
- Drives capacitive loads.
- Low voltage gains compared to bipolar.
- High output resistance.
- High input resistance.
- More noisy.

3. **BiCMOS op-amps :**

BiCMOS technology produces all the advantages of bipolar as well as the MOSFET devices. This type of technology uses both bipolar and MOSFETs to fabricate the op-amps. In this technology, MOSFETs are used to design the input stage and bipolar transistors are used to design the output stage. Due to this it gives high input resistance and low output resistance. It also can sink and source high currents. It produces more noise than the bipolar technology. It produces high unity gain bandwidth. It produces more noise.

Features of BiCMOS op-amps :
- Uses both bipolar transistors and MOSFETs.
- MOSFETs used at the input side and bipolar transistors are used for output side.
- High input resistance.
- Low output resistance.
- Can sink and source high current.
- High unity gain bandwidth.
- Noisy.

The comparison of these technologies is summarized in the table given below.

Table 1.1

Parameter	Bipolar op-amps	CMOS op-amps	BiCMOS op-amps
Input resistance	Moderate	Very large	Very large
Output resistance	Less	Large	Less
Unity gain bandwidth	Moderate	Very large	Very large
Slew rate	1 V/µs	2.5 V/µs	10 V/µs
Current sink/Source capability	Large	Less	Large

1.19 FEATURES OF IC 741 OP-AMP

1. IC 741 op-amp is a internally compensated operational amplifier by Fairchild corporation.
2. No external frequency compensation is required.
3. Provides short circuit protection.
4. Provides offset null capability.
5. Large common mode and differential voltage ranges.
6. Low power consumption.
7. No latch-up problems.

1.20 PIN CONFIGURATION

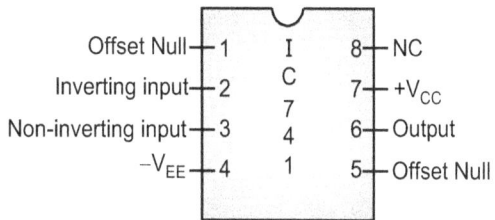

Fig. 1.51: Pin configuration of IC 741

1.21 IC TYPES

There are two types of IC : (i) Digital ICs and (ii) Linear ICs.

Digital ICs are used for gates, counters, multiplexers, demultiplexers, shift registers and others. It uses two levels of voltage high or low.

Linear ICs are equivalent of discrete transistor networks, such as amplifiers, filters, frequency multipliers and modulators. It often requires additional external components for satisfactory operation.

In linear circuits the output electrical signals vary in proportion to the input signals.

Op-amps are classified as :

1. Special purpose op-amps. e.g. LM380.
2. General purpose op-amps. e.g. IC 741C.

Another classification of ICs are :

1. Monolithic ICs
2. Hybrid ICs.

Monolithic is a Greek-based word meaning one stone. Most linear ICs are produced by the monolithic process, in which all transistors and passive elements are fabricated on a single piece of semiconductor material.

In hybrid ICs, passive components and the interconnections between them are placed on a insulating substrate. Active components such as transistors and diodes are then connected to complete a circuit.

Hybrid ICs are divided into two categories :

(1) Thick film and (2) Thin film.

When a suitable material is evaporated on a substrate in forming resistors, capacitors and interconnections, a thin film hybrid IC is obtained.

On the other hand, in a thick film hybrid IC, the resistors, capacitors and interconnections are etched on the substrate by silk screening.

1.22 IC DESIGNATIONS

Manufacturers use a specific code and assign a specific type number to the IC it produces. For example, the IC 741 type of internally compensated op-amp was originally manufactured by Fairchild and is sold as µA 741.

Initials used by some of the well known manufacturers of linear ICs are as follows :

Manufacturer	Initials
Fairchild	µA, µAF
National semiconductor	LM, LH, LF, TBA
Motorola	MC, MFC
RCA	CA, CD
Texas Instruments	SN
Sprague	ULN, ULS, ULX
Intersil	ICL, IH
Siliconix, Inc.	L
Signetics	N/S, NE/SE, SU
Burr-Brown	BB

Fairchild's original µA741 is also manufactured by various other manufacturers under their own designation.

National semiconductor	LM741
Motorola	MCI741
RCA	CA3741
Texas Instruments	SN52741
Signetics	N5741

Some linear ICs are available in different classes such as A, C, E, S and SC.

For example : 741, 741A, 741C, 741E, 741S and 741SC are different versions of op-amp.

The 741 is a military-grade op-amp (− 55°C to 125°C) and 741C is a commercial-grade op-amp (0°C to 70°/75°C).

741A and 741E are improved versions of the 741 and 741C respectively.

1.23 CLASSIFICATION OF ICS

ICs are classified according to the number of components integrated on the same chip.

SSI < 10 components

MSI < 100 components

LSI > 100 components

VLSI > 1000 components

1.24 PACKAGE TYPES

Three basic types of linear IC packages are available. They are :

1. The flat pack,
2. The metal can or transistor pack,
3. The dual in line pack (DIP).

In a flat pack, the chip is enclosed in a rectangular ceramic cage with terminal leads extending through the sides and ends. The flat pack comes with 8, 10, 14 or 16 leads.

In metal can or transistor pack, the chip is encapsulated in a metal or plastic case. The transistor pack is available with 3, 5, 8, 10 or 12 pins. The metal can package is best suited for power amplifiers because metal is a good heat conductor and consequently has better dissipation capability than the flat pack or DIP package. Metal can package permits the use of external heat sinks. Most of the general purpose op-amps come in 8, 10 or 12 pin packages.

In DIP packages, the chip is mounted inside a plastic or ceramic case. The DIP is the most widely used package type because it can be mounted easily. The 8 pin DIP packages are referred as mini-DIP. Dual-in-line packages are also available with 12, 14, 16 and 20 pins.

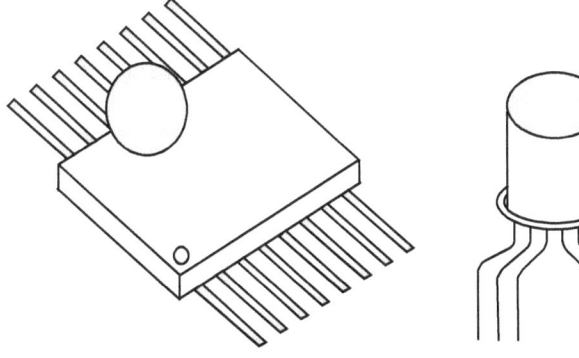
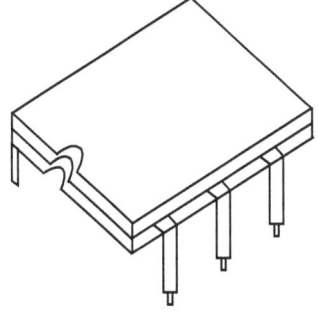

(a) Ceramic flat package   (b) Metal can package   (c) Dual in line package

Fig. 1.52: IC packages

1.25 TEMPERATURE RANGES

All ICs manufactured full into one of the three basic temperature grades :
1. Military temperature range : – 55°C to + 125°C.
2. Industrial temperature range : – 20°C to + 85°C
3. Commercial temperature range : 0°C to + 70°C

1.26 POWER SUPPLIES FOR ICS

Most linear ICs use one or more differential amplifier stages. Differential amplifiers requires both a positive and negative power supplies for proper operation of the circuit. This means most linear ICs need both a positive and negative power supply and some ICs require only a positive supply.

The two power supplies required for a linear IC are usually equal in magnitude + 15 V and – 15 V. These power supply voltages must be referenced to a common point or ground.

1.26.1 Power Supplies for Integrated Circuits

To work properly, op-amp needs power supply voltages. Op-amp needs dual power supply. Op-amp requires the power supply to provide biasing to the transistors internal to op-amp.

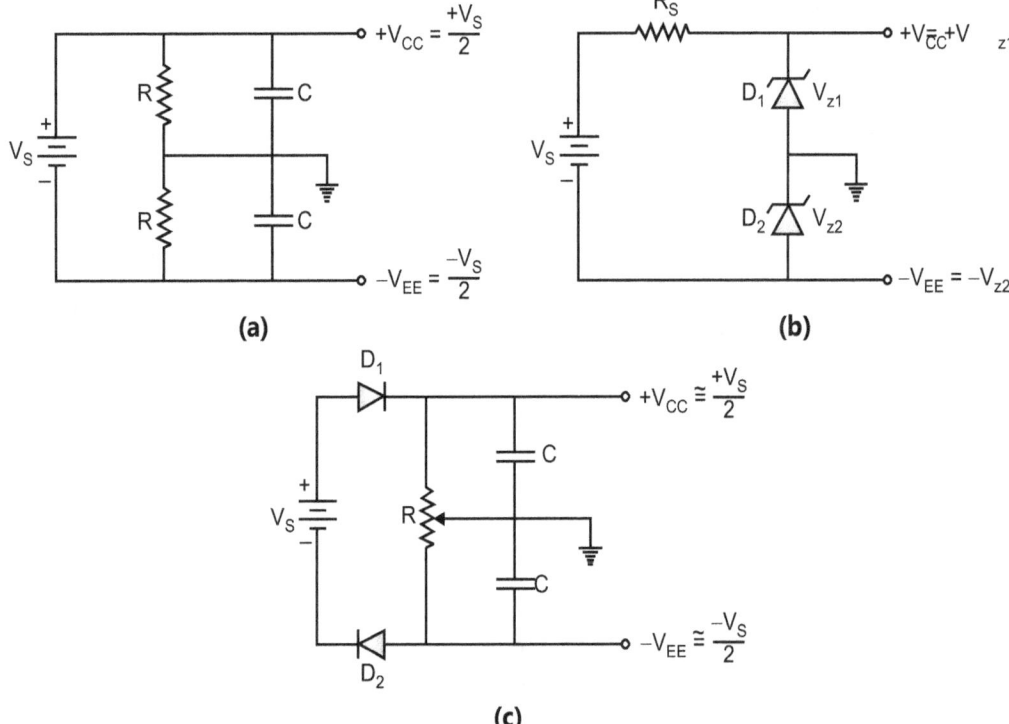

Fig. 1.53 : Different arrangements for obtaining positive and negative supply voltages for an op-amp

Instead of using two power supplies, we can use a single power supply to obtain $+V_{CC}$ and $-V_{EE}$. In Fig. 1.53 the value of the total resistance (2R) should be ≥ 10 kΩ. So that it does not draw much current from the supply V_S. The two capacitors are provided for bypassing of the power supply. They range in value from 0.01 to 10 µF.

In Fig. 1.53, the zener diodes are used to obtain symmetrical supply voltages. The value of R_S should be chosen such that it supplies sufficient current for the diodes to operate in the avalanche mode. The potentiometer used to assure quality between $+V_{CC}$ and $-V_{EE}$ values. Diodes D_1 and D_2 are used to protect the IC if the positive and negative leads of the supply voltage V_S are accidentally reversed.

1.27 MEASUREMENT OF OP-AMP PARAMETERS

1.27.1 Input Offset Voltage (V_{io})

1. **Input offset voltage (V_{io})** :

It is the voltage that must be applied between the two input terminals of an op-amp to null the output. For op-amp IC 741 it is 6 mV.

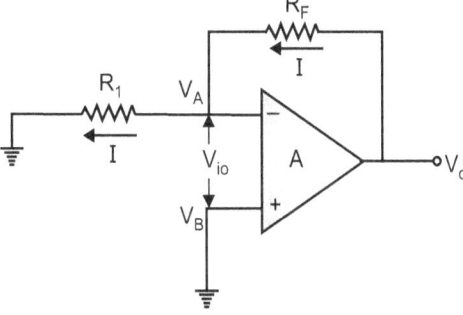

Fig. 1.54

The current flowing through R_F is I and is given as

$$I = \frac{V_o - V_A}{R_F}$$

$$V_A = V_{io}$$

$$I = \frac{V_o - V_{io}}{R_F}$$

and the current flowing through R_1 is also I and is given as

$$I = \frac{V_{io}}{R_1}$$

$$\frac{V_{io}}{R_1} = \frac{V_o - V_{io}}{R_F}$$

$$\boxed{V_o = V_{io}\left[1 + \frac{R_F}{R_1}\right]}$$

Input offset voltage compensation :

To obtain zero output voltage for zero input offset voltage must be compensated.

In most of the op-amps, the offset compensation pins are provided to null the offset voltage. For example, in IC 741 op-amp pin 1 and pin 5 are provided for compensation. A 10 kΩ potentiometer must be connected between pin 1 and 5 and wiper must be connected to the negative supply.

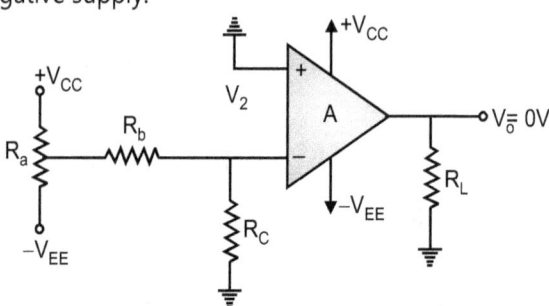

Fig. 1.55 : Offset voltage compensating network

If the op-amp does not contain internal compensating network then external compensating network must be designed.

Fig. 1.55 shows the external compensating network.

To establish a relation between V_{io}, supply voltages and the compensating components, we first have to Thevenize the circuit.

Maximum Thevenin's equivalent resistance occurs when the wiper is at the centre of the potentiometer.

$$R_{max} = \frac{R_a}{2} \parallel \frac{R_a}{2} = \frac{R_a}{4}$$

The maximum Thevenin's voltage V_{max} is equal to either V_{CC} or $-V_{EE}$ when the wiper is uppermost in the potentiometer or lowest in the potentiometer.

$$V_{max} = |V_{CC}| = |-V_{EE}| = V$$

By applying the voltage divider rule to the circuit

$$V_2 = \frac{R_C}{R_{max} + R_b + R_C} V_{max}$$

$$|V_1 - V_2| = V_{io}$$

$$V_{io} = \frac{R_C}{R_{max} + R_b + R_C} V_{max}$$

$$\boxed{V_{io} = \frac{R_C V_{max}}{R_b}}$$

To simplify the equation, we have to assume that

$$R_b > R_{max} > R_C$$
$$R_b > R_a;\ R_b > R_{max}$$
$$R_{max} + R_b + R_C \cong R_b$$

1.27.2 Measurement of Input Offset Current

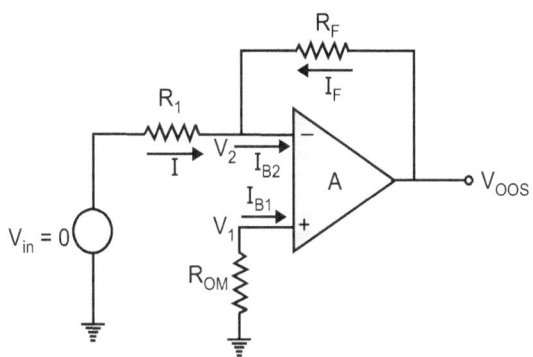

Fig. 1.56 : Measurement of input offset current

Input offset current is the algebraic difference of the two currents that are flowing through the two input terminals.

Analysis :

$$V_1 = I_{B1} R_{OM}$$

$$I_1 = \frac{V_2}{R_1}$$

$$I_1 = \frac{I_{B1} R_{OM}}{R_1} \quad \text{since } V_1 = V_2$$

Apply KCL at node V_2

$$I_F = I_{B2} - I_1$$

$$= I_{B2} - \frac{I_{B1} R_{OM}}{R_1}$$

Apply KVL at inverting terminal from input to output side

$$-V_2 + V_F - V_o = 0$$

$$V_o = V_F - V_2$$

$$V_o = I_F R_F - V_1$$

$$V_o = \left(I_{B2} - \frac{I_{B1} R_{OM}}{R_1}\right) R_F - I_{B1} R_{OM}$$

$$= I_{B2} R_F - \frac{I_{B1} R_F R_{OM}}{R_1} - I_{B1} R_{OM}$$

$$= I_{B2} R_F - I_{B1} R_{OM} \left[\frac{R_F}{R_1} - 1\right]$$

$$R_{OM} = \frac{R_1 R_F}{R_1 + R_F}$$

$$= I_{B2} R_F - I_{B1} \frac{R_1 R_F}{R_1 + R_F} \left[\frac{R_F}{R_1} - 1\right]$$

$$= I_{B2} R_F - I_{B1} \left[\frac{R_F R_F}{R_1 + R_F} - \frac{R_1 R_F}{R_1 + R_F}\right]$$

$$= I_{B2} R_F - I_{B1} \left[\frac{R_F (R_F + R_1)}{(R_1 + R_F)}\right]$$

$$= I_{B2} R_F - I_{B1} R_F$$

$$= R_F [I_{B2} - I_{B1}]$$

$$\boxed{V_o = R_F I_{io}}$$

Input Bias Current Compensation :

Here when input voltage V_{in} is zero, output voltage must be zero but practically currents I_{B1} and I_{B2} flows through non-inverting and inverting terminals respectively. Therefore, practically we get the output voltage due to I_{B1} or I_{B2} as

$$\boxed{V_o = I_{B2} R_F}$$

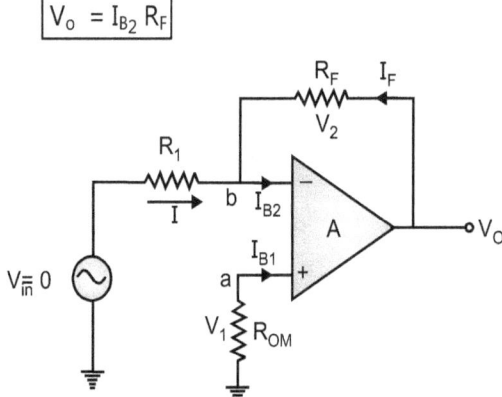

Fig. 1.57 : Input bias current compensation

To compensate this bias current a resistor called R_{OM} is connected at the non-inverting terminal of the op-amp.

Apply KCL at node B, $I_{B2} = I_1 + I_F$

$$I_{B1} = \frac{V_1}{R_1} + \frac{V_2}{R_F}$$

$$\frac{V_1}{R_{OM}} = \frac{V_1}{R_1} + \frac{V_2}{R_F}$$

Since $V_1 = V_2$ due to virtual ground concept.

$$\frac{1}{R_{OM}} = \frac{1}{R_1} + \frac{1}{R_F}$$

$\therefore \quad R_{OM} = R_1 \parallel R_F$

Example 1.18 :

Design a compensating network for LM 307. The op-amp uses ± 10 V supply voltages. The V_{io} = 10 mV.

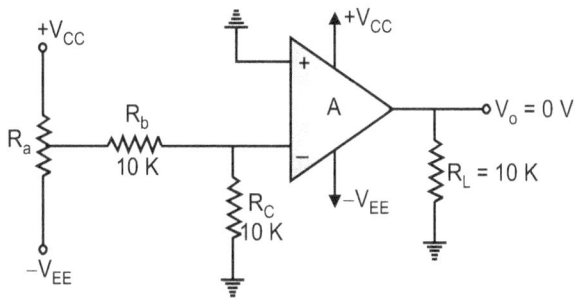

Fig. 1.58

Solution :

$$V = |V_{CC}| = |V_{EE}| = 10 \text{ V}$$
$$V_{ios} = 10 \text{ mV}$$
$$V_{ios} = \frac{R_C}{R_b} \times V_{max}$$
$$10 \text{ mV} = \frac{R_C}{R_b} \times 10 \text{ V}$$
$$R_b = \frac{10 \text{ V}}{10 \text{ mV}} \times R_C$$
$$R_b = 1000 \, R_C$$

If we select $R_C = 10 \, \Omega$.

$$R_b = 1000 \times 10 = 10 \text{ k}\Omega$$

Since, $R_b > R_{max}$ let us choose $R_b = 10 \, R_{max}$ where, $R_{max} = \frac{R_a}{4}$.

$$R_b = 10 \times \frac{R_a}{4}$$
$$R_a = \frac{R_b}{2.5} = \frac{10 \text{ K}}{2.5} = 4 \text{ k}\Omega \text{ potentiometer}$$
$$R_a = 3 \text{ k}\Omega \text{ potentiometer}$$
$$R_b = 10 \text{ k}\Omega$$
$$R_C = 10 \text{ k}\Omega$$

Example 1.19:

For an op-amp the $V_{io} = 12$ mV, the biasing current is 500 nA and $I_{io} = 90$ nA.

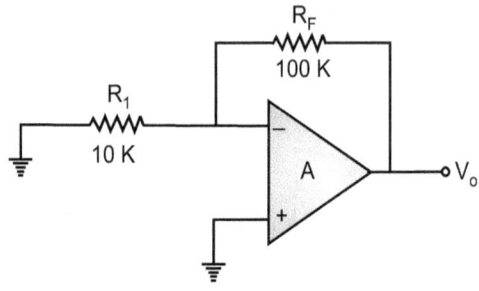

Fig. 1.59

Calculate : (i) V_{oos}, (ii) R_{OM}, (3) V_{oos} with R_{OM}.

Solution :

Offset voltage without compensating resistor.

(i)
$$V_{oos} = V_{io}\left(1 + \frac{R_F}{R_1}\right) + R_F I_B$$

$$= 12 \times 10^{-3}\left(1 + \frac{100\text{ K}}{10\text{ K}}\right) + 100\text{ K} \times 500 \times 10^{-9}$$

$$= 182 \text{ mV}$$

(ii)
$$R_{OM} = R_1 \parallel R_F = \frac{R_1 R_F}{R_1 + R_F}$$

$$\frac{100 \times 1}{100 + 1} = \frac{100}{101} = 9.09 \text{ k}\Omega$$

(iii) V_{oos} with compensating resistor

$$V_{oos} = \left(1 + \frac{R_F}{R_1}\right)V_{io} + R_F I_{io}$$

$$= \left(1 + \frac{100}{1}\right) \times 12 \times 10^{-3} + 100 \times 10^3 \times 90 \times 10^{-9}$$

$$= 141 \text{ mV}$$

1.28 EFFECT OF TEMPERATURE ON OP-AMP PARAMETERS

The op-amp parameter changes with (1) temperature, (2) supply voltage changes, (3) time.

The effect of change in temperature on the parameter is most severe.

(1) Thermal voltage drift :

It is also called as input offset voltage drift.

It is defined as average rate of change of input offset voltage per unit change in temperature. Mathematically, it is given by

$$\text{Input offset voltage drift} = \frac{\Delta V_{io}}{\Delta T}.$$

It is expressed in µV/°C. The drift is not constant and it is non-uniform over specified operating temperature range. The value of the input offset voltage may increase or decrease with the increasing temperature.

$$\text{Input bias current drift} = \frac{\Delta I_b}{\Delta T}$$

$$\text{Input offset current drift} = \frac{\Delta I_{io}}{\Delta T}.$$

(2) Error voltage :

The total output offset voltage is due to input offset voltage and input offset current.

$$\therefore \quad V_{oos} = \left(1 + \frac{R_F}{R_1}\right) V_{io} + R_F I_{io}$$

The change in total offset voltage due to change in temperature is known as error voltage.

$$\frac{\Delta V_{oos}}{\Delta T} = \frac{\Delta V_{io}}{\Delta T}\left(1 + \frac{R_F}{R_1}\right) + R_F \frac{\Delta I_{io}}{\Delta T}$$

$$\Delta V_{oos} = E_V$$

$$E_V = \frac{\Delta V_{io}}{\Delta T}\left(1 + \frac{R_F}{R_1}\right)\Delta T + R_F \frac{\Delta I_{io}}{\Delta T} \Delta T$$

$$V_o = V_i \pm E_V$$

Example 1.20 :

For the non-inverting amplifier shown in Fig. 1.60. $R_1 = 10 \text{ k}\Omega$, $R_F = 50 \text{ k}\Omega$.

(a) What is the maximum output offset voltage due to V_{io} and I_B ? The op-amp is LM 307 with $V_{io} = 10$ mV and $I_B = 300$ nA and $I_{io} = 50$ nA.

(b) Also calculate the value of R_{OM} required to reduce the effect of I_B.

(c) What is the maximum output offset voltage if R_{OM} as calculated in (b) is connected in the circuit.

Given :

V_{io} = 10 mV

I_B = 300 nA

I_{io} = 50 nA

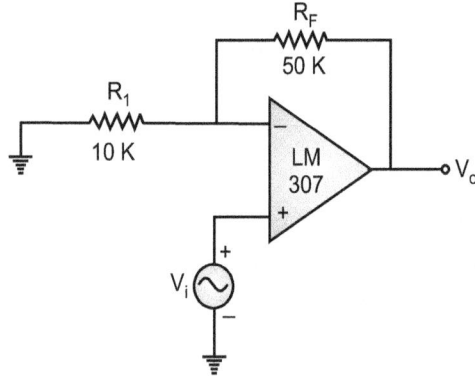

Fig. 1.60

(1) $$V_{oos} = \left(1 + \frac{R_F}{R_1}\right) V_{io} + R_F I_B$$

$$= \left(1 + \frac{50\ K}{10\ K}\right) 10 \times 10^{-3} + 50 \times 10^3 \times 300 \times 10^{-9}$$

$$= 60 \times 10^{-3} + 15 \times 10^{-3}$$

$$= 75\ mV$$

(2) $$R_{OM} = R_1 \| R_F = \frac{R_1 R_F}{R_1 + R_F}$$

$$= \frac{10 \times 50}{10 + 50}$$

$$= 8.33\ k\Omega$$

(3) V_{oos} with R_{OM}

$$V_{oos} = \left(1 + \frac{R_F}{R_1}\right) V_{io} + R_F I_{io}$$

$$= 60\ mV + (50 \times 10^3 \times 50 \times 10^{-9})$$

$$= 60\ mV + 2.5\ mV = 62.5\ mV$$

Example 1.21 :

A non-inverting amplifier with a gain of 120 is nulled at 25°C. Find the output voltage if the temperature increases to 75°C for an offset voltage drift of 0.1 mV/°C.

Solution :

Gain of the op-amp A_{CL} = 120, t_1 = 25°C, t_2 = final temperature = 75°C.

Offset voltage drift = 0.1 mV/°C

Increase in temperature = $t_2 - t_1$ = 75 – 25 = 50°C

∴ Input offset voltage due to increase in temperature = 0.1 × 50 = 5 mV.

Output voltage is gain times the input voltage.

∴ Output voltage = 120 × 5 mV

= 600 mV

= 0.6 V

Example 1.22 :

For an inverting amplifier with R_1 = 1 kΩ and R_F = 50 kΩ, the input offset voltage drift is 10 μV/°C and the input offset current drift is 0.6 nA/°C. The amplifier is nulled at the room temperature of 25°C. Calculate the error voltage and the output voltage at 50°C, if the input is 5 mV DC.

Solution :

R_1 = 1 kΩ, R_F = 50 kΩ, ΔT = $t_2 - t_1$ = 50 – 25 = 25°C.

$$E_V = \left(1 + \frac{R_F}{R_1}\right) \frac{\Delta V_{ios}}{\Delta T} \cdot \Delta T + R_F \left(\frac{\Delta I_{ios}}{\Delta T}\right) \cdot \Delta T$$

$$= \left(1 + \frac{50}{1}\right)(10 \times 10^{-6})\, 25 + (50 \times 10^3)(0.5 \times 10^{-9})\, 25$$

= 12.75 mV + 0.625 mV

= 13.375 mV

(2) **Output voltage :** $V_o = \left(-\frac{R_F}{R_1}\right) V_S \pm E_V$

$= \left(-\frac{50}{1}\right) 5 \times 10^{-3} \pm 13.375$ mV

= (–250 + 13.375) mV or (–250 – 13.375) mV

= –236.625 mV or –263.375 mV

Example 1.23:

For the inverting amplifier shown in Fig. 1.61 the specifications are given for LM 307 are as follows:

$$\frac{\Delta V_{io}}{\Delta T} = 30 \ \mu V/°C \ max$$

$$\frac{\Delta I_{io}}{\Delta T} \ max = 300 \ PA/°A$$

$$V_S = \pm 15 \ V$$

$$R_1 = 1 \ k\Omega, \ R_F = 100 \ k\Omega, \ R_L = 10 \ k\Omega$$

Assume that the amplifier is nulled at 25°C. If V_{in} is a 10 mV peak sine wave at 1 kHz.

(a) Calculate E_v and V_o values at 55°C.
(b) Draw the output voltage.

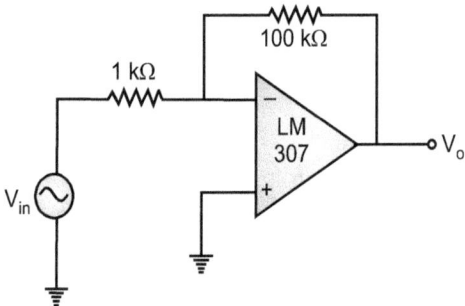

Fig. 1.61

Solution:

The change in temperature,

$$\Delta T = t_2 - t_1 = 55 - 25 = 30°C$$

$$E_v = \left(1 + \frac{R_F}{R_1}\right)\left(\frac{\Delta V_{io}}{\Delta T}\right)\Delta T + R_F \left(\frac{\Delta I_{io}}{\Delta T}\right)\Delta T$$

$$= \left(1 + \frac{100}{1}\right)(30 \times 10^{-6}) \times 30 + 100 \times 10^3 \times 300 \times 10^{-12} \times 30$$

$$= 90.9 \ mV + 0.9 \ mV$$

$$= 91.8 \ mV \ DC$$

$$V_o = \left(-\frac{R_F}{R_1}\right) V_{in} \pm E_v$$

$$= \left(-\frac{100}{1}\right) 10 \times 10^{-3} \pm 91.8 \ mV$$

$$= -1000 \ mV \ peak \pm 91.8 \ mV$$

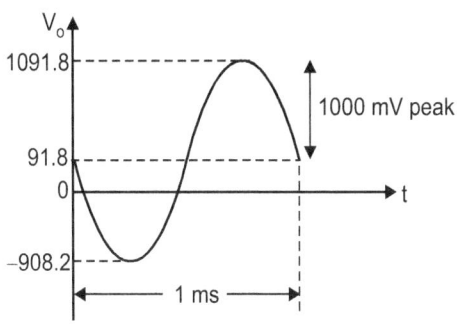

Fig. 1.62

1.29 TRANSIENT RESPONSE CHARACTERISTICS

Transient response : It is the time required to settle the output to it's final value when the input is applied. It is the time domain representation and can be observed for step input and unity gain op-amp configuration.

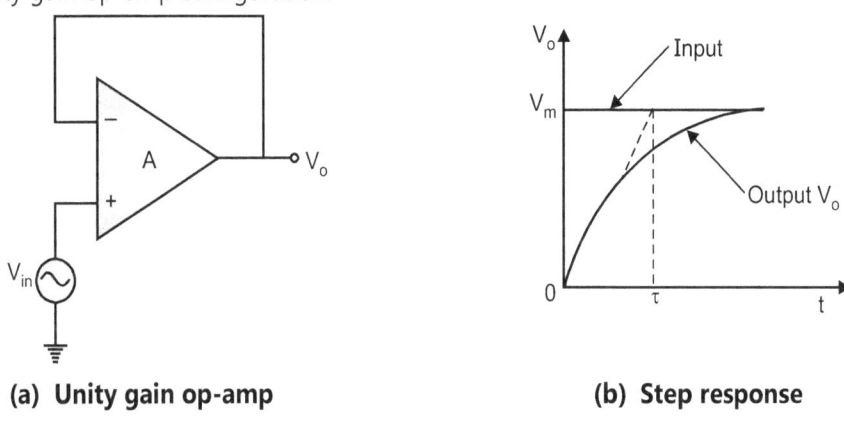

(a) Unity gain op-amp (b) Step response

Fig. 1.63

Consider a unity gain amplifier. The output of the unity gain amplifier is same as input i.e. $V_o = V_{in}$. Suppose the input applied to the amplifier is step input. So the output should step but it is not because practically it takes some finite time to reach the output level. So the output is exponential.

1.30 CLOSED LOOP STABILITY CONSIDERATIONS FOR OP-AMP

In op-amp negative feedback is used to control the gain. The gain with feedback is called closed loop gain. The open-loop gain depends on frequency and denoted as $A_{OL}(f)$.

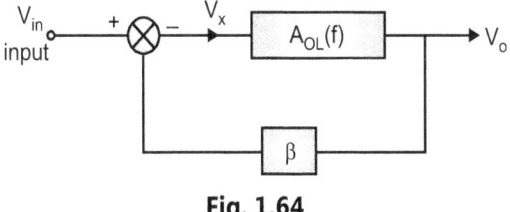

Fig. 1.64

The stability for the closed loop can be calculated as:

$$V_x = V_{in} - \beta V_o \quad \ldots(1.19)$$
$$V_o = V_x [A_{OL}(f)] \quad \ldots(1.20)$$
$$V_x = \frac{V_o}{A_{OL}(f)} \quad \ldots(1.21)$$

Substituting this value in equation (2.1),

$$\frac{V_o}{A_{OL}(f)} = V_{in} - \beta V_o$$

$$\therefore \quad V_o \left[\frac{1}{A_{OL}(f)} + \beta \right] = V_{in}$$

$$\frac{V_o}{V_{in}} = \frac{A_{OL}(f)}{1 + A_{OL}(f)\beta}$$

$\frac{V_o}{V_{in}}$ is the closed loop gain.

$A_{OL}(f)\beta$ is the loop gain.

The stability of the circuit depends on the behaviour of the roots of the equation $1 + A_{OL}(f)\beta$.

$$1 + A_{OL}(f)\beta = 0$$
$$A_{OL}(f)\beta = -1$$
$$A_{OL}(f)\beta = -1 + j0$$
$$|A_{OL}(f)\beta| = \sqrt{1^2 + 0^2}$$
$$|A_{OL}(f)\beta| = 1$$
$$\angle A_{OL}(f) = -\tan^{-1}\frac{0}{1}$$
$$\angle A_{OL}(f) = 0°$$

At a particular frequency, the magnitude and phase angle conditions are satisfied. Oscillations are generated in the amplifier and the system becomes unstable. The system stability can be decided from the following factors by plotting the magnitude plot and phase plot.

(1) Gain crossover frequency :

It is the frequency at which the loop gain magnitude $|A_{OL}(f)\beta| = 1$.

(2) Phase crossover frequency :

It is the frequency at which the loop gain is $-180°$ or $n\pi$ radians.

(3) Gain margin :

The gain measured at the gain crossover frequency is called gain margin.

$$\boxed{G.M. = -20 \log |A_{OL}(f)\beta|}$$ at gain crossover frequency.

(4) Phase margin :

The amount by which angle of the loop gain ($\angle A_{OL}(f)\beta$) differ from the $-180°$ phase shift is called phase margin.

$$\boxed{P.M. = 180° + \angle A_{OL}(f)\beta}$$

If gain margin is positive, the system is stable and similarly, if phase margin is positive, the system is stable.

1.31 FREQUENCY COMPENSATION TECHNIQUES

The rate of change of gain as well as the phase shift can be changed by using specific components with the op-amp. The most commonly used components are resistors and capacitors. The network formed by such components and used for modifying the rate of change of gain and the phase shift is called a compensating network.

The main purpose of the compensating networks is to modify the performance of an op-amp circuit over the desired frequency range by controlling its gain and phase shift.

There are two types of compensating networks :
1. Internal compensation,
2. External compensation.

In internally compensated op-amps, the compensating network is designed into the circuit to control the gain and phase shift of the op-amp. On the other hand, external (discrete) compensating components, that is resistors and/or capacitors, are added at designated terminals in non-compensated op-amps. The 741C is an internally compensated op-amp, whereas 709C is a non-compensated op-amp.

There are two types of external compensation.
1. Dominant pole compensation,
2. Pole-zero (lag) compensation.

1. Dominant pole compensation :

Suppose A_O is the uncompensated transfer function of the op-amp in open-loop condition. A dominant pole can be introduced by adding a RC network in series with op-amp as shown in Fig. 1.65.

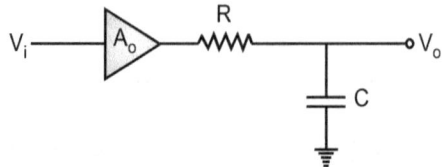

Fig. 1.65: Dominant pole compensation

Then compensated transfer function A_o' becomes

$$A_o' = \frac{V_o}{V_i}$$

$$= A_o \cdot \frac{\frac{-j}{\omega C}}{R - j/\omega C} = \frac{A_o}{1 + j f/f_o}$$

where, $\quad f_o = \dfrac{1}{2\pi RC}$

$$A_o' = \frac{A_{OL}}{(1 + j f/f_o)(1 + j f/f_1)(1 + j f/f_2)(1 + j f/f_3)}$$

where, $f_o < f_1 < f_2 < f_3$

The value of capacitor C can be calculated with the help of equation

$$f_o = \frac{1}{2\pi RC}$$

The advantage of dominant pole compensation is improved system noise immunity as the noise frequency components outside the bandwidth are suppressed. The disadvantage of dominant pole is reduction in open-loop bandwidth.

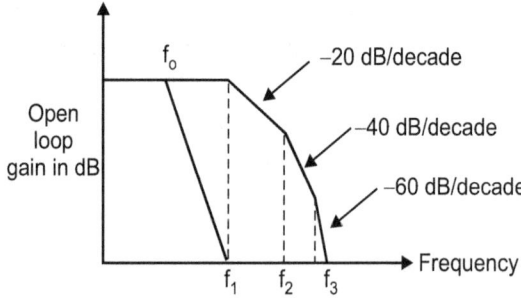

Fig. 1.66: Frequency response of dominant pole compensation network

2. Pole-zero compensation :

In this compensation transfer function A_o can be altered by adding both pole and a zero as shown in Fig. 1.67. The zero should be at higher frequency than a pole.

The transfer function of the compensating network is given as :

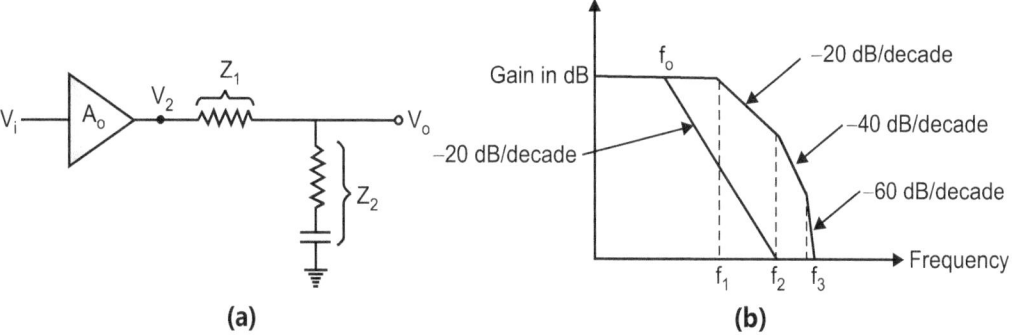

(a)   (b)

Fig. 1.67: Pole zero compensation

$$\frac{V_o}{V_z} = \frac{Z_2}{Z_1 + Z_2} = \frac{R_2}{R_1 + R_2} = \frac{1 + j\,f/f_1}{1 + j\,f/f_o}$$

where, $Z_1 = R_1$, $Z_2 = R_2 + \dfrac{1}{j\omega C_2}$

$$f_1 = \frac{1}{2\pi R_2 C_2}, \quad f_o = \frac{1}{2\pi (R_1 + R_2) C_2}$$

The overall transfer function is given by

$$A_o' = \frac{V_o}{V_i} = \frac{V_o}{V_2} \cdot \frac{V_2}{V_i} = A \cdot \frac{R_2}{R_1 + R_2} \cdot \frac{1 + j\,f/f_1}{1 + j\,f/f_o}$$

$$= \frac{A_{OL}}{(1 + j\,f/f_1)(1 + j\,f/f_2)(1 + j\,f/f_3)} \cdot \frac{R_2}{R_1 + R_2} \cdot \frac{(1 + j\,f/f_1)}{(1 + j\,f/f_o)}$$

$$= \frac{A_{OL}}{(1 + j\,f/f_o)(1 + j\,f/f_2) + (1 + j\,f/f_3)}$$

$0 < f_o < f_1 < f_2 < f_3$

and note that $R_2 \gg R_1$, so that $\dfrac{R_2}{R_1 + R_2} \approx 1$

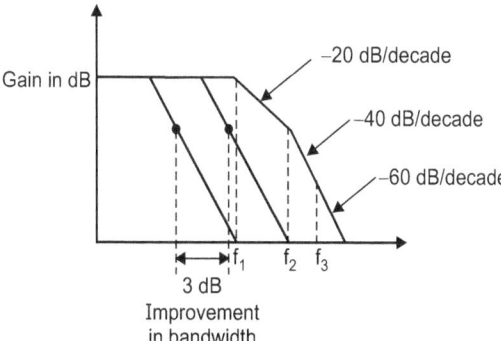

Fig. 1.68: Comparison of dominant pole and pole-zero compensation

3. Feed-forward compensation :

Usually there will be a stage which dominates by providing atleast one pole which overrides the effects of other stages. Therefore, it acts as a bandwidth bottleneck for the overall device. The feed forward compensation is used to provide a high frequency bypass around such dominant stage to avoid its phase lag. Therefore, this stage becomes ineffective due to the compensation and the remaining stages provide a safe value of phase margin by giving sufficient phase lag.

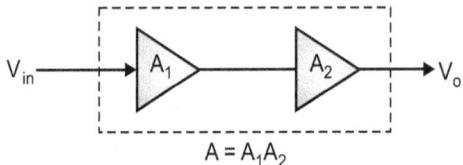

Fig. 1.69 (a) : Feed forward compensation

Consider the multistage amplifier with dominant bottleneck stage with response $A_1(j\omega)$ and all the remaining stages are combined to get the response $A_2(j\omega)$. Fig. 2.69 shows the individual as well as total frequency response without any compensation used.

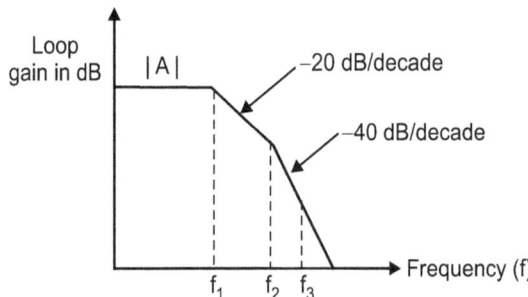

Fig. 1.69 (b) : Frequency response without compensation

As shown in Fig. 1.69 (b), gain crossover frequency occurs in the region of roll off rate −40 dB/decade which gives the instability of the overall system.

In feed-forward compensation an ordinary high-pass function with transfer function H (jω) is used in the system as shown in Fig. 1.70 (a).

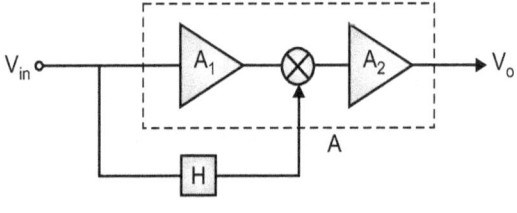

Fig. 1.70 (a)

The transfer function of high pass section is given by

$$H(j\omega) = \frac{j\omega(f/f_o)}{1 + j\omega(f/f_o)}$$

Now due to this function the overall gain function becomes,

$$A' = (A_1 + H)A_2$$
$$= A_1 A_2 + HA_2$$

i.e. $\quad A'(j\omega) = A(j\omega) + H(j\omega) A_2(j\omega)$

$$A(j\omega) = A_1(j\omega) A_2(j\omega)$$

At lower frequencies, $f \to 0$, $H \to 0$ and hence there is no change in uncompensated response. Thus, advantage in low frequency region can be still achieved.

At high frequencies $f \to \infty$, hence $H \to 1$ and $A \to 0$.

∴ $\quad A' = H(j\omega) A_2(j\omega) \approx A_2(j\omega)$ for higher frequencies.

Thus, the system behaviour is controlled by A_2 and effect of critical stage A_1 is completely eliminated. This gives large bandwidth and gain cross-over frequency occurs in low roll off region.

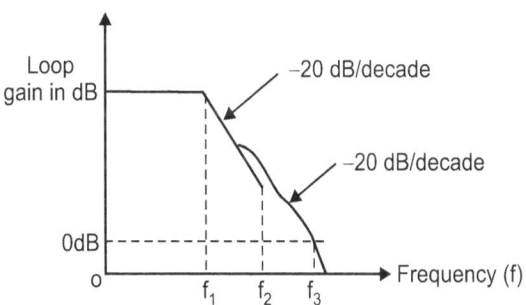

Fig. 1.70 (b)

1.32 INTERNAL COMPENSATION TECHNIQUES

Op-amps such as IC 741 is internally compensated IC. A capacitor value of 10 to 30 pF is fabricated between input and output stage to obtain internal compensation. Such type of compensation is called Miller compensation.

Miller Effect Compensation :

The drawbacks of dominant pole compensation are avoided by using Miller effect compensation. In dominant pole compensation a capacitor is connected to ground whereas in Miller effect compensation it is connected in feedback path in the output stage of op-amp.

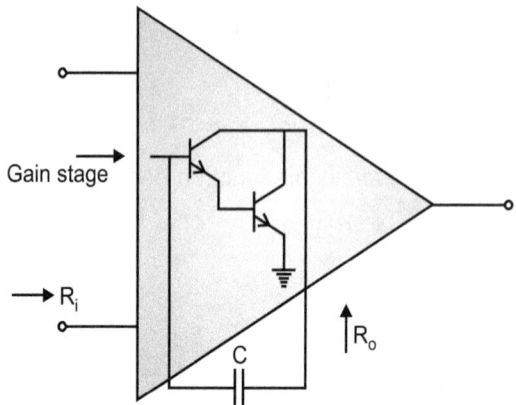

Fig. 1.71 : Miller effect compensation

The C is the compensating capacitor, R_i is the input resistance and R_o is the output resistance. The gain of the Darlington pair is given as

$$a = -G_m R_o$$

where, G_m = Tranconductance of the stage

The capacitor C appears as the Miller capacitance from the input side and from Miller effect we can write,

$$Z_M = \frac{Z_C}{1+a}$$

where, $$Z_M = \frac{1}{j\omega C_M} \text{ and } Z_C = \frac{1}{j\omega C}$$

$$\frac{1}{j\omega C_M} = \frac{\frac{1}{j\omega C}}{(1+a)}$$

$$\boxed{C_M = (1+a)\,C}$$

From the above equation it is clear that C gets multiplied by (1 + a), where a is the gain which is very large. So practically small C values can be used.

The Miller equivalent capacitance C_M forms a low pass RC section with R_i as the input resistance and the corner frequency for this section is given as

$$f_C = \frac{1}{2\pi\, C_M\, R_i}$$

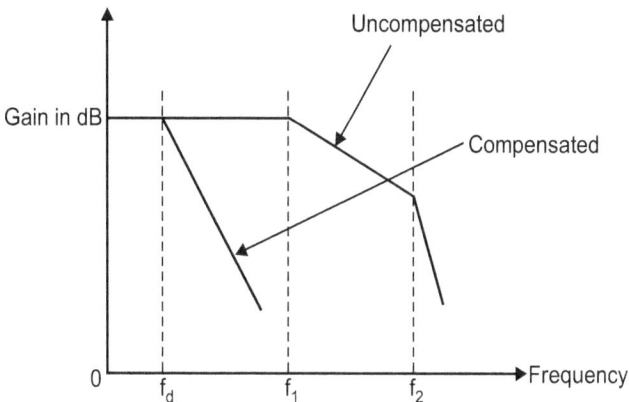

Fig. 1.72 : Magnitude plot with and without compensation

Following op-amps are internally compensated :

- Fairchild µA 741.
- National semiconductor's LM 107, LM 741, LM 112.
- Motorola's MC 1858.

EXERCISE

1. Draw the basic building blocks of op-amp. Explain the function of each block.
2. Define the following terms for differential amplifier.
   (a) Differential gain and common mode gain
   (b) CMRR
3. Draw the circuit diagram of dual input balanced output differential amplifier and find out the differential gain A_d, input impedance R_{in} and output impedance R_0.
4. Justify how a current source is used in place of R_E to improve the CMRR for a differential amplifier.
5. Explain the different methods of improving CMRR in a differential amplifier.
6. With neat circuit diagram, explain the necessity and working of current mirror circuit.
7. With neat circuit diagram, explain the necessity and working of active load for differential amplifier.
8. What are the requirements of output stage in an op-amp? Explain the output stage of IC 741.
9. State the ideal characteristics of op-amp.
10. Explain the effect of temperature on op-amp parameters.
11. Define slew rate of op-amp. State the reasons for limiting the slew rate.

12. Write a short note on constant current sources.

13. The parameters for the differential amplifier are given as: $R_C = 1k\Omega$, $R_S = 1\ k\Omega$, $h_{fe} = 1\ k\Omega$ and $R_E = 2M\Omega$. Neglecting h_{oe}, calculate the difference mode gain and common mode gain. Hence calculate CMRR in dB. The amplifier is in dual input, balanced configuration.

14. When a differential input of 1mV sin ωt is applied to a differential amplifier. The differential output is 0.5 V sin ωt. When both inputs are joined together and 1 V sin ωt is applied the output is 200 mV sin ωt. Determine the CMRR.

15. For a differential amplifier circuit operated from ±5V, assume $V_{BE} = 0.7$ V and $h_{fe} = 100$. If R_C for each is 100 kΩ, calculate the value of R_E so that the quiescent collector emitter voltage for each transistor is 4V.

16. Design a dual input balanced output differential amplifier with a constant current source using diodes to satisfy the following requirements.
    (a) Differential voltage gain, $A_d = 40\pm10$
    (b) Current supplied by the constant current bias circuit = 4mA
    (c) Supply voltages $V_S = \pm10V$

17. Explain the various level shifting networks which are used in a typical op-amp.

18. Explain the various frequency compensation techniques.

19. Define the absolute maximum ratings of a commercial op-amp.

20. The input signal to an op-amp is 0.03 sin 1.5 × 10^5t. what can be the maximum gain of an op-amp with the slew rate of 0.4 v/μsec ?

21. For anon-inverting amplifier R1 = 1 kΩ and Rf = 10 kΩ. Calculate the maximum output offset voltage due to V_{ios} and I_B for an op-amp.

22. V_{ios} = 10 mV ; I_B = 300 nA ; I_{ios} = 50nA. calculate,
    (a) The value of R_{comp} needed to reduce the effect of I_B
    (b) The maximum output offset voltage if R_{comp} as calculated in (i) is connected in the circuit.

Unit II

OP-AMP APPLICATIONS

2.1 INTRODUCTION

In linear applications, output voltage varies linearly w.r.t. the input voltage. In such linear applications a negative feedback is used from the amplifier output to the inverting input terminal. For example, voltage followers or buffers, adder, subtractor, integrator, differentiator, etc.

In non-linear applications, a feedback is provided from the output to the non-inverting input terminal. The feedback may be provided to the inverting input terminals using non-linear elements like diodes, transistors, etc. The non-linear circuits have highly non-linear input to output characteristics.

2.1.1 Realistic Assumptions

1. **Zero Input Current :**

   The current drawn by any of the input terminal is zero. Practically, it is very small of the order of µA or nA. Hence, it is assumed to be zero.

2. **Virtual Ground :**

   For feedback amplifiers using op-amps, the two op-amp terminals will always be approximately equal i.e. $V_1 = V_2$.

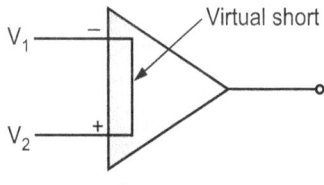

Fig. 2.1 (a)

Since $V_1 = V_2$ for feedback amplifier the two op-amp terminals appears to be shorted together. Such condition in feedback amplifier using op-amp is known as "virtual short".

The application of the concept greatly simplifies the analysis of an op-amp feedback amplifiers.

This means that the differential input voltage V_d between the non-inverting and inverting input terminals is essentially zero.

For example, if $V_o = 5$ V and A_{OL} i.e. open loop gain is 10^4, then

$$V_d = \frac{5}{10^4} = 5 \times 10^{-4} = 0.5 \text{ mV}$$

Hence, V_d is very small.

As $A_{OL} \to \infty$, the $V_d \to 0$ and ideally it is assumed to be zero for analyzing the circuits.

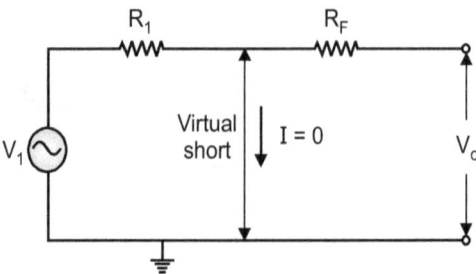

Fig. 2.1 (b) : Showing virtual ground

$$V_d = \frac{V_o}{A_{OL}} \quad \ldots (2.1)$$

$$V_1 - V_2 = \frac{V_o}{\infty} \quad \ldots (2.2)$$

$$V_1 - V_2 = 0 \quad \ldots (2.3)$$

$$V_1 = V_2 \quad \ldots (2.4)$$

Under the linear range of operation there is virtually short circuit between the two input terminals, in the sense these voltages are same. No current flows from the input terminal to the ground.

2.1.2 Ideal Inverting Amplifier

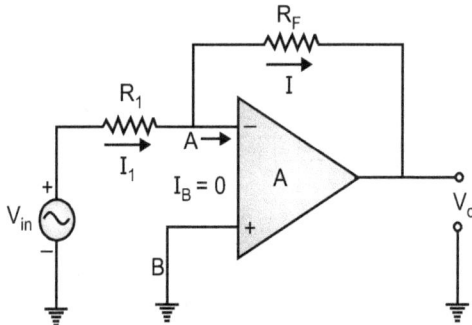

Fig. 2.2 : Inverting amplifier configuration

When the input is applied to the inverting input terminal of the op-amp and non-inverting input terminal is grounded, then the op-amp is said to be in inverting mode configuration.

As node B is grounded, node A is also at ground potential, from the concept of virtual ground.

$$V_A = 0$$

The function of the circuit can be verified by obtaining the expression for the output voltage V_o, which can be obtained from Kirchhoff's current law at node A.

Since, R_i and A of the op-amp are ideally infinite, $I_B = 0$ A and $V_1 = V_2 \cong 0$ V

$$\therefore \quad I_1 = I_B + I \quad \ldots (2.5)$$

The current I_1 can be obtained as

$$I_1 = \frac{V_{in} - V_A}{R_1} \quad \ldots (2.6)$$

The current flowing through R_F can be obtained as :

$$I = \frac{V_A - V_O}{R_F} \quad \ldots (2.7)$$

$$= \frac{0 - V_O}{R_F} \quad \ldots (2.8)$$

$$= \frac{-V_O}{R_F} \quad \ldots (2.9)$$

Since, $I_B = 0$,

$$I = I_1 \quad \ldots (2.10)$$

$$-\frac{V_O}{R_F} = \frac{V_{in}}{R_1} \quad \ldots (2.11)$$

Rearranging the equation, we get

$$\frac{V_O}{V_{in}} = -\frac{R_F}{R_1} \quad \ldots (2.12)$$

$$\therefore \quad \boxed{A_V = \frac{V_O}{V_{in}} = -\frac{R_F}{R_1}} \quad \ldots (2.13)$$

$-\dfrac{R_F}{R_1}$ is the gain of the amplifier while negative (−) sign indicates the phase shift. Hence, it is called a inverting amplifier.

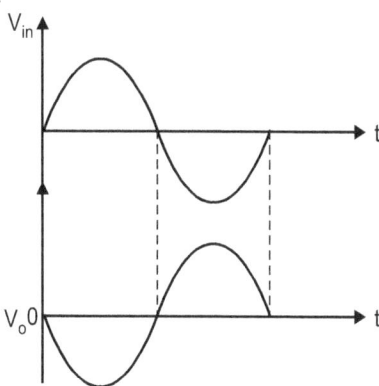

Fig. 2.3 : Input and output waveforms of inverting amplifier

If the ratio of R_F and R_1 is k which is other than one, the circuit is called **scale changer** while for $R_F/R_1 = 1$, it is called a **phase inverter**.

Example 2.1 :

A sine wave of 0.5 V peak voltage is applied to an inverting amplifier using $R_1 = 10\ k\Omega$ and $R_F = 50\ k\Omega$. It uses the supply voltages of ± 12 V. Determine the output and sketch the waveforms.

If now the amplitude of input sine wave is increased to 5 V, what will be the output ? Is it practically possible ? Sketch the waveforms.

Solution :

$$A_v = \frac{V_o}{V_{in}} = \frac{-R_F}{R_1} = \frac{-50}{10} = -5$$

Now, $V_m = 0.5$ V for the input

$$(V_o)_m = (V_{in})_m \times \text{Gain}$$

$$= 5 \times 5 = 25\ V\ \text{peak}$$

But op-amp output saturates at ± 12 V i.e. at supply voltages used. So portion above the + 12 V or below − 12 V will be clipped off from the output. So 25 V peak output is not practically possible.

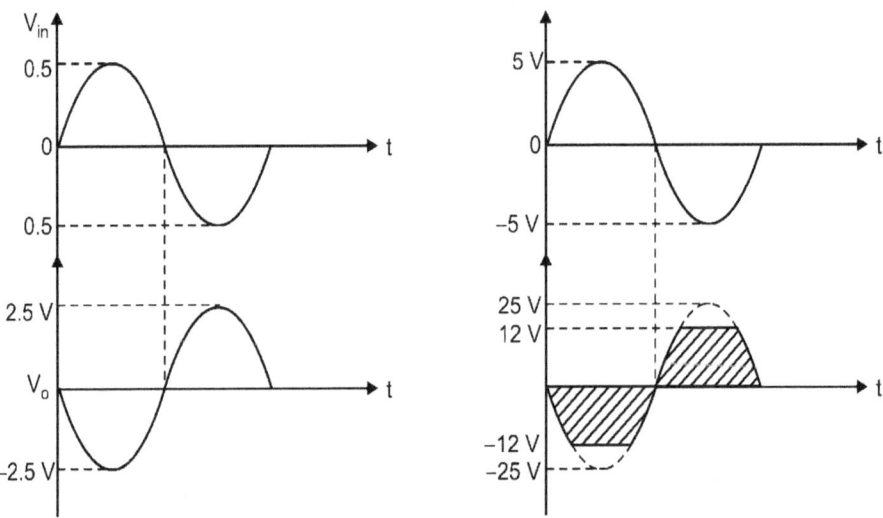

Fig. 2.4 : Input - output waveforms

Example 2.2 :

An inverting amplifier using op-amp has $R_1 = 10$ kΩ and $R_F = 47$ kΩ. It is applied with 2 V peak to peak sine wave. An a.c. voltmeter is used between the output terminal and ground to measure output voltage. Calculate reading on voltmeter. Assume supply voltage to be ± 12 V.

Solution :

$$\text{Gain} = -\frac{R_F}{R_1} = \frac{-47}{10} = -4.7$$

$\therefore \quad V_O \text{ (peak to peak)} = \text{Gain} \times V_{in} \text{ (P-P)}$

$$= 4.7 \times 2 = 9.4 \text{ V}$$

But a.c. voltmeter measures r.m.s. value.

$$V_O \text{ (peak)} = \frac{9.4}{2} = 4.7 \text{ V}$$

$$V_O \text{ (rms)} = \frac{V_O \text{ (peak)}}{\sqrt{2}}$$

$$= \frac{4.7}{\sqrt{2}} = 3.3234 \text{ V}$$

2.1.3 Ideal Non-Inverting Amplifier

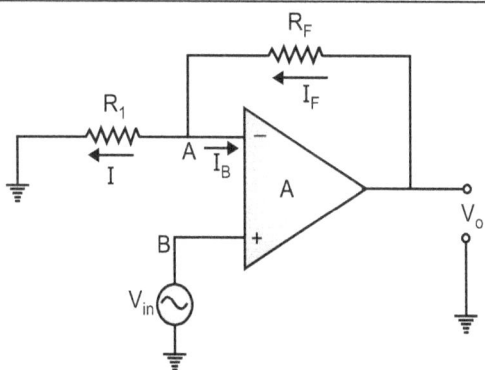

Fig. 2.5 : Non-inverting amplifier

Fig. 2.5 shows the non-inverting amplifier. It is called as non-inverting amplifier because here input is applied to the non-inverting input of the op-amp.

Due to virtual ground concept and as the op-amp is ideal, we can write the Kirchhoff's current law at node A.

$$I + I_B = I_F \qquad \text{... (2.14)}$$

$I_B = 0$ as the op-amp is ideal.

$$\therefore \quad I = I_F \quad \ldots (2.15)$$

$$\frac{V_A - 0}{R_1} = \frac{V_O - V_A}{R_F} \quad \ldots (2.16)$$

$$\frac{V_{in}}{R_1} = \frac{V_O - V_{in}}{R_F} \quad \ldots (2.17)$$

$$\frac{V_{in}}{R_1} = \frac{V_O}{R_F} - \frac{V_{in}}{R_F}$$

$$\frac{V_{in}}{R_1} + \frac{V_{in}}{R_F} = \frac{V_O}{R_F}$$

$$\left(\frac{1}{R_1} + \frac{1}{R_F}\right) V_{in} = \frac{V_O}{R_F}$$

$$\left(\frac{R_F + R_1}{R_1 R_F}\right) R_F = \frac{V_O}{V_{in}}$$

$$A_F = \frac{V_O}{V_{in}} = 1 + \frac{R_F}{R_1} \quad \ldots (2.18)$$

Hence, in non-inverting amplifier, there will not be any phase shift between input and output. The input and output waveforms are shown in Fig. 2.6.

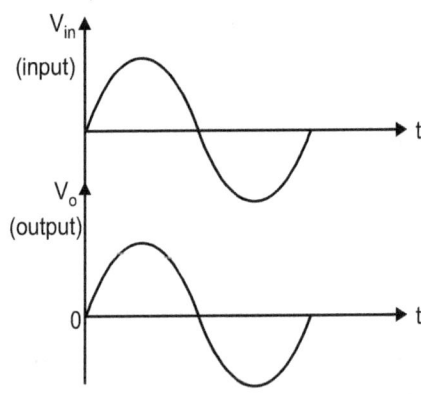

Fig. 2.6 : Waveforms of non-inverting amplifier

Example 2.3 :

Find V_o for the circuit shown in Fig. 2.7.

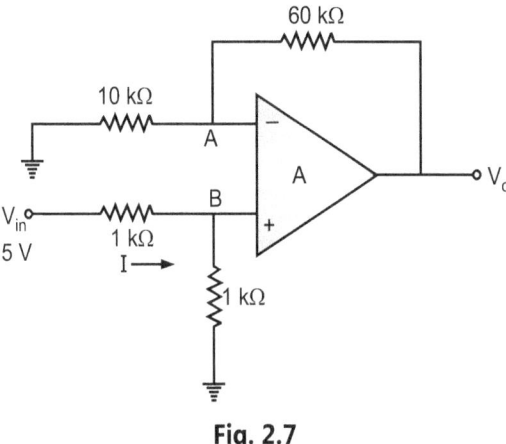

Fig. 2.7

Solution :

The current flowing through the non-inverting input terminal is denoted by I and is given as

$$I = \frac{V_{in}}{(1 + 1) \times 10^3}$$

The voltage at point B is given as

$$V_B = I \times 1$$
$$= \frac{5}{2 \times 10^3} \times 1 \times 10^3 = 2.5 \text{ V}$$

The output voltage of the non-inverting amplifier is calculated as

$$V_o = \left(1 + \frac{R_F}{R_1}\right) \times V_B$$

$$V_o = \left(1 + \frac{60}{10}\right) \times 2.5 \text{ V}$$

$$= (1 + 6) \times 2.5 \text{ V} = 7 \times 2.5 \text{ V}$$

∴ $\boxed{V_o = 17.5 \text{ V}}$

Example 2.4 :

An inverting amplifier shown in Fig. 2.8 with R_1 = 25 kΩ and R_F = 100 kΩ. A load of 10 kΩ is connected to the output with input voltage of 0.5 V. Calculate (i) I_1, (ii) V_o, (iii) I_L, and (iv) total current I_o.

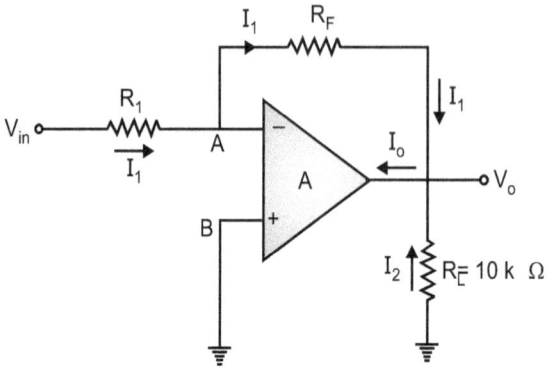

Fig. 2.8

Solution :

(i) $\quad I_1 = \dfrac{V_{in} - V_A}{R_1} = \dfrac{V_{in}}{R_1} = \dfrac{0.5}{25 \times 10^3} = 0.02 \times 10^{-3} = 20\ \mu A$

(ii) $\quad V_o = A \cdot V_{in} = \dfrac{-R_F}{R_1} \cdot V_{in} = \dfrac{-100}{25} \times 0.5 = -2\ V$

(iii) $\quad I_L = \dfrac{V_o}{R_L} = \dfrac{-2}{10 \times 10^3} = 0.2\ mA$

Negative sign indicates it flows from ground towards output terminals.

(iv) Total current, $\quad I_o = I_L + I_1$

$\quad\quad\quad\quad\quad = 0.2 \times 10^{-3} + 20 \times 10^{-6}$

$\quad\quad\quad\quad\quad = 0.22\ mA$

Example 2.5 :

For a non-inverting amplifier shown in Fig. 2.9 calculate (i) A_{CL}, (ii) V_o, (iii) I_L, and (iv) I_o.

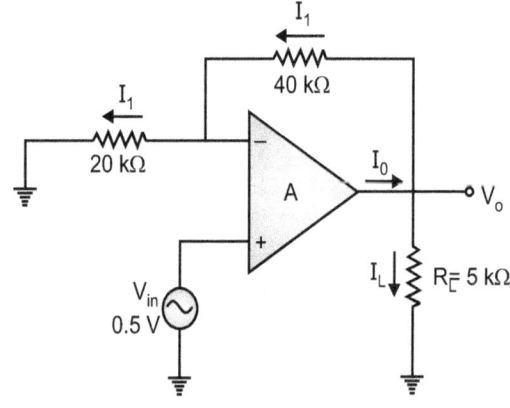

Fig. 2.9

Solution :

As given $V_A = V_B = V_{in} = 0.5$ V

$$I_1 = \frac{V_A}{R_1} = \frac{V_{in}}{R_1}$$

$$= \frac{0.5}{20 \times 10^3} = 0.025 \times 10^{-3} = 25 \, \mu A$$

Same current flows through R_F, as op-amp input current is zero.

$$A_{CL} = 1 + \frac{R_F}{R_1} = 1 + \frac{40}{20} = 3$$

$$V_o = A_{CL} \, V_{in} = 3 \times 0.5 = 1.5 \text{ V}$$

$$I_L = \frac{V_o}{R_L}$$

$$= \frac{1.5}{5 \times 10^3} = 0.3 \times 10^{-3} = 0.3 \text{ mA}$$

Applying KCL at the output node,

$$I_o = I_1 + I_L$$

$$= 25 \times 10^{-6} + 0.3 \times 10^{-3}$$

$$= 0.325 \times 10^{-3}$$

$$I_o = 0.325 \text{ mA}$$

Example 2.6 :

Find the output voltage V_o in terms of V_1 and V_2 for the op-amp circuit shown in Fig. 2.10. Assume ideal op-amps.

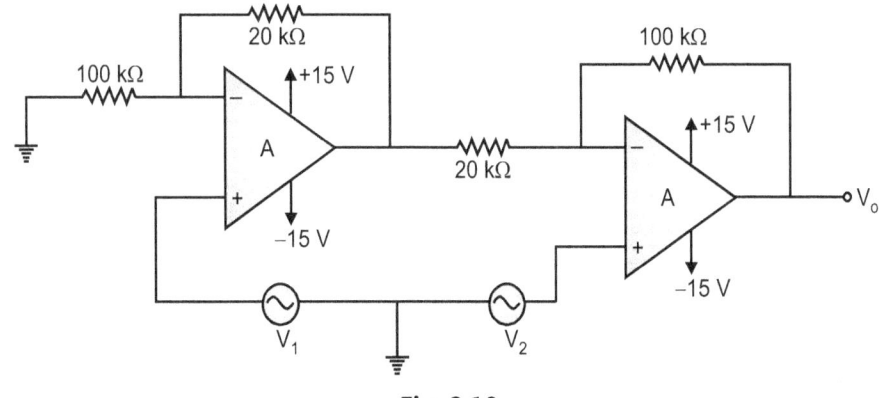

Fig. 2.10

Solution :

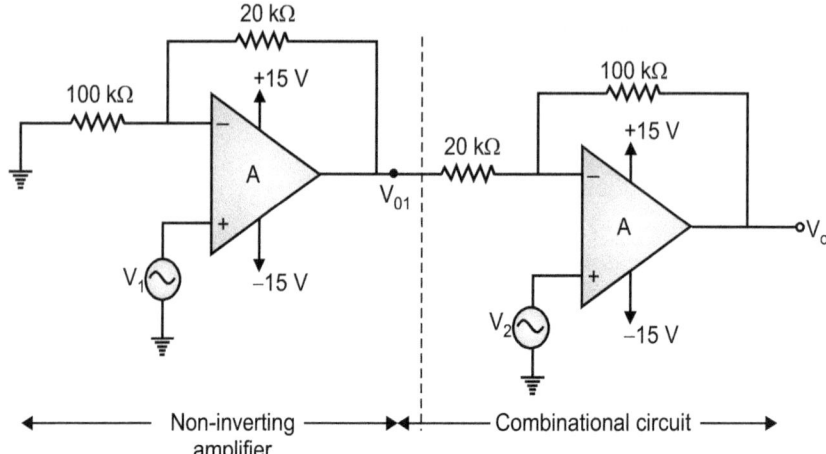

Fig. 2.11

For first stage : $V_{o_1} = \left(1 + \dfrac{R_F}{R_1}\right) V_{in} = \left(1 + \dfrac{20}{100}\right) V_1$

∴ $V_{o_1} = 1.2\, V_1$

For the second stage use superposition principle. Use each input one at a time assuming other input zero.

Assume V_{o_1} active and $V_2 = 0$. This is the inverting amplifier.

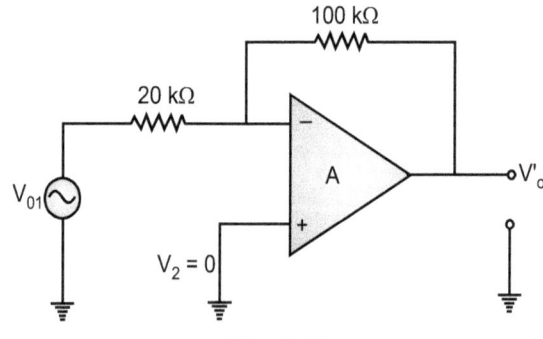

Fig. 2.12

$V'_o = V_{o_1} \left(-\dfrac{R_F}{R_1}\right)$

$ = 1.2\, V_1 \left(-\dfrac{100}{20}\right)$

$ = -6\, V_1$ due to V_{o_1} alone

Now assume V_2 active and $V_{o_1} = 0$ V. This is non-inverting amplifier.

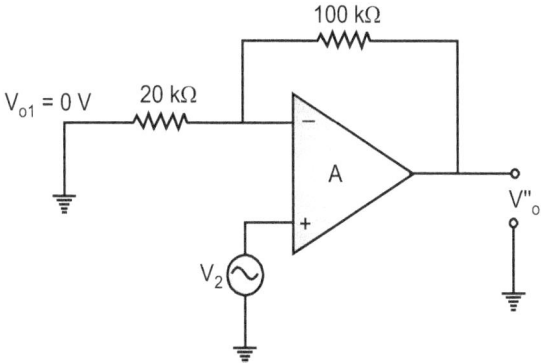

Fig. 2.13

$$\therefore \quad V_o'' = V_2\left(1 + \frac{R_F}{R_1}\right)$$

$$= V_2\left(1 + \frac{100}{20}\right)$$

$$= 6\,V_2 \text{ due to } V_2 \text{ alone}$$

Hence, the net output V_o is summation of V_o' and V_o''.

$$\therefore \quad V_o = V_o' + V_o'' = -6\,V_1 + 6\,V_2$$

$$\therefore \quad V_o = 6\,(V_2 - V_1)$$

2.1.4 Practical Inverting Amplifier

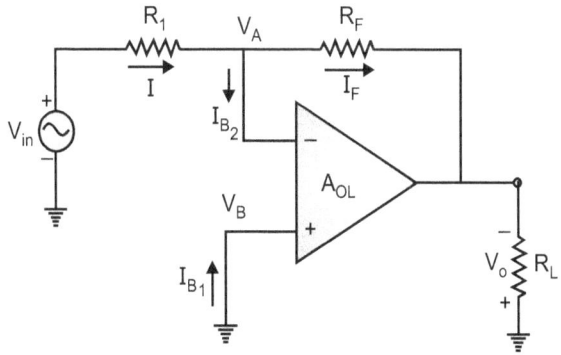

Fig. 2.14 : Practical inverting amplifier

Fig. 2.14 shows the practical inverting amplifier.

Apply KCL at the node A.

$$I = I_F + I_{B_2} \qquad \ldots (2.19)$$

Though input resistance R_{in} is not infinite, it is very very large and hence I_{B_2} is negligible.

$$I = I_F \quad \ldots (2.20)$$

$$\frac{V_{in} - V_A}{R_1} = \frac{V_A - V_o}{R_F} \quad \ldots (2.21)$$

$$V_o = A_{OL} V_{id}$$
$$= A_{OL}(V_1 - V_2) \quad \ldots (2.22)$$

But $V_1 = 0$ and $V_2 = V_A$

$$\therefore \quad V_o = -A_{OL} V_A \quad \ldots (2.23)$$

Substitute this value in equation (2.21),

$$\frac{V_{in} + \dfrac{V_o}{A_{OL}}}{R_1} = \frac{\dfrac{-V_o}{A_{OL}} - V_o}{R_F} \quad \ldots (2.24)$$

$$R_F \left[V_{in} + \frac{V_o}{A_{OL}} \right] = R_1 \left[\frac{-V_o}{A_{OL}} - V_o \right]$$

$$V_{in} R_F + R_F \frac{V_o}{A_{OL}} = -R_1 \frac{V_o}{A_{OL}} - R_1 V_o$$

$$V_{in} R_F = \left[-R_1 \frac{V_o}{A_{OL}} - R_1 V_o - R_F \frac{V_o}{A_{OL}} \right]$$

$$V_{in} R_F = -V_o \left[\frac{R_1}{A_{OL}} + R_1 + \frac{R_F}{A_{OL}} \right] \quad \ldots (2.25)$$

Closed loop gain is A_{CL}.

$$A_{CL} = \frac{V_o}{V_{in}} \quad \ldots (2.26)$$

$$\frac{V_o}{V_{in}} = -\frac{R_F}{\dfrac{R_1}{A_{OL}} + R_1 + \dfrac{R_F}{A_{OL}}} \quad \ldots (2.27)$$

$$A_{CL} = \frac{-R_F A_{OL}}{R_1 + R_F + R_1 A_{OL}}$$

As A_{OL} tends to infinity,

$$A_{OL} R_1 \gg R_1 + R_F$$

$$\therefore \quad A_{CL} = \frac{-R_F A_{OL}}{R_1 A_{OL}}$$

$$\therefore \quad \boxed{A_{CL} = -\frac{R_F}{R_1}} \quad \ldots (2.28)$$

2.1.5 Practical Non-Inverting Amplifier

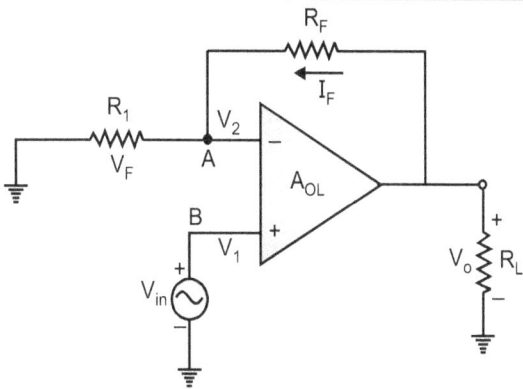

Fig. 2.15 : Practical non-inverting amplifier

Closed loop gain of op-amp is given by

$$A_{CL} = \frac{V_o}{V_{in}} \qquad \text{... (2.29)}$$

The output voltage of non-inverting amplifier is given by

$$V_o = A_{OL} \cdot V_{id} \qquad \text{... (2.30)}$$

By using voltage divider rule, we can write

$$V_2 = \left(\frac{V_o}{R_1 + R_F}\right) R_1 \text{ as } R_{in} >> R_1 \qquad \text{... (2.31)}$$

Substitute this value of V_F in equation (2.30).

$$\therefore \qquad V_o = A_{OL} \cdot V_{id} \qquad \text{... (2.32)}$$

$$V_o = A_{OL}\left[V_{in} - \frac{R_1 V_o}{R_1 + R_F}\right] \qquad \text{... (2.33)}$$

$$V_o = A_{OL} V_{in} - \frac{R_1 A_{OL} V_o}{R_1 + R_F}$$

$$V_o + \frac{R_1 A_{OL} V_o}{R_1 + R_F} = A_{OL} V_{in}$$

$$V_o\left[1 + \frac{R_1 A_{OL}}{R_1 + R_F}\right] = A_{OL} V_{in}$$

$$\frac{V_o}{V_{in}} = \frac{A_{OL}}{1 + \frac{R_1 A_{OL}}{R_1 + R_F}}$$

$$A_{CL} = \frac{V_o}{V_{in}} = \frac{A_{OL}(R_1 + R_F)}{R_1 + R_F + R_1 A_{OL}} \qquad \text{... (2.34)}$$

As A_{OL} is very large which tends to infinity,

$A_{OL} \to \infty$ hence $A_{OL} R_1 >> R_1 + R_F$

$$\frac{V_o}{V_{in}} = \frac{A_{OL}(R_1 + R_F)}{R_1 A_{OL}}$$

$$\frac{V_o}{V_{in}} = \frac{R_1 + R_F}{R_1}$$

$$\boxed{A_{CL} = \frac{V_o}{V_{in}} = 1 + \frac{R_F}{R_1}} \quad \ldots (2.35)$$

2.1.6 Input Resistance with Feedback

To obtain the input resistance with feedback, split R_F into two Miller components using Miller's theorem.

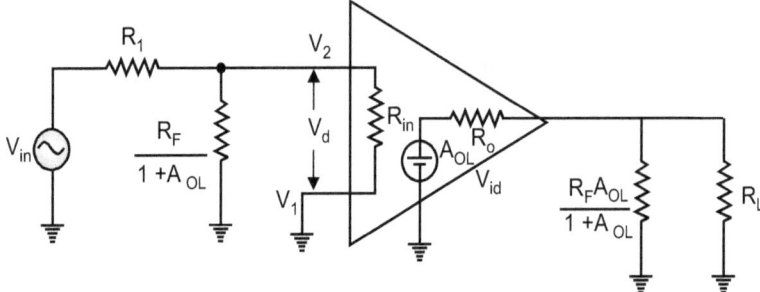

Fig. 2.16 : Input resistance with feedback

The input resistance with feedback which is denoted as R_{inf} and observed from the Fig. 2.16 is given as

$$R_{inf} = R_1 + \left(\frac{R_F}{1 + A_{OL}} \parallel R_{in}\right) \quad \ldots (2.36)$$

$$R_{inf} = R_1 + \left[\frac{\frac{R_F R_{in}}{1 + A_{OL}}}{\frac{R_F}{1 + A_{OL}} + R_{in}}\right] = R_1 + \left[\frac{R_F R_{in}}{1 + A_{OL}} \times \frac{1 + A_{OL}}{R_F + R_{in}(1 + A_{OL})}\right]$$

$$= R_1 + \frac{R_F R_{in}}{R_F + R_{in}(1 + A_{OL})} \quad \ldots (2.37)$$

Ideally, the value of A_{OL} is very very large.

So, $\quad R_{inf} = R_1 \quad \ldots (2.38)$

2.1.7 Voltage Follower or Buffer Amplifier

When the non-inverting amplifier is designed for unity gain, it is called a voltage follower. It means the output voltage is exactly equal to the input voltage both in magnitude and phase.

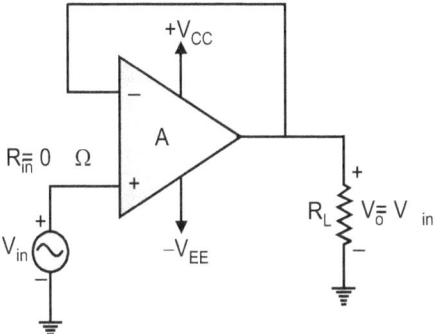

Fig. 2.17 : Voltage follower

The gain of the feedback circuit is 1 ($\beta = 1$).

$$A_F = 1 \qquad \text{... (2.40)}$$

$$R_{iF} = AR_i \qquad \text{... (2.41)}$$

$$R_{OF} = \frac{R_o}{A} \qquad \text{... (2.42)}$$

$$f_F = AF_o \qquad \text{... (2.43)}$$

$$V_{OOT} = \frac{\pm V_{sat}}{A} \qquad \text{... (2.44)}$$

Since, $(1 + A) \cong A$

The voltage follower is also called a non-inverting buffer because, when placed between two networks, it removes the loading effect on the first network.

2.1.8 Voltage Scaling

Op-amps are used extensively in analog circuit design. Fig. 2.18 shows some of the basic scaling applications such as inverting amplifier, non-inverting amplifier and unity-gain amplifier (buffer).

Fig. 2.18 basic voltage scaling applications. The precise operation of all the op-amps circuits shown in Fig. 2.18 is obtained with a minimum number of precise components. In Fig. 2.18 (a) and (b), closed loop gain is determined by simply selecting two register values. The accuracy of the closed loop gain depends entirely upon the resistor value tolerance. The lower limit of the gain for non-inverting circuit depends upon the requirement for maintaining an adequate loop gain to minimise gain error.

Also, closed loop bandwidth decreases with increase in closed loop gain. To obtain high closed loop gains, two op-amp circuits are connected in cascaded mode.

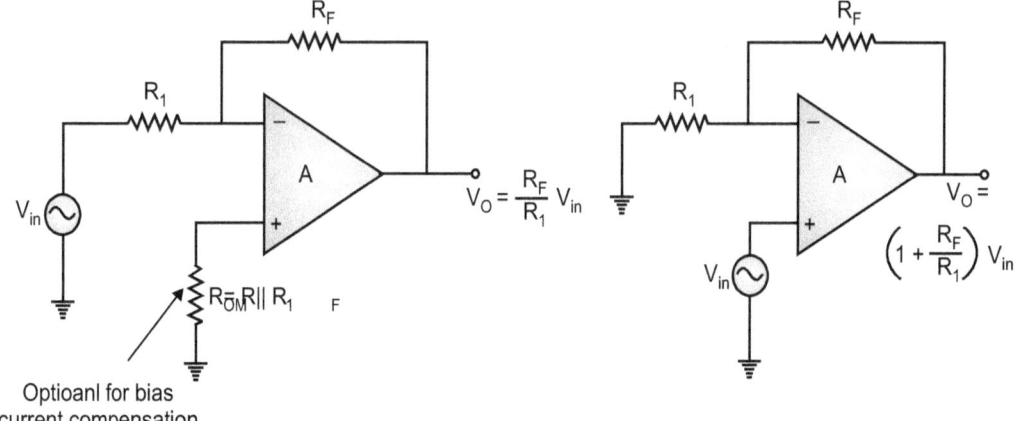

(a) Inverting amplifier   (b) Non-inverting amplifier

(c) Unity-gain amplifier (buffer)

Fig. 2.18 : Basic voltage scaling applications

Both inverting and non-inverting amplifier circuit have low output impedance. This is also the characteristics of negative voltage feedback. The difference between the performance of the non-inverting and inverting circuits is in its input impedance. In case of inverting register R_1 loads the signal source driving the circuit. The non-inverting amplifier present very high input impedance.

The main limitations of the inverting circuit is that its input impedance is effectively equal to the value of the input register R_1. The application may require high input impedance to minimize signal source leading. This demands for a large value for the resistor R_1 and larger value of R_2. Stray capacitance in parallel with a large feedback register limits the bandwidth.

It is difficult to get stable high value of resistors. Therefore in inverting configuration, the need for very high value of feedback resistor is overcome by the use of a T resistance network as shown in Fig. 2.19. This is achieved at the cost of a reduction in loop gain and an increase in noise gain $(-1/\beta)$.

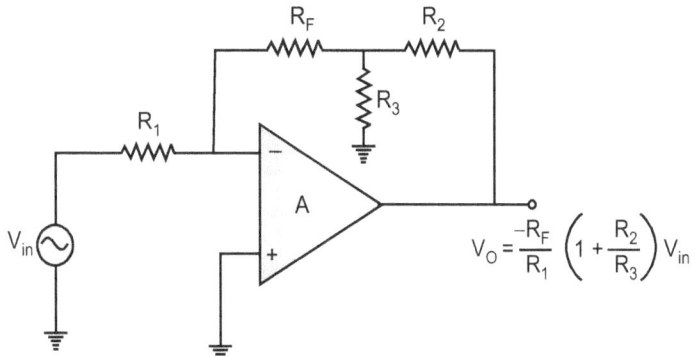

Fig. 2.19 : Inverter circuit using resistive T feedback network

Assume $R_F \gg R_3$

$$\frac{1}{\beta} \approx \left(1 + \frac{R_F}{R_1}\right)\left(1 + \frac{R_2}{R_3}\right)$$

The non-inverting circuit achieves high input impedance without using large value resistors. The high input impedance of the non-inverting circuit makes it a better choice than the inverting circuit in many applications. It also has the limitations for the input. The voltage applied to the non-inverting input must not be allowed to exceed the maximum common mode voltage for the op-amp.

The buffer circuit shown in Fig. 2.18 (c) has high input impedance and low output impedance. It is used to avoid interaction between a signal source and load. Buffer are used in sallen and key filter circuit to prevent interaction between filter stages and to allow simple design rules.

Variable Gain Control :

Instead of fixed value resistors, potentiometers are used to set the gain. Fig. 2.20 shows the variable gain from zero to very high value.

The disadvantages of this is that the scaling factor does not vary linearly with respect to potentiometer rotation. Another disadvantages is that the input impedance falls as the gain is increased.

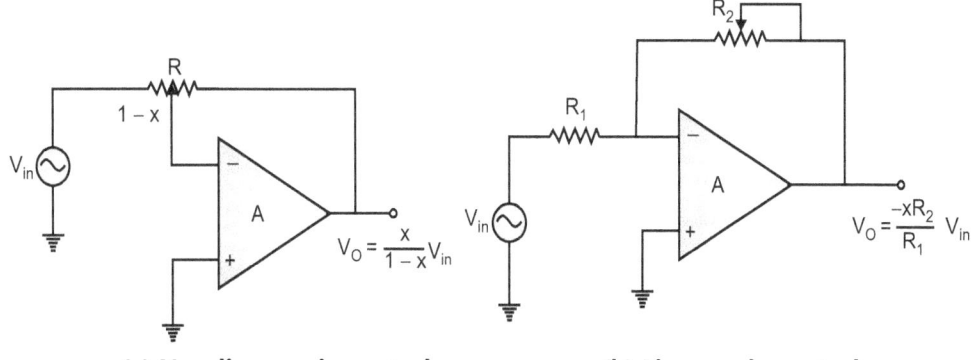

(a) Non-linear gain control (b) Linear gain control

Fig. 2.20 : Variable scale factor

The circuit in Fig. 2.20 (b) gives a narrower range of scale factor variation from zero to R_2/R_1, but the gain variation is linear w.r.t. potentiometer setting and the input impedance remains constant i.e. equal to R_1.

The changes in the closed loop gain changes the closed loop bandwidth. Also, changes in the value of gain setting resistor produces a change in the offset error due to op-amp bias current. Offset errors due to bias current are minimized by using a bias current FET input op-amp.

Switched Scaling Factor :

Gain setting resistors can be switched into circuit. Different values of scale setting resistors are switched into the signal path which allows switching of the gain between preset value. Switching can be performed by a manual control of a mechanical switch, by an electromechanical switch or by means of some form of solid state switch. Fig. 2.21 shows the use of analog switch in a programmable gain circuit.

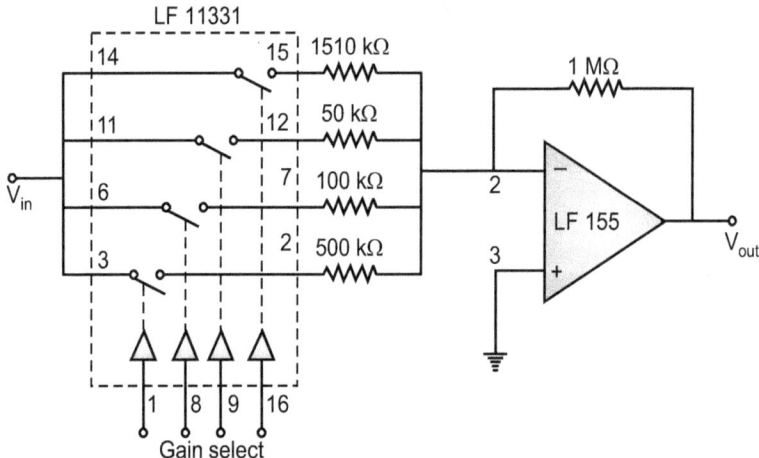

Fig. 2.21 : Programmable gain operated amplifier

Voltage Controlled Gain :

Voltage controlled gain requires a voltage controlled resistive element. Junction gate FETs when operated below pinch-off behaves as a linear resistors with channel resistance (R_{ds}) determined by the value of the gate source voltage. They exhibit bilateral characteristics for small values of drain source voltage.

Linear voltage controlled gain can be obtained by using a feedback arrangement between the drain and gate of the FET. The voltage swing across the FET can be kept small by including it in T-network as shown in Fig. 2.22.

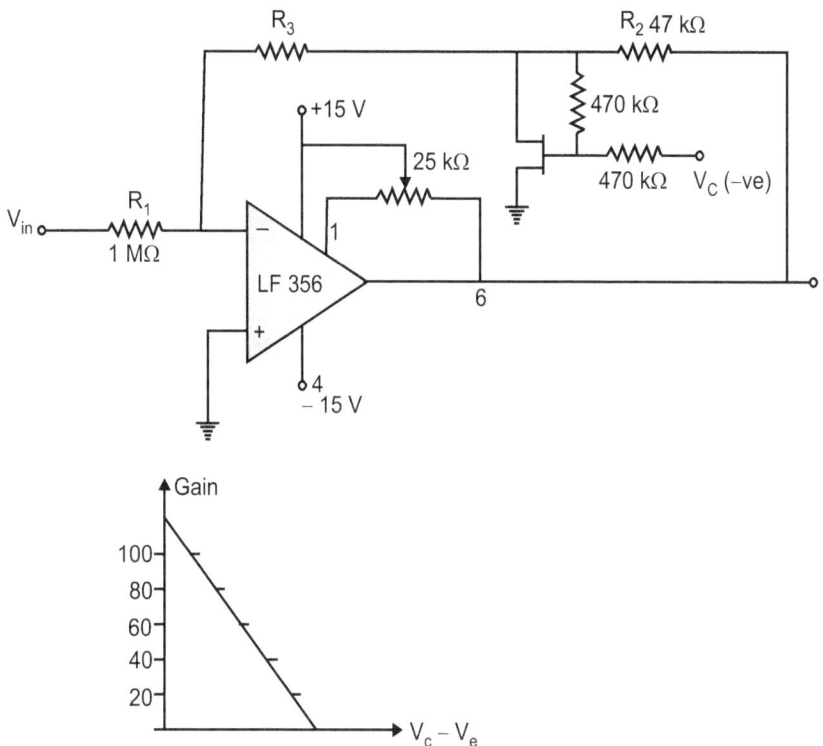

Fig. 2.22 : Voltage controlled scaling factor

The effective resistance of the resistive T when connected to the op-amp summing point is

$$R_e = R_2 + R_3 + \frac{R_2 R_3}{R_{ds}}$$

where R_{ds} is the drain source resistance of the FET.

Which is determined by the relationship as

$$R_{ds} = \frac{r_o}{1 - \frac{V_d}{2V_p}}$$

where r_o = drain source resistance for $V_{ds} = 0$, $I_{ds} = 0$
 V_p = Pinch-off voltage
 V_c = Control voltage applied to the gate of the FET via a series resistor.

Therefore, $$R_e = R_2 + R_3 + \frac{R_2 R_3 \left(1 - \frac{V_c}{2V_p}\right)}{r_o}$$

which is a linear function of V_c.

The closed loop signal gain of the circuit, $-R_e/R_1$, also varies linearly with the value of V_c. The range of gain variation obtainable depends upon the r_o of the FET used in the circuit.

Example 2.7 :

The 741C op-amp having the following parameters is connected as a non-inverting amplifier with $R_1 = 1\ k\Omega$ and $R_F = 10\ k\Omega$.

$A = 200{,}000$ Supply voltages $= \pm 15$ V

$R_i = 2\ M\Omega$ Output voltage swing $= \pm 13$ V

$R_o = 75\ \Omega$

$f_o \cong 5$ Hz

Compute the voltage values of A_F, R_{iF}, R_{OF}, f_F and V_{OOT} for the voltage follower.

Solution :

For the voltage follower, $\beta \cong 1$; therefore $1 + A\beta = 200{,}000$. To compute the closed-loop parameters substitute the known values in equations for A_F, R_{iF}, R_{OF}, f_F, V_{OOT}.

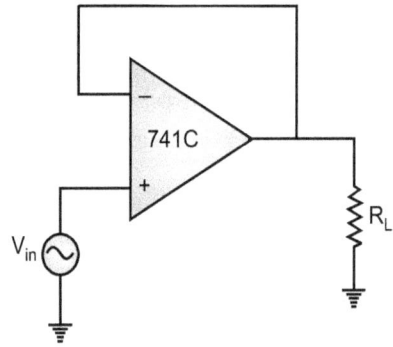

Fig. 2.23

$$A_F = 1$$

$$R_{iF} = 2\ M\Omega\ (200{,}000) = 400\ G\Omega$$

$$R_{OF} = \frac{75}{200{,}000} = 0.375\ m\Omega$$

$$f_F = (5\ Hz)(200{,}000) = 1\ MHz$$

∴ $$V_{OOT} = \frac{\pm 13}{200{,}000} = \pm 65\ \mu V$$

Thus, the input and output resistances of the voltage follower approach ideal values, and the bandwidth is equal to the maximum operating frequency of the op-amp.

2.1.9 Inverting Adder Circuit

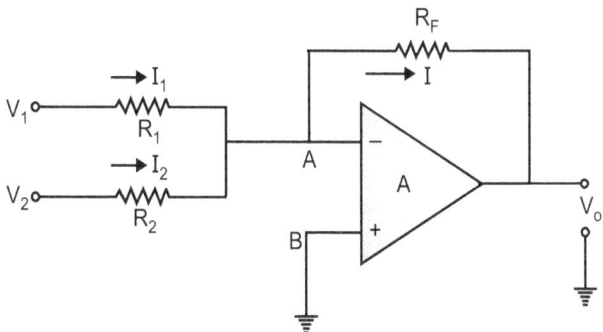

Fig. 2.24 : Inverting adder

$V_A = V_B = 0$ - due to virtual ground concept ... (2.45)

The current flowing through R_1 is I_1.

$$I_1 = \frac{V_1 - V_A}{R_1} = \frac{V_1}{R_1} \quad \ldots (2.46)$$

$$I_2 = \frac{V_2 - V_A}{R_2} = \frac{V_2}{R_2} \quad \ldots (2.47)$$

Using Kirchhoff's current law,

$$I = I_1 + I_2 \quad \ldots (2.48)$$

$$= \frac{V_1}{R_1} + \frac{V_2}{R_2}$$

$$I = \frac{V_A - V_O}{R_F} = \frac{-V_O}{R_F} \quad \ldots (2.49)$$

$$\frac{-V_O}{R_F} = \frac{V_1}{R_1} + \frac{V_2}{R_2}$$

If $R_1 = R_2 = R_F$

$$\boxed{V_O = -(V_1 + V_2)} \quad \ldots (2.50)$$

Here the negative sign indicates that the output is obtained with phase shift i.e. 180°.

2.1.10 Non-inverting Adder

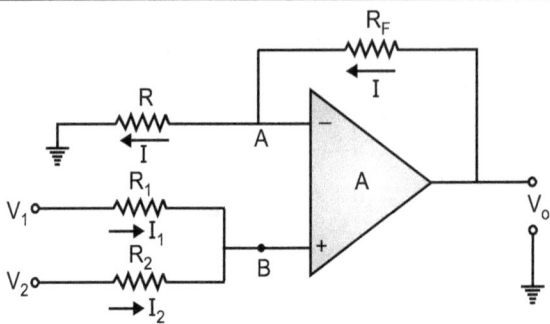

Fig. 2.25 : Non-inverting adder

$V_A = V_B = 0$ due to virtual ground concept ... (2.51)

The current flowing through R_1 is I_1

$$I_1 = \frac{V_1 - V_B}{R_1} \quad \text{... (2.52)}$$

and the current flowing through R_2 is I_2

$$I_2 = \frac{V_2 - V_B}{R_2} \quad \text{... (2.53)}$$

Applying Kirchhoff's current law,

$$I_1 + I_2 = I_{B_1} \quad \text{Since } I_{B_1} = 0 \text{ ... (2.54)}$$

$$= \frac{V_1 - V_B}{R_1} + \frac{V_2 - V_B}{R_2} = 0$$

$$\frac{V_1}{R_1} + \frac{V_2}{R_2} = \frac{V_B}{R_1} + \frac{V_B}{R_2}$$

$$\frac{V_1}{R_1} + \frac{V_2}{R_2} = V_B \left(\frac{R_1 + R_2}{R_1 R_2}\right)$$

$$V_B = \frac{R_2 V_1 + R_1 V_2}{R_1 R_2} \times \frac{R_1 R_2}{R_1 + R_2}$$

$$V_B = \frac{R_1 V_2 + R_2 V_1}{R_1 + R_2} \quad \text{... (2.55)}$$

$$I = \frac{V_A}{R} = \frac{V_B}{R} \quad \text{... (2.56)}$$

and
$$I = \frac{V_O - V_A}{R_F} = \frac{V_O - V_B}{R_F} \quad \ldots (2.57)$$

$$\frac{V_B}{R} = \frac{V_O - V_B}{R_F}$$

$$V_B(R_F) = R(V_O - V_B)$$

$$V_B R_F + RV_B = RV_O$$

$$V_B(R_F + R) = RV_O$$

$$V_O = V_B \left(\frac{R + R_F}{R}\right)$$

$$V_O = \left(\frac{R + R_F}{R}\right) \times \frac{R_2 V_1 + R_1 V_2}{R_1 + R_2}$$

When $R_1 = R_2 = R = R_F$, we get

$$V_O = \frac{R + R}{R} \times \frac{R(V_1 + V_2)}{R + R}$$

$$\boxed{V_O = V_1 + V_2} \quad \ldots (2.58)$$

Example 2.8 :

Determine the output voltage for the circuit shown in Fig. 2.26 for $V_1 = 2$ V and $V_2 = 4$ V.

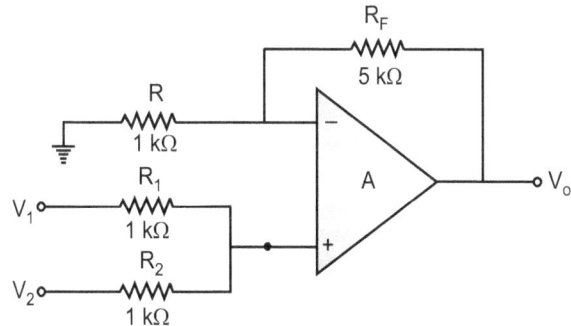

Fig. 2.26

Solution :

$$R_1 = R_2 = 1 \text{ k}\Omega$$

$$V_B = \frac{R_2 V_1 + R_1 V_2}{R_1 + R_2}$$

$$= \frac{V_1 + V_2}{2}$$

$$V_B = \frac{2+4}{2} = 3 \text{ V}$$

$$V_O = \left(1 + \frac{R_F}{R_1}\right) V_B$$

$$V_O = \left(1 + \frac{5}{1}\right) \times 3 = (1+5) \times 3 = 6 \times 3 = 18$$

∴ $\boxed{V_O = 18 \text{ V}}$

Example 2.9 :

Determine the output voltage for the circuit shown in Fig. 2.27.

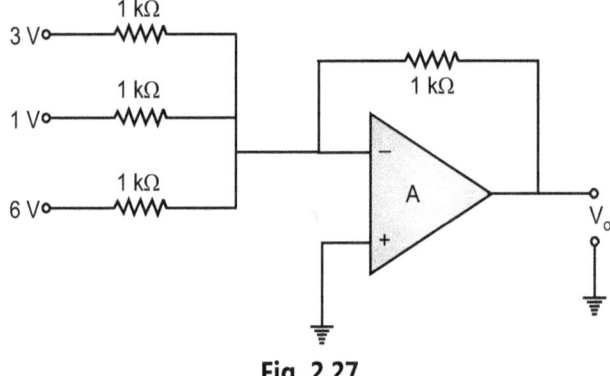

Fig. 2.27

Solution :

From Fig. 2.27, $R_1 = R_2 = R_3 = 1 \text{ k}\Omega$

$R_F = 1 \text{ k}\Omega$

$$V_O = -\left[\frac{R_F}{R_1} V_1 + \frac{R_F}{R_1} V_2 + \frac{R_F}{R_1} V_3\right]$$

$$V_O = -\frac{R_F}{R}[V_1 + V_2 + V_3]$$

$$= -[V_1 + V_2 + V_3] = -(3 + 1 + 6) = -10 \text{ V}$$

∴ $\boxed{V_O = -10 \text{ V}}$

2.1.11 Averaging Circuit

The average circuit is a circuit in which the output voltage is equal to the average of all the input voltages. This is obtained by using all the input resistors of equal values. When $R_a = R_b = R_c = R$. As well as the gain by which each input is amplified must be equal to 1 over the number of inputs i.e.

$$\frac{R_F}{R} = \frac{1}{n}$$

where n is the number of inputs.

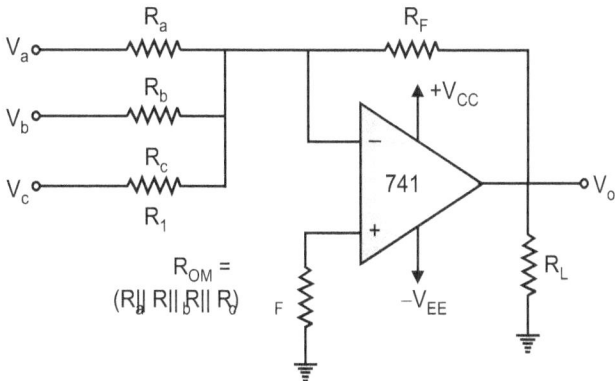

Fig. 2.28 : Inverting configuration can be used as a averaging amplifier

If there are three inputs,

$$\frac{R_F}{R} = \frac{1}{3}$$

$$V_o = -\left(\frac{V_a + V_b + V_c}{3}\right)$$

The offset minimizing resistor R_{OM} is used to minimize the effect of input bias currents on the output offset voltage.

2.1.12 Subtractor or Difference Amplifier

A basic differential amplifier can be used as a subtractor as shown in Fig. 2.29.

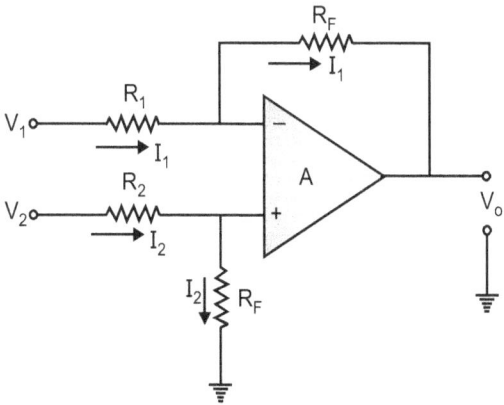

Fig. 2.29 : Subtractor or difference amplifier

Use superposition principle to find the relation between input and output. Consider V_1 is acting alone.

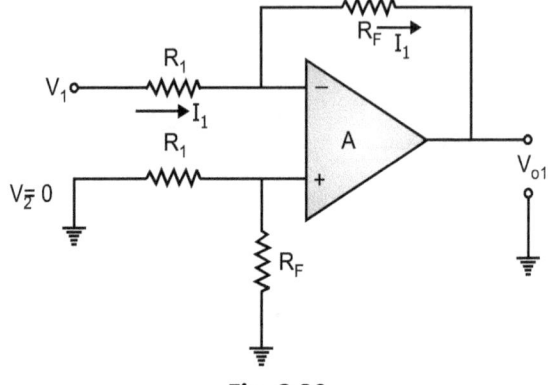

Fig. 2.30

Now the op-amp acts in inverting amplifier mode. So,

$$V_{o_1} = \frac{-R_F}{R_1} V_1 \qquad \ldots (2.59)$$

Now consider V_2 is acting alone.

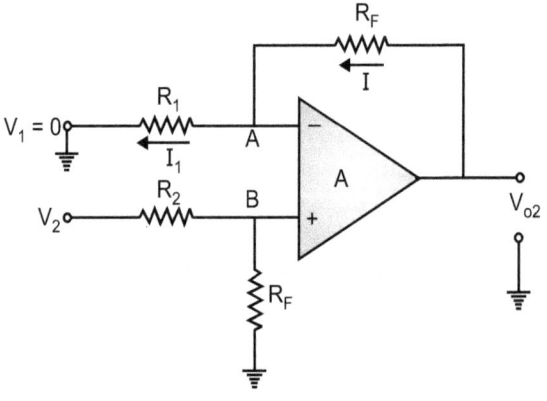

Fig. 2.31

The voltage at non-inverting input is V_B and is given by

$$V_B = \frac{R_F}{R_2 + R_F} \times V_2 \qquad \ldots (2.60)$$

$$I = \frac{V_A}{R_1} = \frac{V_B}{R_1} \qquad \ldots (2.61)$$

$$I = \frac{V_{o_2} - V_A}{R_F} = \frac{V_{o_2}}{R_F} \qquad \ldots (2.62)$$

$$\frac{V_B}{R_1} = \frac{V_{o_2} - V_B}{R_F}$$

$$V_B R_F = R_1 V_{O_2} - R_1 V_B$$

$$V_{O_2} = \frac{V_B R_F + R_1 V_B}{R_1} = \frac{V_B(R_1 + R_F)}{R_1} = \left[\frac{R_1 + R_F}{R_1}\right] V_B$$

$$V_{O_2} = \left(1 + \frac{R_F}{R_1}\right)\left(\frac{R_F}{R_1 + R_F}\right) V_2 \qquad \ldots (2.63)$$

$$V_O = V_{O_1} + V_{O_2} \qquad \ldots (2.64)$$

$$= \frac{-R_F}{R_1} V_1 + \left(\frac{R_1 + R_F}{R_1}\right)\left(\frac{R_F}{R_1 + R_F}\right) V_2$$

$$= \frac{-R_F}{R_1} V_1 + \frac{R_F}{R_1} V_2 = \frac{R_F}{R_1}[V_2 - V_1]$$

When $R_F = R_1 = R$, then

$$V_O = V_2 - V_1$$

The above circuit acts as subtractor.

2.2 INTEGRATOR

2.2.1 Passive Integrator

A low pass circuit with large time constant can be called as passive integrator which is made of passive component such as R and C.

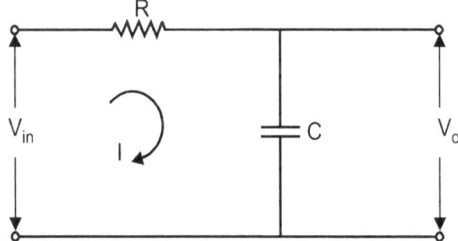

Fig. 2.32 : Passive integrator

The voltage drop across C can be made negligible by selecting proper values of R and C so that the entire input voltage V_{in} appears across R.

Voltage across R, $V_R = V_{in} = IR$

i.e. $I = \dfrac{V_{in}}{R}$

The output voltage is taken across capacitor C,

$$V_O = \frac{1}{C} \int I \, dt$$

$$= \frac{1}{RC} \int V_{in} \, dt$$

Hence, the output voltage is the integration of the input voltage.

2.2.2 Active Integrator

The circuit whose output voltage waveform is the integral of the input voltage waveform is called integrator. It can be obtained by using basic inverting amplifier configuration if the feedback resistor R_F is replaced by a capacitor C_F.

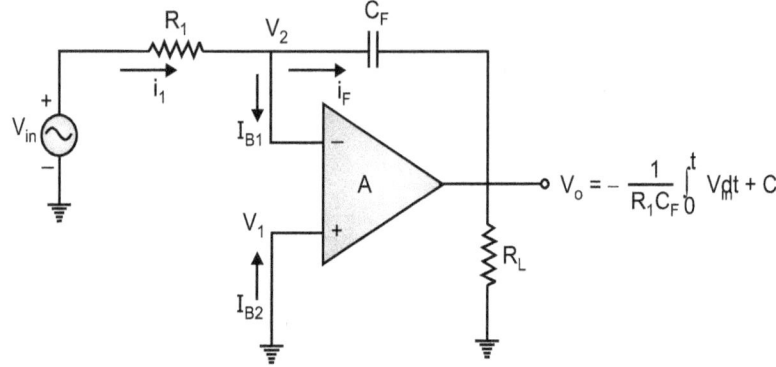

Fig. 2.33 : Active integrator

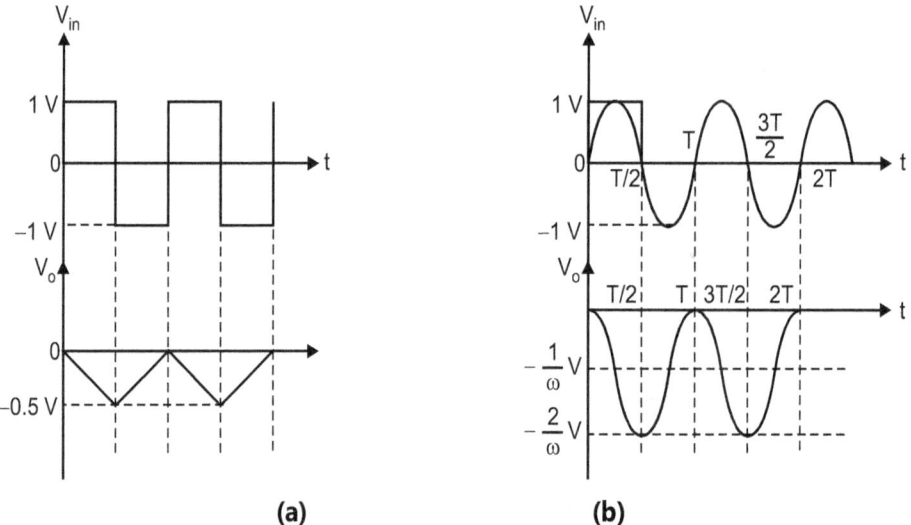

(a) (b)

Fig. 2.34 : Input/output waveforms when input is square wave and sinusoidal signal

The output voltage V_O can be obtained by writing Kirchhoff's current law at node V_2.

$$i_1 = I_B + i_F \qquad \text{... (2.65)}$$

Since, I_B is small and negligible,

$$i_1 = i_F \qquad \text{... (2.66)}$$

The current through capacitor is given by

$$i_C = C\frac{dV_C}{dt} \qquad \text{... (2.67)}$$

Therefore, $\dfrac{V_{in} - V_2}{R_1} = C_F \dfrac{d}{dt}(V_2 - V_o)$ ... (2.68)

However, $V_1 = V_2 = 0$ because A is very large.

Therefore, $\dfrac{V_{in}}{R_1} = C_F \dfrac{d}{dt}(-V_o)$ ... (2.69)

The output voltage can be obtained by integrating both sides with respect to time.

$$\int_0^t \dfrac{V_{in}}{R_1} dt = \int_0^t C_F \cdot \dfrac{d}{dt}(-V_o) dt$$

$$= C_F(-V_o) + V_o|_{t=0}$$

Therefore, $V_o = -\dfrac{1}{R_1 C_F} \int_0^t V_{in}\, dt + C$ ... (2.70)

where C is the integration constant and is proportional to the value of the output voltage V_o at time t = 0 seconds. The above equation shows that the output voltage is directly proportional to the negative integral of the input voltage and inversely proportional to the time constant $R_1 C_F$.

2.2.3 Frequency Response of Active Integrator

Consider the output equation of an ideal integrator.

$$V_o(t) = -\dfrac{1}{R_1 C_F} \int_0^t V_{in}\, dt \quad ...(2.71)$$

Assume the initial voltage $V_o(0)$ as zero. By taking the Laplace transform of this equation, we get

$$V_o(S) = -\dfrac{1}{SR_1 C_F} V_{in}(S) \quad ...(2.72)$$

To get the frequency response replace S by jω.

$$V_o(j\omega) = \dfrac{1}{-j\omega R_1 C_F} V_{in}(j\omega) \quad ...(2.73)$$

$$\dfrac{V_o(j\omega)}{V_{in}(j\omega)} = \dfrac{1}{-j\omega R_1 C_F}$$

To obtain the frequency response, obtain the magnitude of the gain as

$$A = \left|\frac{V_o(j\omega)}{V_{in}(j\omega)}\right| = \left|-\frac{1}{j\omega R_1 C_F}\right|$$

$$A = \frac{1}{\omega R_1 C_F} = \frac{1}{2\pi f R_1 C_F} \qquad \ldots (2.74)$$

f_b is the frequency at which the gain is 0 dB and is given by

$$f_b = \frac{1}{2\pi R_1 C_F} \qquad \ldots (2.75)$$

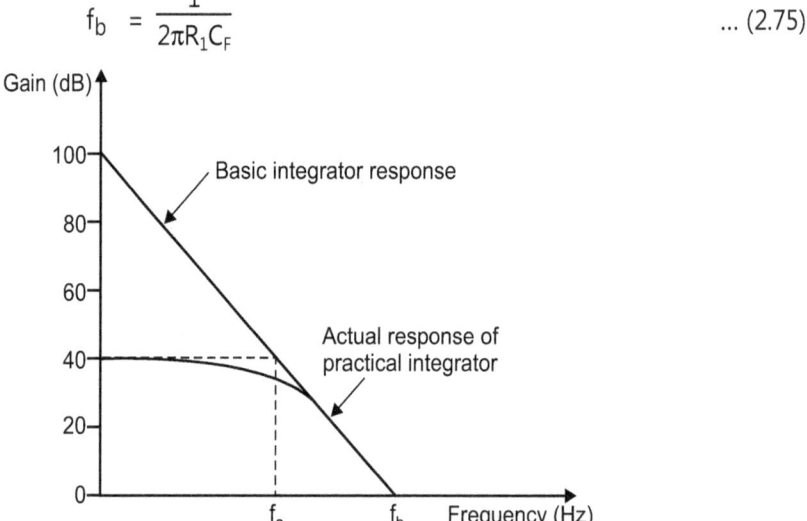

Fig. 2.35 : Frequency response of basic and practical integrators

2.2.4 Errors in Basic Integrator

1. Error voltage :

When $V_{in} = 0$, the op-amp acts as an open-loop amplifier. This is because capacitor C_F acts as open circuit to the input offset voltage V_{ios}. The input offset voltage V_{ios} and the part of the input current charges capacitor C_F which produces an error voltage at the output of the integrator. Output waveform may be distorted due to such an error voltage.

2. Limitations in bandwidth :

Due to stability problems and the low-frequency roll-off problems the basic integrator is suitable for small frequency range of input.

To remove these errors in basic integrator, a resistor R_F is connected across the feedback capacitor C_F. R_F resistor limits the low-frequency gain and hence minimizes the variations in the output voltage.

Both the stability and the low frequency roll-off problems can be corrected by the addition of a resistor R_F.

Stability refers to a constant gain as frequency of an input signal is varied over a certain range.

Low frequency roll-off means to the rate of decrease in gain at lower frequencies.

2.2.5 Practical Integrator

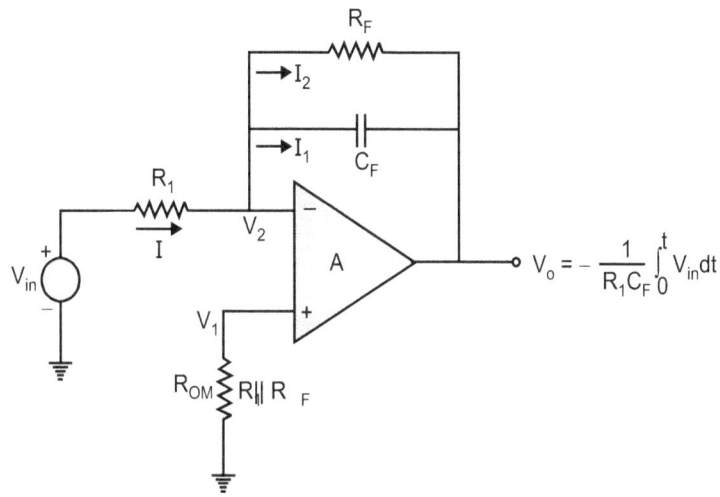

Fig. 2.36 : Practical integrator

Fig. 2.36 shows the practical integrator circuit in which the resistance R_F reduces the low frequency gain of the op-amp.

From Fig. 2.36,
$$I = \frac{V_{in} - V_2}{R_1} = \frac{V_{in}}{R_1} \text{ as } V_1 = V_2 = 0 \quad \ldots (2.76)$$

Similarly,
$$I_1 = C_F \frac{d(V_2 - V_o)}{dt} = -C_F \frac{dV_o}{dt} \text{ as } V_2 = 0 \quad \ldots (2.77)$$

$$I_2 = \frac{V_2 - V_o}{R_F} = \frac{-V_o}{R_F} \quad \ldots (2.78)$$

Applying KCL at node V_2,
$$I = I_1 + I_2 \quad \ldots (2.79)$$

$$\frac{V_{in}}{R_1} = -C_F \frac{dV_o}{dt} - \frac{V_o}{R_F}$$

Taking Laplace of this equation,

$$\frac{V_{in}(S)}{R_1} = -S C_F V_o(S) - \frac{V_o(S)}{R_F}$$

$$\frac{V_{in}(S)}{R_1} = -V_o(S) \left[SC_F + \frac{1}{R_F} \right]$$

$$\frac{V_{in}(S)}{R_1} = \frac{-V_o(S)[1 + SC_F R_F]}{R_F}$$

$$V_o(S) = -\frac{R_F}{R_1}\left[\frac{1}{1 + SC_F R_F}\right] V_{in}(S) \qquad \ldots (2.80)$$

$$V_o(S) = -\frac{1}{SR_1 C_F + \dfrac{R_1}{R_F}} V_{in}(S)$$

As R_F is very large than R_1/R_F,

$$V_o(S) = -\frac{1}{SR_1 C_F} V_{in}(S)$$

Replacing S by t,
$$\boxed{V_o(t) = -\frac{1}{R_1 C_F} \int_0^t V_{in}(t)\, dt} \qquad \ldots (2.81)$$

2.2.6 Frequency Response of Practical Integrator

Consider the equation (2.80),

$$V_o(S) = -\frac{R_F}{R_1}\left[\frac{1}{1 + SC_F R_F}\right] V_{in}(S)$$

$$\frac{V_o(S)}{V_{in}(S)} = -\frac{R_F/R_1}{1 + SC_F R_F}$$

To obtain the frequency response replace S by $j\omega$.

$$\frac{V_o(j\omega)}{V_{in}(j\omega)} = \frac{-R_F/R_1}{1 + j\omega\, C_F R_F}$$

$$A = \frac{-R_F/R_1}{1 + j\, 2\pi f\, C_F R_F}$$

$$A = \frac{R_F/R_1}{1 + j\, f/f_a}$$

where,
$$f_a = \frac{1}{2\pi C_F R_F}$$

$$|A| = \frac{R_F/R_1}{\sqrt{1 + (f/f_a)^2}} \qquad \ldots (2.82)$$

At $f = 0$,
$$|A| = \frac{R_F}{R_1}$$

$$20 \log |A| = 20 \log (R_F/R_1) \text{ dB}$$

At $f = f_a$,
$$|A| = \frac{R_F/R_1}{\sqrt{2}} = 0.707 (R_F/R_1) \quad \ldots (2.83)$$

$$20 \log |A| = 20 \log 0.707 + 20 \log (R_F/R_1)$$
$$= -3 \text{ dB} + \text{DC gain} \quad \ldots (2.84)$$

At $f = f_a$, the gain drops by 3 dB frequency.

Here f is some relative operating frequency and for frequencies f to f_a, the gain R_F/R_1 is constant and after f_a the gain decreases at a rate of 20 dB/decade. That means between f_a and f_b the circuit acts as an integrator. The gain limiting frequency f_a is given by

$$f_a = \frac{1}{2\pi R_F C_F} \quad \ldots (2.85)$$

Generally, the value of f_a and in turn $R_1 C_F$ and $R_F C_F$ values should be selected such that $f_a < f_b$ for example, $f_a = f_b/10$, then $R_F = 10 R_1$.

The input signal is integrated properly if the time period T of the signal is larger or equal to $R_F C_F$.

$$T \geq R_F C_F \quad \ldots (2.86)$$

where,
$$R_F C_F = \frac{1}{2\pi f_a}$$

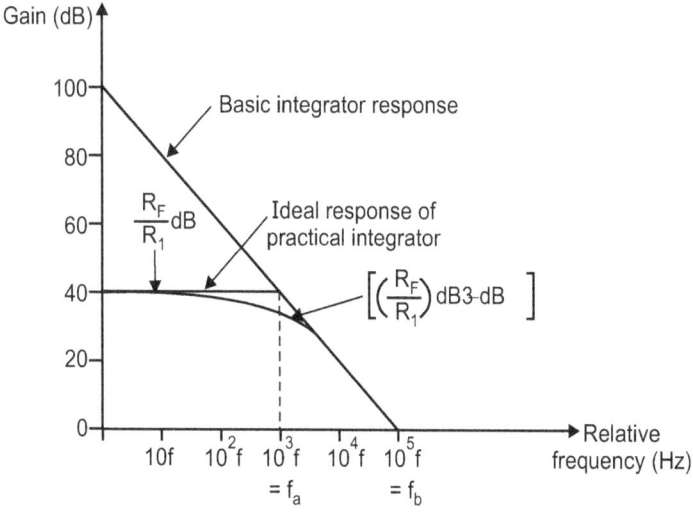

Fig. 2.37 : Frequency response of basic and practical integrators

$$f_a = \frac{1}{2\pi R_F C_F} \text{ and } f_b = \frac{1}{2\pi R_1 C_F}$$

2.2.7 Integrator Run, Set and Hold Modes

In a practical integrator circuit it is necessary to provide setting of a initial value of the integrator output voltage at the start of the integration period. In some systems, it is also essential to stop the integrator at any time and for the integrator output then to remain constant at the value it has reached at that time. the switching of the integrator between its various modes of operation are shown in Fig. 2.38.

Different types of switching can be used such as manual switching, relay switching or solid state switching etc.

When the switch is kept in 'set' position, it allows to set the initial value of the integrator output at any desired value within the output capability of the amplifier.

$$V_{o\,(t=0)} = \frac{-R_2}{R_1} V_{ref}$$

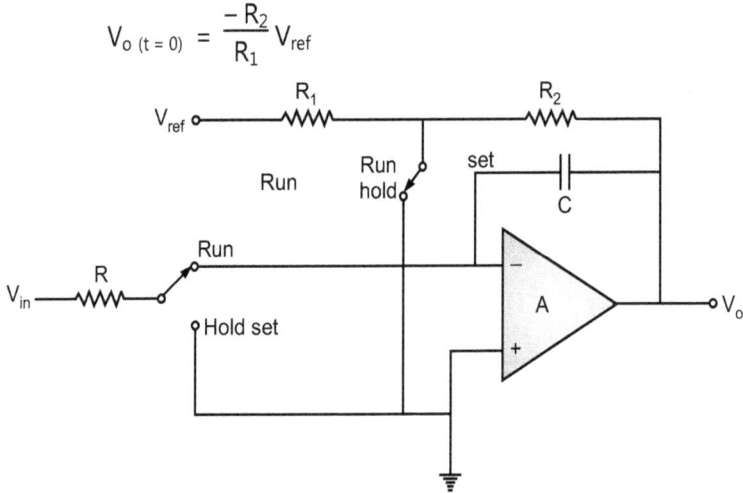

Fig. 2.38 : Integrator run, set and hold modes

The integrator output does not immediately take on this value when switched to the set mode. It reaches to the desired value exponentially according the following relationship.

$$V_o = V_{o\,(t=0)} + (V_o' - V_{o\,(t=0)}) \exp\left(\frac{-t}{R_1 C}\right)$$

where V_o' is the value of V_o at the instant of switching set mode.

When the switch is kept on 'run mode, the circuit integrator the input voltage and output voltage is

$$V_o = V_{o\,(t=0)} - \frac{1}{CR} \int_0^t V_{in}\, dt$$

When the integrator is switched to the 'Hold' mode, integration is stopped and ideally the output of the integrator remains constant. In both 'run' and 'hold' modes, the drift causes an integrator error.

2.2.7.1 Integrator Errors

1. Offset and drift errors in practical integrators :

The greatest source of error in practical integrators is due to offset and drift of the op-amp with no input applied. The op-amps input offset voltage and bias current causes a continuous charging of the feedback capacitor. When the output voltage of a practical free running integrator changes continuously, the output of the op-amp drift into either positive or negative saturation.

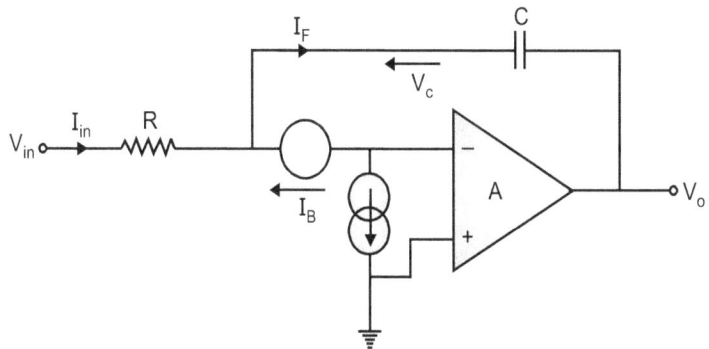

Fig. 2.39 : Equivalent circuit to estimate errors due to input offset voltage and bias current

Integrator output voltage drift with time can be reduced to zero by cancelling the effects of the amplifier offsets with a suitable balance control. Amplifier offsets depends upon, temperature, supply voltage and time. If the drift condition established with a balance control is not maintained, the integrator goes into saturation. The integrator error due to amplifier input offset voltage and bias current is reduced with the help of the following circuit connections shown in Fig. 2.39.

Consider that the open-loop gain and open-loop input impedance of the amplifier are infinite. Then we can write

$$I_f = I_{in} - I_B$$

where $I_{in} = (V_{in} - V_{io})/R$

Now, $$V_c = V_{io} - V_o = \frac{\int I_f \, dt}{C}$$

V_o = Ideal performance equation − Error due to offset and bias current.

$$V_o = -\frac{1}{RC} \int V_{in} \, dt + \frac{1}{RC} \int V_{io} \, dt + \frac{1}{C} \int I_B \, dt + V_{io}$$

The percentage error after a particular integration time may be written as

$$\frac{V_{io} + I_B R}{V_{in}} \times 100\%$$

The error component due to amplifier bias current can be reduced by connecting a resistor equal to the value to that of the integrating resistor between the non-inverting input terminal of the amplifier and earth.

There are practical considerations that limit the capacitance value. A large value of C requires a corresponding small value of R for a particular CR value. The input impedance of the integrator is set by the value of the resistor R. Capacitor leakage represents an additional capacitors source of integrator drift. Large value, high performance capacitors are expensive and should have dielectric leakage current that less than the amplifier bias current. The dielectric absorption of a capacitor will also caused drift. Polypropylene and polystyrene dielectrics have lowest absorption, whereas electrolytic and tantalum have the highest.

To get low drift integrators with long-term stability, low current FET input op-amps are used.

Integrator errors due to finite open-loop gain, finite input impedance and finite bandwidth :

The performance of the practical circuit is near about same as ideal only when the loop gain βA_{OL} is large.

In a practical integrator, finite open-loop gain causes integrator performance errors for very low frequency input signals and finite bandwidth causes errors for high frequency input signals.

(a) Errors at high frequency due to finite open-loop bandwidth :

At frequencies approaching and exceeding the amplifier unity gain frequency f_1

$$\beta \to 1, \; A_{OL\,(jf)} \to -j\,(f_1/f)$$

and

$$\frac{V_{o\,(jf)}}{V_{in\,(jf)}} = -\frac{1}{j2\pi fCR}\left[\frac{1}{1+j\,f/f_1}\right]$$

This equation represents the equation for an ideal integrator when cascaded with a first order low-pass function having a break frequency equal to the open-loop unity gain frequency of the op-amp. The attenuation and phase shift produced by this first order function represents the errors in the steady/state sinusoidal response of the integrator at frequencies approaching f_1. The output of a practical integrator exhibits a time lag in response to an input step signal is shown in Fig. 2.40. The time lag is inversely proportional to the open-loop unity gain frequency f_1 of the op-amp.

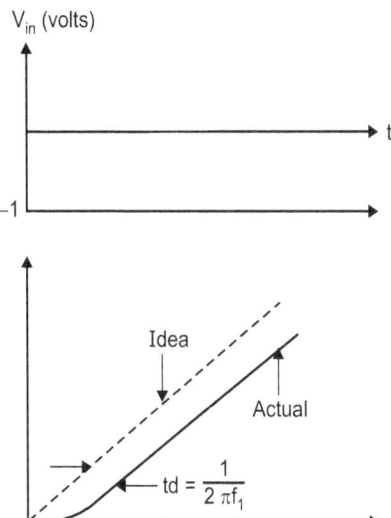

Fig. 2.40 : Time-lag in integrator due to finite open-loop bandwidth

(b) Errors at low frequencies due to finite open-loop gain :

The gain of the ideal integrator increases as the signal frequency is decreased, but in a practical integrator the gain cannot be greater than the open-loop gain of the amplifier A_o.

At frequencies less than f_1/A_o, $A_{OL\,(jf)} \rightarrow A_o$.

and
$$\frac{1}{\beta\,A_{OL\,(jf)}} = \frac{1}{A_o} + \frac{1}{j\,2\pi f\,A_o\,CR'} \cong \frac{1}{j2\pi f\,A_o\,CR'}$$

$\therefore$
$$\frac{V_{o\,(jf)}}{V_{in\,(jf)}} = -\frac{1}{j2\pi fCR}\left[1 + \left(\frac{1}{\frac{1}{j2\pi f\,A_o\,CR'}}\right)\right] = \frac{A_o\frac{R'}{R}}{1 + j2\pi f\,A_o\,CR'}$$

for $f < f_c$.

The above equation is equivalent to the response of an ideal op-amp with infinite gain and infinite input resistance. It has a feedback impedance consisting of a capacitor C in parallel with a resistor A_oR' as shown in Fig. 2.41 below.

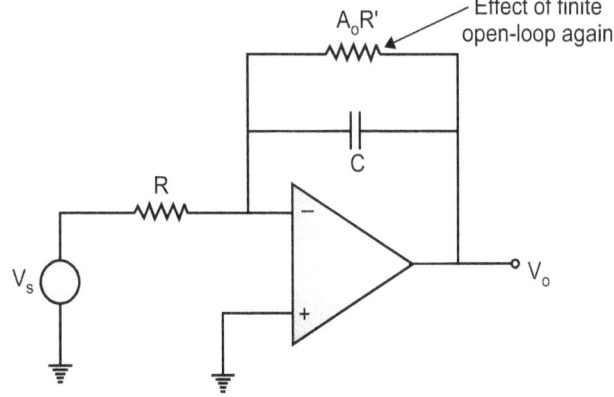

Fig. 2.41 : Integrator low frequency equivalent circuit

Connecting the input resistor R to a constant D.C. voltage produces a linear ramp generator. In such applications, low frequency errors due to finite open-loop gain causes departures from the ramp linearity. The output response of the low frequency equivalent circuit to an input step voltage V_s is determined by the relationship.

$$V_{o(t)} = -A_o \frac{R'}{R} \cdot V_s \left[1 - \exp\left(\frac{-t}{A_o CR'}\right)\right]$$

(c) Finite open-loop gain causes errors in hold mode :

If during integration process the input voltage to the integrator is switched to zero, the output of the integrator should ideally remain constant at any value it may have reached. Finite open-loop gain and finite input resistance in addition to amplifier offsets, contribute errors in the hold mode.

The error can be minimised by open circuiting the input resistor R_1. This makes the effective leakage resistance $A_o R'$ equal to $A_o R_d$ due to amplifiers finite open-loop gain and finite input resistance. This effective leakage resistance tends to discharge any fixed voltage stored across the integrating capacitor and the equivalent circuit is shown in Fig. 2.42 below. It may be used to compute drift error in the hold ode.

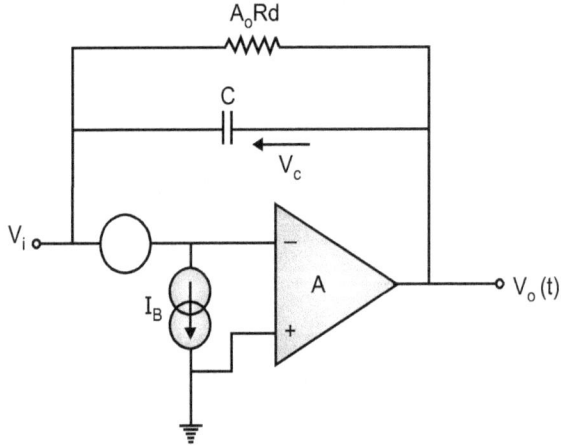

Fig. 2.42

(d) Slew rate errors :

Fast integrators require an output voltage that changes rapidly. Slew rate limitations can cause performance errors. Slew rate limitations arises from the basic mechanism of capacitor charging. The slew rate is determined by the charging of the op-amps frequency compensating capacitor.

2.2.8 Extensions to a Basic Integrator

To change the response characteristics and to extend the usefulness of the integrator, variety of external circuit modifications can be made to the basic integrator.

(a) Summing Integrator :

A single amplifier is used to perform both summation and the integration at the same time.

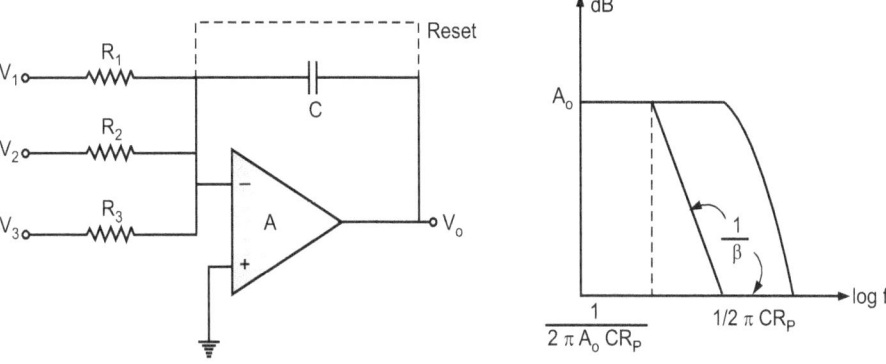

Fig. 2.43

$$V_o = -\left[\frac{1}{CR_1}\int V_1\,dt + \frac{1}{CR_2}\int V_2\,dt + \frac{1}{CR_3}\int V_3\,dt\right]$$

Low frequency errors due to finite gain occur at frequency approaching and below the frequency at which the Bode plot for $1/\beta$ and the open-loop gain intersect.

For summing integrator $1/\beta$ is determined by the parallel sum of all input resistors R_p.

$$\frac{1}{\beta} = 1 + \frac{1}{j2\pi fC\,R_p}$$

(b) Augmenting Integrator :

When a resistor is connected in series with the feedback capacitor of a basic integrator, the circuit produce a composite output consisting of a component proportional to the input signal added to a component proportional to the time integral of the input signal.

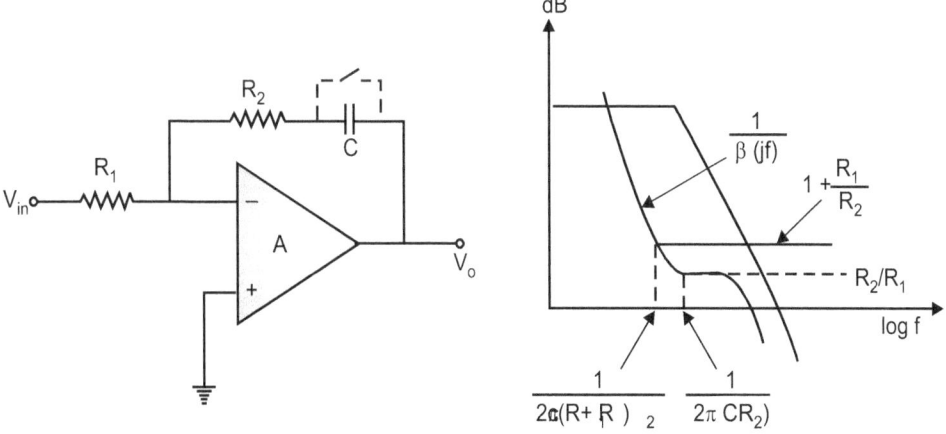

Fig. 2.44 : Augmenting integrator

This principal may also be adapted to the summing integrator by connecting a resistor in series with the feedback capacitor.

(c) Differential Integrator :

The subtraction principle can be applied to give a circuit in which a single differential input op-amp produces an output signal proportional to the time integral of the difference between two input signals.

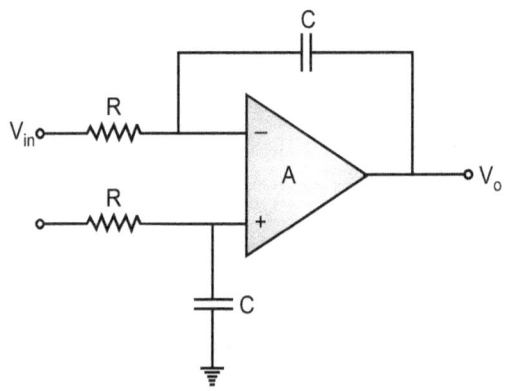

Fig. 2.45 : Differential integrator

$$V_o = \frac{1}{CR} - \int (V_2 - V_1)\, dt + \underbrace{\frac{1}{CR}\int V_{io}\, dt + \frac{1}{C}\int I_{io}\, dt + V_{io}}_{\text{error due to input offset current and input offset voltage}}$$

The error occurs in the output due to input offset voltage, input offset current, finite open-loop gain, and bandwidth. The error occurs due to two capacitors with a single amplifier. Therefore, it is convient to use the two-amplifier one capacitor circuit as shown in Fig. 2.46 to perform the differential integrator operation.

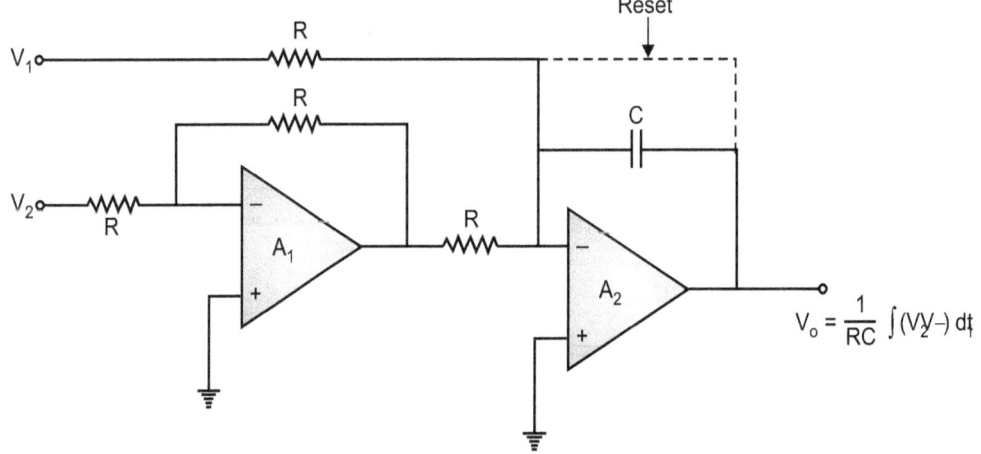

Fig. 2.46 : Differential integrator using two op-amps

Here one amplifier acts as a simple inverter and the other acts as a summing integrator. The CMRR circuit depends upon the accurate resistor matching.

(d) Current Integrator :

Sometimes it is required to form an output signal voltage proportional to the integral with respect to time of input current rather than input voltage.

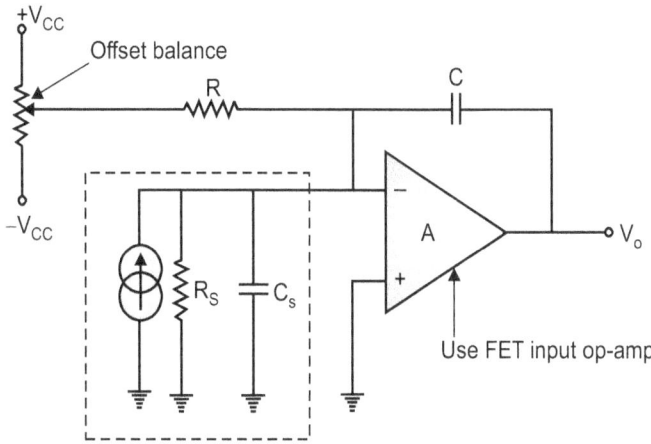

Fig. 2.47 : Current integrator

Such type of circuit is suitable for integrating small high impedance currents to earth. It produces a negligible voltage intrusion into the measurement circuit.

With suitable precautions and the offsets are nulled, the circuit provides accurate integration for small input currents. If external leakage is reduced to negligible proportions, the accuracy limitations are set by the amplifier bias current drift. A FET input op-amp has low bias current drift and should be used.

(e) Integrator Reset :

Integrator output does not return to zero when the input signal is made zero unlike a normal amplifier circuit. Therefore, it is necessary to provide some means of resetting its output voltage to zero.

Switching of the integrator between its various modes of operation may be done with the help of mechanical switches or solid state switches.

Reset switches are connected in parallel with the integrator feedback capacitor. A low leakage reset which can be implemented using two MOSFETs as shown in Fig. 2.48.

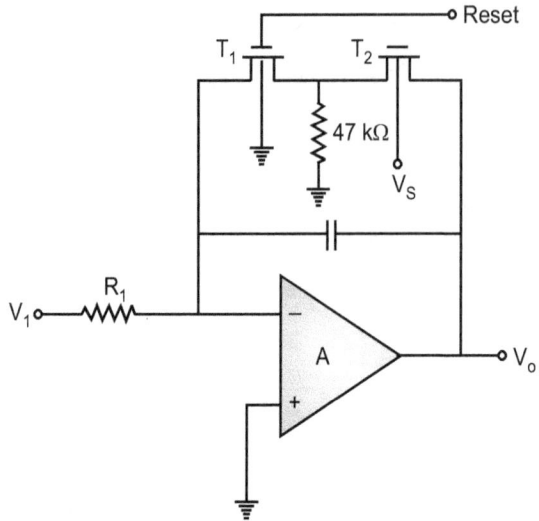

Fig. 2.48 : Low leakage integrator reset

When P-channel MOS switches are used, the source substrate junction must not be forward biased. The substrate must not become negative w.r.t. the input signal. The leakage current of a MOS switch in the OFF state occurs mainly across the substrate to drain junction.

2.2.9 Applications of Integrator

1. Used in analog computers.
2. Used in analog to digital converters.
3. Used in signal-wave shaping circuits.

Example 2.10 :

In the circuit as shown in Fig. 2.49, $R_1 C_F = 1$ second and the input is a step (DC) voltage. Determine the output voltage and sketch it. Assume that the op-amp is initially nulled.

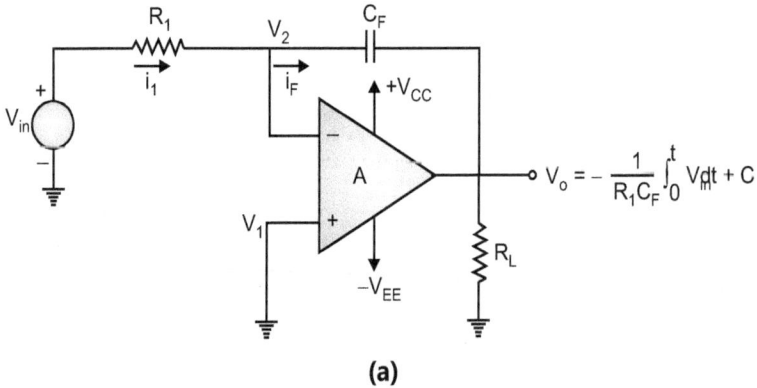

(a)

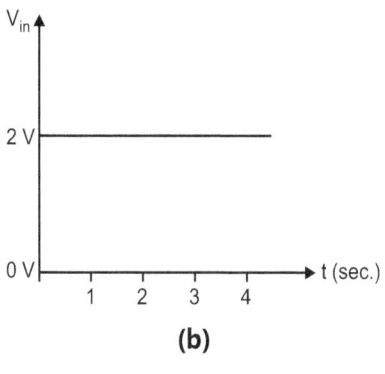

(b)

Fig. 2.49

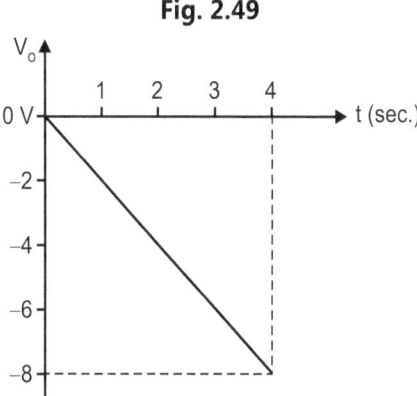

Fig. 2.50 : Input and output waveforms

Solution :

The input function is constant beginning at t = 0 seconds. That is V_{in} = 2 V for $0 \leq t \leq 4$.

Therefore, $V_O = -\int_0^{t=4} 2\, dt$

$$= -\left[\int_0^1 2\, dt + \int_1^2 2\, dt + \int_2^3 2\, dt + \int_3^4 2\, dt\right]$$

$$= -(2 + 2 + 2 + 2) = -8 \text{ V}$$

The output waveform is called a ramp function. The slope of the ramp is – 2V/s. Thus with a constant voltage applied at the input, the integrator gives a ramp at the output.

Example 2.11 :

Implement the following equation.

$$V_O = -\int_0^t (2V_1 + 3V_2 + 4V_3)\, dt$$

Solution :

The output of the summing integrator with three inputs is

$$V_o = -\int_0^t \left(\frac{1}{R_1 C_F} V_1 + \frac{1}{R_2 C_F} V_2 + \frac{1}{R_3 C_F} V_3\right) dt$$

Comparing this with the given equation,

$$\frac{1}{R_1 C_F} = 2, \quad \frac{1}{R_2 C_F} = 3, \quad \frac{1}{R_3 C_F} = 4$$

Choose $C_F = 10\ \mu F$, hence,

$$R_1 = \frac{1}{2 \times 10 \times 10^{-6}} = 50\ k\Omega$$

$$R_2 = \frac{1}{3 \times 10^{-6} \times 10} = 33.33\ k\Omega$$

$$R_3 = \frac{1}{4 \times 10 \times 10^{-6}} = 25\ k\Omega$$

The circuit is shown in Fig. 2.51.

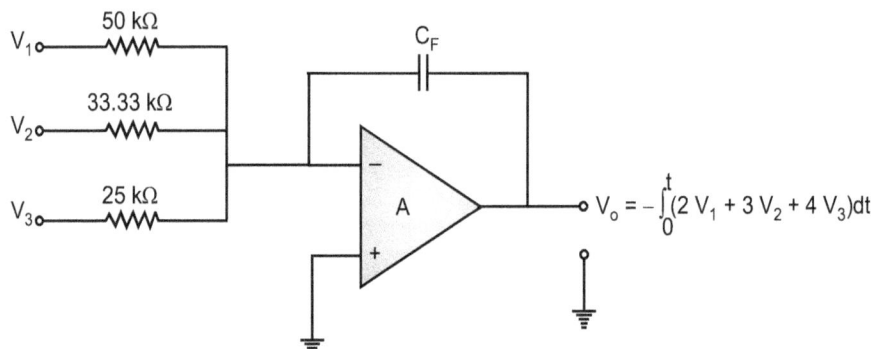

Fig. 2.51 : Summing integrator with three inputs

Example 2.12 :

Design a practical integrator circuit with a DC gain of 10, to integrate a square wave of 10 kHz.

Solution :

$$|A|\ DC = R_F / R_1$$

$$10 = R_F / R_1$$

$$f = 10\ kHz$$

For the proper operation, $f \geq 10 f_a$

$$\frac{f}{f_a} = 10$$

$$f_a = \frac{f}{10} = \frac{10 \times 10^3}{10} = 1 \text{ kHz}$$

Now for practical integrator,

$$f_a = \frac{1}{2\pi R_F C_F}$$

$$1000 = \frac{1}{2\pi R_F C_F}$$

$$R_F C_F = \frac{1}{2\pi \times 1000} = 1.5915 \times 10^{-4}$$

Choose $R_1 = 10 \text{ k}\Omega$

$$R_F = 10 R_1 = 10 \times 10 = 100 \text{ k}\Omega$$

$$C_F = \frac{1.5915 \times 10^{-4}}{100 \times 10^3} = 1.5915 \times 10^{-9} \cong 16 \text{ nF}$$

$$R_{OM} = R_1 \| R_F$$

$$R_{OM} = \frac{10 \times 100}{10 + 100} = \frac{1000}{110} = 9.09 \text{ k}\Omega$$

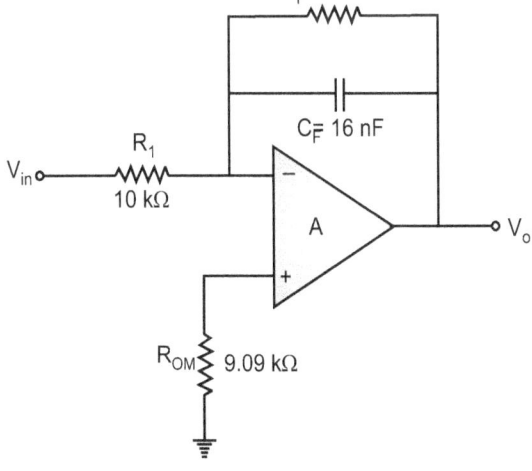

Fig. 2.52

Example 2.13 :

Find R_1 and R_F in lossy integrator so that the peak gain is 40 dB and the gain 3 dB down from its peak occurs at a frequency of 1.25 kHz. Use capacitance of 0.01 µF.

Solution :

The peak gain is the DC gain.

$$20 \log (R_F/R_1) = 40 \text{ dB}$$
$$\log (R_F/R_1) = 2$$
$$R_F/R_1 = 100$$

At f = 1.25 kHz, the gain is down by 3 dB from its peak value 40 dB.

So at f = 1.25 kHz, Gain = 40 – 3 = 37 dB

$$20 \log \left[\frac{R_F/R_1}{\sqrt{1 + (f/f_a)^2}} \right] = 37$$

$$20 \log \left[\frac{100}{\sqrt{1 + \left(\frac{1.25 \times 10^3}{f_a}\right)^2}} \right] = 37$$

$$\log \left[\frac{100}{\sqrt{1 + \left(\frac{1.25 \times 10^3}{f_a}\right)^2}} \right] = 1.85$$

$$\frac{100}{\sqrt{1 + \left(\frac{1.25 \times 10^3}{f_a}\right)^2}} = 70.794$$

$$\sqrt{1 + \left(\frac{1.25 \times 10^3}{f_a}\right)^2} = 1.4125$$

$$1 + \left(\frac{1.25 \times 10^3}{f_a}\right)^2 = 1.4125$$

$$\frac{1.25 \times 10^3}{f_a} = 0.9952$$

$$f_a = 1.253 \text{ kHz}$$

$$f_a = \frac{1}{2\pi C_F R_F} \text{ and } C_F = 0.01 \text{ µF}$$

$$R_F = 12.70 \text{ k}\Omega$$

$$R_1 = \frac{R_F}{100} = 127 \text{ }\Omega$$

2.3 DIFFERENTIATOR

The circuit which produces the differentiation of the input voltage at its output is called differentiator.

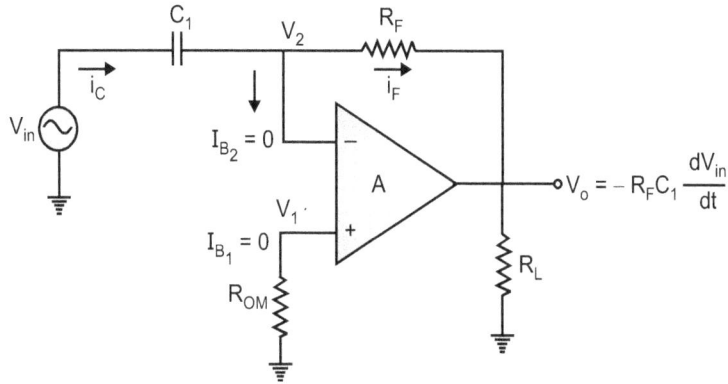

Fig. 2.53 : Basic differentiator circuit

The differentiator may be designed from a basic inverting amplifier if an input resistor R_1 is replaced by a capacitor C_1.

We can obtain the equation for the output voltage from Kirchhoff's current law applying at node V_2.

$$i_C = I_B + i_F \qquad \ldots (2.87)$$

Since $I_B \cong 0$, as op-amp is ideal.

$$i_C = i_F$$

$$C_1 \frac{d}{dt}(V_{in} - V_2) = \frac{V_2 - V_o}{R_F}$$

But $V_1 = V_2 = 0$

$$\therefore \quad C_1 \frac{d}{dt}(V_{in}) = -\frac{V_o}{R_F}$$

$$V_o = -R_F C_1 \frac{dV_{in}}{dt} \qquad \ldots (2.88)$$

Thus, the output V_o is equal to $R_F C_1$ times the negative instantaneous rate of change of the input voltage V_{in} with time. Since, the differentiator performs the reverse of the integrator's function, a cosine wave input will produce a sine wave output or a triangular input will produce a square wave output.

2.3.1 Frequency Response of Ideal Differentiator

The output voltage of ideal differentiator is

$$V_o(t) = -R_F C_1 \frac{dV_{in}}{dt} \qquad ...(2.89)$$

Taking Laplace transform of this equation, we get,

$$V_o(S) = -S R_F C_1 V_{in}(S) \qquad ...(2.90)$$

To get the frequency response, replace S by jω

$$V_o(j\omega) = -j\omega R_F C_1 V_{in}(j\omega) \qquad ...(2.91)$$

$$\frac{V_o(j\omega)}{V_{in}(j\omega)} = -j\, 2\pi f\, R_F\, C_1$$

$$A = \left|\frac{V_o(j\omega)}{V_{in}(j\omega)}\right| = \left|-j\, 2\pi f\, R_F\, C_1\right|$$

$$A = \omega R_F C_1 = 2\pi f R_F C_1 \qquad ...(2.92)$$

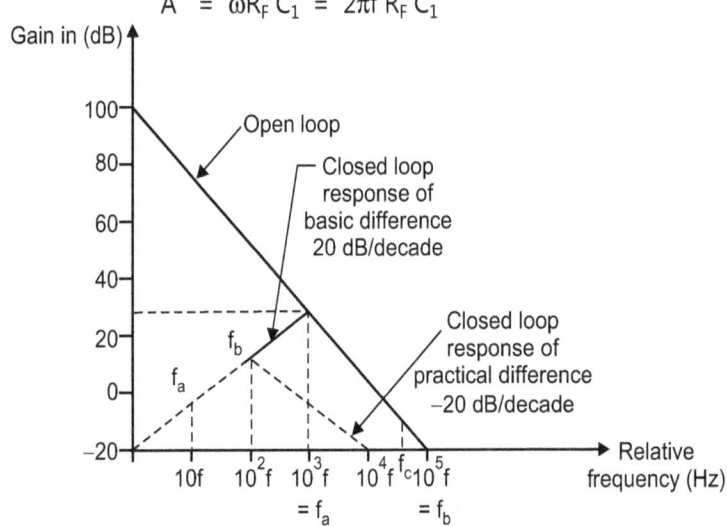

Fig. 2.54 : Frequency response

So at low frequency i.e. DC, the gain is zero and as the frequency increases, the gain also increases.

$$A = \frac{f}{f_a} \qquad ...(2.92\text{ a})$$

where,

$$f_a = \frac{1}{2\pi R_F C_1}$$

The frequency f_a is the frequency at which the gain becomes 1 or 0 dB. The increase in the gain is at a rate of 20 dB/decade.

When $f < f_a$, the ratio f/f_a becomes less than unity. So the rate of 20 dB/decade is negative. When $f > f_a$, the gain increases with a rate of + 20 dB/decade.

2.3.2 Disadvantages of Basic Differentiator

1. At high frequency the differentiator becomes unstable and oscillations are produced. So the op-amp goes into saturation.
2. As frequency increases, the input impedance decreases. The circuit becomes sensitive to the noise. When the noise is amplified, the noise may override the output. Therefore, noise cannot be removed from the output.

Both the stability and high frequency noise problems can be corrected by the addition of two components : R_1 and C_F. That is the practical differentiator.

2.3.3 Practical Differentiator

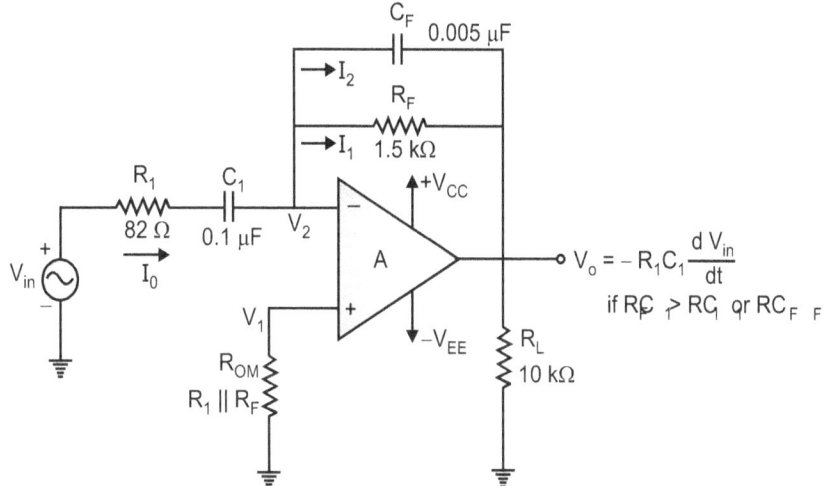

Fig. 2.55 : Practical differentiator

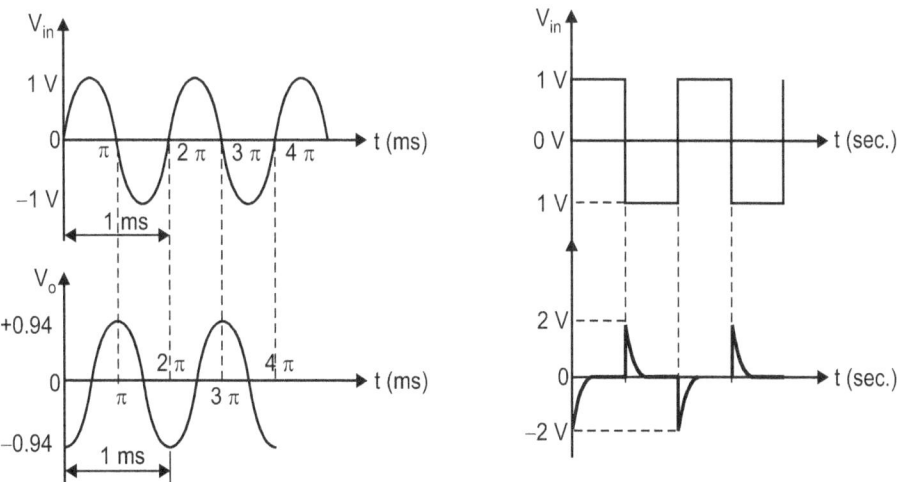

Fig. 2.56 : Input and output waveforms

The current flowing through R_1 and C_1 is given as I_0.

$$I_0 = \frac{V_{in} - V_2}{Z_1} = \frac{V_{in}}{Z_1} \text{ as } V_2 = V_1 = 0 \qquad \ldots (2.93)$$

where,
$$Z_1 = R_1 + \frac{1}{SC_1} \qquad \ldots (2.94)$$

$$= \frac{1 + SR_1C_1}{SC_1}$$

$$I_0 = \frac{V_{in}(S) \, SC_1}{1 + SR_1C_1} \qquad \ldots (2.95)$$

The current flowing through the feedback resistors is I_1 and is given as:

$$I_1 = \frac{V_2 - V_o}{R_F} = \frac{-V_o}{R_F} \text{ as } V_2 = 0 \qquad \ldots (2.96)$$

$$I_1 = -\frac{V_o(S)}{R_F}$$

and current through feedback capacitor C_F is I_2 and is given by

$$I_2 = C_F \frac{d(V_2 - V_o)}{dt} \qquad \ldots (2.97)$$

$$= -C_F \frac{dV_o}{dt}$$

$$= -SC_F V_o(S) \qquad \ldots (2.98)$$

Using Kirchhoff's current law at node V_2,

$$I = I_1 + I_2 \qquad \ldots (2.99)$$

$$\frac{V_{in}(S) \, SC_1}{1 + SR_1C_1} = \frac{-V_o(S)}{R_F} - SC_F V_o(S) \qquad \ldots (2.100)$$

$$= -V_o(S)\left[SC_F + \frac{1}{R_F}\right]$$

$$\frac{V_{in}(S) \, SC_1}{1 + SR_1C_1} = -V_o(S)\left[\frac{1 + SR_FC_F}{R_F}\right]$$

$$V_o(S) = \frac{-SR_FC_1V_{in}(S)}{(1 + SR_1C_1)(1 + SR_FC_F)} \qquad \ldots (2.101)$$

If $R_FC_F = R_1C_1$, then

$$V_o(S) = \frac{-SR_FC_1V_{in}(S)}{(1 + SR_1C_1)^2} \qquad \ldots (2.102)$$

The time constant R_FC_1 is much greater than R_1C_1 or R_FC_F and hence the equation becomes

$$V_O(S) = -SR_FC_1 V_{in}(S) \qquad \text{...(2.103)}$$

$$V_O(t) = -R_FC_1 \frac{dV_{in}(t)}{dt} \qquad \text{...(2.104)}$$

where, $\qquad R_FC_1 \leq T$

2.3.4 Frequency Response of Practical Differentiator

Using equation (2.102),

$$\frac{V_O(S)}{V_{in}(S)} = \frac{-SR_FC_1}{(1+SR_1C_1)^2} \qquad \text{...(2.105)}$$

where, $\qquad R_FC_F = R_1C_1$

To obtain frequency response replace S by $j\omega$

$$\frac{V_O(\omega)}{V_{in}(\omega)} = \frac{-j\omega R_FC_1}{(1+j\omega R_1C_1)^2} \qquad \text{...(2.106)}$$

$$\frac{V_O(\omega)}{V_{in}(\omega)} = \frac{-j 2\pi f R_FC_1}{(1+j 2\pi f R_1C_1)^2}$$

Now let $f_b = \dfrac{1}{2\pi R_1C_1}$ and $f_a = \dfrac{1}{2\pi R_FC_1}$

$$\frac{V_O(\omega)}{V_{in}(\omega)} = \frac{-j(f/f_a)}{(1+j f/f_b)^2}$$

f_a and f_b are two break frequencies.

$$A = \left| \frac{V_O(j\omega)}{V_{in}(j\omega)} \right| = \frac{f/f_a}{\left[\sqrt{1+(f/f_b)^2}\right]^2}$$

$$A = \frac{f/f_a}{1+(f/f_b)^2} \qquad \text{...(2.107)}$$

As R_FC_1 is much larger than R_1C_1, $f_a < f_b$. Hence as frequency increases, the gain increases till $f = f_b$ at a rate of +20 dB/decade. After $f = f_b$ occurs due to the combination of R_1C_1 and R_FC_F.

2.3.5 Applications of Practical Differentiator

1. Used in wave shaping circuits to detect high frequency components in an input signal.
2. It acts as a rate of change detector in FM modulators.

2.3.6 Designing Steps for a Practical Differentiator

1. Select f_a equal to the highest frequency of the input signal to be differentiated.
2. Select value of $C_1 < 1$ µF and calculate the value of R_F.
3. Choose $f_b = 20\, f_a$ and calculate the values of R_1 and C_F so that $R_1 C_1 = R_F C_F$.

Example 2.14 :

(a) Design a differentiator to differentiate an input signal that varies in frequency from 10 Hz to about 1 kHz.

(b) If a sine wave of 1 V peak at 1000 Hz is applied to the differentiator of part (a) and draw its output waveform.

Solution :

To design a differentiator, simply follow the design procedure as mentioned before.

(1) $\quad f_a = 1 \text{ kHz} = \dfrac{1}{2\pi R_F C_1}$

Let $C_1 = 0.1$ µF, then $R_F = \dfrac{1}{(2\pi)(10^3)(10^{-7})} = 1.59 \text{ k}\Omega$

Let R_F be 1.5 kΩ.

(2) $\quad f_b = 20 \text{ kHz} = \dfrac{1}{2\pi R_1 C_1}$

Hence, $\quad R_1 = \dfrac{1}{(2\pi)(2)(10^4)(10^{-7})} = 79.5\ \Omega$

Let R_1 be 82 Ω. Since, $R_1 C_1 = R_F C_F$

$$C_F = \dfrac{(82)(10^{-7})}{1.5 \text{ k}\Omega} \cong 0.0055 \text{ µF}$$

Let C_F be 0.005 µF. Finally $R_{OM} = R_F \cong 1.5$ kΩ

(b) Since, $V_p = 1$ V and $f = 1000$ Hz, the input voltage is

$$V_{in} = V_p \sin \omega t$$
$$= \sin (2\pi)(10^3)\, t$$

Hence,
$$V_o = -R_F C_1 \frac{dV_{in}}{dt}$$
$$= -(1.5 \text{ k}\Omega)(0.1 \text{ μF}) \frac{d}{dt}\left[\sin(2\pi)(10^3)t\right]$$
$$= -(1.5 \text{ k}\Omega)(0.1 \text{ μF})(2\pi)(10^3)\cos\left[2\pi(10^3)t\right]$$
$$= -0.94 \cos\left[(2\pi)(10^3)t\right]$$

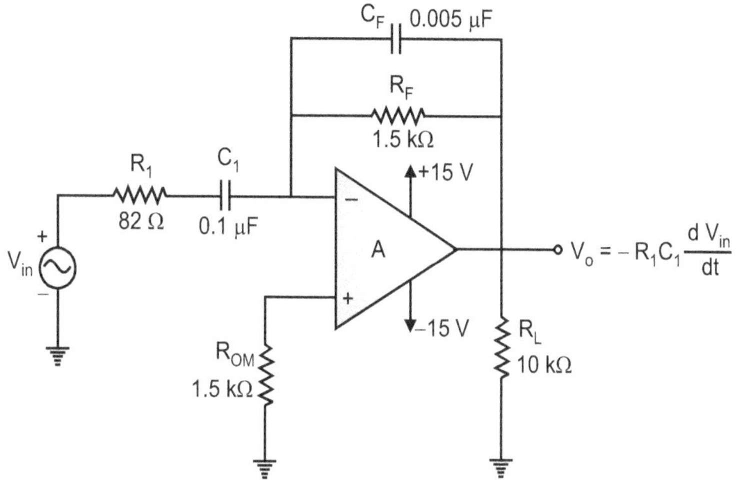

Fig. 2.57

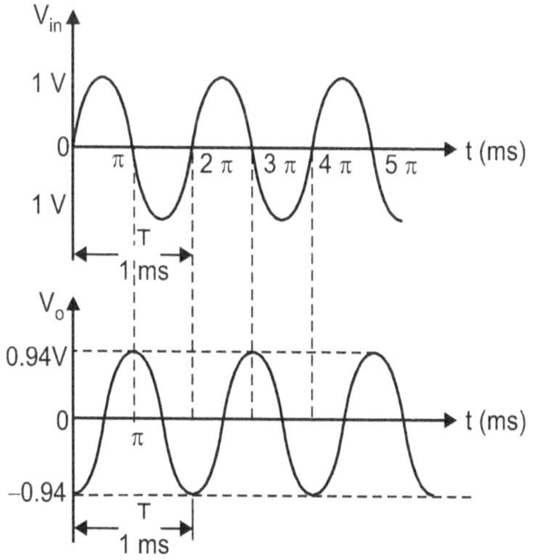

Fig. 2.58 : Input and output waveforms

Example 2.15 :

Design a practical differentiator circuit that will differentiate an input signal with the $f_{max} = 100$ Hz.

Solution :

$$f_a = f_{max} = 100 \text{ Hz}$$

Choose $C_1 = 1 \, \mu F$

$$f_a = \frac{1}{2\pi R_F C_1}$$

$$100 = \frac{1}{2\pi R_F \times 1 \times 10^{-6}}$$

$$R_F = \frac{1}{2\pi \times 100 \times 10^{-6}}$$

$$R_F = 0.0159 \times 10^6 = 1.59 \text{ k}\Omega$$

Now,
$$f_b = 10 \, f_a$$

$$f_b = 10 \times 100 = 1000$$

$$f_b = \frac{1}{2\pi R_1 C_1}$$

$$1000 = \frac{1}{2\pi \times R_1 \times 1 \times 10^{-6}}$$

$$R_1 = \frac{1}{2\pi \times 1000 \times 10^{-6}} = 159 \, \Omega$$

$$R_1 C_1 = R_F C_F$$

$$159 \times 1 \times 10^{-6} = 1.59 \times 10^3 \times C_F$$

$$C_F = \frac{159 \times 10^{-6}}{1.59 \times 10^3}$$

$$C_F = 0.159 \, \mu F$$

$$R_{OM} = R_1 \| R_F$$

$$= \frac{159 \times 1.59 \times 10^3}{159 + 1.59 \times 10^3}$$

$$= \frac{252.81 \times 10^3}{159 + 0.00159}$$

$$= \frac{252.81 \times 10^3}{159.00159}$$

$$= 1.58 \times 10^3 = 1.58 \text{ k}\Omega$$

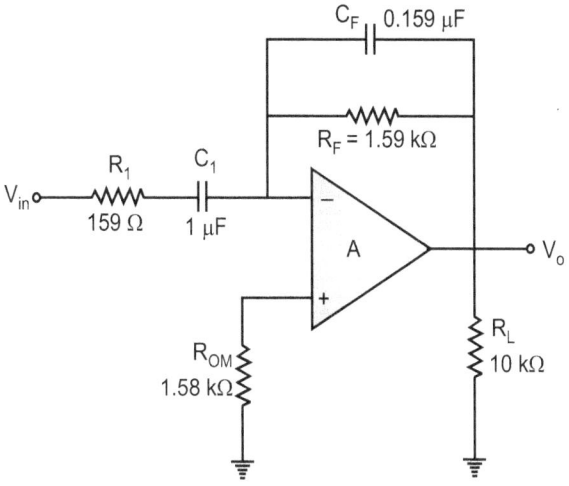

Fig. 2.59

Example 2.16 :

Design a differentiator to differentiate an input signal whose frequency varies from 50 Hz to 2 kHz.

Solution :

Choose f_a as the highest frequency.

$$f_a = 2 \text{ kHz} = f_{max}$$

Choose $C_1 = 0.1 \ \mu F$

$$f_a = \frac{1}{2\pi R_F C_1}$$

i.e.

$$2000 = \frac{1}{2\pi R_F \times 0.1 \times 10^{-6}}$$

∴ $R_F = 7.957 \ k\Omega$

$f_b = 10 f_a = 20 \text{ kHz}$

$$f_b = \frac{1}{2\pi R_1 C_1}$$

$$2000 = \frac{1}{2\pi R_1 \times 0.1 \ \mu F}$$

$R_1 = 795.77 \ \Omega$

$R_1 C_1 = R_F C_F$

∴ $C_F = \dfrac{795.77 \times 0.1 \times 10^{-6}}{7.957 \times 10^3} = 1 \text{ nF}$

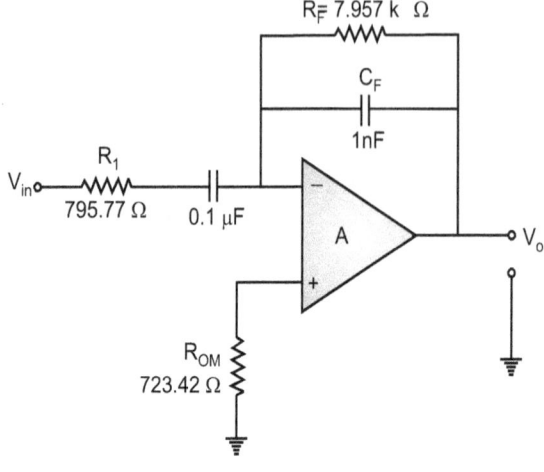

Fig. 2.60

$$R_{OM} = R_1 \| R_F = \frac{R_1 R_F}{R_1 + R_F} = \frac{795.77 \times 7.95 \times 10^3}{795.77 + 7.95 \times 10^3} = 723.42 \, \Omega$$

2.4 PEAK AMPLIFIERS

The circuit which gives the frequency response that peaks at a certain frequency is called as peaking amplifier. This is obtained by using a parallel LC network with the op-amp. Fig. 2.61 shows the peak amplifier circuit and its frequency response.

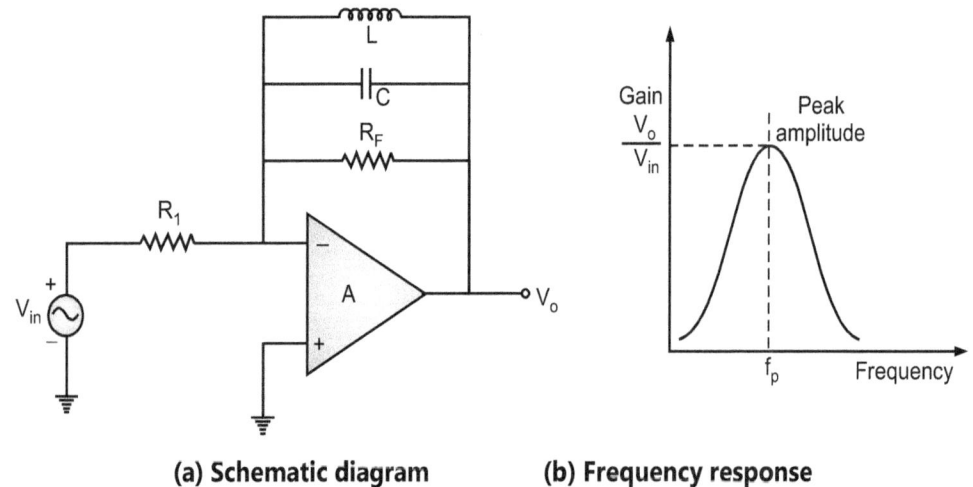

(a) Schematic diagram (b) Frequency response

Fig. 2.61

The peak frequency at which the peak occurs is given by

$$f_p = \frac{1}{2\pi \sqrt{LC}} \text{ if } Q_{coil} \geq 10 \qquad \ldots (2.108)$$

where Q_{coil} = figure of merit of the coil.

The impedance of the parallel LC network is very large at the resonant frequency.

The gain of the amplifier is maximum at peak frequency and is given by

$$A_f = \frac{-R_F \| R_p}{R_1} \qquad \ldots (2.109)$$

where R_p = Equivalent parallel resistance of the tank circuit = $(Q_{coil}^2 R)$

R = Internal resistance of the coil

The impedance of the parallel LC network below and above the peak frequency is less than R_p. Therefore, the gain of the amplifier is less than $(R_F \| R_p | R_1)$ at any other frequency than f_p.

The bandwidth of the peak amplifier is determined as follows :

$$B_w = \frac{f_p}{Q_p} \qquad \ldots (2.110)$$

where, f_p = Peaking frequency

Q_p = Figure of merit of the parallel resonant circuit = $(R_F \| R_p | X_L)$

2.5 AC AMPLIFIERS

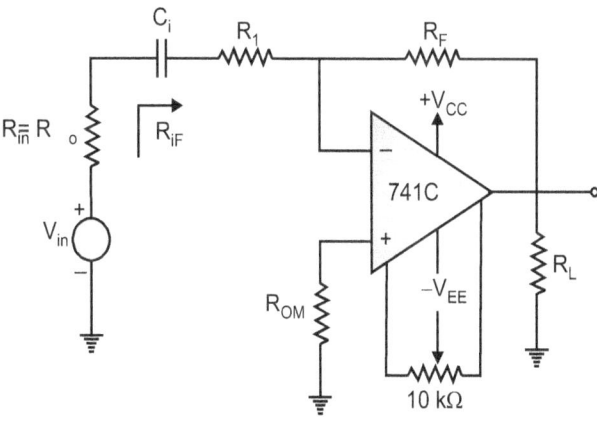

Fig. 2.62 : Inverting AC amplifier

To study the AC response characteristics of the op-amp i.e. lower and higher frequency limits, AC amplifier is used. For example, in an audio receiver system that consists of a number of stages, because of thermal drift, component tolerances and variations, the DC level is produced. To prevent the amplification of such DC levels, coupling capacitors must be used between the stages. Fig. 2.62 and 2.63 shows the AC inverting and non-inverting amplifiers with coupling capacitors respectively.

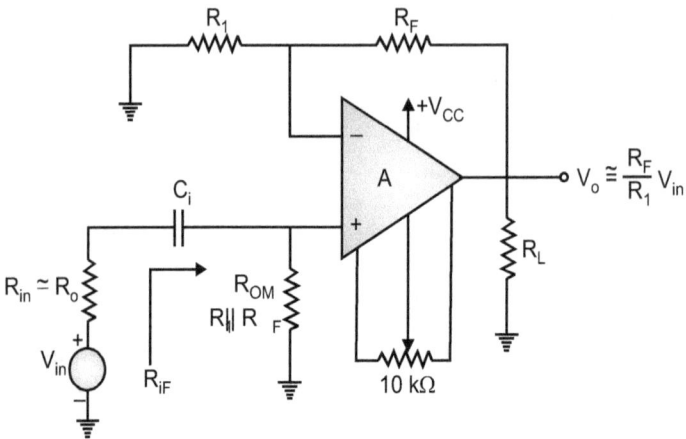

Fig. 2.63 : Non-inverting AC amplifier

The coupling capacitor is used to block the DC voltage as well as to set the lower frequency cut-off limit and is given by

$$f_L = \frac{1}{2\pi C_i (R_{iF} + R_o)} \quad \ldots (2.111)$$

where, f_L = Lower frequency cut-off

C_i = Capacitance between two stages being coupled or DC blocking capacitance

R_{iF} = AC input resistance

R_o = AC output resistance

The closed loop gain of the AC inverting amplifier is

$$A_F \cong -\frac{R_F}{R_1} \quad \ldots (2.112)$$

The closed loop gain of the non-inverting amplifier is

$$A_F \cong 1 + \frac{R_F}{R_1} \quad \ldots (2.113)$$

Example 2.17 :

In an AC inverting amplifier, R_{in} = 50 Ω, C_i = 0.1 μF, R_1 = 100 Ω, R_F = 1 kΩ, R_L = 10 kΩ and supply voltage = ± 15 V. Determine the bandwidth of the amplifier.

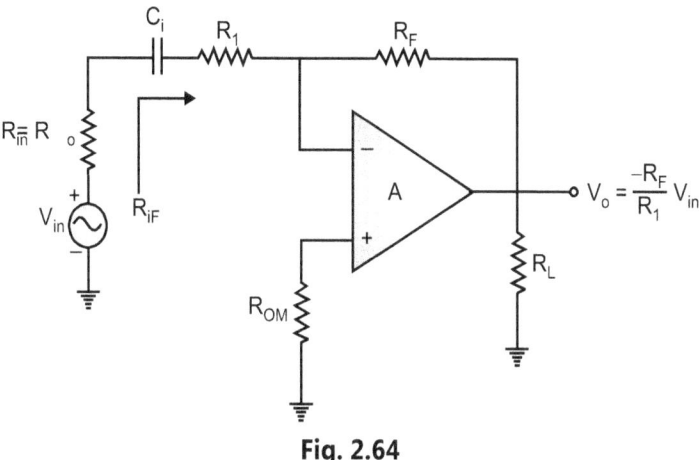

Fig. 2.64

Solution :

The input resistance of the inverting amplifier with feedback is

$$R_{iF} = R_1 = 100 \; \Omega$$

The source resistance, $R_{in} = R_o = 50 \; \Omega$

Therefore,

$$f_L = \frac{1}{2\pi C_i (R_{iF} + R_o)}$$

$$= \frac{1}{2\pi \times (0.1 \times 10^{-6}) \times (100 + 50)} = \frac{1}{2\pi \times 10^{-7} \times 150}$$

$$= 10.6 \text{ kHz}$$

Since

$$A_F = -\frac{R_F}{R_1} = -10$$

The high cut-off frequency f_H is given as :

$$f_H = \frac{(V_{GB}) K}{A_F}$$

where,

V_{GB} = Unity gain bandwidth

$$K = \frac{R_F}{R_1 + R_F}$$

$$f_H = \frac{(10^6) \times (0.909)}{10} \cong 90.9 \text{ kHz}$$

Thus, BW = 90.9 kHz – 10.6 kHz = 80.3 kHz

2.6 AF AMPLIFIER IC LM 380

In audio applications, much higher current delivered than that supplied by general purpose op-amps. The loads such as speakers and motors requiring substantial currents cannot be driven directly by the output of the general purpose op-amps. One solution for this is to use discrete or monolithic power transistors called power boosters at the output of the op-amp and another solution is to use specialized ICs designed as power amplifiers.

2.6.1 Monolithic Power Amplifiers

A variety of monolithic as well as hybrid power amplifiers are commercially available. National Semiconductor's LM380 audio power amplifier is more popular.

2.6.2 LM380 Audio Power Amplifier

National semiconductor's LM380 is audio power amplifier designed to deliver a minimum of 2.5 watt (rms) to an 8 Ω load and hence it is ideal for consumer applications.

2.6.3 Features of LM380 Audio Power Amplifier

- Internally fixed gain of 50 (34 dB).
- Output automatically self-centering to one-half of the supply voltage.
- Output short circuit proof with internal thermal limiting.
- Unique input stage allowing inputs to be ground referenced or AC coupled.
- Wide supply voltage range from 5 V to 22 V.
- High peak current capability – 1.3 A maximum.
- High impedance of 150 kΩ.
- Low total harmonic distortion (THD).
- Has a bandwidth of 100 kHz.

Fig. 2.65 shows the block diagram, connection diagram and schematic diagram of the LM380.

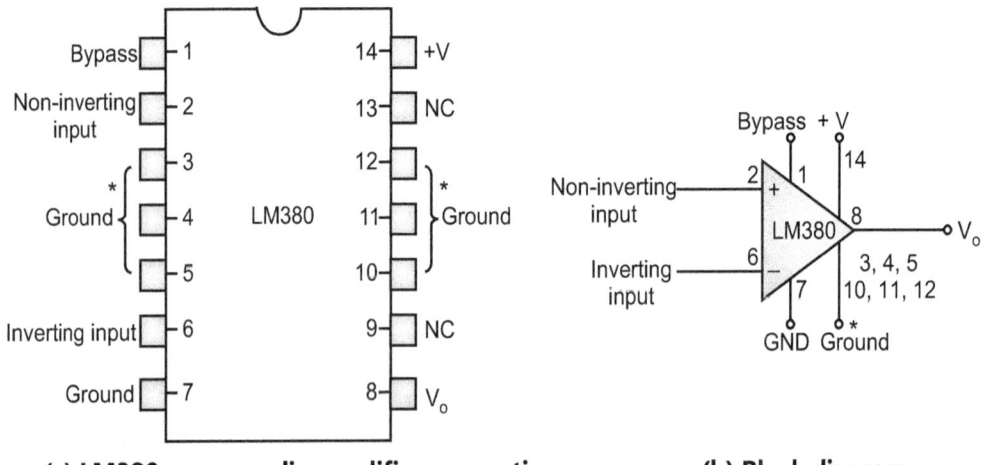

(a) LM380 power audio amplifier connection diagram

(b) Block diagram

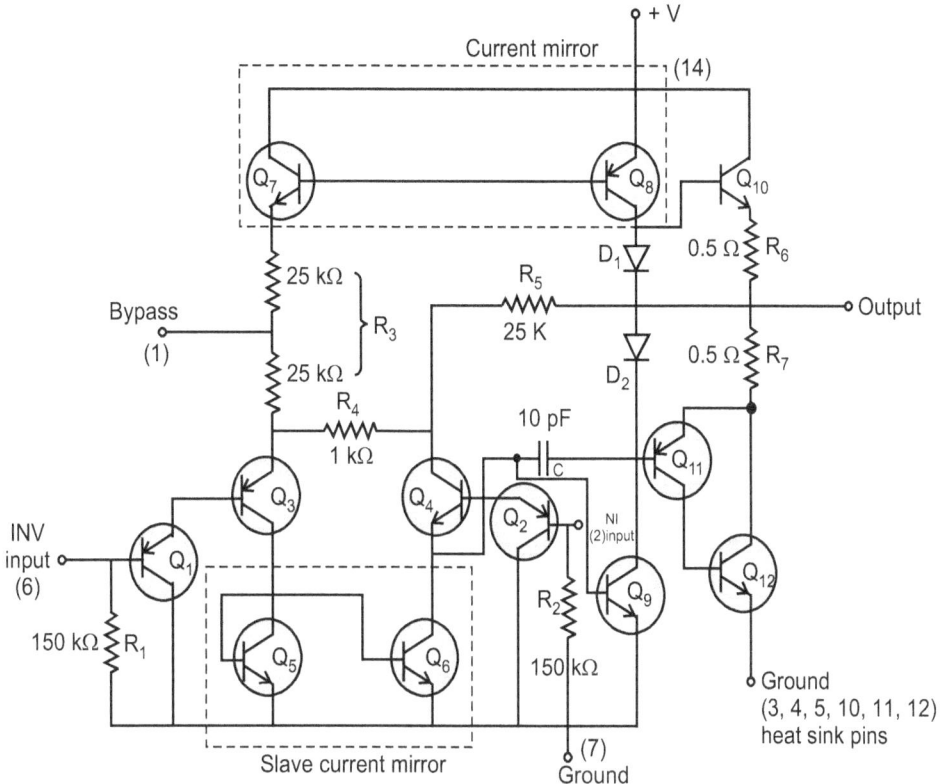

(c) Schematic diagram

Fig. 2.65

The schematic diagram of the LM380 is composed of four stages : PNP emitter follower, differential amplifier, common emitter and quasi-complementary emitter follower.

The input stage is an emitter follower composed of PNP transistors Q_1 and Q_2, which drives the PNP Q_3 - Q_4 differential pair. The current in the PNP differential pair Q_3 - Q_4 is established by Q_7, R_3 and +V. The current mirror formed by transistors Q_7, Q_8 and associated resistors then establishes the collector current of Q_9. Transistors Q_5 and Q_6 constitute collector loads for the PNP differential pair. The output of the differential amplifier is taken at the junction of Q_4 and Q_6 transistors and is applied as an input to the common emitter voltage-gain stage.

The common emitter amplifier stage is formed by transistors Q_9 with D_1, D_2 and Q_8 as a current source load. The capacitor C between base and collector of Q_9 provides internal compensation and helps to establish the upper cut-off frequency of 100 kHz at 2 W for 8 Ω load. Since, Q_7 and Q_8 form a current mirror, the current through D_1 and D_2 is approximately the same as the current through R_3. In addition, D_1 and D_2 are temperature compensating diodes for transistors Q_{10} and Q_{11}. Therefore, the current through Q_{10} and (Q_{11} - Q_{12}) is approximately equal to current through diodes D_1 and D_2.

The output stage is a quasi-complementary pair emitter follower formed by NPN transistors Q_{10} and Q_{12}. The combination of PNP transistor Q_{11} and NPN transistor Q_{12} has the power capability of an NPN transistor but the characteristics of a PNP transistor.

The negative DC feedback applied through R_5 balances the differential amplifier so that the DC output voltage is stabilized at +V/2.

2.6.4 Applications of LM380

1. Audio Power Amplifier :

Fig. 2.66 shows the simplest and most basic application of LM380 as an audio power amplifier. The amplifier requires very few external components because of the internal biasing, compensation and the fixed gain. When the power amplifier is used in the non-inverting configuration, usually capacitor is connected between the inverting terminal and ground if the input has a high internal impedance. In either configuration the supply voltage +V should be decoupled by connecting a capacitor between the +V terminal and ground. As a precautionary measure, an RC combination should be used at the output terminal to eliminate 5 to 10 MHz oscillation.

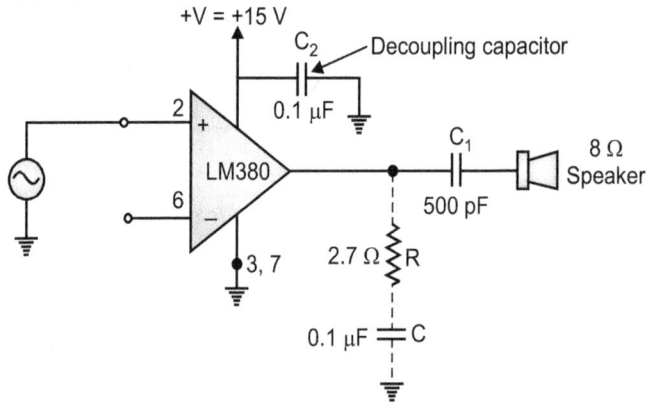

Fig. 2.66 : LM380 audio power amplifier

The gain of the LM380 is internally fixed at 50, it can be changed with the use of external components. Gains upto 300 are possible with the use of positive feedback. Variable gains upto 50 are obtained with the use of a potentiometer across the two input terminals as shown in Fig. 2.67.

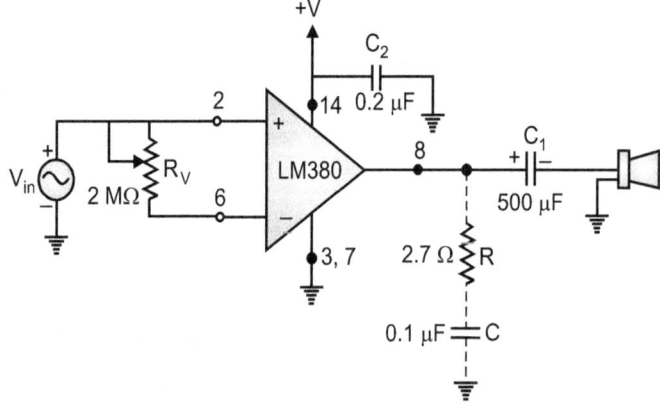

(a) LM380 with a variable gain (volume control) upto 50 using a potentiometer across the two input terminals

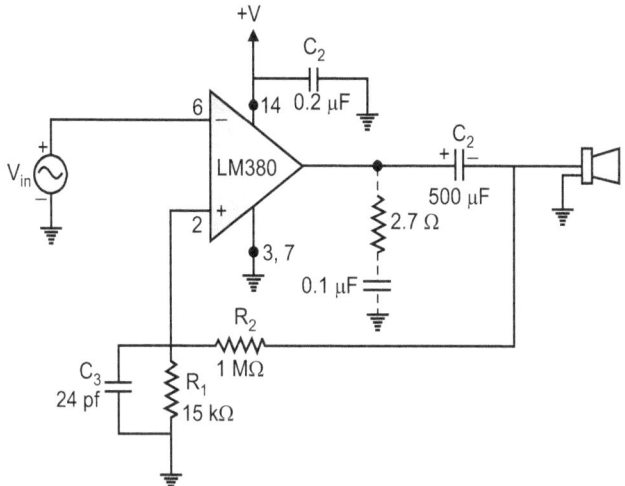

(b) LM380 configured for a gain of 200 using positive feedback
Fig. 2.67

2. Bridge Power Audio Amplifier :

The applications where more power is required than a single LM380 amplifier, two LM380s can be used in the bridge configuration. Fig. 2.68 shows the bridge configuration of LM380 to provide more power.

In this arrangement, the maximum output voltage swing will be twice that of a single LM380 amplifier, therefore, the power delivered to the load will be four times as much. For improved performance potentiometer R_4 should be used to balance the offset voltages of the LM380s.

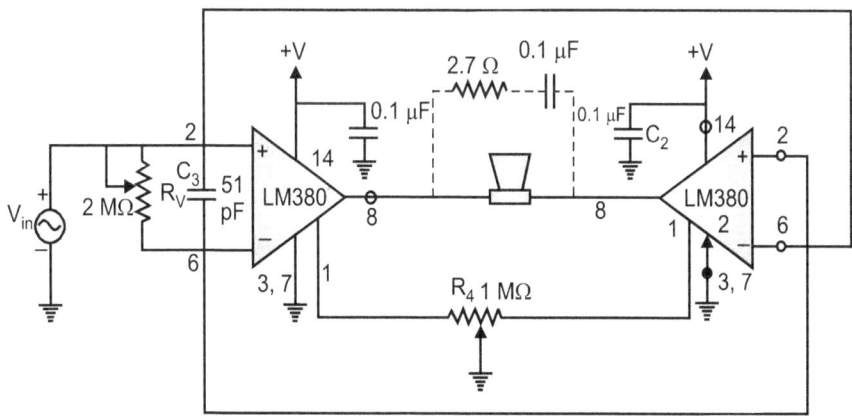

Fig. 2.68 : LM380s used in bridge configuration to provide more power

3. Intercom Systems :

A simple and inexpensive intercom system can be formed by using the LM380 as shown in Fig. 2.69. The speakers used in this configuration are permanent magnet types and hence acts as microphones as well. The talk and listen modes are defined with reference to a master station.

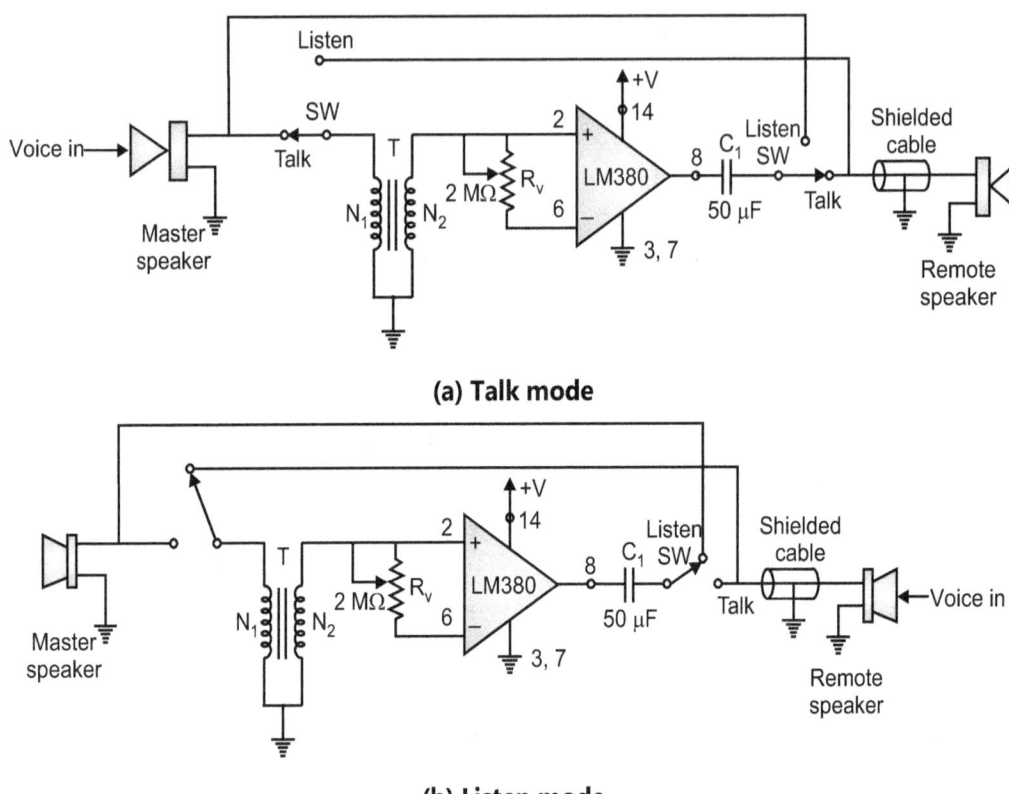

(a) Talk mode

(b) Listen mode

Fig. 2.69 : Intercom systems using the LM380

When the switch is in the talk position, the master speaker acts as a microphone. On the other hand, when the switch is in listen mode, the remote speaker acts as a microphone. In either position, the overall gain of the circuit is the same and depends on the turns ratio of the transformer T as well as the internal gain of LM380.

2.7 ANALOG COMPUTATION

Analog computer is a circuit which uses op-amps to perform linear operations such as multiplication, addition, integration etc. It can also be used to solve the differential equations. The basic building block of the analog computer consists of op-amps used as a inverter scale changer, integrator, etc. Integrators are widely used in analog computers, whereas differentiators are avoided because of the following reasons :

1. Stabilization of differentiators are difficult compared to integrators.
2. Input impedance does not remain constant.
3. The differentiator is more sensitive to noise compared to integrator.
4. Setting of initial conditions in differentiator is difficult.

The analog computers are used for :
(i) Implementation of given equation.
(ii) To provide a solution of a linear differential equation.
(iii) To solve two simultaneous equations.
(iv) Simulation of a transfer function.

2.7.1 Basic Building Blocks of Analog Computers

The building blocks of analog computers consists of inverter, summing amplifier or integrators etc.

(i) Summing amplifier :

It is mainly used to add the different voltages. Fig. 2.70 below shows the summing amplifier.

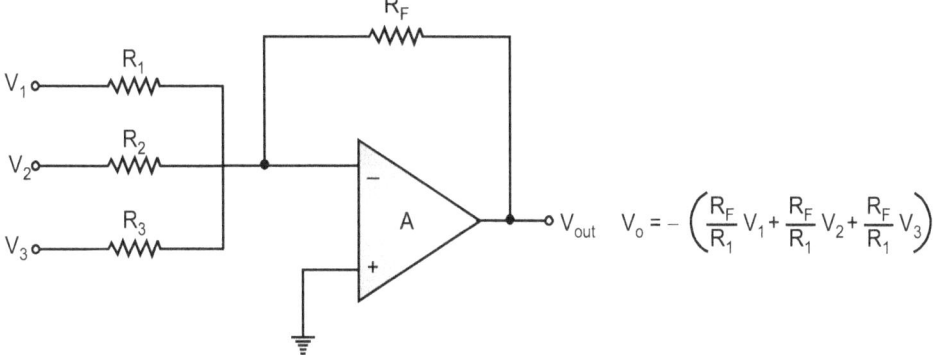

Fig. 2.70

$$V_o = -\left(\frac{R_F}{R_1}V_1 + \frac{R_F}{R_2}V_2 + \frac{R_F}{R_3}V_3\right) \quad \ldots (2.114)$$

when $R_F = R_1 = R_2 = R_3$
$V_o = -(V_1 + V_2 + V_3)$

Thus, it acts a summing amplifier.

(ii) Integrator :

Integrators are widely used in analog computers. Fig. 2.71 shows a integrator circuit used in analog computers.

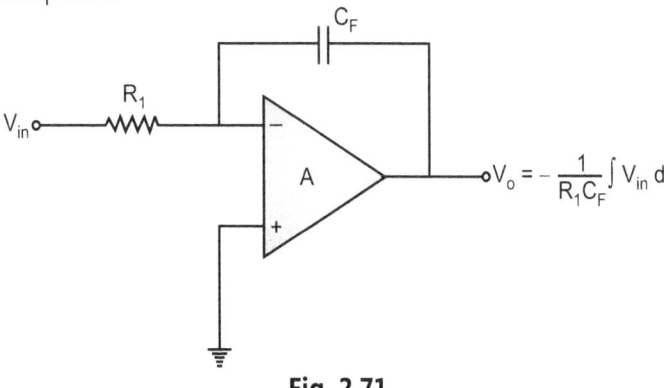

Fig. 2.71

2.7.2 Implementation of a given Equation in Analog Computer

The analog computers are used to implement the given equation for example.

Consider $\quad V_o = a_1 V_1 + a_2 V_2 - a_3 V_3$

To implement this equation we require inverting summing amplifier, an inverter and a subtractor. Fig. 2.72 shows how the above equation is implemented using basic building blocks of a analog computer.

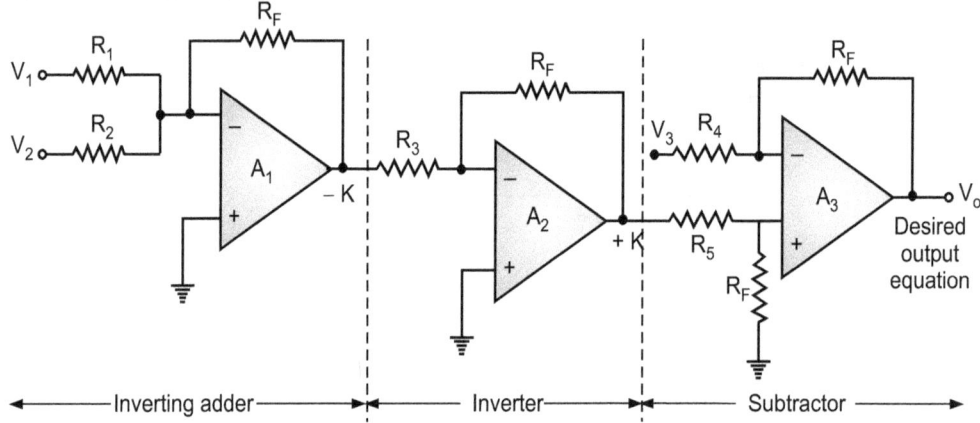

Fig. 2.72 : Implementation of a given equation using analog computer

In inverting adder, $\dfrac{R_F}{R_1} = a_1, \dfrac{R_F}{R_2} = a_2$

When $R_F = R_1 = R_2 = 1$ the output is $-K$. When this output is given as a input to the inverter then it becomes $+K$.

The subtractor output $V_o = V_2 - V_1$ when $R_F = R_4 = R_5$.

$$V_o = K - V_3$$
$$= a_1 V_1 + a_2 V_2 - a_3 V_3$$

This proves that any equation can be implemented using analog computer.

2.7.3 Solution of a Basic Linear Differential Equation

The analog computer is used to solve the linear differential equations. Consider the linear differential equation as :

$$\dfrac{d^2 y}{dt^2} + k_1 \dfrac{dy}{dt} + k_2 y(t) = x(t) \qquad \ldots (2.115)$$

where x and y are the functions of time and k_1 and k_2 are positive constants.

The initial conditions are given as

$$y(0) = -k_3 \text{ and } \left.\dfrac{dy}{dt}\right|_{t=0} = y'(0) = -k_4$$

The first step to solve the equations is assume that $\frac{d^2y}{dt} = y''$. To integrate high order terms to obtain the required signals, integrators are preferred. So we can write the above equation as,

$$y'' = k_1 y' - k_2 y + x \qquad \ldots (2.116)$$

The equation (2) shows that three terms must be added with proper sign and scale factor. For that blocks used are integrator, summer and scale change or inverter.

Fig. 2.73 shows the integrator 1. Select $R_1 C_F$ time constant as unity to get the output $-y'$.

To obtain the required initial condition close the switch S before applying the y" as input.

When switch is closed, the capacitor get charged control the voltage across the capacitor using potentiometer POT.

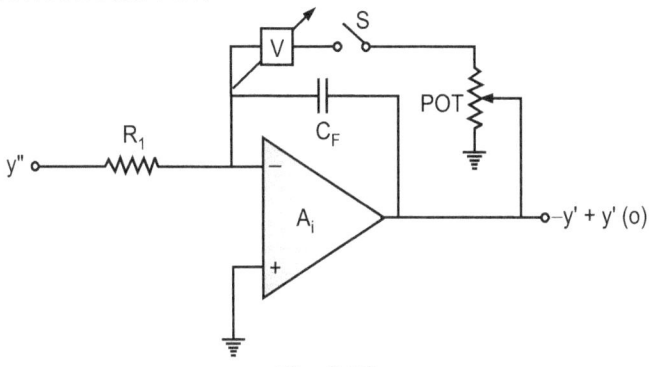

Fig. 2.73

To get the proper sign of the initial condition adjust the polarity of V.

To adjust the coefficient K_1, another variable resistance of multiplier is used as shown in Fig. 2.74.

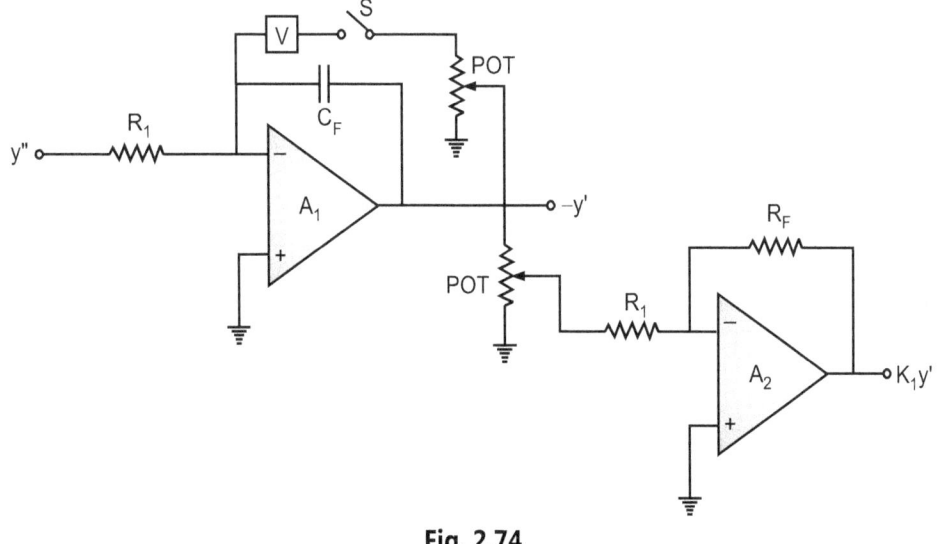

Fig. 2.74

Due to POT, the signal is changed to $-XY'$ where X is constant, then R_F/R_1 can be adjusted as $\dfrac{K_1}{X}$ to get the output

$$-x \cdot y' \times \dfrac{K_1}{X} = +K_1 y' \text{ as} \qquad \ldots (2.117)$$

shown in Fig. 2.75

In the similar way obtain the simulation of y(t) from y' by adjusting coefficient K_2.

Another circuit is used to input x(t) signal, which must be available at the output to get y". The output point then may be connected back to input to complete the entire set up to solve the differential equation.

The signal $+K_1y'$ output is inverted by the op-amp A_4 to get $-K_1y'$ at the output.

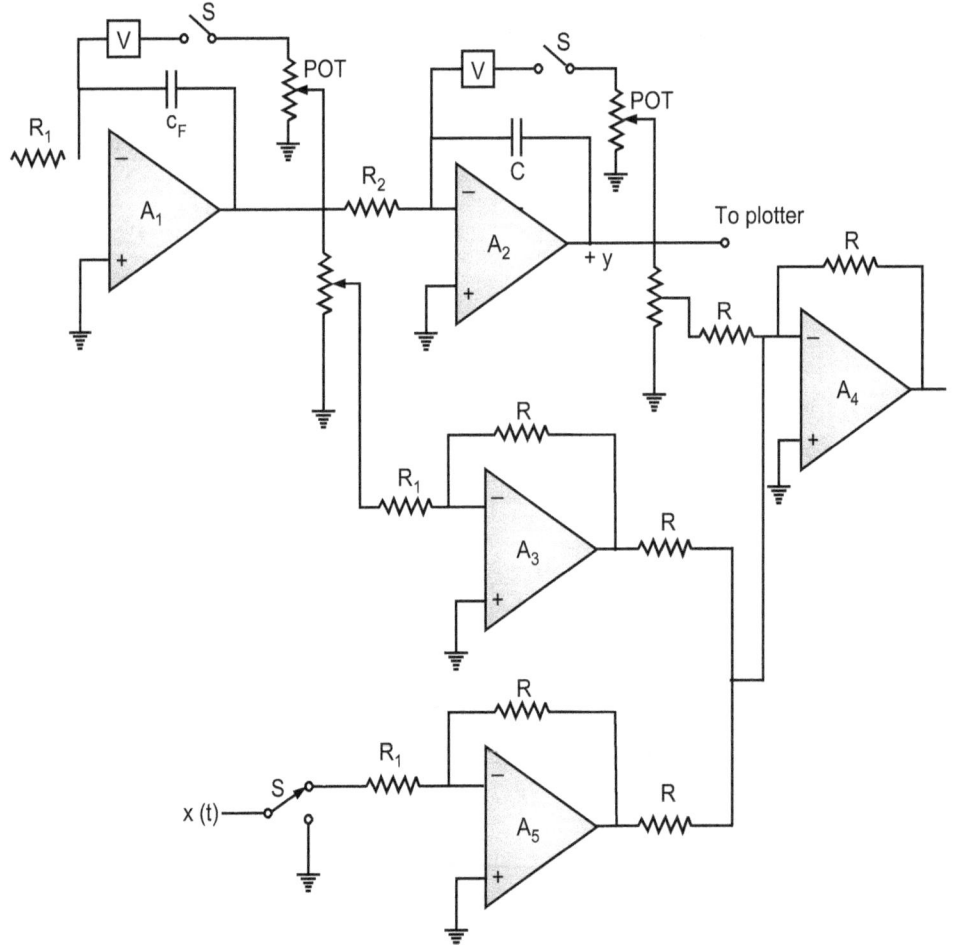

Fig. 2.75 : Simulation of second order linear differential equation

The entire set up can be redrawn by using analog computer symbols as shown in Fig. 2.76.

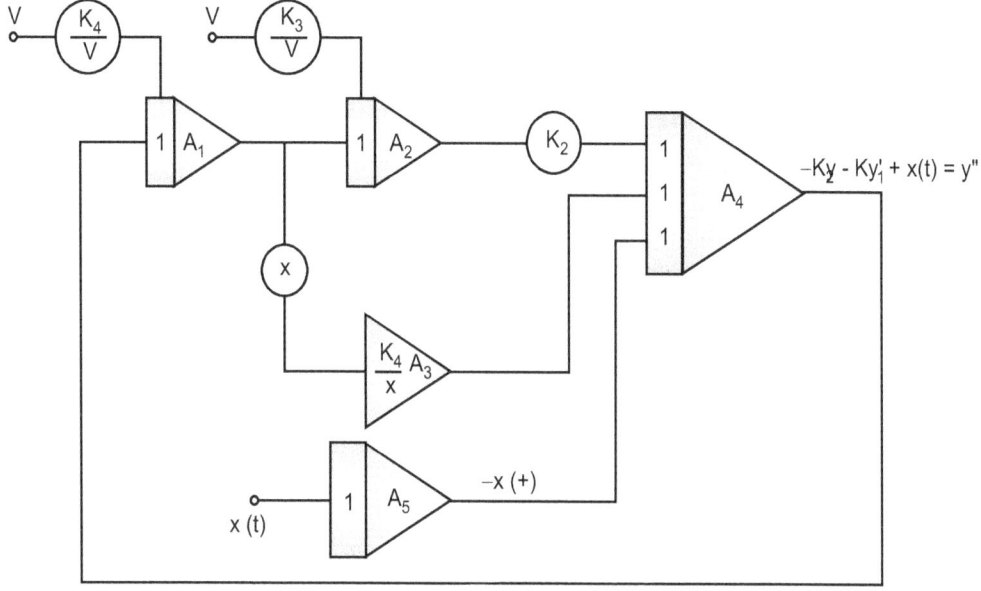

Fig. 2.76

Example 2.18 :

Obtain the analog computer set up to solve differential equation

$$\frac{d^2y}{dt^2} + 8\frac{dy}{dt} + 0.5y = x(t)$$

with $y(0) = +2.8$ and $y'(0) = -3.4$.

Solution : Assume y'' is available and rewrite the equation as

$$y'' = -8y' - 0.5y + x$$

The initial conditions are set up by keeping switches S_3 and S_4 open and switches S_1 and S_2 close. Once the initial conditions are set up then close switch S_3 and S_4 and open switch as S_1 and S_2. The potentiometers are used to 1 kΩ to set the initial conditions.

The time constant can be selected as unity by $R_1 = 1$ kΩ and $C_F = 1$ µF.

The intermediate potentiometers are used to get precisely the coefficients of y' and y which are 8 and 0.5 respectively.

Fig. 2.77 shows the simulation set up.

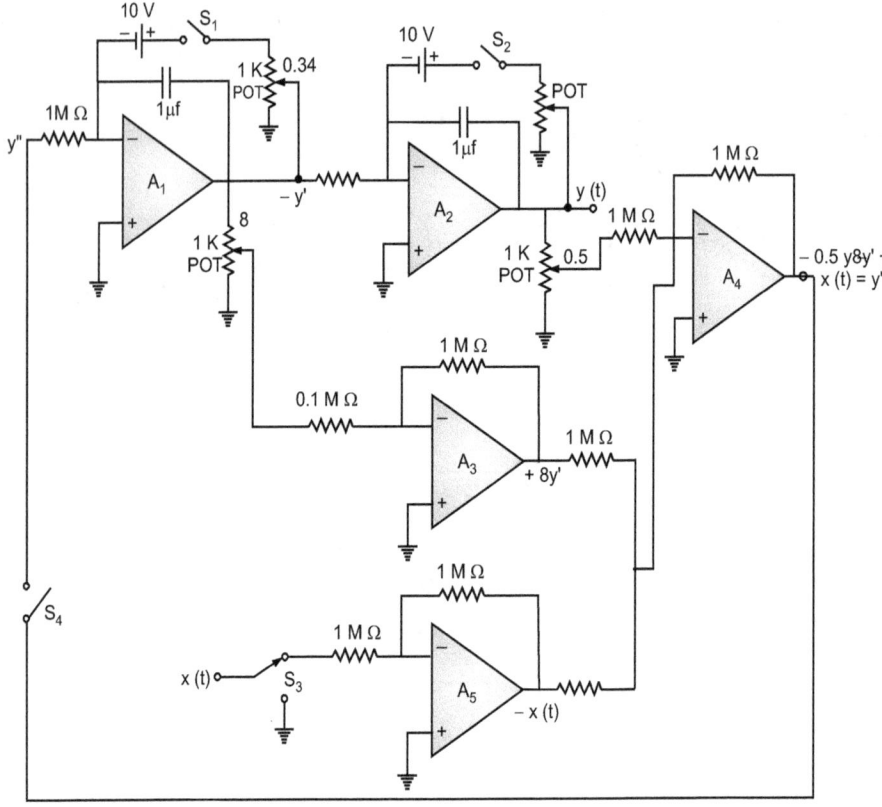

Fig. 2.77

The symbolic representation is shown in Fig. 2.78.

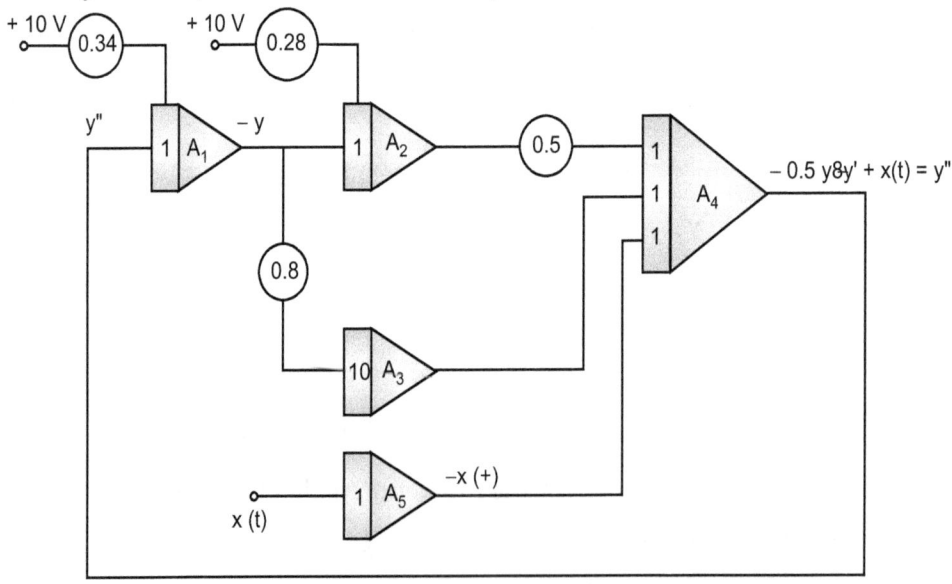

Fig. 2.78

2.8 DIFFERENCE AMPLIFIERS

The basic difference amplifier using op-amp gives the output as difference between the two applied input. Hence, it can be considered as a instrumentation amplifier.

Limitations of difference amplifiers :

(1) The input impedance of the difference amplifier is low as well as the input impedances seen by the signal sources V_1 and V_2 are not same. This inequality of the input impedances is the major limitation to work as a instrumentation amplifier because instrumentation amplifier requires high as well as balanced input impedance.

(2) Imbalance is there in circuit components and ideal equations which cannot be satisfied by the external resistors.

Hence, the difference amplifier is not used as a instrumentation amplifier.

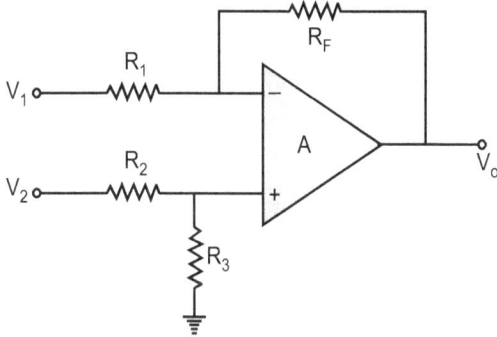

Fig. 2.79 : Difference amplifier

2.9 INSTRUMENTATION AMPLIFIERS

The measurement and control of physical quantities are very important in many industrial and consumer applications.

Examples are :

1. Measurement of temperature and humidity inside a dairy or meat plant to maintain the product quality.

2. Precise temperature control of a plastic furnace is needed to produce a particular type of plastic.

Generally, transducers are used to convert one form of energy into another form. An instrumentation amplifier is used to measure the output signal produced by a transducer and to control the physical signal producing it. Fig. 2.80 shows the simplified block diagram of such a system.

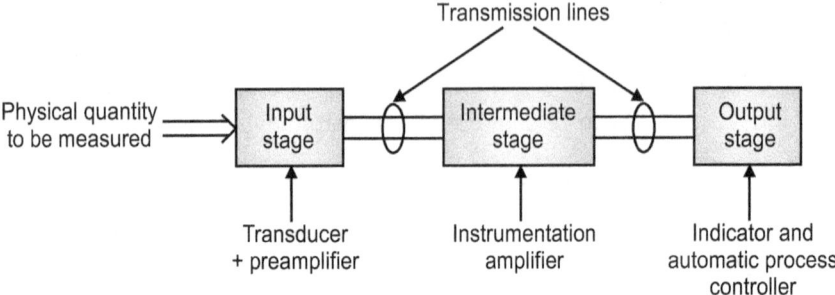

Fig. 2.80 : Block diagram of an instrumentation amplifier

The input stage is composed of a preamplifier and some sort of transducer, depending on the physical quantity to be measured. The output stage may be devices such as meters, oscilloscopes, charts or magnetic recorders. The connecting lines between the blocks represents transmission lines, used when the transducer is at remote test site monitoring hazardous conditions. For example, high temperatures of liquid levels of flammable chemicals. The length of the transmission line depends upon the physical quantities to be monitored and an system requirements. The input to the instrumentation amplifier is the output of the transducer. Some transducers produce outputs with sufficient strength to use it directly, but many do not permit to use it directly. To amplify the low level output of the transducer, instrumentation amplifier is used.

Instrumentation amplifier is used to amplify the low level output of the transducer.

Requirements of Instrumentation Amplifier

- Low level signal amplification where low noise, low thermal and time drifts.
- High input resistance.
- Accurate closed loop gain.
- Low power consumption.
- High common-mode rejection ratio.
- High slew rate.

There are many instrumentation amplifiers such as µA 725, ICL 7605 and LH 0036.

The requirements for instrumentation op-amp is more rigid than those for general purpose applications. Most of the instrumentation amplifiers use a transducer in a bridge circuit.

2.9.1 Instrumentation Amplifier using Transducer Bridge

Fig. 2.81 shows the simplified differential instrumentation amplifier using a transducer bridge. A resistive transducer whose resistance changes as a function of some physical energy is connected in one arm of the bridge with a small circle around it and is denoted by ($R_T \pm \Delta R$), where R_T is the resistance of the transducer and ΔR is the change in resistance R_T.

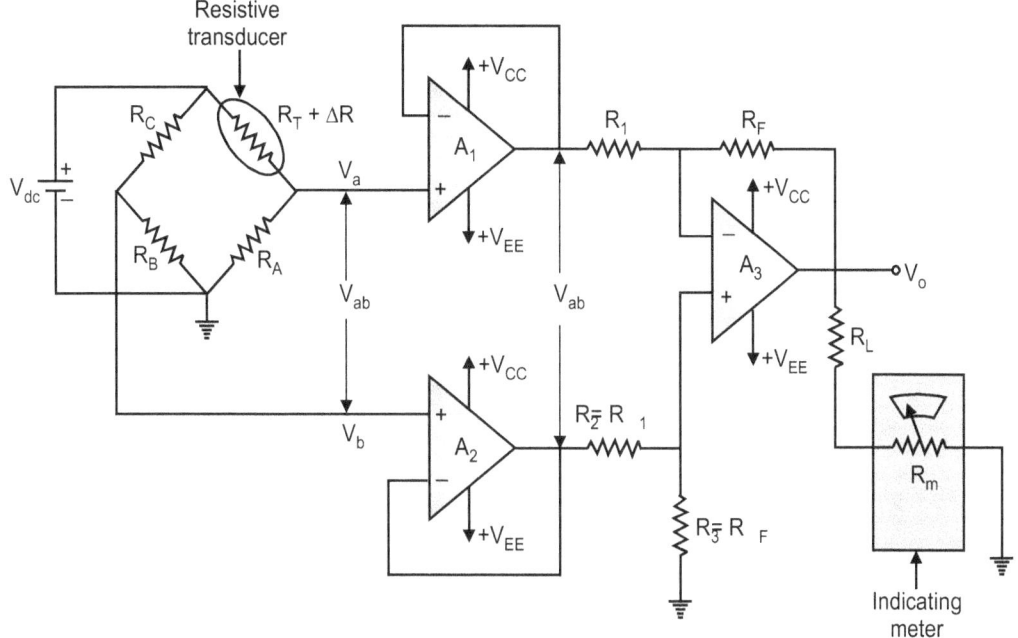

Fig. 2.81 : Differential instrumentation amplifier using a transducer bridge

The bridge is excited by DC. The bridge balance condition is

$$V_b = V_a$$

or

$$\frac{R_B (V_{dc})}{R_B + R_C} = \frac{R_A (V_{dc})}{R_A + R_T}$$

That is

$$\frac{R_C}{R_B} = \frac{R_T}{R_A}$$

Generally, resistors R_A, R_B and R_C are selected so that they are equal in value to the transducer resistance R_T at some reference condition.

The bridge is balanced at some reference condition. As the physical quantity to be measured changes, the resistance of the transducer also changes which causes the bridge to unbalance ($V_a \neq V_b$).

Let the change in resistance of the transducer be ΔR. Since, R_B and R_C are fixed, the voltage V_b will be constant. Voltage V_a varies as a function of the change in transducer resistance.

Therefore, according to voltage divider rule,

$$V_a = \frac{R_A (V_{dc})}{R_A + (R_T + \Delta R)}$$

$$V_b = \frac{R_B (V_{dc})}{R_B + R_C}$$

The voltage V_{ab} across the output terminals of the bridge is

$$V_{ab} = V_b - V_a$$

$$= \frac{R_A V_{dc}}{R_A + R_T + \Delta R} - \frac{R_B V_{dc}}{R_B + R_C}$$

However, if $R_A = R_B = R_T = R$, then

$$V_{ab} = \frac{R V_{dc}}{2R} - \frac{R V_{dc}}{2R + \Delta R}$$

$$= \frac{(2R^2 + R \Delta R - 2R^2) V_{dc}}{2R (2R + \Delta R)}$$

$$= \frac{R \Delta R V_{dc}}{2R (2R + \Delta R)}$$

$$= \frac{\Delta R V_{dc}}{2 (2R + \Delta R)}$$

The output voltage V_{ab} is then applied to the differential instrumentation amplifier composed of three op-amps. The voltage follower is used to avoid the loading effect of the bridge circuit. The gain of the basic differential amplifier is $(-R_F/R_1)$, therefore, the output V_o of the circuit is

$$V_o = V_{ab} (-R_F/R_1)$$

$$= \frac{(\Delta R) V_{dc}}{2 (2R + \Delta R)} \times \frac{R_F}{R_1}$$

Generally, the change in resistance of the transducer ΔR is very small. Therefore, we can approximate $(2R + \Delta R) \cong 2R$.

$$\therefore \quad V_o = \frac{R_F}{R_1} \cdot \frac{\Delta R}{4R} V_{dc} \qquad \ldots (2.118)$$

It indicates that the V_o is directly proportional to the change in resistance ΔR of the transducer.

2.9.2 Instrumentation Amplifier Using Three Op-amps

The op-amps A_1 and A_2 are the non-inverting amplifiers forming the input stage of the instrumentation amplifier. The op-amp A_3 is the normal difference amplifier forming an output stage of the amplifier.

$$V_o = \frac{R_2}{R_1} \left(V_{o_2} - V_{o_1} \right) \qquad \ldots (2.119)$$

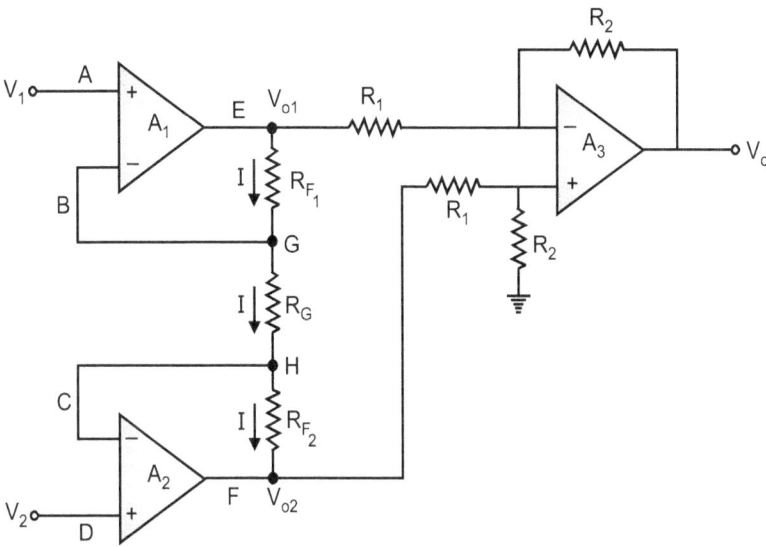

Fig. 2.82 : Instrumentation amplifier using three op-amps

From the realistic assumptions potential of node B is also at V_1 and hence potential of G is also at V_1. The potential of node C is at V_2 and hence potential of H is also at V_2.

As the input currents for op-amps are zero, current I remains same through R_{F_1}, R_G and R_{F_2}.

Apply Ohm's law between node E and F, the current I will be

$$I = \frac{V_{o_1} - V_{o_2}}{R_{F_1} + R_G + R_{F_2}}$$

$$R_{F_1} = R_{F_2} = R_F$$

$$I = \frac{V_{o_1} - V_{o_2}}{2R_F + R_G}$$

Now from the observation of nodes G and H,

$$I = \frac{V_G - V_H}{R_G} = \frac{V_1 - V_2}{R_G}$$

$$\frac{V_{o_1} - V_{o_2}}{2R_F + R_G} = \frac{V_1 - V_2}{R_G}$$

$$\left(\frac{R_G}{2R_F + R_G}\right) V_{o_1} - V_{o_2} = V_1 - V_2$$

$$V_{o_1} - V_{o_2} = \frac{2R_F + R_G}{R_G}(V_1 - V_2)$$

$$V_{O_2} - V_{O_1} = \frac{2R_F + R_G}{R_G}(V_2 - V_1)$$

$$V_O = (V_{O_2} - V_{O_1})A$$

$$= \frac{R_2}{R_1}\left(\frac{2R_F + R_G}{R_G}\right)(V_2 - V_1)$$

$$V_O = \frac{R_2}{R_1}\left(1 + \frac{2R_F}{R_G}\right)(V_2 - V_1) \qquad \ldots (2.120)$$

2.9.3 Differential Amplifier using Two Op-amps

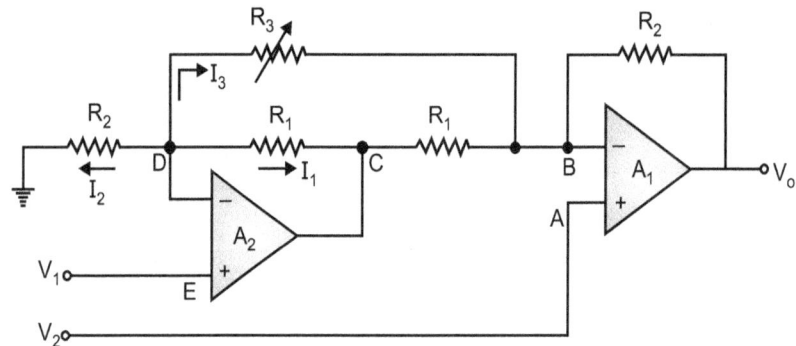

Fig. 2.83

For amplifier A, potential of node A is same as that of node B.

$$\therefore \quad V_A = V_B = V_2$$

Similarly, for amplifier A_2, the potential of node E is same as that of node D.

$$\therefore \quad V_E = V_D = V_1$$

Now,
$$I_2 = \frac{V_D}{R_2} = \frac{V_1}{R_2}$$

$$I_1 = \frac{V_D - V_C}{R_1} = \frac{V_1 - V_C}{R_1}$$

$$I_3 = \frac{V_D - V_B}{R_3} = \frac{V_1 - V_2}{R_3}$$

Applying KCL at node D, $I_1 + I_2 + I_3 = 0$

$$\therefore \quad \frac{V_1 - V_C}{R_1} + \frac{V_1}{R_2} + \frac{V_1 - V_2}{R_3} = 0$$

$$\therefore \quad V_1\left[\frac{1}{R_1} + \frac{1}{R_2} + \frac{1}{R_3}\right] - \frac{V_2}{R_3} = \frac{V_C}{R_1}$$

Similarly, applying KCL at node B and neglecting input current of op-amps,

$$\frac{V_B - V_D}{R_3} + \frac{V_B - V_C}{R_1} + \frac{V_B - V_O}{R_2} = 0$$

∴ $$\frac{V_2 - V_1}{R_3} + \frac{V_2 - V_C}{R_1} + \frac{V_2 - V_O}{R_2} = 0$$

∴ $$V_2\left[\frac{1}{R_3} + \frac{1}{R_1} + \frac{1}{R_2}\right] - \frac{V_1}{R_3} - \frac{V_O}{R_2} = \frac{V_C}{R_1}$$

Equating the expressions for V_C/R_1,

$$V_1\left[\frac{1}{R_1} + \frac{1}{R_2} + \frac{1}{R_3}\right] - \frac{V_2}{R_3} = V_2\left[\frac{1}{R_3} + \frac{1}{R_1} + \frac{1}{R_2}\right] - \frac{V_1}{R_3} - \frac{V_O}{R_2}$$

$$\frac{V_1[R_2R_3 + R_1R_3 + R_1R_2] - R_1R_2V_2}{R_1R_2R_3} = \frac{V_2[R_1R_2 + R_2R_3 + R_1R_3] - R_1R_2V_1 - R_1R_3V_O}{R_1R_2R_3}$$

$$V_1[R_2R_3 + R_1R_3 + 2R_1R_2] - V_2[R_2R_3 + R_1R_3 + 2R_1R_2] = -R_1R_3V_O$$

$$R_1R_3V_O = V_2 - V_1[R_2R_3 + R_1R_3 + 2R_1R_2]$$

∴ $$\frac{V_O}{(V_2 - V_1)} = 1 + \frac{R_2}{R_1} + \frac{2R_2}{R_3}$$

The $V_2 - V_1$ is the differential input while V_O is the output voltage. Thus, the voltage gain of this circuit is

$$A_V = 1 + \frac{R_2}{R_1} + \frac{2R_2}{R_3} \qquad \ldots (2.121)$$

2.9.4 Differential Input and Differential Output Amplifier

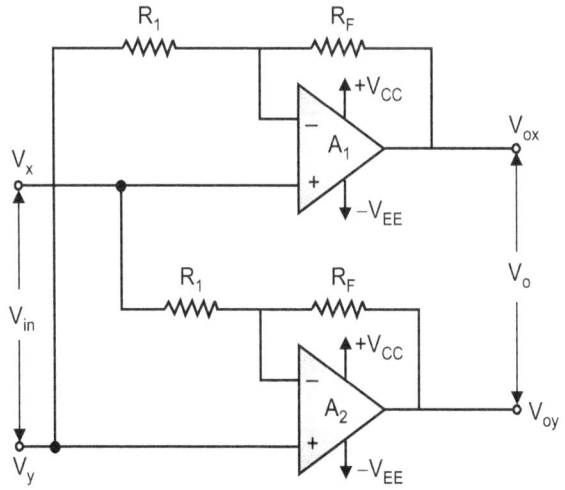

Fig. 2.84

In some applications a differential output is required. The differential input and differential output is mostly used as a preamplifier and in driving push-pull arrangement.

Fig. 2.84 shows the arrangement of a differential input and differential output amplifier using two identical op-amps, that is dual op-amps. The analysis of the circuit can be obtained by determining the output of each op-amp due to differential input.

Using the superposition theorem, the output V_{ox} due to inputs V_x and V_y is

$$V_{ox} = \left(1 + \frac{R_F}{R_1}\right) V_x - \left(\frac{R_F}{R_1}\right) V_y \qquad \ldots (2.122)$$

Similarly, the output V_{oy} is

$$V_{oy} = \left(1 + \frac{R_F}{R_1}\right) V_y - \left(\frac{R_F}{R_1}\right) V_x \qquad \ldots (2.123)$$

However, the differential output V_o is

$$V_o = V_{ox} - V_{oy}$$

Therefore, the equations (2.122) and (2.123),

$$V_o = \left(1 + \frac{R_F}{R_1}\right) V_x - \left(\frac{R_F}{R_1}\right) V_y - \left(1 + \frac{R_F}{R_1}\right) V_y + \left(\frac{R_F}{R_1}\right) V_x$$

$$= \left(1 + \frac{2R_F}{R_1}\right) (V_x - V_y)$$

or $\qquad V_o = \left(1 + \frac{2R_F}{R_1}\right) V_{in} \qquad \ldots (2.124)$

This means that the differential input and output are in phase or of the same polarity provided that $V_{in} = V_x - V_y$ and $V_o = V_{ox} - V_{oy}$.

The above circuit is very useful in noisy environments, especially if the input signal is relatively smaller, because it rejects the common-mode noise voltage.

2.9.5 Monolithic Instrumentation Amplifiers

Instrumentation amplifiers are available using dedicated ICs such as AD 521/524/624/625 and the AMP-01 and AMP-05 (analog devices).

Fig. 2.85 shows the simplified diagram of the AMP-01.

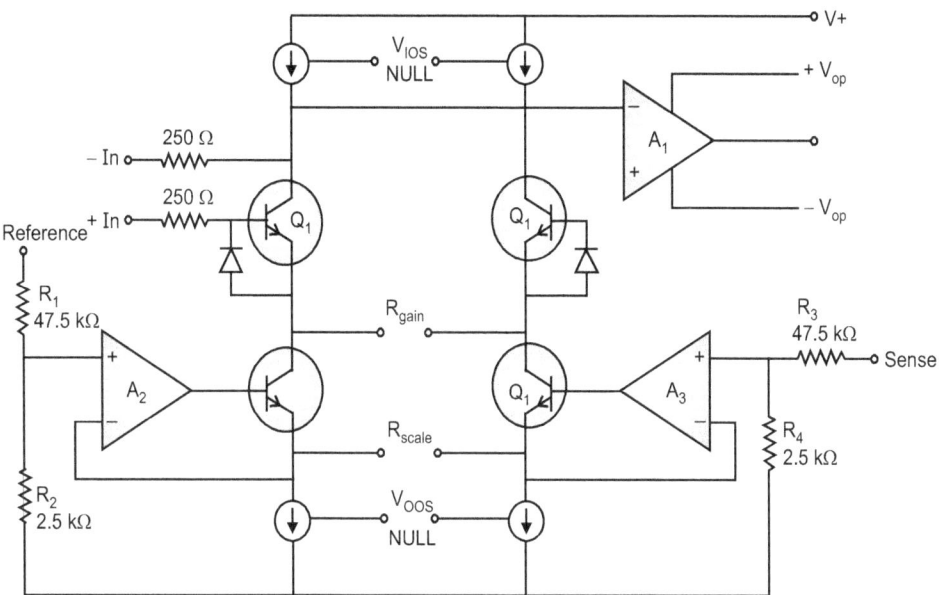

Fig. 2.85 : Simplified circuit diagram of the AMP-01 low-noise precision IA

Operation :

Apply a differential signal between the input which unbalances the current through Q_1 and Q_2. Op-amp A_1 reacts to this by unbalancing Q_1 and Q_2 in the opposite direction to restore the balanced condition $V_N = V_P$ at its own input. A_1 achieves this by applying a suitable drive to the bottom transistor pair via A_3. The amount of drive needed depends on the ratio R_S/R_G as well as on the magnitude of the input difference. This drive forms the output of the instrumentation amplifier. Fig. 2.86 shows belows gives the connection diagram for AMP 01.

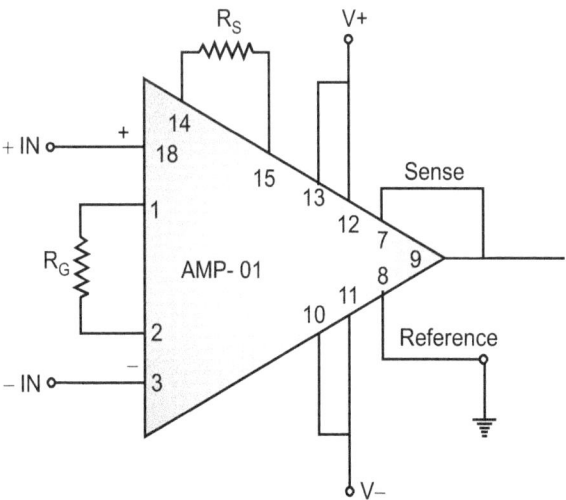

Fig. 2.86 : Basic AMP-01 connection

$$\text{Voltage gain, G} = \left(\frac{20 \times R_S}{R_G}\right) \qquad \ldots (2.125)$$

Salient features of AMP-01.

1. Offset voltage = 15 µV.
2. Offset voltage drift = 0.1 µV/°C.
3. Noise = 0.2 µ V_{PP} (0.1 Hz to 10 Hz).
4. Output drive = ± 10 V @ ± 50 mA.
5. Capacitive load stability = to 1 µF.
6. Range gain = 0.1 to 10,000.
7. Linearity = 16 bit at G = 1000 V/V.
8. CMRR dB = 140 dB at G = 1000 V/V.
9. Bias current = 1 nA.

2.9.6 Flying Capacitor Instrumentation Amplifiers

To achieve high CMRRs flying-capacitor technique is used. It is so called because it flips a capacitor back and forth between source and amplifier. Fig. 2.87 shows the connection diagram of flying capacitor Instrumentation Amplifier (IA).

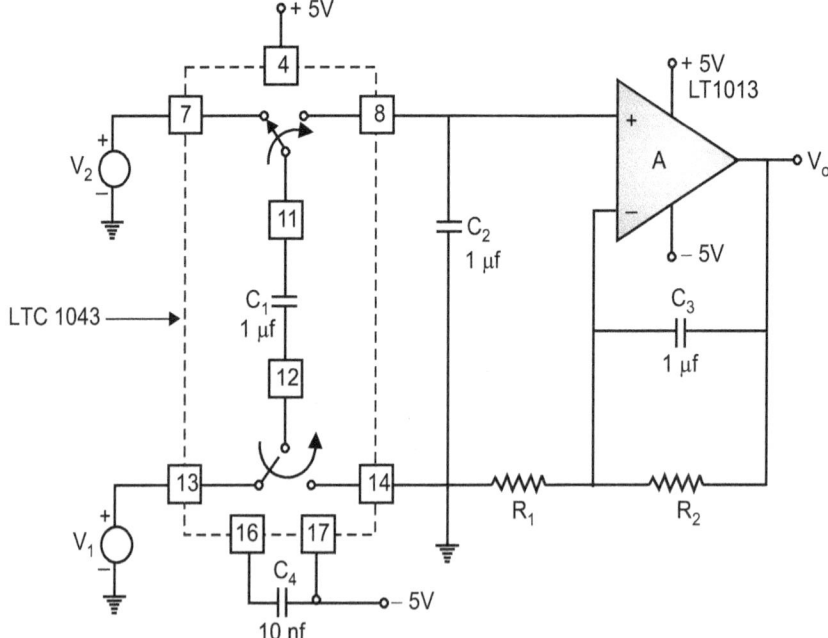

Fig. 2.87 : Flying-capacitor IA

Operation :

Flipping the switches to the left chares C_1 to the voltage difference $(V_2 - V_1)$ and flipping the switches to the right transfers charge from C_1 to C_2. Continuous switch clocking causes C_2 to charge up until the equilibrium condition is reached in which the voltage across C_2 becomes equal to that across C_1. This voltage is magnified by the non-inverting amplifier to give.

$$r_o = (1 + R_2/R_1)(V_2 - V_1) \qquad \ldots (2.126)$$

To obtain high performance, the circuit uses LTC 1043 precision instrumentation switches capacitor building block and the LT 1013 precision op-amp. The switches are operated at a frequency set by C_4. The function of C_3 is to provide low-pass filtering to ensure a clean output.

2.9.7 Instrumentation Amplifier with Active Guard Drive

In applications for e.g. monitoring of hazardous industrial conditions, source and amplifier may be located far apart from each other. To reduce the effect of noise pickups as well as ground-loop interference, the input signal is transmitted in double ended from over a pair of shielded wires and then processed with a difference amplifier. The advantage of double-ended over single-ended transmission is that since the two wires tend to pick-up identical noise this noise will appear as a common-mode component and will thus be rejected by the IA. The purpose of shielding is to help reduce differential-mode noise pickup.

Because of the distributed capacitance of the cable another problem arises called as CMRR degradation with frequency. It is analyzed using the Fig. 2.88 given below. Fig. 2.88 shows the model of non-zero source resistance and distributed cable capacitance.

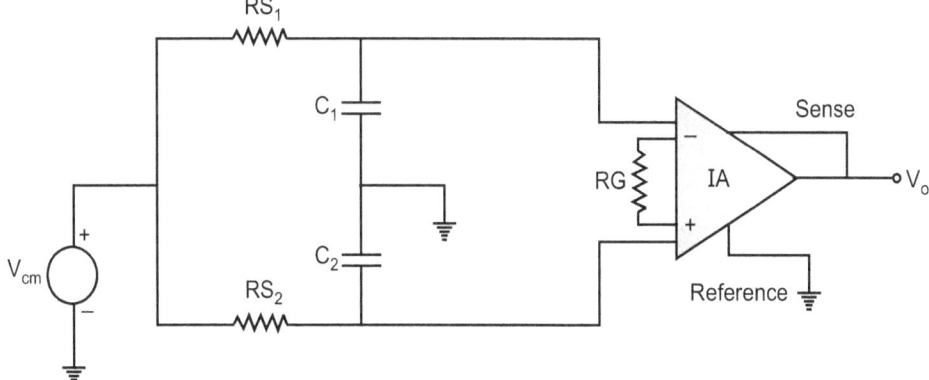

Fig. 2.88 : Model of non-zero resistance and distributed cable capacitance

Since the differential-mode component has assumed to be zero, so the IA output should be zero but practically, the time-constant $R_{S1}C_1$ and $R_{S2}C_2$ are different and variations in V_{cm} will result in uneven signal variation or $V_1 \neq V_2$ thus the output is not zero. This results the non-zero output signal even if there is no differential-mode component at the source. This represents degradation in CMRR.

The CMRR due to RC imbalance is

$$CMRR_{dB} \cong 20 \log_{10} \frac{1}{2\pi f\, R_{dm}\, C_{cm}} \qquad \ldots (2.127)$$

where $R_{dm} = |R_{S1} - R_{S2}|$ source resistance imbalance

$C_{cm} = (C_1 + C_2)/2$ – common mode capacitance between each wire and the grounded shield.

f is the frequency of common mode input component.

The effect of C_{cm} can be neutralized by driving the shield with the common-mode voltage itself to reduce the common-mode voltage itself to reduce the common-mode swing across C_{cm} to zero. Fig. 2.90 shows the arrangement to achieve this.

$$V_{cm} = \frac{V_1 + V_2}{2} = \frac{(V_1 + V_3 + V_2 - V_3)}{2}$$

$$= \frac{V_{o1} + V_{o2}}{2}$$

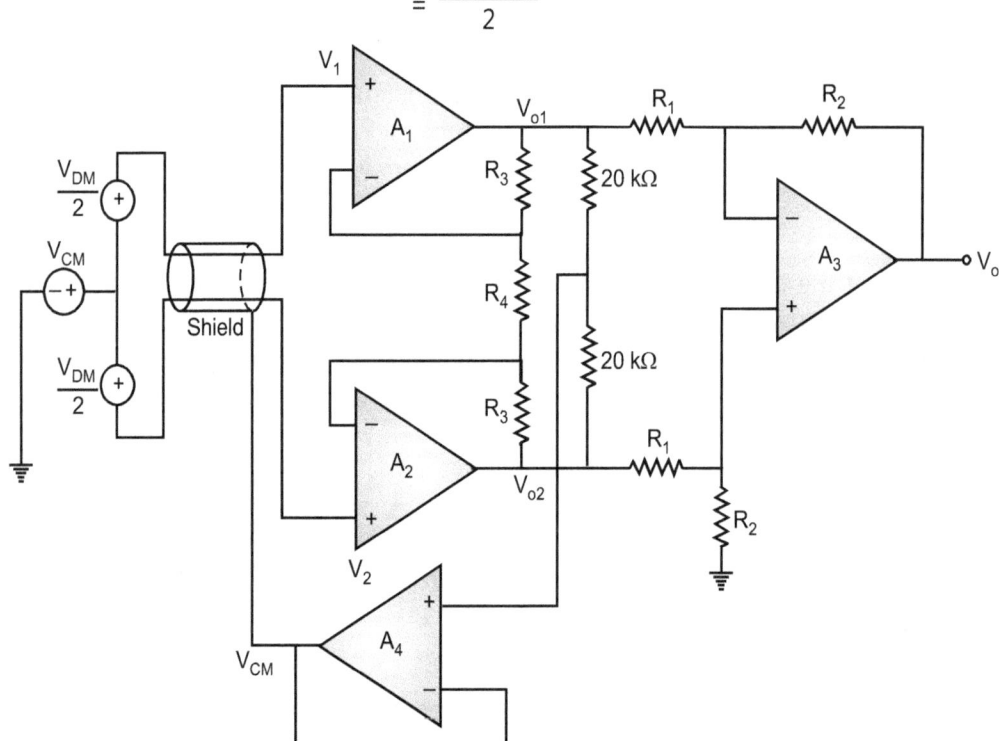

Fig. 2.90 : Instrumentation amplifier with active guard drive

2.9.8 Digitally Programmable Gain Instrumentation Amplifiers

In data acquisition systems it is required to program the gain of the instrumentation amplifier. This can be achieved by using the method given in Fig. 2.73. It programs the first-stage gain A_1 using a string of symmetrically valued resistors and a string of simultaneously activated switch pairs to select the tap pair corresponding to a given gain.

At any given time only one switch pair is closed and all others are open

$$A_1 = 1 + \frac{R_{outside}}{R_{inside}} \qquad \ldots (2.128)$$

where R_{inside} is the sum of the resistances located between the two selected switches and $R_{outside}$ is the sum of all remaining resistances.

The advantages of this topology is that the current flowing through any closed switch is the negligible input current of the corresponding op-amp.

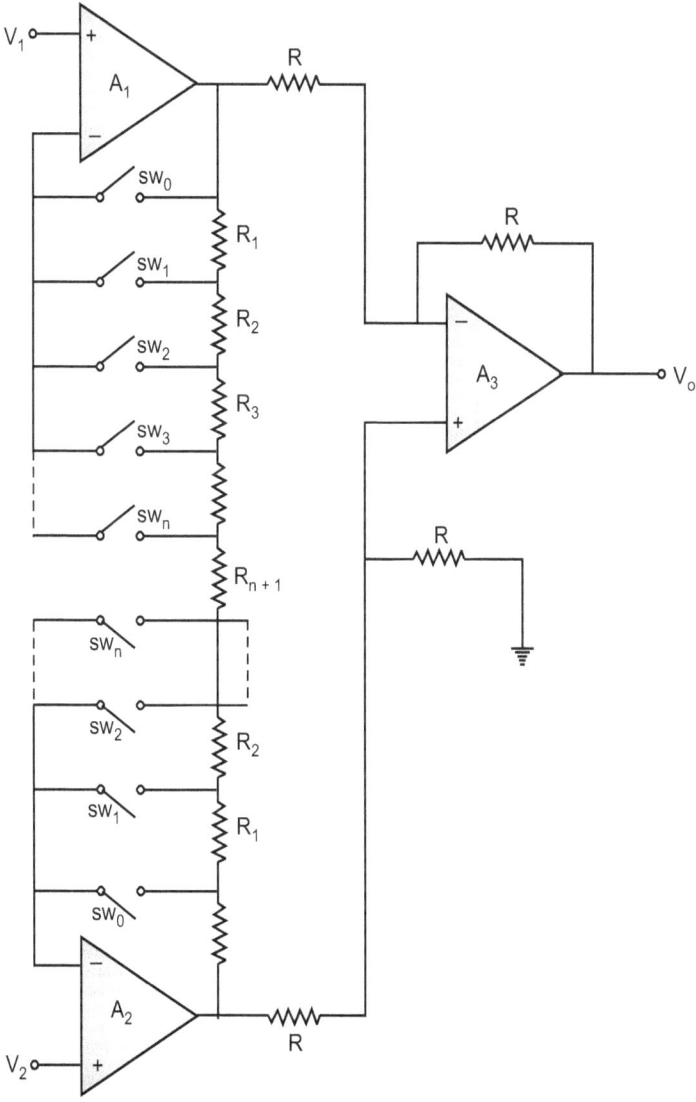

Fig. 2.91 : Digitally programmable IA

2.9.9 Output-Offset Control in IA

There are some applications which require some amount of offset at the output of an IA. For example, when IA is connected to a voltage-to-frequency converter, which requires that its input range be of only one polarity at that time the IA must be suitably offset to ensure a unipolar range. Fig. 2.92 shows the IA with output offset control.

In the Fig. 2.92 the reference node is driven by a voltage V_{ref}. This voltage is obtained from the wiper of the pot and is buffered by A_4, where low output resistance prevents disturbance of the bridge balance.

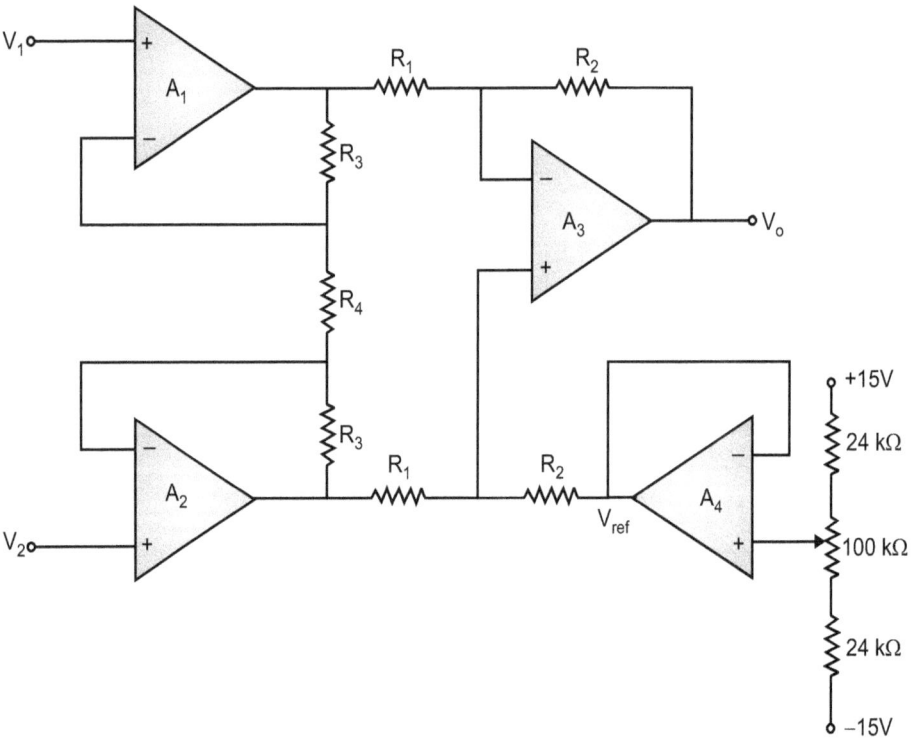

Fig. 2.92 : IA with output offset control

By applying superposition rule, we get

$$V_o = A(V_2 - V_1) + (1 + R_2/R_1) \times [R_1/(R_1 + R_2)] V_{ref}$$

$$V_o = A(V_2 - V_1) + V_{ref} \qquad \ldots (2.129)$$

V_{ref} is variable from -10 V to $+10$ V.

2.9.10 Current Output Instrumentation Amplifiers

By turning the second storage into a flow and circuit we can configure the three op-amp IA for current output operation. This is desirable when signals are transmitted over long wires because the stray wire resistance does not degrade current signals. Fig. 2.93 shows the current output IA.

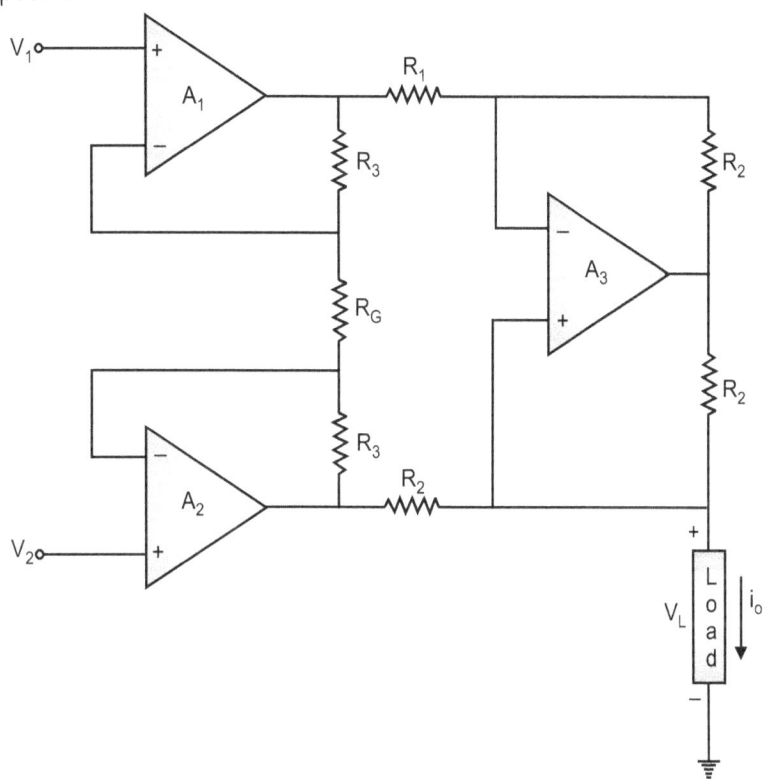

Fig. 2.93

$$i_o = \frac{1 + 2R_3/R_G}{R_1}(V_2 - V_1) \quad \ldots (2.130)$$

2.9.11 Applications of Instrumentation Amplifiers

1. Temperature control,
2. Temperature indicator,
3. Light intensity meter,
4. Measurement of flow and thermal conductivity,
5. Analog weight scale,
6. Data acquisition systems.

1. Temperature controller : Temperature controller circuit can be constructed by using a thermister in the bridge circuit and by replacing a meter with a relay in the circuit shown in Fig. 2.80. The output of the differential instrumentation amplifier drives a relay that controls the current in the heat generating circuit.

2. Light intensity meter : The circuit in Fig. 2.80 can be used as light intensity meter if a transducer is a photocell. The bridge can be balanced for darkness conditions. Therefore, when exposed to light, the bridge will be unbalanced and cause the meter to deflect.

The light intensity meter using an instrumentation bridge amplifier is more accurate and stable than single input inverting or non-inverting configurations because common mode (noise) voltages are effectively rejected by the differential configuration.

2.10 INSTRUMENTATION AMPLIFIER IC μA 725

2.10.1 Description

The μA 725 is a monolithic instrumentation operational amplifier constructed using the Fairchild Planner Epitaxial Process. It is intended for precise, low level signal amplification applications where low noise, low drift and accurate closed loop gain are required. The offset null capability, low power consumption, very high voltage gain as well as wide power supply range provide superior performance for a wide range of instrumentation applications. The μA 725 is a lead compatible with the popular μA 741 operational amplifier.

2.10.2 Specification Features of μA 725

- Low input noise current – 0.15 PA/$\sqrt{Hz}$ at 1.0 kHz typically.
- High open loop gain – 3,000,000 typically.
- Low input offset current – 2.0 nA typically.
- Low input voltage drift – 0.6 μV/°C typically.
- High common mode rejection – 120 dB.
- High input voltage range - ± 14 V typically.
- Wide power supply range = ± 3.0 V to ± 22 V.
- Offset null capability.

2.10.3 Absolute Maximum Ratings

Storage temperature range :
    Metal can : 65°C to + 175°C
    Molded DIP : – 65°C to + 150°C
Operating temperature range
    Extended (μA 725 AM, μA 725 M) : – 55°C to + 125°C
    Commercial (μA 725 CE, μA 725 C) : 0°C to + 70°C

Lead temperature

    Metal can : 300°C

    Molded DIP : 265°C

Internal power dissipation.

    8L – Metal can : 1.00 W

    8L – Molded DIP : 0.93 W

    Supply voltage : ± 22 V

    Differential input voltage : ± 5.0 V

    Input voltage : ± 22 V

    Voltage between offset null and V^+ : ± 0.5 V

2.10.4 Connection Diagram

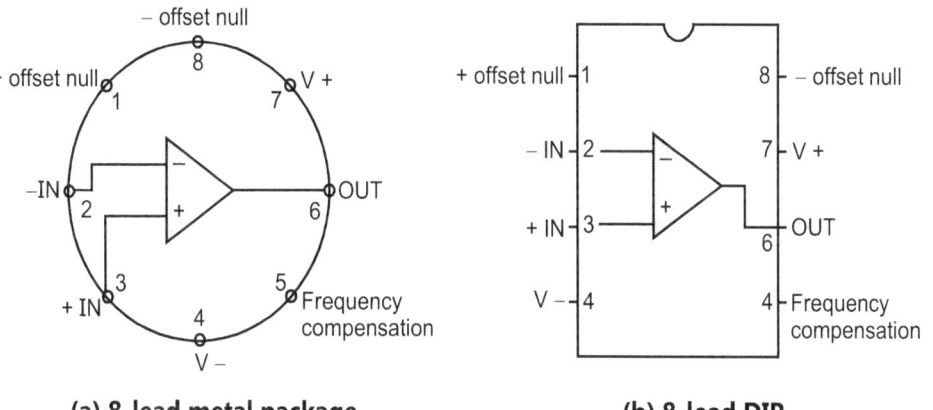

(a) 8-lead metal package   (b) 8-lead DIP

Fig. 2.94

2.11 BRIDGE AMPLIFIER

The four resistances and op-amp forms the basic bridge amplifier. Among the four resistances one of the resistance is a transducer. Transducers is a device that converts physical quantity into electrical signal. The example of such transducer are thermisters or temperature dependent resistors whose resistance changes according to the change in temperature or photoresistors or photoconductive cell whose resistance changes according to light intensity etc.

If such transducers are placed in one of the arm of the bridge then the circuit is called as transducer bridge amplifier. Fig. 2.95 shows the bridge amplifier.

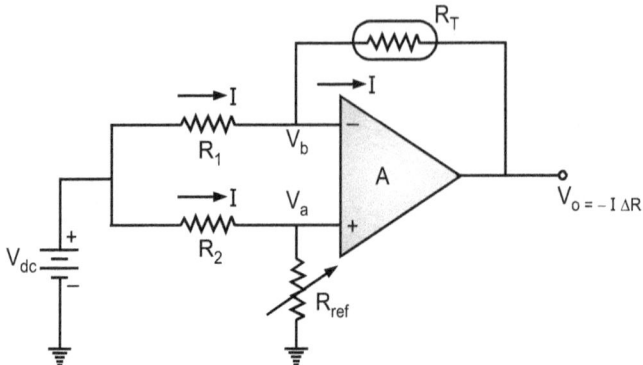

Fig. 2.95 : Bridge amplifier

Applying KVL to the non-inverting input side.

$$I = \frac{V_{dc}}{R_1 + R_{ref}}$$

$$V_a = I \cdot R_{ref}$$

whenever the temperature changes, the resistance of transducer changes by ΔR

$$\therefore \quad R_T = R_{ref} + \Delta R \quad \ldots (2.131)$$

When the bridge is balanced $R_T = R_{ref}$

Apply KVL at the inverting input,

$$I = \frac{V_{dc} - V_b}{R_1}$$

Same current flows through the transducer, as the input currents to the op-amp are zero.

$$I = \frac{V_b - V_o}{R_{ref} + \Delta R}$$

$$\frac{V_{dc} - V_a}{R_1} = \frac{V_b - V_o}{R_{ref} + \Delta R}$$

Due to virtual ground concepts $V_a = V_b$

$$\frac{V_{dc} - V_a}{R_1} = \frac{V_a - V_o}{R_{ref} + \Delta R}$$

$$\frac{V_o}{R_{ref} + \Delta R} = \frac{V_a}{R_{ref} + \Delta R} + \frac{V_a}{R_1} - \frac{V_{dc}}{R_1}$$

$$\frac{V_o}{R_{ref} + \Delta R} = V_a \left[\frac{1}{R_{ref} + \Delta R} + \frac{1}{R_1} \right] - \frac{V_{dc}}{R_1}$$

$$\frac{V_o}{R_{ref} + \Delta R} = I \cdot R_{ref} \left[\frac{1}{R_{ref} + \Delta R} + \frac{1}{R_1} \right] - \frac{I}{R_1}(R_1 + R_{ref})$$

$$\frac{V_o}{R_{ref} + \Delta R} = I\left[\frac{R_{ref}}{R_{ref} + \Delta R} + \frac{R_{ref}}{R_1} - \frac{R_1 + R_{ref}}{R_1}\right]$$

$$\frac{V_o}{R_{ref} + \Delta R} = -\frac{I \Delta R}{(R_{ref} + \Delta R)}$$

$$V_o = -I \Delta R$$

$$V_o = \frac{V_{dc} \Delta R}{(R_1 + R_{ref})} \qquad \ldots (2.132)$$

Thus, $V_o \propto \Delta R$

2.12 CURRENT TO VOLTAGE CONVERTER

This is the special case of the inverting amplifier in which an input current is converted into a proportional output voltage.

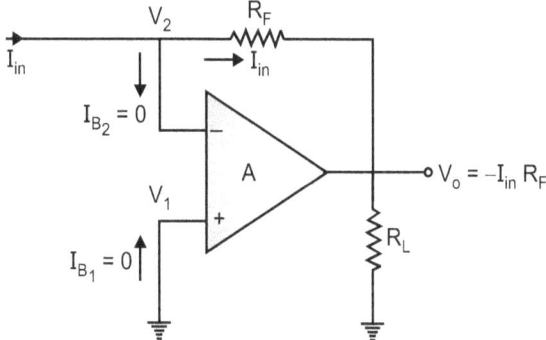

Fig. 2.96 : Current to voltage converter

The ideal voltage gain of the inverting amplifier is given as

$$\frac{V_o}{V_{in}} = -\frac{R_F}{R_1} \qquad \ldots (2.133)$$

Therefore, rearranging the above equation, we get

$$V_o = -\left(\frac{V_{in}}{R_1}\right) R_F$$

However, since $V_1 = 0$ V and $V_1 = V_2$

$$\frac{V_{in}}{R_1} = I_{in} \qquad \ldots (2.134)$$

and $\qquad V_o = -I_{in} R_F \qquad \ldots (2.135)$

This means that if we replace the V_{in} and R_1 combination by a current source I_{in}, the output voltage V_o becomes proportional to the input current I_{in}.

Applications of I-V Converter :
1. In sensing the current from photodetectors.
2. Digital-to-analog converter applications.

2.12.1 DAC using Current to Voltage Converter

Fig. 2.97 shows a combination of a DAC and current to voltage converter. The eight-digit binary signal is the input to MC 1408 DAC, and V_o corresponding analog output of the current to voltage converter.

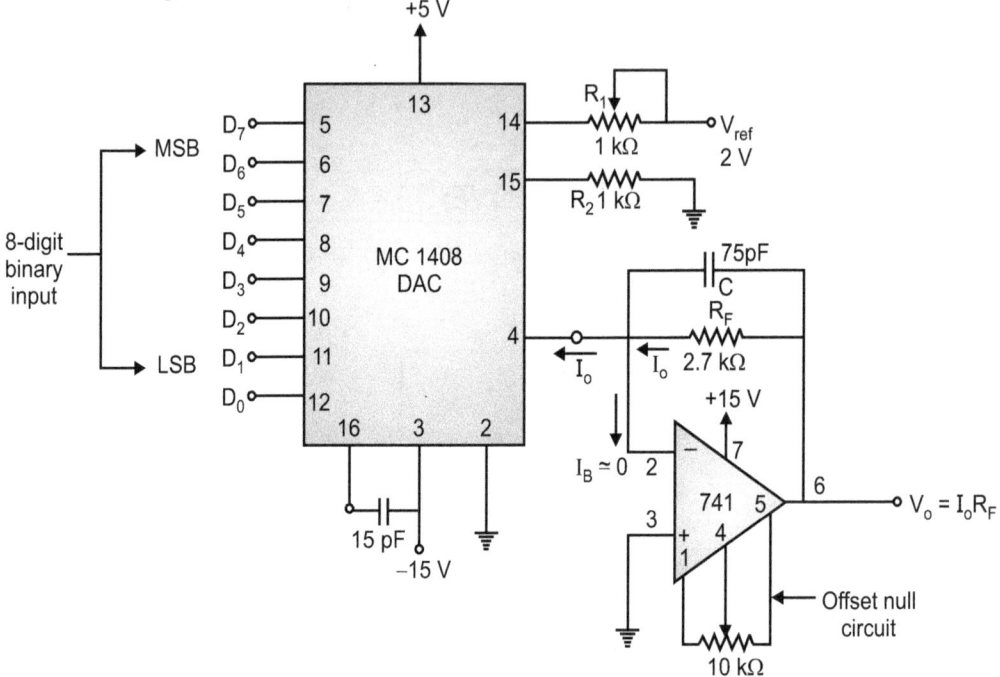

Fig. 2.97 : DAC using current to voltage converter

The output of the MC 1408 is current I_o. The value of I_o depends on the logic state of the binary inputs as shown in equation (2.121)

$$I_o = \frac{V_{ref}}{R_1}\left(\frac{D_7}{2} + \frac{D_6}{4} + \frac{D_5}{8} + \frac{D_4}{16} + \frac{D_3}{32} + \frac{D_2}{64} + \frac{D_1}{128} + \frac{D_0}{256}\right) \qquad \text{... (2.136)}$$

where,
I_o = Output current of the DAC (mA)
R_1 = Resistance (kΩ)
V_{ref} = Reference voltage (volts)
D_0 through D_7 = Eight binary inputs

I_o is zero when all the inputs are logic 0 and I_o is maximum when all the inputs are logic 1. The variation in I_o can be converted into a desired output voltage range by selecting a proper value for R_F. Since,

$$V_o = I_o R_F \qquad \text{... (2.137)}$$

Capacitor C is connected to minimize overshoot and ranging. The output voltage V_o of the current to voltage converter is positive because the direction of input current I_o is opposite to that in Fig. 2.97.

2.13 VOLTAGE TO CURRENT CONVERTER WITH FLOATING LOAD

Fig. 2.98 shows a voltage to current converter in which load resistor R_L is floating (i.e. not connected to ground).

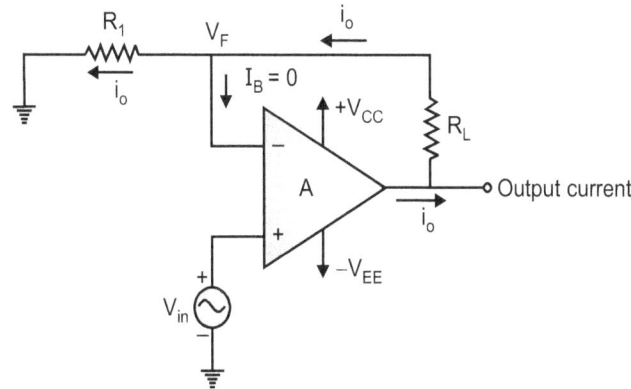

Fig. 2.98 : Voltage to current converter with floating load

Input voltage is applied to non-inverting input terminal and the inverting input is driven by the feedback voltage across R_1. This type of circuit is also called a current series negative feedback amplifier because the feedback voltage across R_1 depends on the output current i_o and it is in series with the input difference voltage V_{id}.

Applying Kirchhoff's voltage equation for the input loop,

$$V_{in} = V_{id} + V_f \qquad \ldots (2.138)$$

But $V_{id} \approx 0$ V. Since, A is very large, therefore,

$$V_{in} = V_f$$
$$V_{in} = R_1 i_o \qquad \ldots (2.139)$$

or

$$i_o = \frac{V_{in}}{R_1} \qquad \ldots (2.140)$$

Thus, it is shown that an input voltage V_{in} is converted into an output current of V_{in}/R_1.

2.14 VOLTAGE TO CURRENT CONVERTER WITH GROUNDED LOAD

Fig. 2.99 shows another version of the voltage to current converter. In this, one terminal of the load is grounded and load current is controlled by an input voltage.

Apply Kirchhoff's current law at node V_1.

$$I_1 + I_2 = I_L \qquad \ldots (2.141)$$

$$\frac{V_{in} - V_1}{R} + \frac{V_o - V_1}{R} = I_L$$

$$V_{in} + V_o - 2V_1 = I_L R$$

Therefore,

$$V_1 = \frac{V_{in} + V_o - I_L R}{2} \qquad \ldots (2.142)$$

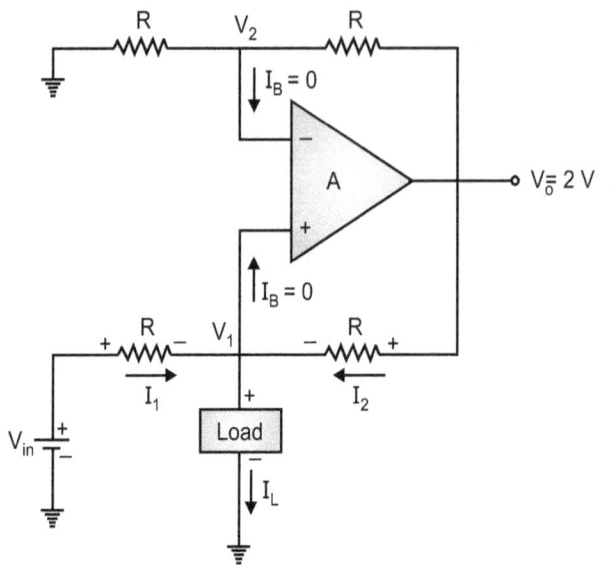

Fig. 2.99 : Voltage to current converter with grounded load

As the op-amp is connected in the non-inverting mode, the gain of the circuit is 1 + R/R = 2. Then, the output voltage is

$$V_O = 2V_1 \qquad \ldots (2.143)$$
$$V_O = V_{in} + V_O - I_L R$$
$$V_{in} - I_L R = 0$$

That is
$$V_{in} = I_L R$$

∴
$$I_L = \frac{V_{in}}{R} \qquad \ldots (2.144)$$

It shows that the load current depends on the input voltage V_{in} and resistor R.

The voltage to converter with grounded load may be used in testing devices such as zener and LEDs. The circuit will perform satisfactorily when the load size ≤ R value.

Applications of voltage to current converters :

1. Low voltage DC and AC voltmeters.
2. Diode match finders.
3. Light emitting diodes (LEDs) and zener diode testers.

2.14.1 Low Voltage DC Voltmeter

If the load resistor R_L is replaced by an ammeter with a full-scale deflection of 1 mA in the voltage to current converter with floating load, the resulting circuit is the DC voltmeter. It requires the external offset voltage compensating network.

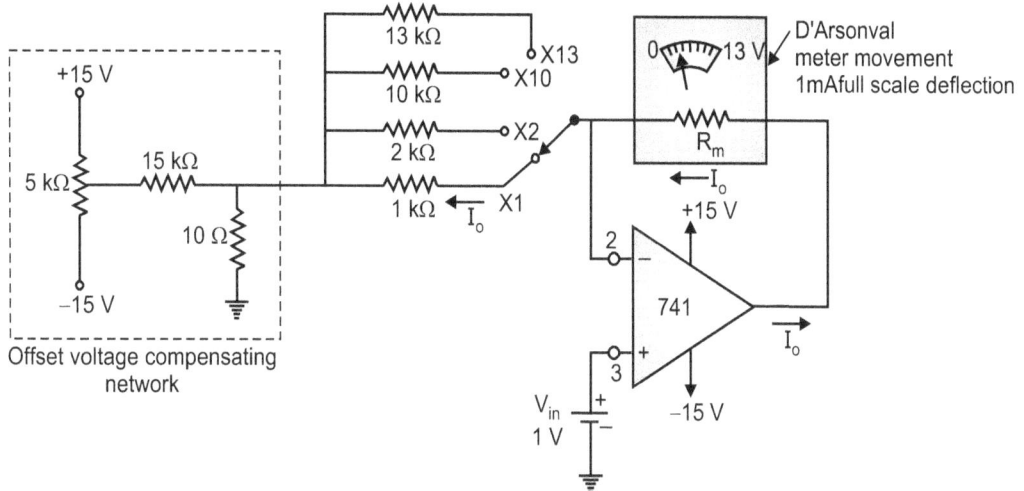

Fig. 2.100 : DC voltmeter with 1 to 13 V full-scale range

By calibrating the face of the ammeter in volts, a DC voltmeter with a full-scale voltage range of 1 to 13 V can be constructed. A centered zero ammeter can be used to measure positive as well as negative input voltages. To improve the accuracy of voltage measurements, the ammeter should be nulled each time before input voltage is applied.

2.14.2 Low Voltage AC Voltmeter

A combination of an ammeter and a full-wave rectifier can be employed in the feedback loop to form an AC voltmeter. In this, circuit an alternative current is converted into a direct current.

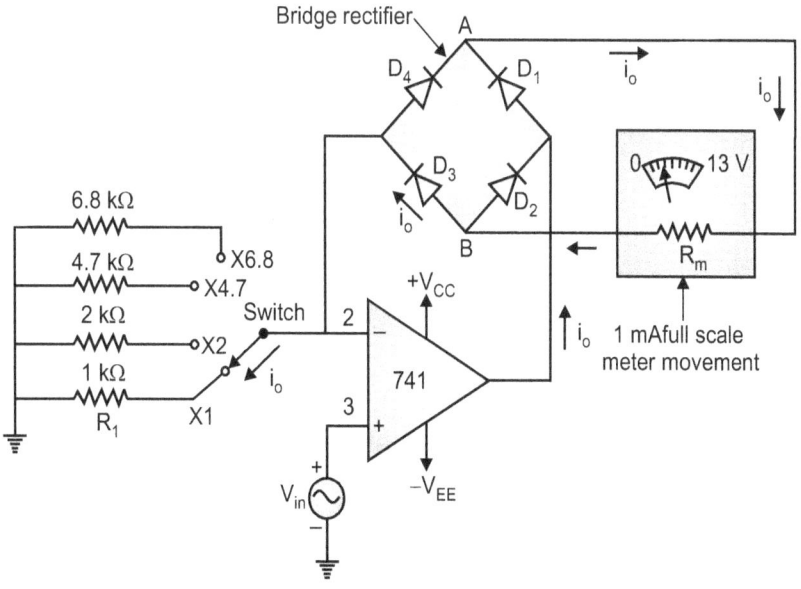

Fig. 2.101 : AC voltmeter

During the positive half-cycle of AC input, diodes D_1 and D_3 conduct, whereas diodes D_2 and D_4 conduct during the negative half-cycle of V_{in}. Therefore, the current through the ammeter flows only in one direction for the entire cycle of the AC input. For full wave rectification, meter current can be expressed as :

$$i_o = \frac{0.9 \, V_{in}}{R_1} \quad \text{... (2.145)}$$

$$V_{in} = (1.1 \, R_1) \, i_o \quad \text{... (2.146)}$$

2.14.3 Diode Match Finder

In ring modulator and foster-seely discriminator, it is necessary to have matched diodes with equal voltage drops at a particular value of diode current. The circuit diagram which is used as diode match finder is shown in Fig. 2.102 by replacing R_L with a diode.

When the switch is in position 1, rectifier diode 1N4001 is placed in the feedback loop; the current through this loop is set by the input voltage V_{in} and resistor R_1. For $V_{in} = 1$ V and $R_1 = 100 \, \Omega$, the current through the diode is

$$I_o = \frac{V_{in}}{R_1} = \frac{1}{100} = 10 \text{ mA} \quad \text{... (2.147)}$$

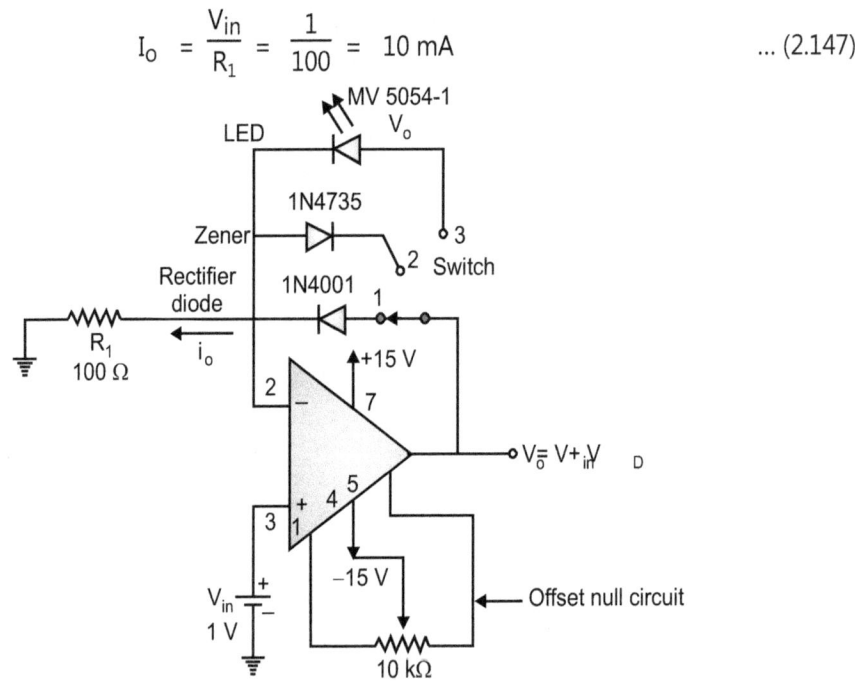

Fig. 2.102 : Diode match finder

When V_{in} and R_1 are constant, the current I_o will be constant. The voltage drop across the diode can be found either by measuring the voltage across it or the output voltage. The output voltage is equal to $(V_{in} + V_D)$. To avoid an error in output voltage, the op-amp should be initially nulled.

2.15 ANALOG MULTIPLIERS AND DIVIDERS

An analog multiplier is a three-terminal device that will perform the mathematical operations of multiplication and division by approximate terminal connections. Fig. 2.103 below shows a conceptual block representing a multiplier.

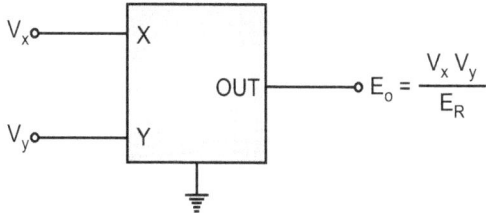

Fig. 2.103 : Conceptual multiplier

For the given value of the inputs, V_x and V_y and the output will be $V_x V_y/E_R$, where E_R is a dimensional constant, usually equal to 10 volts.

The simplest electronic multipliers use logarithmic amplifiers. The computation relies on the fact that the antilog of the sum of the logs of two numbers is the product of those numbers as shown in Fig. 2.104 below.

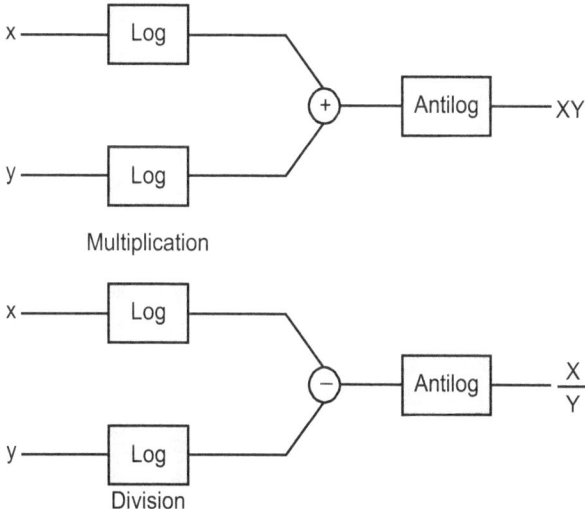

Fig. 2.104 : Multiplication and division using log amplifiers

The disadvantages of this type of multiplication amplifier the very limited bandwidth and single quadrant operation. A far better type of multiplier uses the 'Gilbert cell'. This structure was invented by Barrier Gilbert in the late 1960s.

2.15.1 Gilbert Cell Multiplier

There is a linear relationship between the collector current of a silicon junction transistor and its transconductance (gain) which is given by

$$dI_C/dV_{BE} = qI_C/KT \qquad \ldots (2.148)$$

where
- I_C = The collector current
- V_{BE} = The base-emitter voltage
- q = The electron change $(1.60219 \times 10^{-19})$
- K = Boltzman's constant $(1.38062 \times 10^{-23})$
- T = The absolute temperature

This relationship may be exploited to construct a multiplier with a long-tailed pair of silicon transistors as shown in Fig. 2.105.

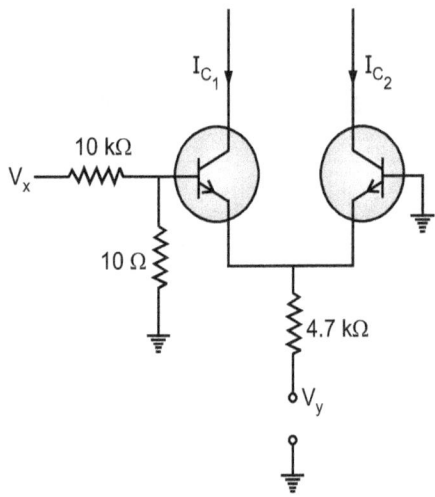

Fig. 2.105 : Basic transconductance amplifier

$$I_{C1} - I_{C2} = \Delta IC = \frac{q}{KT}\left(\frac{V_y + V_{bc}}{4.7 \times 10^3}\right)\left(\frac{10}{10010}\right) V_z = 8.3 \times 10^{-6} (V_y + 0.6) V_x$$

This is rather poor multiplier because (1) the Y input is offset by the V_{BE}, which changes non-linearly with V_y; (2) the X input is non-linear as a result of the exponential relationship between I_C and V_{BE} and (3) the scale factor varies with temperature.

The Gilbert multiplier cell is a modification of the emitter coupled cell and this allows four quadrant multiplication. Therefore, it forms the basic of most of the integrated circuit balanced multipliers. Gilberts multiplier cell is formed by two cross-coupled emitter coupled pairs in series connection with an emitter coupled pair.

The collector currents of Q_3 and Q_4 are given by

$$I_{C3} = \frac{I_{C1}}{1 + e^{(-V_1/V_T)}} \qquad \ldots (2.149)$$

and

$$I_{C4} = \frac{I_{C1}}{1 + e^{V_1/V_T}} \qquad \ldots (2.150)$$

Similarly the collector currents of Q_5 and Q_6 are given by

$$I_{C5} = \frac{I_{C2}}{1 + e^{V_1/V_T}} \quad \ldots (2.151)$$

$$I_{C6} = \frac{I_{C2}}{1 + e^{-V_1/V_T}} \quad \ldots (2.152)$$

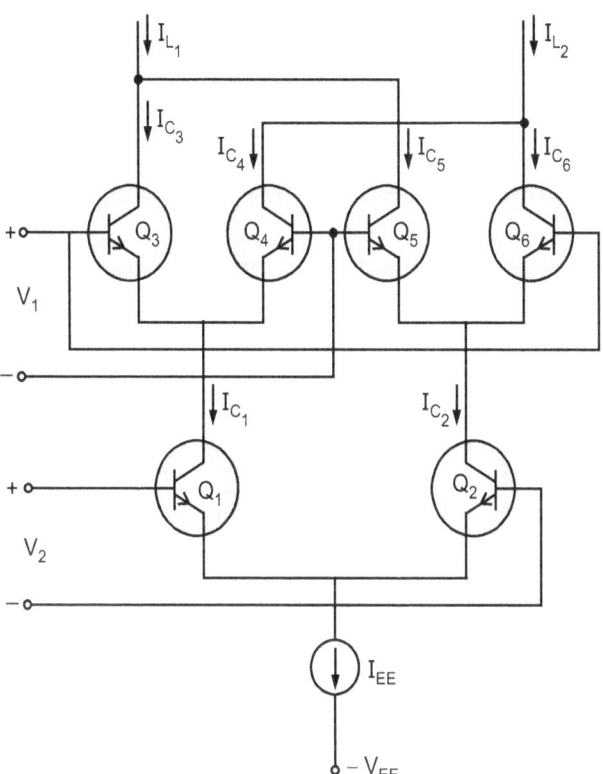

Fig. 2.106 : Gilbert multiplier cell

The collector currents I_{C1} and I_{C2}, of transistors Q_1 and Q_2 can be expressed as,

$$I_{C1} = \frac{I_{EE}}{1 + e^{-V_2/V_T}} \quad \ldots (2.153)$$

$$I_{C2} = \frac{I_{EE}}{1 + e^{V_2/V_T}} \quad \ldots (2.154)$$

Substituting equation (2.153) in (2.149) and (2.150) equations

$$I_{C3} = \frac{I_{EE}}{[1 + e^{-V_1/V_T}][1 + e^{-V_2/V_T}]} \quad \ldots (2.155)$$

$$I_{C4} = \frac{I_{EE}}{[1 + e^{V_1/V_T}][1 + e^{-V_2/V_T}]} \qquad \ldots (2.156)$$

Similarly substituting equations (2.154) in equation (2.151) and (2.152), we get

$$I_{C5} = \frac{I_{EE}}{[1 + e^{V_1/V_T}][1 + e^{-V_2/V_T}]} \qquad \ldots (2.157)$$

$$I_{C6} = \frac{I_{EE}}{[1 + e^{-V_1/V_T}][1 + e^{V_2/V_T}]} \qquad \ldots (2.158)$$

The differential output current ΔI is given by

$$\Delta I = I_{L1} - I_{L2}$$
$$\Delta I = (I_{C3} + I_{C5}) - (I_{C4} + I_{C6})$$
$$\Delta I = (I_{C3} - I_{C6}) - (I_{C4} - I_{C5}) \qquad \ldots (2.159)$$

Substituting equation (2.155), (2.156), (2.157), (2.158) in equation (2.159) and employing exponential formulae for hyperbolic functions, we get

$$\Delta I = I_{EE}\left[\tanh\left(\frac{V_1}{2V_T}\right)\tanh\left(\frac{V_2}{2V_T}\right)\right] \qquad \ldots (2.160)$$

The above equation shows that when V_1 and V_2 are small, the Gilbert cell shown in Fig. 2.106 above can be used as a four quadrant analog multiplier with the use of current-to-voltage converters.

2.15.2 Analog Multiplier ICs

Analog multiplier is a circuit whose output voltage at any instant is proportional to the product of instantaneous value of two individual input voltages. The important applications of these multipliers are multiplication, division, squaring and square-rooting of signals, modulation and demodulation. These analog multipliers are available as integrated circuits consisting of op-amps and other circuit elements. The schematic of a typical analog multiplier namely AD633 is shown in Fig. 2.107.

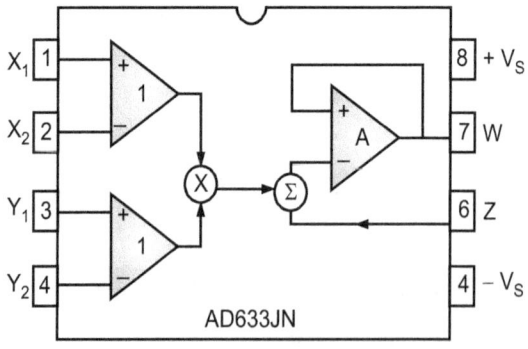

Fig. 2.107 : Schematic symbol of AD 633 multiplier IC

The AD 633 multiplier is a four-quadrant analog multiplier.

2.15.2.1 Features of AD633

- Possesses high input impedance.
- Negligible loading effect on the signal source.
- Operate with supply voltages ranging from ± 8 V to ± 18 V.
- Does not require any external components.
- Calibration of user is not necessary.
- Typical range of the two input signals is ± 10 V.

2.15.2.2 Applications of Multiplier ICs

The multiplier ICs are used for the following purpose :

(i) Voltage squarer.

(ii) Frequency doubler.

(iii) Voltage divider.

(iv) Square rooter.

(v) Phase angle detector.

(vi) Rectifier.

2.16 LOG AMPLIFIER

The response of the op-amp is determined by the choice of elements used in the feedback network of op-amp. When resistors are used in the feedback, the circuit shows a linear relationship between input and output. But when non-linear elements are connected in the feedback path such as diode or transistor, then non-linear relationship is developed between input and output. The resulting circuit is called as log or antilog amplifiers.

2.16.1 Basics of Log Amplifier

The current flowing through diode is given as

$$I = I_o (e^{V/\eta V_T} - 1) \quad \ldots (2.161)$$

where $\quad$ I = Diode current

I_o = Reverse saturation current

V = Diode voltage

η = Constant for Ge = 1 and Si = 2

V_T = Voltage equivalent of temperature

V_T = K.T.

where $\quad$ K = Boltzman's constant = 8.62×10^{-5} eV/°K

T = Temperature in °K

or $V_T = 26$ mV

From the V-I characteristics of diode, the diode voltage is positive and the exponential term has positive coefficient. Therefore $1 << e^{V/\eta V_T}$ and can be neglected.

Therefore, the diode current becomes the forward bias current

$$I_F = I_0 e^{V/\eta V_T}$$

2.16.2 Basic Log Amplifier using Diode

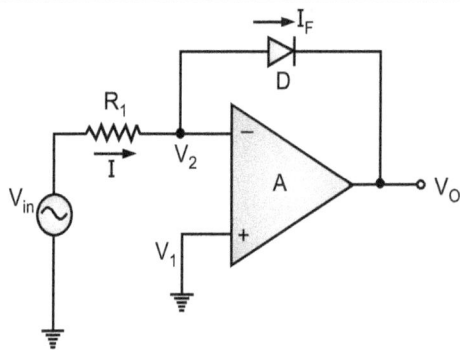

Fig. 2.108 : Basic log amplifier

Fig. 2.108 shows the basic log amplifier circuit using diode. According to virtual concept.

$$V_1 = V_2 = 0$$

$$\therefore \quad I = \frac{V_{in} - V_2}{R} = \frac{V_{in}}{R}$$

As the input currents to the op-amp are zero

$$I = I_F$$

From diode's current equation, we can write

$$V = \eta V_T \ln \left[\frac{I_F}{I_0} \right]$$

For this circuit $V = V_2 - V_o = -V_o$

$$-V_o = \eta V_T \ln \left[\frac{I_F}{I_0} \right]$$

But $I_F = \dfrac{V_{in}}{R}$

$$V_o = -\eta V_T \ln \left[\frac{V_{in}}{RI_0} \right]$$

$I_o R$ is a constant d.c. voltage and it can be called as reference voltage.

$$V_o = -\eta V_T \ln\left[\frac{V_{in}}{V_{ref}}\right] \qquad \ldots (2.162)$$

This equation gives the relation between input and output voltage. The output voltage is proportional to natural logarithm to base of input voltage.

2.16.2.1 Revision of Some Basic Equations of Transistors

The transistor collector current is given by

$$I_C = \alpha I_S (e^{V_{BE}/V_T} - 1)$$

where
- I_C = Collector current
- I_S = Emitter saturation currents
- V_{BE} = Base to emitter voltage
- α = Constant = 1

$$\frac{I_C}{I_S} = (e^{V_{BE}/V_T} - 1)$$

$$\frac{I_C}{I_S} + 1 = e^{V_{BE}/V_T}$$

As the saturation current is very small and $1 \ll I_C/I_S$. So $\frac{I_C}{I_S} + 1 \approx \frac{I_C}{I_S}$.

Apply natural logarithm on both sides.

$$\therefore \quad \ln\left(\frac{I_C}{I_S}\right) = \ln(e^{V_{BE}/V_T})$$

$$\frac{V_{BE}}{V_T} = \ln\left[\frac{I_C}{I_S}\right]$$

$$V_{BE} = V_T \ln\left[\frac{I_C}{I_S}\right] \qquad \ldots (2.163)$$

2.16.3 Basic Log Amplifier using Transistor

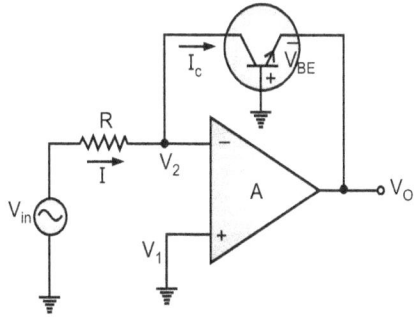

Fig. 2.109 : Basic log amplifier using transistor

Fig. 2.109 shows the basic log amplifier using transistor. A transistor is connected in the feedback path.

From Fig. 2.109. Node V_2 is also at virtual ground.

∴ $$V_1 = V_2 = 0$$

$$I = \frac{V_{in} - V_2}{R} = \frac{V_{in}}{R}$$

Due to realistic assumptions

$$I = I_C = \frac{V_{in}}{R}$$

Substitute this value in equation 2.137.

From the output side.

$$V_{BE} = -V_o$$

So we can write

$$-V_o = V_T \ln\left[\frac{I_C}{I_S}\right]$$

$$V_o = V_T \ln\left[\frac{I_C}{I_S}\right]$$

$$V_o = -V_T \ln\left[\frac{V_{in}}{R\,I_S}\right]$$

$$V_o = -V_T \ln\left[\frac{V_{in}}{V_{ref}}\right] \quad \ldots (2.164)$$

This equation is same as the equation obtained for the log amplifier using diodes.

2.16.4 Temperature Compensated Log Amplifier

The reverse saturation current depends on the temperature. When temperature increases by 10° celcius, the reverse saturation current doubles. As well as the reverse saturation current varies from one transistor to another with respect to temperature.

The accuracy of the basic log amplifier is affected by the temperature. Therefore, temperature compensation must be provided of the basic log amplifier.

Fig. 2.110 below shows temperature compensated log amplifier with necessary modification.

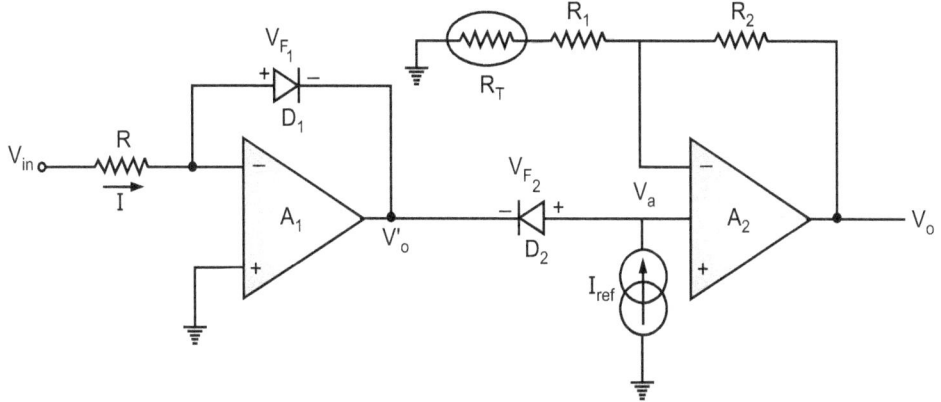

Fig. 2.110 : Temperature compensated log amplifier

Here diodes D_1 and D_2 are selected such that their V_T and I_o values are same. With the help of I_{ref}, a constant reference voltage is generated.

From Fig. 2.110, we can write

$$V_a = V_o' + V_{F2} \quad \ldots (2.165)$$

Op-amp A_1 is the basic log amplifier and the output of log amplifier is

$$V_o' = -\eta V_T \ln\left[\frac{I_{in}}{R\,I_o}\right]$$

The voltage across diode D_2 is V_{f2}

$$V_{F2} = \eta V_T \ln\left[\frac{I_{F2}}{I_o}\right]$$

Here $\quad I_{F2} = I_{ref}$

$$V_{F2} = \eta V_T \ln\left[\frac{I_{ref}}{I_o}\right]$$

Substituting the value of V_{F2} and V_o' in equation (2.165)

$$V_a = -\eta V_T \ln\left[\frac{V_{in}}{R\,I_o}\right] + \eta V_T \ln\left[\frac{I_{ref}}{I_o}\right]$$

$$V_a = -\eta V_T \left[\ln\left(\frac{V_{in}}{R}\right) - \ln(I_o) - \ln(I_{ref}) + \ln(I_o)\right]$$

$$V_a = -\eta V_T \left[\ln\left(\frac{V_{in}}{R}\right) - \ln(I_{ref})\right]$$

$$V_a = -\eta V_T \ln\left[\frac{V_{in}}{R \cdot I_{ref}}\right]$$

$$V_a = \eta V_T \ln\left[\frac{V_{in}}{V_{ref}}\right]$$

Thus, the reverse saturation current I_o is cancelled. But still the term V_T depends on temperature. If the gain of the op-amp A_2 is made temperature dependent.

$$V_o = V_a \cdot \left[1 + \frac{R_F}{R_1 + R_T}\right]$$

$$V_o = -\eta V_T \left[\frac{R_1 + R_T + R_F}{R_1 + R_T}\right] \ln\left[\frac{V_{in}}{R\,I_{ref}}\right]$$

The resistance R_T has positive temperature coefficient. Therefore, when temperature increases, resistance R_T also increases and the overall term remains constant.

$$V_o = -K \ln\left[\frac{V_{in}}{V_{ref}}\right] \qquad \ldots (2.166)$$

Now, the circuit is completely independent of temperature changes.

2.17 ANTILOG AMPLIFIER

If the non-linear element like diode or transistor is connected at the input side of the op-amp then the op-amp circuit acts as a antilog amplifier.

Fig. 2.111 shows the basic antilog amplifier.

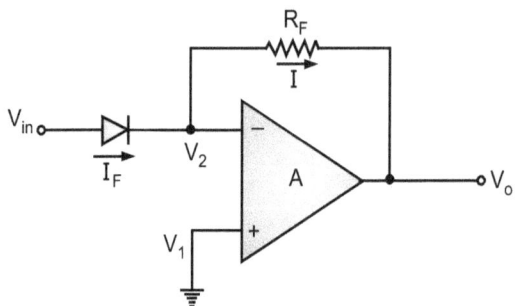

Fig. 2.111 : Basic antilog amplifier

Due to virtual ground concept.

$$V_1 = V_2 = 0$$

The current flowing through diode is given as

If $\qquad I_F = I_o\, e^{V_{in}/\eta V_T}$

$\qquad I = I_F$ for the op-amp

$$I = I_F = \frac{V_2 - V_o}{R_F} = \frac{-V_o}{R_F}$$

$$-\frac{V_o}{R_F} = I_o\, e^{V_{in}/\eta V_T}$$

$$V_o = -(I_o\,R_F)\,e^{V_{in}/\eta V_T}$$

$$V_o = -V_{ref}\,e^{V_{in}/\eta V_T} \qquad \ldots (2.167)$$

where $\quad V_{ref} = I_o\,R_F$

Thus, the output voltage is proportional to the exponential function (antilog) of the V_{in}.

2.17.1 Basic Antilog Amplifier using Transistor

Fig. 2.112 shows the circuit which gives the antilog of the input voltage using transistor.

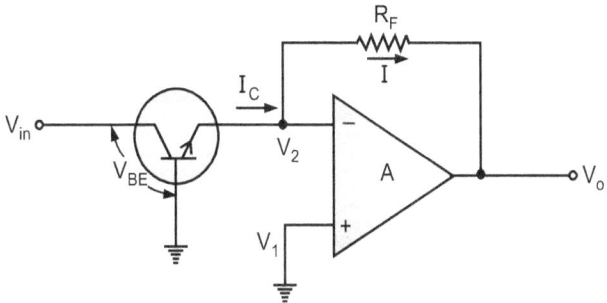

Fig. 2.112 : Antilog amplifier using transistor

Due to virtual ground concept $V_1 = V_2 = 0$. We know the collector current equation of transistor.

$$I_C = I_S\,e^{V_{BE}/V_T}$$

Here $\quad V_{BE} = V_{in}$

$$I_C = I_S\,e^{V_{in}/V_T}$$

From Fig. 2.112,

$$I_C = I = \frac{V_2 - V_o}{R_F}$$

$$I_C = I = \frac{-V_o}{R_F}$$

$$\frac{-V_o}{R_F} = I_S\,e^{V_{in}/V_T}$$

$$V_o = -I_S\,R_f\,e^{V_{in}/V_T} \qquad \ldots (2.168)$$

Thus, the output voltage is proportional to the antilog of the input voltage.

Again the terms I_o, I_S and V_T are temperature dependent. Therefore, the antilog amplifier also needs. Some temperature compensation to increase the performance.

2.17.2 Temperature Compensated Antilog Amplifier

Fig. 2.113 shows the temperature compensated antilog amplifier.

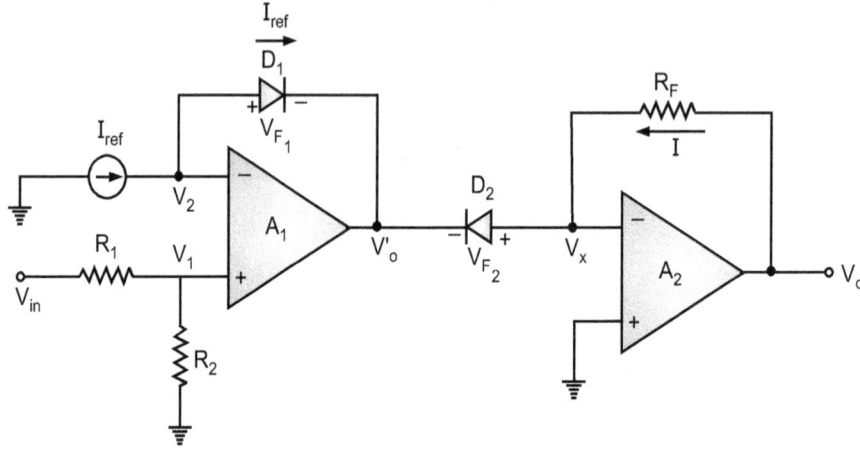

Fig. 2.113 : Temperature compensated antilog amplifier

The voltage V_2 can be calculated by using voltage divider rule.

$$V_1 = \frac{V_{in} R_2}{R_1 + R_2} \quad \ldots (2.169)$$

As the input currents of op-amp are zero, the current source I_{ref} provides the current to the diode.

$$V_o' = V_2 - V_{F1} \quad \ldots (2.170)$$

From the diode equation (b),

$$V_{F1} = \eta V_T \ln\left(\frac{I_F}{I_o}\right)$$

Therefore, V_o' becomes

$$V_o' = V_{in}\left(\frac{V_2}{R_1 + R_2}\right) - \eta V_T \ln\left(\frac{I_F}{I_o}\right)$$

For op-amp A_2, $\quad V_o' = -V_{F2} \quad \ldots (2.171)$

$$V_{F2} = \eta V_T \ln\left(\frac{I_{F2}}{I_o}\right) \quad \ldots (2.172)$$

But $\quad I_{F2} = I = \dfrac{V_o - V_x}{R_F} = \dfrac{V_o}{R_F} \quad \ldots (2.173)$

While $\quad I_{F1} = I_{ref}$

Substitute (2.172) and (2.173) in equation (2.171)

$$V_o' = -\eta V_T \ln\left(\frac{V_o}{I_o R_F}\right)$$

Now we have two equations for V_o'

$$V_{in}\left(\frac{R_2}{R_1 + R_2}\right) - \eta V_T \ln\left(\frac{I_{ref}}{I_o}\right) = -\eta V_T \ln\left(\frac{V_o}{I_o R_F}\right)$$

$$\therefore \quad V_{in}\left(\frac{R_2}{R_1 + R_2}\right) = \eta V_T\left[\ln(I_{ref}) - \ln(I_o) - \ln\left(\frac{V_o}{R_F}\right) + \ln(I_o)\right]$$

$$V_{in}\left(\frac{R_2}{R_1 + R_2}\right) = \eta V_T \ln\left(\frac{I_{ref} R_F}{V_o}\right)$$

$$V_{in}\left(\frac{R_2}{R_1 + R_2}\right) = -\eta V_T \ln\left(\frac{V_o}{I_{ref} R_F}\right)$$

$$\ln\left(\frac{V_o}{I_{ref} R_F}\right) = \frac{-V_{in} R_2}{\eta V_T (R_1 + R_2)}$$

Take antilog on both sides

$$V_o = I_{ref} R_F \ln\left[\frac{-V_{in} R_2}{\eta V_T (R_1 + R_2)}\right] \qquad \ldots (2.174)$$

Since I_o gets cancelled, but still V_T term exists in the output equation. If the input resistive divider is made temperature sensitive using thermister the effect of V_T will get cancelled.

EXERCISE

1. Explain the working of op-amp inverting amplifier. Derive the expression for its voltage gain.

2. Draw the instrumentation amplifier using three op-amps and derive the expression for output voltage.

3. Design the op-amp circuit to get the output expression as $V_0 = \frac{1}{2} V_1 + V_2 + 5V_3$.

4. Show how op-amp can be used as logarithmic amplifier and explain the function of logarithmic amplifier.

5. With suitable circuit diagram, show how op-amp can be used as log and anti-log amplifiers. Derive the expression for output voltages in both cases.

6. Show how an op-amp can be used as an integrator and a differentiator by obtaining the expression for output voltages.

7. Draw the circuit of a temperature compensated log amplifier and obtain an expression for the output voltage.
8. Write a short note on op-amp integrator.
9. Write short note on bridge amplifier.
10. Why stability compensation is required for log amplifier? How it is provided?
11. Explain with neat circuit diagram of operation of following circuits using log and antilog amplifiers: (a) Analog multiplier, (b) Analog divider.
12. Can a basic difference amplifier be used as an instrumentation amplifier? Explain
13. In an inverting adder circuit, the input voltages are 0.3 V, 0.5 V, 0.1 V while $R_1 = R_2 = R_3 = 1$ kΩ. If $R_F = 10$ kΩ, calculate the output voltage.
14. Design the practical differentiator circuit to differentiate a sine wave signal of 2 sin (2π300t), draw the output waveform.
15. Find R_1 and R_F in the lossy integrator so that the peak gain is 20 dB and the gain is 3 dB down from its peak when ω = 10000 rad/sec. use C_F = 0.01μF.
16. Explain with a suitable example, the use of analog computer setup in
    (a) implementing given equation (b) solving linear differential equation

Unit III

ACTIVE FILTERS AND VOLTAGE REGULATORS

3.1 ACTIVE FILTERS

A filter is a circuit that is designed to pass a specified band of frequencies while attenuating all the signal outside the band. It is also called as a frequency selective device.

Advantages of Active Filters :
1. Small size and weight because all components are available in integrated form.
2. Low cost.
3. Op-amp gain can be easily controlled in closed loop mode. Therefore, active filter input signal is not attenuated.
4. Tuning of the active filters is easy due to flexibility in gain and frequency adjustments.
5. Loading effect of the source or load is avoided.
6. Since inductors are not used, modern active filters are more economical.
7. Active filters can be realized under number of class of functions such as butterworth, Thomson, Chebyshev, Cauver, etc.
8. Improved frequency response compared to passive filters.
9. Design procedure is simple.

Disadvantages or Limitations of Active Filters :
1. Bandwidth is restricted upto 500 kHz, whereas the passive filters can be used upto 500 MHz.
2. Active elements are much sensitive to the temperature changes or environmental changes than passive components.
3. It requires power supply for its operation. The passive filters do not require the DC supply.

Types of Filters :

The active filters are classified into four categories :
1. Low-pass filters
2. High-pass filters
3. Band-pass filters
4. Band-reject filters.

Time domain and frequency domain analysis of active filters.

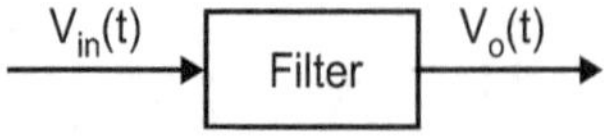

$V_{in}(t) \rightarrow \boxed{\text{Filter}} \rightarrow V_o(t)$

(a) Time domain representation

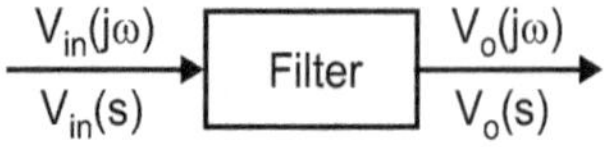

$\begin{matrix} V_{in}(j\omega) \\ V_{in}(s) \end{matrix} \rightarrow \boxed{\text{Filter}} \rightarrow \begin{matrix} V_o(j\omega) \\ V_o(s) \end{matrix}$

(b)

Fig. 3.1

$$H(S) = \frac{V_o(S)}{V_{in}(S)} \quad \ldots (3.1)$$

$$H(j\omega) = \frac{V_o(j\omega)}{V_{in}(j\omega)} \quad \ldots (3.2)$$

$$H(j\omega) = |H(j\omega)| \angle H(j\omega)$$

Thus, the magnitude of the transfer function $|H(j\omega)|$ is called the gain of the filter.

The filter in which denominator polynomial of its transfer function is a Butterworth polynomial is called a Butterworth filter.

3.1.1 First Order Low pass Butterworth Filter

Fig. 3.2 shows a first order low-pass butterworth filter that uses an RC network for filtering. Op-amp is used in the non-inverting configuration, hence there is no load on the RC network. Resistors R_1 and R_F determine the gain of the filter.

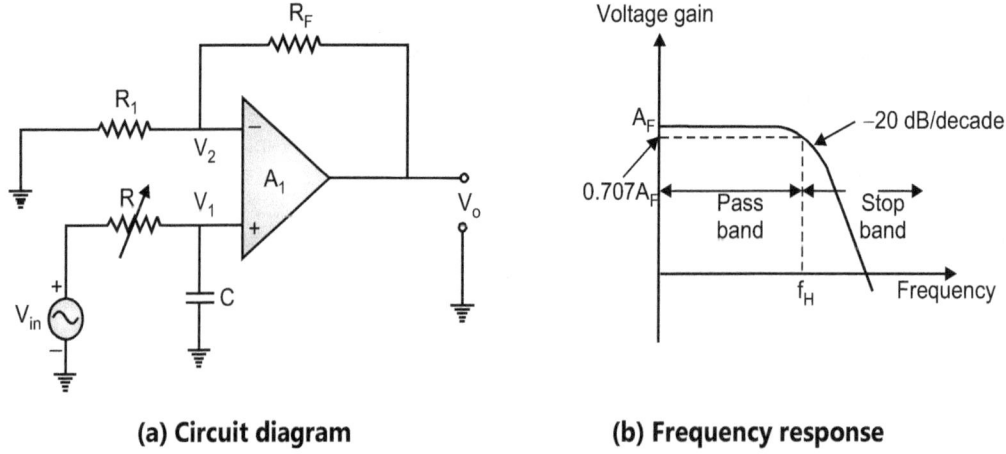

(a) Circuit diagram   (b) Frequency response

Fig. 3.2 : First order low-pass butterworth filter

According to the voltage divider rule, the voltage at the non-inverting terminal (across capacitor C) is

$$X_C = \frac{1}{2\pi fC} = -jX_C$$

$$V_1 = \frac{-jX_C}{R - jX_C} \cdot V_{in} \qquad \text{... (3.3)}$$

where, $j = \sqrt{-1}$ and $-jX_C = \frac{1}{j2\pi fC}$

$$V_1 = \frac{-j\left(\frac{1}{2\pi fC}\right)}{R - j\left(\frac{1}{2\pi fC}\right)} \cdot V_{in} = \frac{\frac{-j}{2\pi fC}}{\frac{2\pi f_R R_C - j}{2\pi fC}} \cdot V_{in}$$

$$= \frac{-j}{2\pi fC} \times \frac{2\pi fC}{2\pi f\,RC - j} \cdot V_{in}$$

$$= \frac{-j}{2\pi f\,RC - j} \cdot V_{in}$$

$$-j = \frac{1}{j} \; ; \; -\frac{1}{j} = j$$

$$V_1 = \frac{V_{in}}{1 + j\,2\pi f\,RC}$$

and output voltage, $V_O = \left(1 + \frac{R_F}{R_1}\right) V_1$

$$V_O = \left(1 + \frac{R_F}{R_1}\right) \cdot \frac{V_{in}}{1 + j\,2\pi f\,RC}$$

$$\frac{V_O}{V_{in}} = \frac{A_F}{1 + j\,(f/f_H)} \qquad \text{... (3.4)}$$

where, $\frac{V_O}{V_{in}}$ = Gain of the filter as a function of frequency

$A_F = 1 + \frac{R_F}{R_1}$ = Passband gain of the filter

f = Frequency of the input signal

$f_H = \frac{1}{2\pi RC}$ = High cut off frequency of the filter

The gain magnitude and phase angle equations are obtained by converting equation (3.3) into its polar form as follows :

$$\left|\frac{V_o}{V_{in}}\right| = \frac{A_F}{\sqrt{1 + (f/f_H)^2}} \qquad \text{... (3.5)}$$

$$\phi = -\tan^{-1}\left(\frac{f}{f_H}\right)$$

The operation of the low pass filter can be varied from the gain-magnitude equation (6.10).

(1) At very low frequencies, i.e. $f < f_H$,

$$\left|\frac{V_o}{V_{in}}\right| \cong V_F \qquad \text{... (3.6)}$$

(2) At $f = f_H$,

$$\left|\frac{V_o}{V_{in}}\right| = \frac{A_F}{\sqrt{2}} = 0.707 \, A_F \qquad \text{... (3.7)}$$

(3) At $f > f_H$,

$$\left|\frac{V_o}{V_{in}}\right| < A_F \qquad \text{... (3.8)}$$

Example 3.1 :

Design a low pass filter at a cut-off frequency of 15.9 kHz with a passband gain 1.5.

Solution :

$$f_H = 15.9 \text{ kHz}$$

Choose $\quad C = 0.001 \, \mu F$

$$f_H = \frac{1}{2\pi RC}$$

$$15.9 \times 10^3 = \frac{1}{2 \times \pi \times R \times 0.001 \times 10^{-6}}$$

$$R = 10 \text{ k}\Omega$$

For frequency scaling use 20 K pot.

$$A_F = 1.5$$

$$\therefore \quad 1.5 = 1 + \frac{R_F}{R_1}$$

$$\therefore \quad \frac{R_F}{R_1} = 1.5 - 1 = 0.5$$

$$\therefore \quad R_F = 0.5 \, R_1 \quad \text{where } R_1 = 10 \text{ k}\Omega$$

$$\therefore \quad R_F = 0.5 \times 10 \text{ k}\Omega = 5 \text{ k}\Omega$$

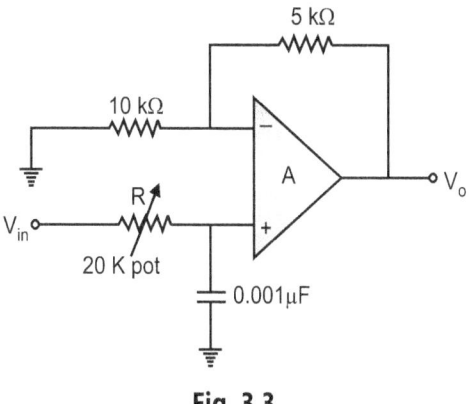

Fig. 3.3

Filter Design :

A low pass filter can be designed by implementing the following steps :
1. Choose a higher cut-off frequency value f_H.
2. Select a value of C less than or equal to 1 µF. Mylar or tantalum capacitors are recommended for better performance.
3. Calculate the value of R using

$$R = \frac{1}{2\pi f_H C}$$

4. Finally select values of R_1 and R_F dependent on the desired passband gain A_F using

$$A_F = 1 + \frac{R_F}{R_1}$$

3.1.2 Second Order Low Pass Butterworth Filter

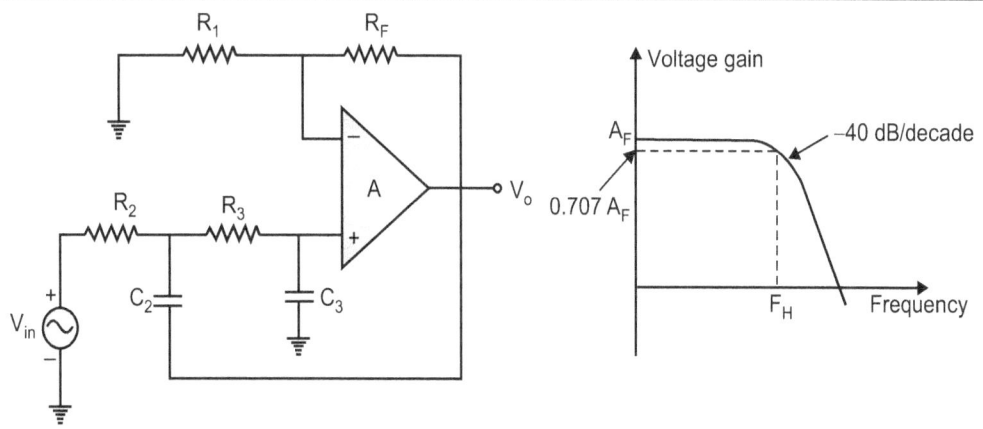

(a) Circuit diagram (b) Frequency response

Fig. 3.4 : Second order low pass butterworth filter

A stop band response having a 40 dB/decade roll-off is obtained with the second order low pass filter. A first order low pass filter can be converted into a second order type simply by using an additional RC network. The gain of the second order filter is set by R_1 and R_F, while the high cut-off frequency f_H is determined by R_2, C_2, R_3 and C_3 as follows :

For determining the expression for the cut-off frequency, replace the input RC network in Laplace domain.

Fig. 3.4 (c) : Laplace domain representation of input RC network

$$I_1 = I_2 + I_3$$

$$\frac{V_{in} - V_1}{R_2} = \frac{V_1 - V_o}{\left(\frac{1}{SC_2}\right)} + \frac{V_1 - V_2}{\left(R_3 + \frac{1}{SC_3}\right)} \quad \ldots (3.9)$$

Using potential divider rule, we can write

$$V_2 = V_1 \left(\frac{\frac{1}{SC_3}}{R_3 + \frac{1}{SC_3}}\right) = \frac{V_1}{1 + SR_3C_3}$$

$$V_1 = V_A(1 + SR_3C_3)$$

Substitute this value of V_1 in equation (3.9),

$$\frac{V_{in} - V_A(1 + SR_3C_3)}{R_2} = \frac{V_A(1 + SR_3C_3) - V_o}{\left(\frac{1}{SC_2}\right)} + \frac{V_A(1 + SR_3C_3) - V_A}{R_3 + \frac{1}{SC_3}}$$

$$\frac{V_{in}}{R_2} - \frac{V_A(1 + SR_3C_3)}{R_2} = \frac{V_A(1 + SR_3C_3)}{\left(\frac{1}{SC_2}\right)} - \frac{V_o}{\left(\frac{1}{SC_2}\right)} + \frac{V_A(1 + SR_3C_3 - 1)}{R_3 + \frac{1}{SC_3}}$$

$$\frac{V_{in}}{R_2} + \frac{V_o}{(1/SC_2)} = \frac{V_A(1 + SR_3C_3)}{(1/SC_2)} + \frac{V_A(1 + SR_3C_3)}{R_2} + \frac{V_A(SR_3C_3)}{R_3}$$

$$\frac{V_{in}}{R_2} + V_o(SC_2) = V_A\left[\frac{1 + SR_3C_3}{1/SC_2} + \frac{1 + SR_3C_3}{R_2} + \frac{1 + SR_3C_3}{R_3} - \frac{1}{R_3}\right]$$

$$\frac{V_{in}}{R_2} + V_o(SC_2) = V_A\left[\frac{R_2R_3SC_2(1 + SR_3C_3) + R_3(1 + SR_3C_3) + R_2(1 + SR_3C_3) - R_2}{R_2R_3}\right]$$

$$V_{in}R_3 + V_oSR_3R_2C_2 = V_A\left[(1 + SR_3C_3)(R_2R_3SC_2 + R_3 + R_2) - R_2\right]$$

$$(V_{in}R_3 + V_oSR_2R_3C_2) = V_A\left[(1 + SR_3C_3)(R_2R_3SC_2 + R_2 + R_3) - R_2\right]$$

$$V_2 = \frac{R_3V_{in} + SR_2R_3C_2V_o}{\left[(1 + SR_3C_3)(R_3 + R_2R_3C_2S + R_2) - R_2\right]}$$

$$V_o = A_F V_2$$

$$V_o\left[1 - \frac{SR_2R_3C_2}{(1 + SR_3C_3)(R_3 + R_2R_3C_2S + R_2) - R_2}\right] = \left[\frac{A_FR_3V_{in}}{(1 + SR_3C_3)(R_3 + R_2R_3C_2S + R_2) - R_2}\right]$$

$$A_FR_3V_{in} = V_o\left[(1 + SR_3C_3)(R_3 + R_2R_3C_2S + R_2) - R_2 - SR_2R_3C_2\right]$$

$$\frac{V_o}{V_{in}} = \frac{A_F}{S^2 + \left(\dfrac{R_3C_3 + R_2C_3 + R_2C_2 - A_FR_2C_2}{R_2R_3C_2C_3}\right)S + \dfrac{1}{R_2R_3C_2C_3}}$$

$$\frac{V_o}{V_{in}} = \frac{A}{S^2 + 2\xi\omega_n S + \omega_n^2} \qquad \text{... (3.10)}$$

A = Overall gain
ξ = Damping of system
ω_n = Natural frequency of oscillation

$$\omega_n^2 = \frac{1}{R_2R_3C_2C_3}$$

$$(2\pi f_H)^2 = \frac{1}{R_2R_3C_2C_3}$$

$$f_H = \frac{1}{2\pi\sqrt{R_2R_3C_2C_3}}$$

$$\frac{V_o}{V_{in}} = \frac{A_F}{\sqrt{1 + (f/f_H)^4}} \qquad \text{... (3.11)}$$

Filter Design :

The design steps of the second order filter are identical to those of the first order filter as follows :

1. Choose a value for the high cut-off frequency f_H.
2. To simplify the design calculations, set $R_2 = R_3 = R$ and $C_2 = C_3 = C$. Then choose value of $C \leq 1$ µF.
3. Calculate the value of R using equation

$$R = \frac{1}{2\pi f_H C}$$

4. Finally, because of equal resistor ($R_2 = R_3$) and capacitor ($C_2 = C_3$) values, the passband voltage gain $A_F = \left(1 + \dfrac{R_F}{R_1}\right)$ of the second order low-pass filter has to be equal to 1.586. That is $R_F = 0.586\, R_1$. Hence, choose a value of $R_1 \leq 100\ k\Omega$ and calculate the value of R_F.

Example 3.2 :

Design a second order low-pass filter at a high cut-off frequency of 1 kHz.

Solution :

To design the second order low-pass filter, simply follow the steps just mentioned above.

1. $f_H = 1\ kHz$
2. Let $C_2 = C_3 = 0.0047\ \mu F$
3. Then $R_2 = R_3 = \dfrac{1}{(2\pi)(10^3)(47)(10^{-10})} = 33.86\ k\Omega$

   (Use $R_2 = R_3 = 33\ k\Omega$)
4. Since, R_F must be equal to $0.586\, R_1$, let $R_1 = 27\ k\Omega$.

   $\therefore \quad R_F = (0.586)(27\ k\Omega) = 15.82\ k\Omega$

   (Use $R_F = 20\ k\Omega$ pot)

   $R_2 = R_3 = 33\ k\Omega$
   $C_2 = C_3 = 0.0047\ \mu F$
   $R_1 = 27\ k\Omega$ and $R_F = 15.8\ k\Omega$ (20 kΩ pot)

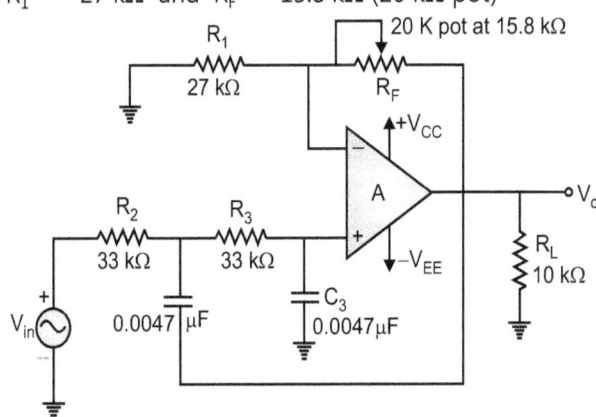

Fig. 3.5

3.1.3 First Order High Pass Butterworth Filter

First order high pass filter is formed from a first order low pass type by interchanging components R and C. Fig. 3.6 shows a first order high pass Butterworth filter with a low cut-off frequency of f_L. All frequencies higher than f_L are passband frequencies.

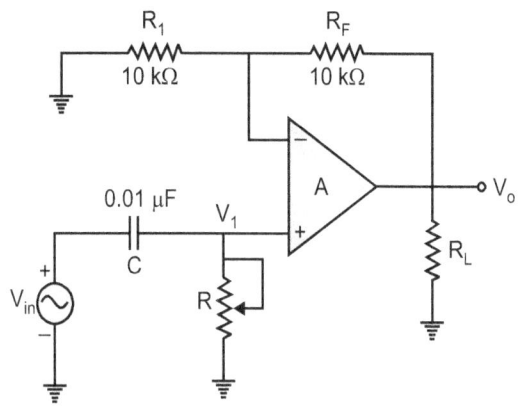
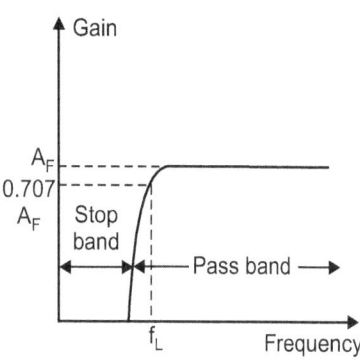

(a) First order high pass Butterworth filter

(b) Its frequency response

Fig. 3.6

By the voltage divider rule,

$$V_1 = V_{in} \cdot \frac{R}{R - jX_C}$$

$$= V_{in} \cdot \left[\frac{R}{-jX_C\left(1 + \frac{R}{-jX_C}\right)}\right]$$

$$-\frac{1}{j} = j$$

$$\frac{1}{-jX_C} = \frac{j}{X_C} = \frac{j}{\left(\frac{1}{2\pi fC}\right)} = j2\pi fC$$

$$\therefore \quad V_1 = V_{in}\left[\frac{R/-jX_C}{1 + \frac{R}{-jX_C}}\right]$$

$$= V_{in}\left[\frac{j2\pi fRC}{1 + j2\pi fRC}\right]$$

This can be represented as

$$V_1 = V_{in}\left[\frac{j(f/f_L)}{1 + j(f/f_L)}\right]$$

where, $\quad f_L = \dfrac{1}{2\pi RC}$

The output voltage is

$$V_o = \left(1 + \frac{R_F}{R_1}\right) V_1$$

$$= \left(1 + \frac{R_F}{R_1}\right) V_{in} \left[\frac{j(f/f_L)}{1 + j(f/f_L)}\right]$$

$$\frac{V_o}{V_{in}} = A_F \left[\frac{j(f/f_L)}{1 + j(f/f_L)}\right] \quad \ldots (3.12)$$

where,

$$A_F = 1 + \frac{R_F}{R_1} = \text{Passband gain of the filter}$$

$$f = \text{Frequency of the input signal (Hz)}$$

$$f_L = \frac{1}{2\pi RC} = \text{Low cut-off frequency (Hz)}$$

Hence, the magnitude of the voltage gain is

$$\left|\frac{V_o}{V_{in}}\right| = \frac{A_F (f/f_L)}{\sqrt{1 + (f/f_L)^2}} \quad \ldots (3.13)$$

(1) So at low frequencies, $f < f_L$

$$\left|\frac{V_o}{V_{in}}\right| < A_F \quad \ldots (3.14)$$

(2) At $f = f_L$,

$$\left|\frac{V_o}{V_{in}}\right| = 0.707 \, A_F \quad \ldots (3.15)$$

(3) At $f > f_L$,

$$\left|\frac{V_o}{V_{in}}\right| \cong A_F \quad \ldots (3.16)$$

At high frequencies, 1 can be neglected as compared to (f/f_L) from denominator.

Example 3.3 :

Design a high-pass filter with a cut-off frequency of 10 kHz with a passband gain of 1.5. Also plot the frequency response for the designed filter.

Solution :

Given : $f_L = 10 \text{ kHz}$

Choose C less than 1 µF

$$C = 0.02 \, \mu F$$

Calculate R.

$$f_L = \frac{1}{2\pi RC}$$

$$\therefore \quad 10 \times 10^3 = \frac{1}{2\pi R \times 0.02 \times 10^{-6}}$$

$$\therefore \quad R = 795.77\ \Omega$$

For frequency scaling use a pot of 1 kΩ.

$$A_F = 1.5$$

$$1 + \frac{R_F}{R_1} = 1.5$$

$$\therefore \quad \frac{R_F}{R_1} = 0.5$$

$$\therefore \quad R_F = 0.5\ R_1$$

Select $R_1 = 10\ k\Omega$

$$\therefore \quad R_F = 5\ k\Omega$$

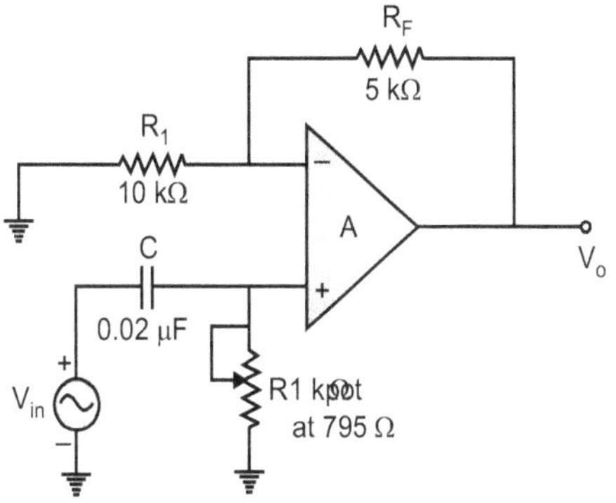

Fig. 3.7

3.1.4 Second Order High-pass Butterworth Filter

The analysis, design and the scaling procedure for this filter is exactly same as that of second order low pass butterworth filter.

$$\left|\frac{V_o}{V_{in}}\right| = \frac{A_F}{\sqrt{1 + (f_L/f)^4}} \qquad ...(3.17)$$

$$f_L = \frac{1}{2\pi\sqrt{R_2 R_3 C_2 C_3}}$$

$$A_F = 1.586$$

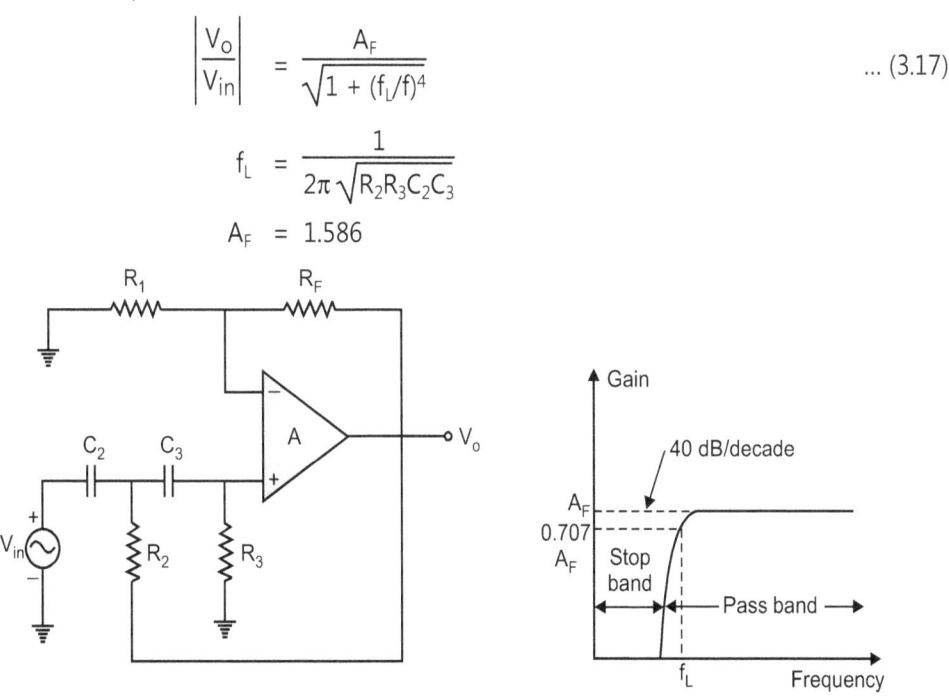

(a) Circuit diagram (b) Frequency response

Fig. 3.8 : Second order high-pass Butterworth filter

Butterworth Approximations :

η	Polynomials
1	(S + 1)
2	$S^2 + \sqrt{2}\,S + 1$
3	$(S^2 + S + 1)(S + 1)$
4	$(S^2 + 0.76536\,S + 1)(S^2 + 1.84776\,S + 1)$
5	$(S + 1)(S^2 + 0.6180\,S + 1)(S^2 + 1.6180\,S + 1)$
6	$(S^2 + 0.5176\,S + 1)(S^2 + \sqrt{2}\,S + 1)(S^2 + 1.6180\,S + 1)$
7	$(S + 1)(S^2 + 0.4450\,S + 1)(S^2 + 1.2456\,S + 1)(S^2 + 1.8022\,S + 1)$

Example 3.4 :

Design a fourth order butterworth low pass filter having upper cut-off frequency 1 kHz.

Solution :

$$f_H = 1\text{ kHz} = \frac{1}{2\pi RC}$$

Let $C = 0.1\ \mu F$, $R = 1.6\ k\Omega$

For n = 4, we get 2 damping factors namely $\alpha_1 = 0.765$, $\alpha_2 = 1.848$

$$A_{O_1} = 3 - \alpha_1 = 3 - 0.765 = 2.235$$

$$A_{O_2} = 3 - \alpha_2 = 3 - 1.848 = 1.152$$

The transfer function of the fourth order butterworth filter is

$$\frac{2.235}{S^2 + 0.765\,S + 1} \cdot \frac{1.152}{S^2 + 1.848\,S + 1}$$

Now,

$$A_{O_1} = 1 + \frac{R_{F_1}}{R_1} = 2.235$$

$$\frac{R_{F_1}}{R_1} = 1.235$$

$$R_1 = 10\ k\Omega,\quad R_{F_1} = 12.35\ k\Omega$$

$$A_{O_2} = 1 + \frac{R_{F_2}}{R_2} = 1.152$$

$$R_2 = 100\ k\Omega,\quad R_{F_2} = 0.152 \times 100\ k\Omega = 15.2\ k\Omega$$

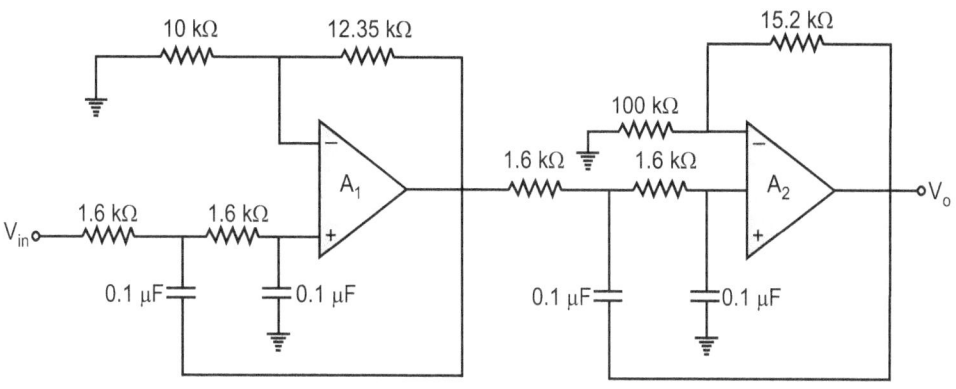

Fig. 3.9

3.1.5 Band-Pass Filters

A band-pass filter has a passband between two cut-off frequencies f_H and f_L such that $f_H > f_L$. Any input frequency outside this passband is attenuated. Basically, there are two types of band-pass filters : (1) Wide band-pass filter, (2) Narrow band-pass filters.

Filters are divided as wide band-pass if its figure of merit or quality factor Q < 10. When Q > 10, then the filter is called as narrow band-pass filter. Q is the measure of selectivity, more the value of Q, the more selective is the filter or narrower is its bandwidth (BW).

$$Q = \frac{f_C}{BW} = \frac{f_C}{f_H - f_L}$$

For wide band-pass filter the centre frequency f_C can be defined as

$$f_C = \sqrt{f_H f_L}$$

where, f_H = High cut-off frequency (Hz)

f_L = Low cut-off frequency of the wide band filter (Hz)

3.1.5.1 Wide Band-Pass Filter

A wide band-pass filter can be formed by simply cascading high-pass and low-pass sections and is generally the choice for simplicity of design and performance.

To obtain a ± 20 dB/decade band-pass, first order high pass and first order low pass sections are cascaded. Fig. 3.10 shows the ± 20 dB/decade wide band-pass filter which is composed of first order high-pass and first order low-pass filters. To obtain a band-pass response f_H must be larger than f_L.

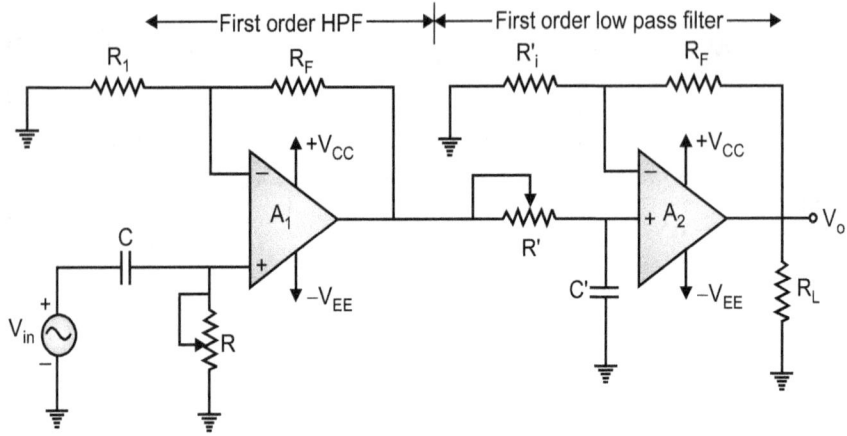

(a) ± 20 dB/decade wide band-pass filter

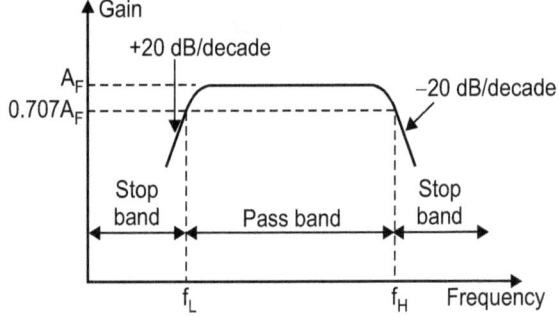

(b) Its frequency response

Fig. 3.10

$$\left|\frac{V_o}{V_{in}}\right| = \frac{A_F}{\sqrt{1 + (f/f_H)^2}} \quad \text{for low pass}$$

$$\left|\frac{V_o}{V_{in}}\right| = \frac{A_F (f/f_L)}{\sqrt{1 + (f/f_L)^2}} \quad \text{for high pass}$$

As the two circuits are in cascade, the overall gain of wide band-pass filter is the product of the two gains.

$$\left|\frac{V_o}{V_{in}}\right| = \frac{A_{F_T} (f/f_L)}{\sqrt{[1 + (f/f_L)^2][1 + (f/f_H)^2]}} \quad \ldots (3.18)$$

where, $A_{F_T} = A_1 A_2$

Example 3.5 :

Design a wide band-pass filter with f_L = 200 Hz, f_H = 1 kHz, and a pass band gain of 4.

(a) Draw the frequency response plot of this filter.

(b) Calculate the value of Q for the filter.

Solution :

(1) Design the low pass filter.

$$f_H = 1 \text{ kHz}$$

Let $\quad C = 0.01 \text{ }\mu F$

$$f_H = \frac{1}{2\pi R'C'}$$

$$R' = \frac{1}{2\pi \times 1 \times 10^3 \times 0.01 \times 10^{-6}} = 15.9 \text{ k}\Omega$$

(2) Design the high pass filter.

$$f_L = 200 \text{ Hz}$$

$$C = 0.05 \text{ }\mu F$$

$$R = \frac{1}{2\pi f_L C} = \frac{1}{2\pi \times (200) \times 5 \times 10^{-8}}$$

$$= 15.9 \text{ k}\Omega$$

$$A_{F_T} = A_1 A_2$$

$$A_1 A_2 = 2$$

$$A_1 = A_2 = 1 + \frac{R_F}{R_1} = 2$$

$$\therefore \quad \frac{R_F}{R_1} = 1$$

Select $R_F = R_1 = 10 \text{ k}\Omega$

$$f_C = \sqrt{f_H f_L} = \sqrt{1 \times 10^3 \times 200} = 447.2 \text{ Hz}$$

$$BW = f_H - f_L = 1000 - 200 = 800 \text{ Hz}$$

$$Q = \frac{f_C}{BW} = \frac{447.2}{1000 - 200} = 0.56$$

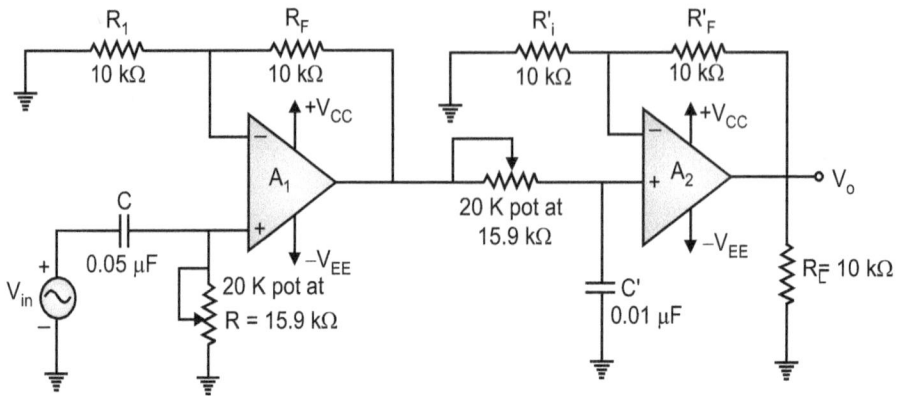

Fig. 3.11

3.1.5.2 Narrow Band-Pass Filter

This filter is unique as it has two feedback paths. Hence, it is called as multiple-feedback filter.

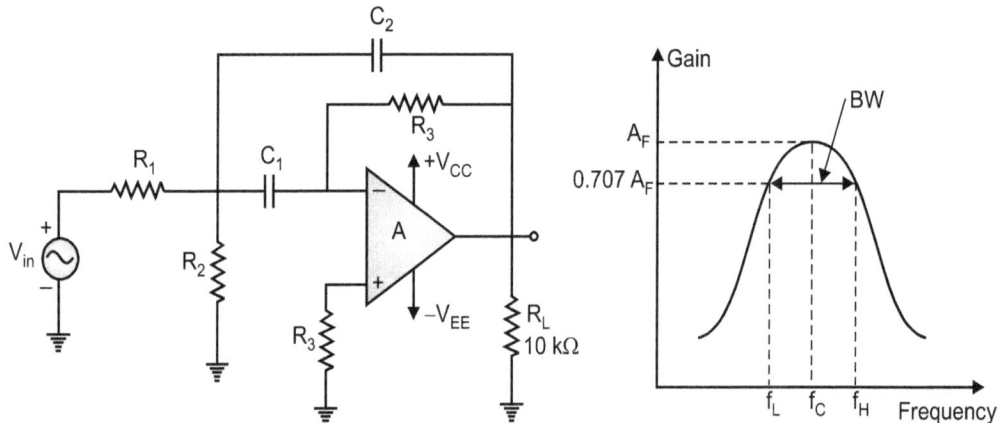

(a) Multiple feedback narrow band-pass filter   **(b) Its frequency response**

Fig. 3.12

Generally, the narrow band-pass filter is designed for specific values of centre frequency f_C and Q or f_C and bandwidth. The circuit components are determined from the following relationships.

Choose $\quad C_1 = C_2 = C$

$$R_1 = \frac{Q}{2\pi f_C \, C A_F} \qquad \ldots (3.19)$$

$$R_2 = \frac{Q}{2\pi f_C \, C \, (2Q^2 - A_F)} \qquad \ldots (3.20)$$

$$R_3 = \frac{Q}{\pi f_C \, C} \qquad \ldots (3.21)$$

where A_F is the gain at f_C given by

$$A_F = \frac{R_3}{2R_1} \qquad \ldots (3.22)$$

The gain A_F, must satisfy the condition

$$A_F < 2Q^2$$

The advantage of multiple feedback filter is that its centre frequency f_C can be changed to a new frequency f'_C without changing gain or bandwidth.

$$R'_2 = R_2 \left(\frac{f_C}{f'_C}\right)^2 \qquad \ldots (3.23)$$

Example 3.6 :

Design the narrow band-pass filter with two feedback paths with f_C = 1.5 kHz, Q = 7 and A_F = 15. Calculate the new value of resistance in the circuit which will change f_C to 2 kHz.

Solution :

Choose $\quad C_1 = C_2 = 0.02\ \mu F$

$$R_1 = \frac{Q}{2\pi f_C\, CA_F} = \frac{7}{2\pi \times 1.5 \times 10^3 \times 0.02 \times 10^{-6} \times 15} = 2.47\ k\Omega$$

$$R_2 = \frac{Q}{2\pi f_C\, C\, (2Q^2 - A_F)}$$

$$= \frac{1}{2\pi \times 1.5 \times 10^3 \times 0.02 \times 10^{-6}\, (2 \times 7^2 - 15)} = 447.4\ \Omega$$

$$R_3 = \frac{Q}{\pi f_C \cdot C} = \frac{7}{\pi \times 1.5 \times 10^3 \times 0.02 \times 10^{-6}}$$

$$= 74.27\ k\Omega$$

The resistance R_2 can be changed to get R'_2

$$f_C = 2\ kHz$$

$$R'_2 = R_2 \left(\frac{f_C}{f'_C}\right) = 447.4 \times \left(\frac{1.5}{2}\right)^2 = 251.66\ \Omega$$

3.1.6 Band-Reject Filters

The band-reject filter is also called a band-stop or band-elimination filter. Band-reject filter rejects the frequencies in the stop band, while other frequencies are passed.

Depending upon Q factor the band-reject filters are divided into two categories :
1. Wide band-reject filter,
2. Narrow band-reject filter or notch filter.

Because of high Q factor i.e. Q > 10, the bandwidth of the narrow band-reject filter is much smaller than that of the wide band-reject filter.

3.1.6.1 Wide Band-Reject Filter

Fig. 3.13 shows the wide band-reject filter using a low pass filter, a high pass filter and a summing amplifier. To realize a band-reject response, the low cut-off frequency f_L of the high pass filter must be larger than the high cut-off frequency f_H of the low pass filter. The passband gain of both the high pass and low pass sections must be equal.

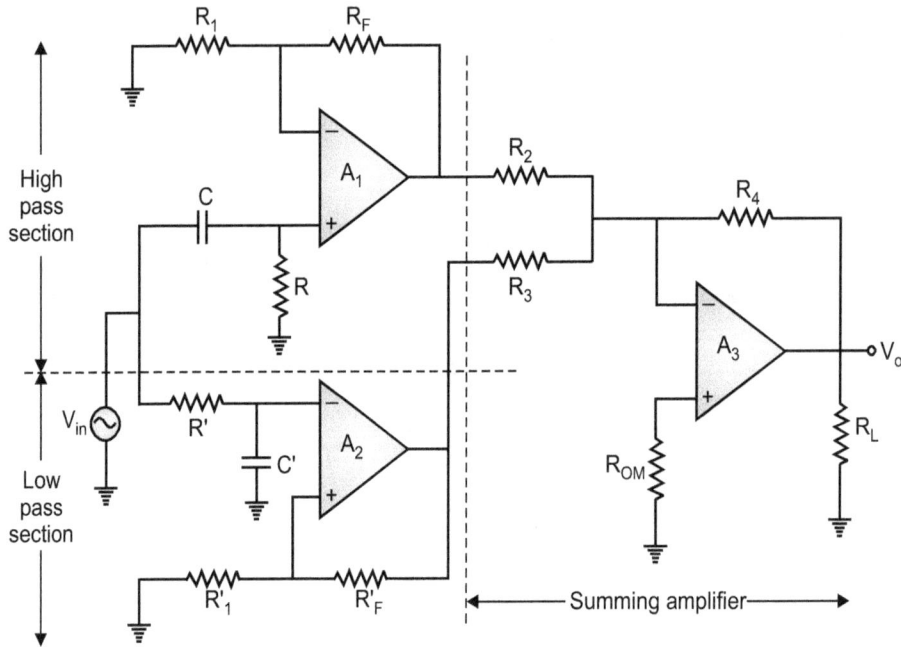

(a) Circuit diagram

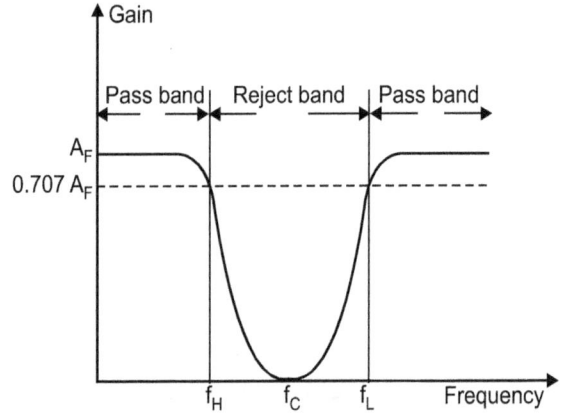

(b) Frequency response

Fig. 3.13 : Wide band-reject filter

Here $R_2 = R_3 = R_4$

$$R_{OM} = R_2 \| R_3 \| R_4 = \frac{R}{3}$$

$$f_C = \sqrt{f_L \cdot f_H} \qquad \ldots (3.24)$$

Example 3.7 :

Design a wide band-reject filter having $f_H = 200$ Hz and $f_L = 1$ kHz. Assume suitable data.

Solution :

$$f_H = 200 \text{ Hz} \text{ and } f_L = 1 \text{ kHz}$$

Assume $A_F = 2$ for both sections.

For high pass section, $f_L = 1$ kHz

Choose $C = 0.01 \, \mu F$

Now, $f_L = \dfrac{1}{2\pi RC}$

$$R = \frac{1}{2\pi f_L C}$$

$$= \frac{1}{2\pi \times 1000 \times 0.01 \times 10^{-6}}$$

$$= 15.91 \text{ k}\Omega$$

For low pass section, $f_H = 200$ Hz

Choose $C' = 0.05 \, \mu F$

Now, $f_H = \dfrac{1}{2\pi R'C'}$

$$R' = \frac{1}{2\pi f_H C'} = \frac{1}{2\pi \times 200 \times 0.05 \times 10^{-6}}$$

$$= 15.9 \text{ k}\Omega$$

$$A_F = 1 + \frac{R_F}{R_1} = 2$$

Choose $R_F = R_1 = 10 \text{ k}\Omega$

For summing amplifier let gain be 1.

∴ $R_2 = R_3 = R_4 = 10 \text{ k}\Omega$

and $R_{OM} = \dfrac{R}{3} = \dfrac{10}{3} = 3.33 \text{ k}\Omega$

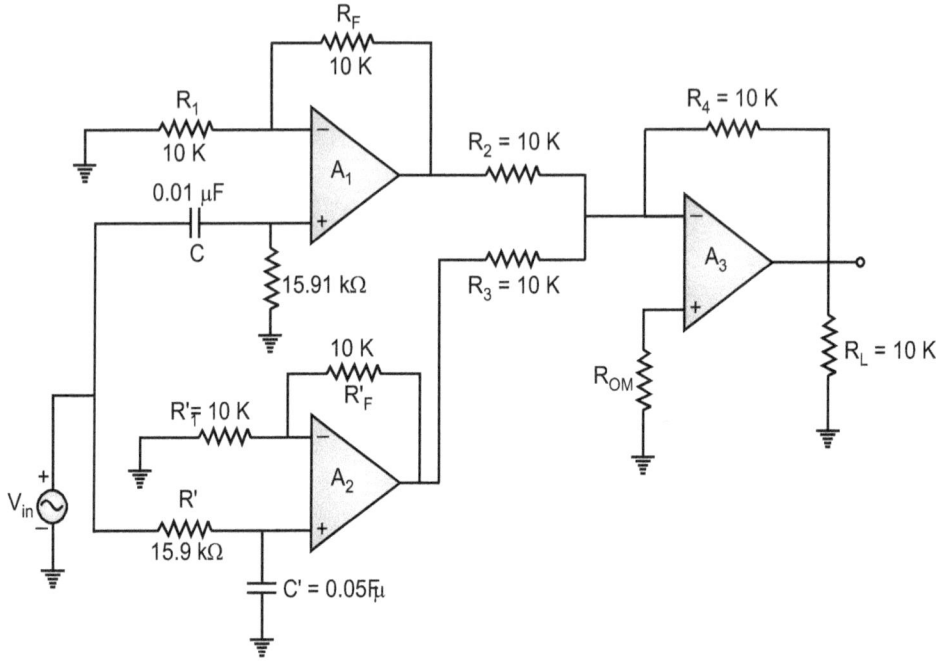

Fig. 3.14

3.1.6.2 Narrow Band-Reject Filter

The narrow band-reject filter often called as Notch filter, is commonly used for a rejection of a single frequency such as 60 Hz power line frequency hum. The most commonly used notch filter is the twin-T network as shown in Fig. 3.15 (a).

This is a pass filter composed of two T-shaped networks. One T-network is made up of two resistors and a capacitor, while the other uses two capacitors and a resistor.

The notch frequency is the frequency at which maximum attenuation occurs and it is given as

$$F_N = \frac{1}{2\pi RC}$$

(a) Twin-T notch filter

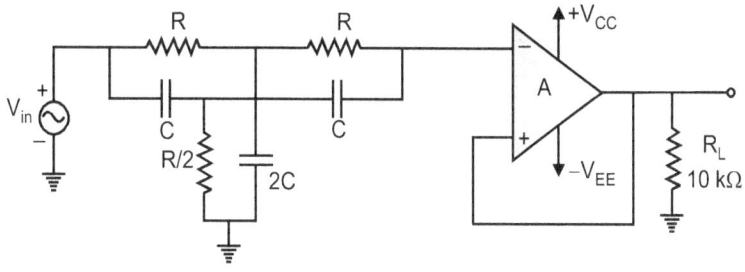

(b) Active notch filter

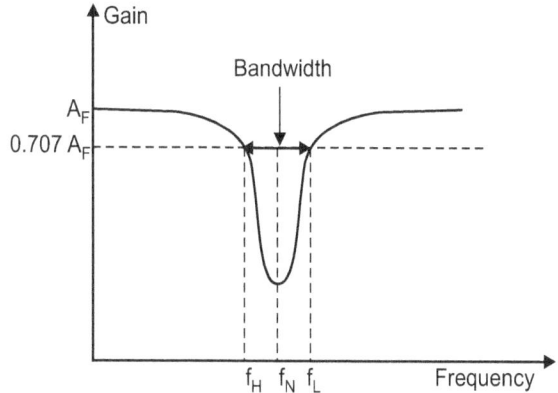

(c) Frequency response of the active notch filter

Fig. 3.15

Q-factor for the passive network is very low, hence two networks are preferred. The Q of the network can be increased significantly if it is used with the voltage follower. The frequency response of the active notch filter is shown in Fig. 3.15 (c).

To design an active notch filter for a specific notch out frequency f_N, choose the value of $C \leq 1$ µF and then calculate the required value of R.

3.1.6.3 Second Order Notch Filter

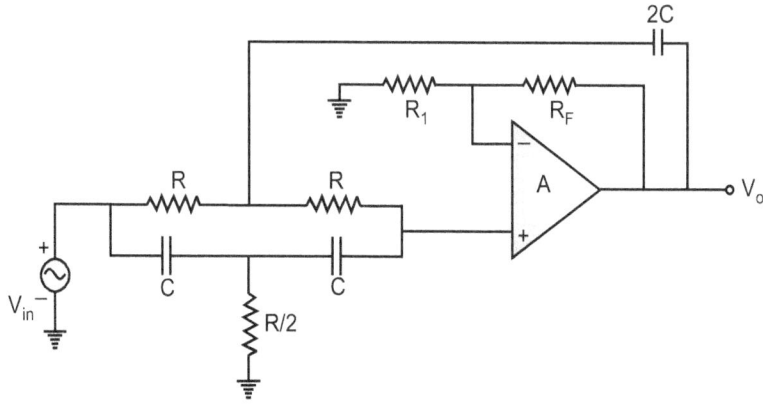

Fig. 3.16 : Second order notch filter

To improve the frequency response, second order notch filter is used. The transfer function of this circuit is given as :

$$\frac{V_o}{V_{in}} = \frac{1 + (f/f_N)^2}{1 - (f/f_n)^2 + \left(\frac{1}{Q}\right) j \, (f/f_n)} \quad \text{... (3.25)}$$

$$f_N = \frac{1}{2\pi RC} \quad \text{... (3.26)}$$

$$Q = \frac{1}{2(2 - A_F)} \quad \text{... (3.27)}$$

$$A_F = 1 + \frac{R_F}{R_1} \quad \text{... (3.28)}$$

To obtain stability A_F must be less than 2.

3.1.7 Low Pass Sallen-Key Filters or KRC Filters

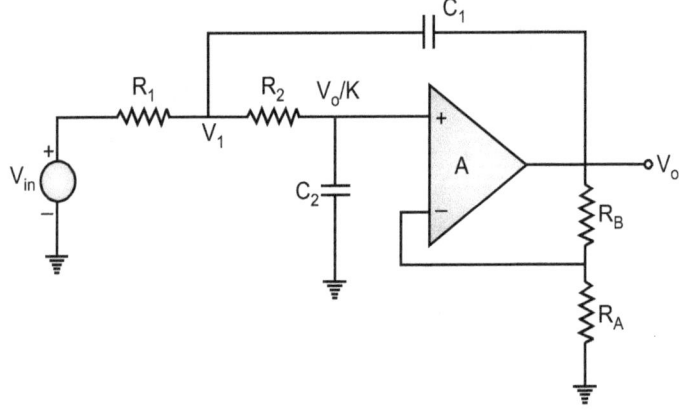

Fig. 3.17 : Low pass KRC filter

In Fig. 3.17 the gain block is implemented with an op-amp operating as a non-inverting amplifier.

$$K = 1 + \frac{R_B}{R_A} \quad \text{... (3.29)}$$

Output is taken from the output node of the op-amp.

$$V_o = K \frac{1}{R_2 C_2 S + 1} V_1 \quad \text{... (3.30)}$$

Summing currents at node V_1,

$$\frac{V_{in} - V_1}{R_1} + \frac{V_o/K - V_1}{R_2} + \frac{V_o - V_1}{1/C_1 S} = 0$$

Eliminating V_1 and collecting, we get

$$H(S) = \frac{V_o}{V_{in}} = \frac{K}{R_1C_1R_2C_2S^2 + [(1-K)R_1C_1 + R_1C_2 + R_2C_2]S + 1}$$

Put $S = j\omega$ ... (3.31)

$$H(j\omega) = K\frac{1}{1 - \omega^2 R_1C_1R_2C_2 + j\omega[(1-K)R_1C_1 + R_1C_2 + R_2C_2]}$$

Put this function in the standard form

$$H(j\omega) = H_{OLP} H_{LP}(j\omega) \qquad \ldots (3.32)$$

Equate the coefficients pairwise.

By observation, $\quad H_{OLP} = K \qquad \ldots (3.33)$

Let $\quad \omega^2 R_1C_1R_2C_2 = (\omega/\omega_o)^2$ gives

$$\omega_o = \frac{1}{\sqrt{R_1C_1R_2C_2}} \qquad \ldots (3.34)$$

Indicating that ω_o is the geometric mean of the individual stage frequency

$$\omega_1 = \frac{1}{R_1C_1} \text{ and } \omega_2 = \frac{1}{R_2C_2}$$

Finally, letting $j\omega[(1-K)R_1C_1 + R_1C_2 + R_2C_2] = (j\omega/\omega_o)/Q$ gives

$$Q = \frac{1}{(1-K)\sqrt{R_1C_1/R_2C_2} + \sqrt{R_1C_2/R_2C_1} + \sqrt{R_2C_2/R_1C_1}} \qquad \ldots (3.35)$$

Observe that K and Q depend on component ratios, while ω_o depends on component products.

Two common designs are the equal component and the unity gain designs.

3.1.7.1 Equal Component KRC Circuit

Using $R_1 = R_2 = R$ and $C_1 = C_2 = C$,

$$H_{OLP} = K, \quad \omega_o = \frac{1}{RC}, \quad Q = \frac{1}{3-K} \qquad \ldots (3.36)$$

The design equations are then

$$RC = \frac{1}{\omega_o}, \quad K = \frac{3-1}{Q}, \quad R_B = (K-1)R_A \qquad \ldots (3.37)$$

3.1.7.2 Unity-Gain KRC Circuit

Imposing K = 1 minimizes the number of components and also maximizes the bandwidth of the op-amp.

To simplify put $R_2 = R$, $C_2 = C$, $R_1 = mR$ and $C_1 = nC$.

$$H_{OLP} = \frac{1\,V}{V}, \quad \omega_o = \frac{1}{\sqrt{mn}\,RC}, \quad Q = \frac{\sqrt{mn}}{m+1} \qquad \ldots (3.38)$$

For a given n, Q is maximized when m = 1 i.e. when the resistances are equal. with m = 1, n = $4Q^2$.

3.1.8 High Pass KRC Filters

Interchanging the components of a low pass R-C stage with each other a high pass C-R stage can be obtained.

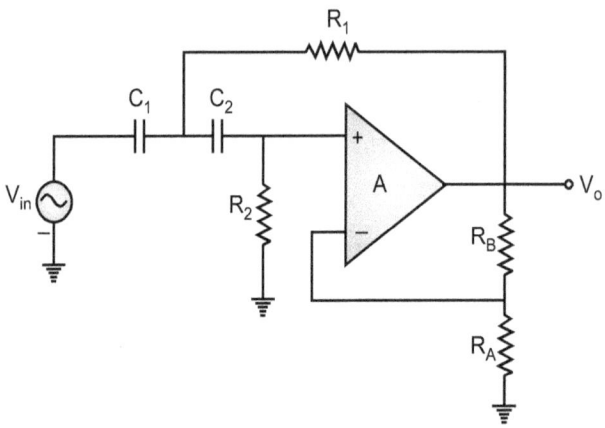

Fig. 3.18 : High pass KRC filter

$$\frac{V_o}{V_i} = H_{OHP}\, H_{HP} \qquad \ldots (3.39)$$

$$H_{OHP} = K, \quad \omega_o = \frac{1}{\sqrt{R_1 C_1 R_2 C_2}} \qquad \ldots (3.40)$$

$$Q = \frac{1}{(1-K)\sqrt{R_2 C_2 / R_1 C_1} + \sqrt{R_1 C_2 / R_2 C_1} + \sqrt{R_1 C_1 / R_1 C_2}} \qquad \ldots (3.41)$$

3.1.9 Band-pass KRC Filters

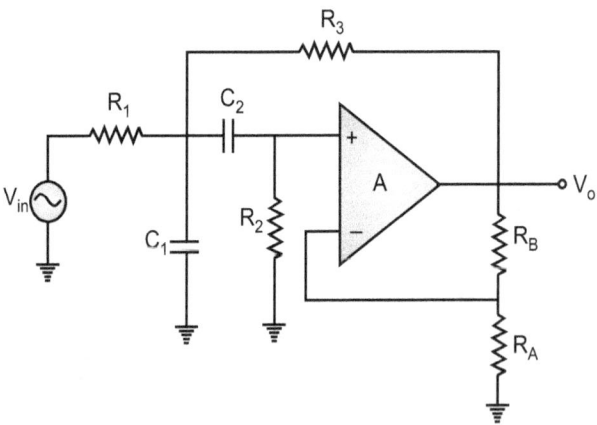

Fig. 3.19 : Band pass KRC filters

The circuit shown in Fig. 3.19 consists of an R-C stage followed by a C-R stage to synthesize a band-pass block and a gain block to provide positive feedback via R_3. This feedback is designed to bolster the response near $\omega/\omega_o = 1$.

$$\frac{V_o}{V_{in}} = H_{OBP} H_{BP} \quad \ldots (3.42)$$

$$H_{OBP} = \frac{K}{1 + (1-K) R_1/R_3 + (1+ C_1/C_2) R_1/R_2} \quad \ldots (3.43)$$

$$\omega_o = \frac{\sqrt{1 + R_1/R_3}}{\sqrt{R_1 C_1 R_2 C_2}} \quad \ldots (3.44)$$

$$Q = \frac{\sqrt{1 + R_1/R_3}}{[1 + (1-K) R_1/R_3] \sqrt{R_2 C_2/R_1 C_1} + \sqrt{R_1 C_2/R_2 C_1} + \sqrt{R_1 C_1/R_2 C_2}} \quad \ldots (3.45)$$

If $Q = 7\sqrt{2}/3$ then $R_1 = R_2 = R_3 = R$ and $C_1 = C_2 = C$.

$$H_{OBP} = \frac{K}{4-K}, \quad \omega_o = \frac{\sqrt{2}}{RC}, \quad Q = \frac{\sqrt{2}}{4-K} \quad \ldots (3.46)$$

The corresponding design equations are

$$RC = \sqrt{2}/\omega_o, \quad K = 4 - \sqrt{2}/Q, \quad R_B = (K-1) R_A \quad \ldots (3.47)$$

3.1.10 Band-Reject KRC Filter

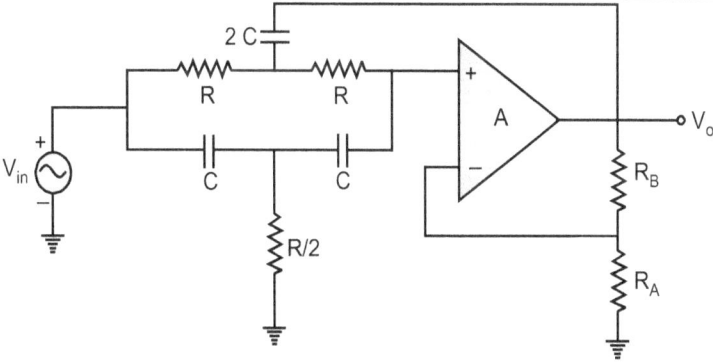

Fig. 3.20 : Band-reject KRC filter

The circuit shown in Fig. 3.20 consists of a twin-T-network and a gain block to provide positive feedback via the top capacitance. The T-network provides alternative forward paths through which V_{in} can reach the amplifier's input; the low-frequency path R-R and the high frequency path C-C, indicating $H \to K$ at the frequency extremes.

The AC analysis of the circuit gives $V_o/V_i = H_{ON} H_N$, where H_N is given as

$$H_{ON} = K, \quad \omega_o = \frac{1}{RC}, \quad Q = \frac{1}{4 - 2K} \quad \ldots (3.48)$$

3.2 TYPES OF VOLTAGE REGULATORS

Regulators are basically classified depending upon where the control element is connected in the regulator circuit.

1. Series voltage regulator. 2. Shun voltage regulator.

3.2.1 Series Voltage Regulator

It the control element is connected in series with the load, then the voltage regulator is called series voltage regulator circuit. Fig. 3.21 shows the block diagram of series voltage regulator circuit.

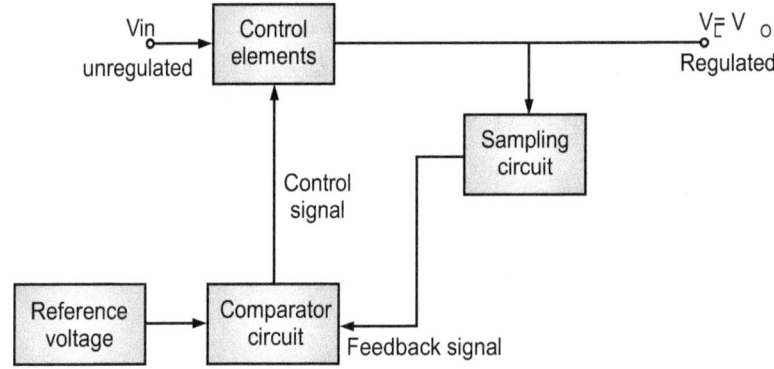

Fig. 3.21 : Block diagram of series voltage regulator

Input to the circuit is unregulated d.c. voltage. The control element controls the input voltage. The sampling circuit provides the necessary feedback signal. Comparator compares the feedback with the reference voltage to generate the appropriate control signal.

3.2.1.1 Series Regulator Using op-amp

Fig. 3.22 shows the series regulator using op-amp. Here the op-amp acts as a comparator to compare the output from the potential divider which gives the feedback signal with reference voltage generated by the zener diode. Thus, the output of comparator drives the transistor Q_1 which acts as a control element.

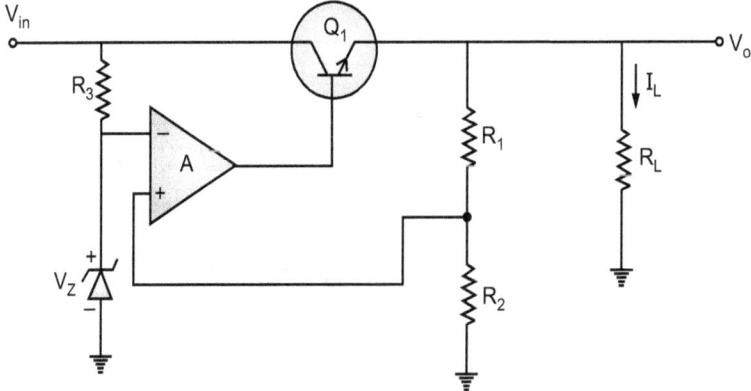

Fig. 3.22 : Series regulator using op-amp

If the output changes, the control element i.e. transistor conduction is controlled by the control signal from op-amp.

The output voltage can be obtained as

$$V_o = \left(1 + \frac{R_L}{R_2}\right) V_z \qquad ...(3.49)$$

3.2.2 Shunt Voltage Regulator

If the control element is connected in parallel with the load, the type of regulator is called as shunt voltage regulator. Fig. 3.23 shows the block diagram of shunt voltage regulator.

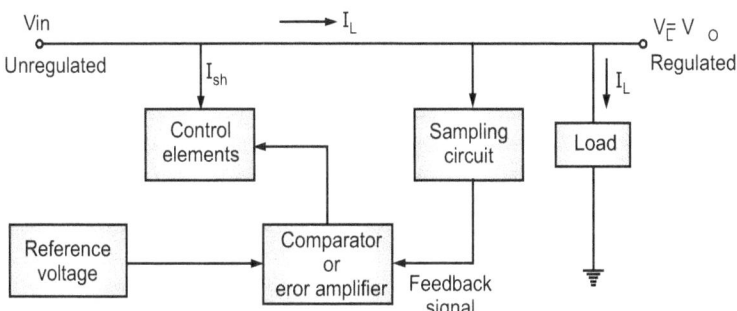

Fig. 3.23 : Black diagram of shunt voltage regulator

The unregulated supply is given as input. It supplies the load current but the part of the load current is drawn by the control element to provide constant voltage at the output load. If the load voltage changes, the sampling circuit gives the feedback signal to the comparator. Comparator compares the feedback signal with the reference voltage. It gives the control signal to the control element. Thus, the output gets controlled or remains constant.

3.2.2.1 Shunt Regulator Using op-amp

The comparator circuit used in the block diagram of shunt regulator is nothing but the op-amp. Fig. 3.24 shows the shunt regulator using op-amp.

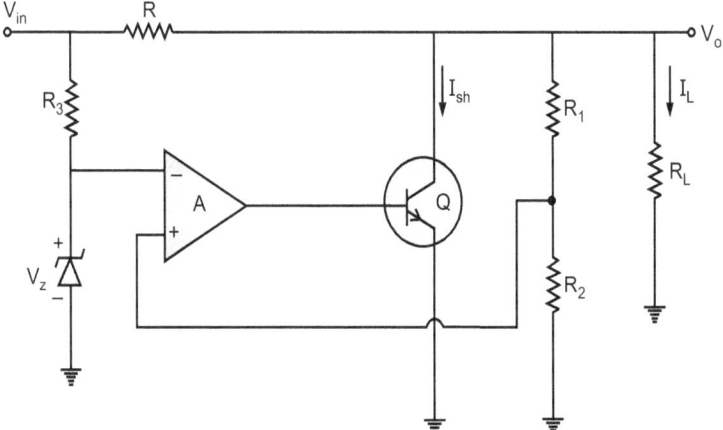

Fig. 3.24 : Shunt regulator using op-amp

The feedback signal given to the comparator is obtained using potential divider formed by R_1 and R_2. The op-amp compares the feedback signal with the reference signal generated by R_3 and zener diode. The current through resistance R is controlled by dropping the voltage across R. Thus, the output remains constant.

The shunt regulator suffers from the limitations such as
1. Limitation in supply of maximum load current.
2. Wastage of power in zener diode and R.
2. Poor stability.

3.3 IC μA 723 VOLTAGE REGULATOR

The μA 723 is a precision integrated-circuit voltage regulator.

3.3.1 Features of I_C μA723

1. 150-mA load current without external power transistor.
2. Adjustable current limiting capability.
3. Input voltages up to 40 V.
4. Output adjustable from 2 V to 37 V.
5. High ripple rejection.
6. Excellent input and load regulation.
7. Excellent temperature stability.

The μA 723 is a precision integrated circuit voltage regulator. The circuit consists of a temperature-compensated reference-voltage amplifier, an error amplifier, a 150-mA output transistor and an adjustable-output current limiter. The μA 723 is designed for use in positive or negative power supplies as a series, shunt, switching or floating regulator. For output currents exceeding 150 mA, additional pass elements can be connected.

3.3.2 Functional Block Diagram

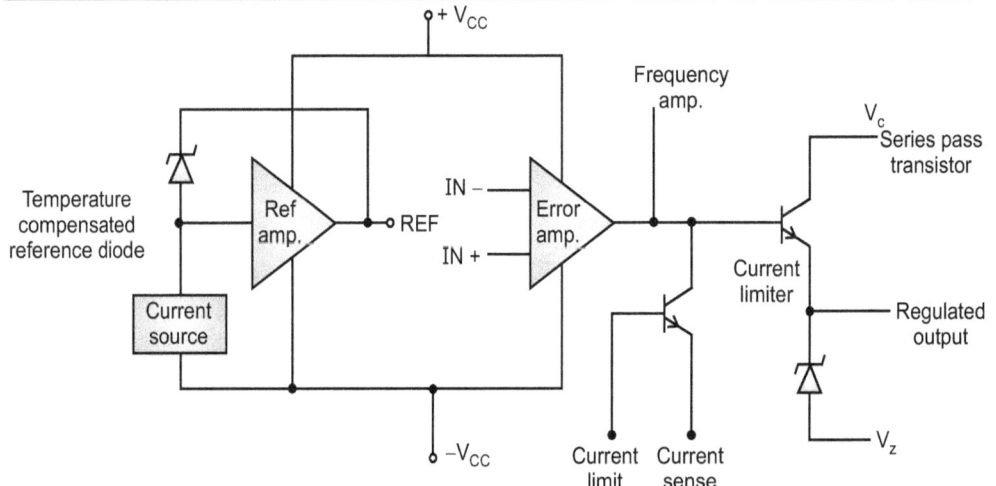

Fig. 3.25 : Functional Block Diagram

Fig. 3.25 shows the block diagram of I_C μA 723. It is divided into four parts.
1. Temperature compensated voltage reference source.
2. Op-amp used as an error amplifier.
3. A series pass transistor capable of 150 mA output current.
4. Transistor to limit the output current.

The reference element consists of temperature compensated zener diode, constant current source and reference amplifiers. Zener diode is forced by the constant current source to operate at a fixed voltage. The output voltage is compared with the reference voltage of 7 V. V_{ref} is connected to the non-inverting input of the error amplifier.

The error amplifier is a high gain differential amplifier. The error amplifier controls the series pass transistor Q_1, which acts as a variable resistor. The series pass transistor is a small power transistor having about 800 mw dissipation.

Transistor Q_2 acts as a current limiter for short circuit condition. The frequency compensation terminal controls the frequency response of the error amplifier. The required roll-off is obtained by connecting a small capacitor of 100 pF between frequency compensation and inverting input terminals.

Fig. 3.26 below shows the pin diagram of I_C μA 723.

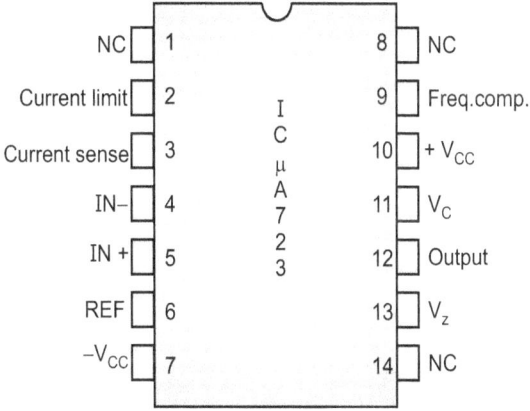

Fig. 3.26 : D or N package

3.3.3 Specification of IC μA 723

Table 3.1 shows the electrical specifications of I_C 723.
Absolute maximum ratings over operating free-air temperature range.

Table 3.1

Peak voltage from $V_{CC}+$ to V_{CC} (tw ≤ 50 ms)	50 V
Continuous voltage from V_{CC}^+ to V_{CC}^-	40 V
Input to output voltage differential	40 V
Differentials input voltage to error amplifier	± 5 V
Voltage between non-inverting input and V_{CC}^-	8 V
Current from V_z	25 mA
Current from V_{ref}	15 mA

Table 3.2 shows the recommended operating conditions.

Table 3.2

	Minimum	Maximum	Unit
Input voltage, V_i	9.5	40	V
Output voltage, V_o	2	37	V
Input-to-output voltage differential ($V_c - V_o$)	3	38	V
Output current, I_o	–	150	mA
Operating free-air temperature range TA	0	70	°C

3.3.4 Applications of I_C µA 723

Different types of regulator circuits can be designed using I_C 723.

1. Basic low voltage regulator : Fig. 3.27 shows the basic low voltage regulator whose output voltage can be obtained between 2 V to 7 V.

The resistor R_{sc} is connected between pin CL and CS.

The value of R_{sc} can be obtained as

$$R_{sc} = \frac{V_{sense}}{I_{limit}} = \frac{0.6}{I_{limit}}$$

I_{limit} can be selected as 1.2 to 1.5 times the maximum load current.

A potential divider made up of R1 and R2 is connected between v_{ref} and non-inverting terminals.

$$V_{non\text{-}inverting} = V_{ref} \times \frac{R_2}{R_1 + R_2}$$

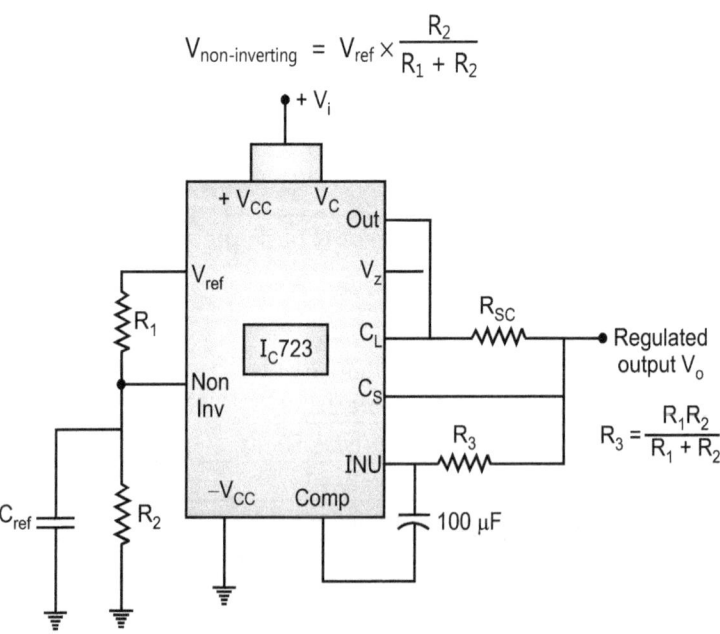

Fig. 3.27 : Basic low voltage regulator

Series pass transistor works as a emitter follower.

$$V_o = V_{ref} \times \frac{R_2}{R_1 + R_2}$$

$$R_3 = R_1 \| R_2 = \frac{R_1 R_2}{R_1 + R_2}$$

Maximum load current can be 150 mA.

2. **Basic high voltage regulator (V_o = 7 V to 37 V)** : Fig. 3.28 shows basic positive high voltage regulator. The output varies from 7 V to 37 V.

The gain $A = 1 + \dfrac{R_1}{R_2}$

The output voltage is calculated as

$$V_o = V_{ref}\left(1 + \frac{R_1}{R_2}\right)$$

$$= V_{ref}\left(\frac{R_1 + R_2}{R_2}\right)$$

$$R_{sc} = \frac{0.6}{I_{limit}} = \frac{V_{sense}}{I_{sc}}$$

$$R_3 = R_1 \| R_2 = \frac{R_1 R_2}{R_1 + R_2}$$

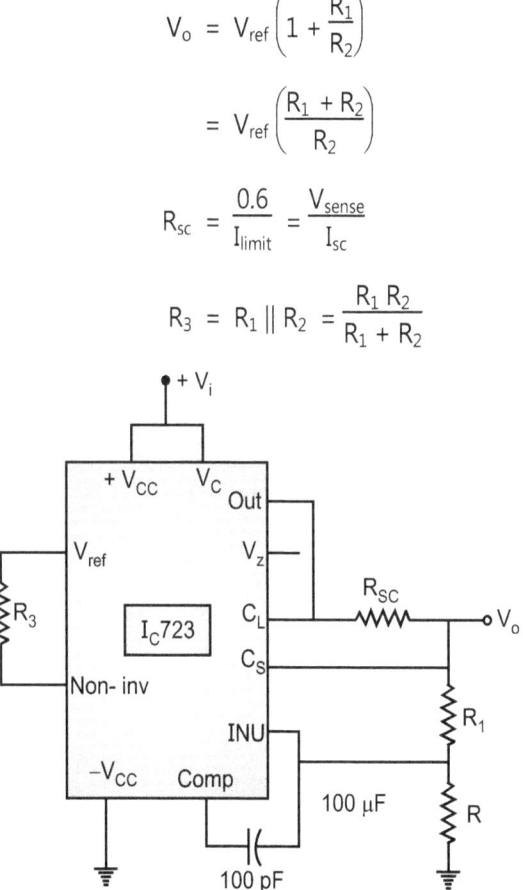

Fig. 3.28 : **Basic high voltage regulator**

3. Negative voltage regulator :

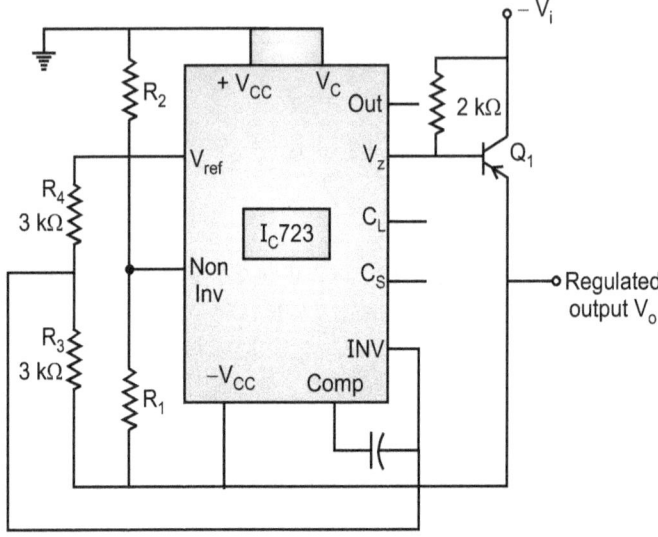

Fig. 3.29 : Negative voltage regulator

Fig. 3.29 shows the I_C µA 723 to obtain negative voltage regulator. An external PNP transistor, Q_1 is connected. Resistance can be used from 1 kΩ to 10 kΩ.

$$R_3 = R_4$$

$$V_{out} = \left[\frac{V_{ref}}{2} + \frac{R_1 + R_2}{R_1} \right]$$

If magnitude of $-V_i$ is less than 9 V, connect V_{CC}^+ and V_C to a positive supply such that V_{CC}^+ to V_{CC}^- is grater than 9 V, for proper functioning of the I_C.

Example 3.8 :

Design a regulator using I_C 723 to meet the following specifications :
$V_o = 5$ V; $I_o = 100$ mA
$V_{in} = 15 \pm 20\%$, $I_{SC} = 150$ mA, $V_{sense} = 0.7$ V

Solution :

Here
$$R_{SC} = \frac{V_{sence}}{I_{SC}} = \frac{0.7}{150 \times 10^{-3}} = 4.67 \Omega$$

Neglecting input bias current of an error amplifier we can write,

$$R_1 = \frac{V_{ref} - V_o}{I_D}$$

Where, I_D = Potential divider current = 1 mA
V_{ref} = 7.15 V for I_C 723

∴ $$R_1 = \frac{7.15 - 5}{1 \times 10^{-3}} = 2.15 \text{ k}\Omega$$

Use 2.2 kΩ standard resistance.

Now
$$V_o = V_{ref} \cdot \frac{R_2}{R_1 + R_2}$$

$$5 = 7.15 \cdot \frac{R_2}{(2.2 + R_2)}$$

∴ $\quad 2.2 + R_2 = 1.43\, R_2$

$\quad R_2 = 5.11\ k\Omega$

Use 5.1 kΩ standard resistor.

$$R_3 = R_1 \| R_2 = \frac{2.2 \times 5.1}{2.2 + 5.1} = 1.536\ k\Omega$$

Use 1.5 kΩ resistor.

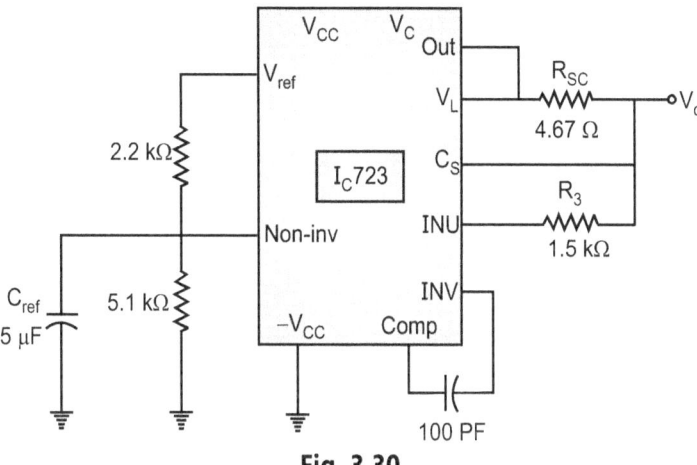

Fig. 3.30

3.4 VOLTAGE REGULATORS

A voltage regulator is a circuit that provides a constant voltage even if there is a change in input voltage, or change in load current or change in temperature.

IC voltage regulators are versatile and relatively inexpensive. These ICs are available with various features such as :
- Programmable output,
- Current / Voltage boosting,
- Internal short-circuit current limiting,
- Thermal shutdown,
- Floating operation for high voltage applications.

3.4.1 Types of Voltage Regulators
- Fixed output voltage regulators,
- Adjustable output voltage regulators,
- Switching regulators,
- Special regulators.

Except the switching regulators, all other types are called linear regulators.

The impedance of a linear regulator's active element may be continuously varied to supply a desired current to the load.

In switching regulator a switch is turned ON and OFF at a rate such that the regulator delivers the desired average current in periodic pulses to the load.

Switching regulator is more efficient than the linear regulators because it dissipates negligible power in either the ON or OFF state.

3.4.2 Advantages of Voltage Regulators

- Simple to use.
- Reliable.
- Low in cost.
- Availability in a variety of voltage and current ratings.

3.4.3 Applications of Voltage Regulators

- Used for on-card regulation.
- Used for laboratory type power supplies.
- Switching regulators are used in pulse width modulation.
- Switching regulators are used in push-pull bridges and series type switch mode supplies.

3.4.4 Fixed Voltage Regulators

Positive Voltage Regulators :

The 7800 series is a three terminal positive voltage regulator with seven voltage options as 5, 6, 8, 12, 15, 18, 24V. These ICs are designed with adequate heat sinking which can deliver output currents in excess of 1 A. These ICs do not require external components. Internal thermal overload protection and internal short circuit current limiting is provided.

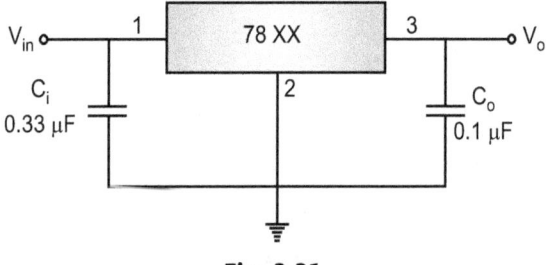

Fig. 3.31

The difference between input and output voltages ($V_{in} - V_o$), called **dropout voltage**, must be typically 2.0 V even during the low point on the input ripple voltage.

The capacitor C_i is used when the regulator is located an appreciable distance from a power supply filter. C_o is used to improve the transient response of the regulator.

3.4.5 Performance Parameters of Voltage Regulators

- Line regulation.
- Load regulation.
- Temperature stability.
- Ripple rejection.
- Line regulation is defined as the change in output voltage for a change in the input voltage and usually expressed in millivolts or as a percentage of output voltage V_O.
- Load regulation is the change in output voltage for a change in load current and is also expressed in millivolts or a percentage of V_O.
- Temperature stability or average temperature coefficient of output voltage (TCV_O) is the change in output voltage per unit change in temperature and is expressed in millivolts/°C or parts per million (ppm)/°C.
- Ripple rejection is the measure of a regulator's ability to reject ripple voltages. It is usually expressed in decibels.

The smaller the value of load regulation, line regulation and temperature stability, the better will be the regulator.

Application of 7800 Regulator as a Current Source :

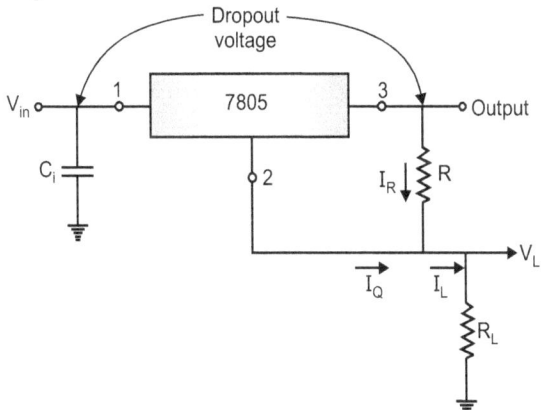

Fig. 3.32 : 7805C as a 0.5 A current source

Fig. 3.32 shows the 7805C as a 0.5 A current source. The current supplied to the load is given by

$$I_L = \frac{V_R}{R} + I_Q$$

where,

I_Q = Quiescent current
= 4.3 mA typically for 7805C

$V_R = V_{23} = 5$ V and $R = 10\ \Omega$

$I_L \cong 0.5$ A

The output voltage V_O w.r.t. ground is

$$V_O = V_R + V_L$$

where, $V_L = I_L R_L$

Load resistance, $R_L = 10 \, \Omega$

Hence $V_L = 5$ V. Therefore, $V_O = 10$ V

Since, the dropout voltage for the 7805C is 2 V, the minimum input voltage required is given as

$$V_{in} = V_O + \text{(Dropout voltage)} = 12 \text{ V}$$

Finally, a current source circuit using a voltage regulator can be designed for a desired value of load current I_L. Here V_{in} depends upon the size of R_L and also the dropout voltage of the regulator.

Negative Voltage Regulator Series :

The 7900 series of fixed output negative voltage regulators are complements to the 7800 series devices. There are also available in the same seven options as the 7800 series. In addition, two extra voltage options, – 2 V and –5.2 V are also available in the negative 7900 series.

3.4.6 Adjustable Voltage Regulators

Adjustable voltage regulators gives the answers to the excessive inventory and production costs because a single device satisfies many voltage requirements from 1.2 V upto 37 V.

3.4.6.1 Advantages of Adjustable Voltage Regulators over Fixed Voltage Regulators

- Improved system performance by having better line and load regulation.
- Improved overload protection allows greater output current over operating temperature range.
- Improved system reliability with each device being subjected to 100% thermal limit burn-in.

The LM317 is the most commonly used general purpose adjustable voltage regulator.

3.4.6.2 LM 317 Regulator

LM317 series is a adjustable three terminal positive voltage regulators. The different grades are available in the series with output of 1.2 to 37 V and output current from 0.1 A to 1.5 A. The three terminals are V_{IN}, V_{OUT} and ADJUSTMENT (ADJ). Fig. 3.33 shows the diagram for the LM317 regulator.

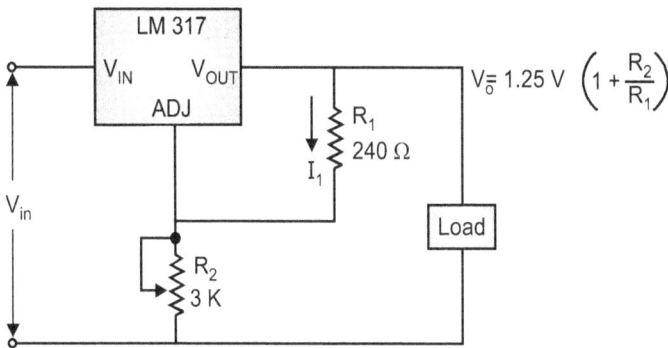

Fig. 3.33 : Typical connection diagram for LM317 regulator

When configured as shown in Fig. 3.33, the LM317 develops a nominal 1.25 V, referred to as the reference voltage V_{REF} between the output and adjustment terminal. This reference voltage is generated across resistor R_1 and since the voltage is constant, the current I_1 is also constant for a given value of R_1. Because resistor R_1 sets current I_1, it is called current set or program resistor.

In addition to the current I_1, the current I_{ADJ} from the adjustment terminal also flows through the output set resistor R_2.

The LM317 is designed such that I_{ADJ} is very small and constant with line and load changes. The maximum value of adjustment pin current I_{ADJ} is 100 µA.

From Fig. 3.33, the output voltage V_O is

$$V_O = R_1 I_1 + R_2 (I_1 + I_{ADJ})$$

where,
$$I_1 = \frac{V_{REF}}{R_1}$$

R_1 = Current (I_1) set resistor

R_2 = Output (V_O) set resistor

I_{ADJ} = Adjustment pin current

Substituting the value of I_1 and rearranging, we get

$$V_O = V_{ref}\left(1 + \frac{R_2}{R_1}\right) + I_{ADJ} R_2$$

where, V_{REF} = 1.25 V

Since I_{ADJ} is very small and constant, the voltage drop across R_2 due to I_{ADJ} is also very small and can be neglected.

$$V_O = 1.25\left(1 + \frac{R_2}{R_1}\right)$$

3.4.6.3 Practical Circuit Diagram of LM317 Voltage Regulator

Normally no capacitors are needed unless the LM317 is situated far from the power supply filter capacitors.

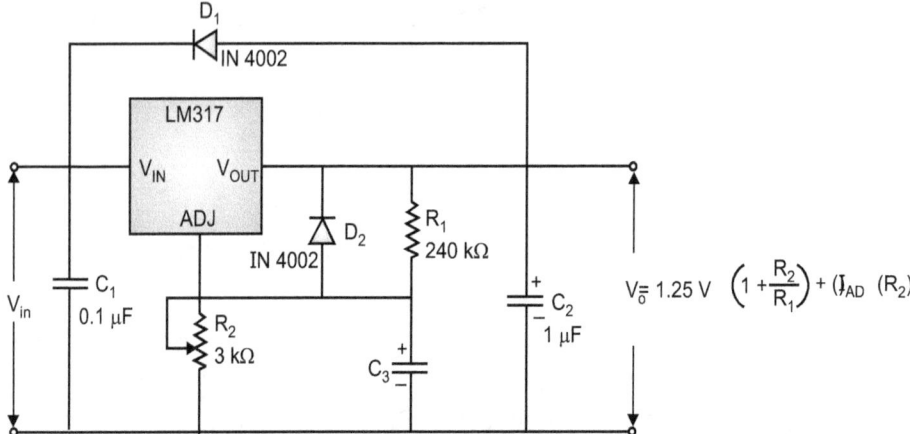

Fig. 3.34 : Practical LM317 regulator with capacitors and protective diodes

A 0.1 µF disc or 1 µF tantalum capacitor is suitable for input bypassing. Also an output capacitor C_2 can be added to improve transient response. Output capacitors in the range of 1 to 1000 µF of aluminium or tantalum electrolytic are commonly used to provide improved impedance and rejection of transients. The adjustment terminal can be bypassed with C_3 to obtain very high ripple rejection ratios, with a 10 µF bypass capacitor C_3, 80 dB ripple rejection is obtainable at any output level. Protection diodes are used to prevent the capacitors from discharging through low current points into the regulator. Protection diodes are included for use with outputs greater than 25 V and high values of output capacitance.

The important specifications of LM 317/LM 337 are given below :

Power dissipation (based on the package)	– 0.6 W to 20 W
Adjustable output voltage	– 1.2 V to 37 V
Line regulations	– 0.1 % / V (Typ)
Load regulation	– 0.1 % (Typ)
Standard 3-lead transistor packages	– TO_3, TO-39, TO-200 TO-202 and TO-92
Ripple rejection	– 80 dB

Example 3.9 :

An LM 317 regulator shown in Fig. has R_1 = 240 Ω. and R_2 = 2 kΩ. If I_{AD3} = 50 µA.

Solution :

$$V_o = V_{ref}\left(1 + \frac{R_2}{R_1}\right) + I_{AD3}\, R_2$$

$$= 1.25\left(1 + \frac{2000}{240}\right) + 50 \times 10^{-6} \times 2 \times 10^3 = 11.77 \text{ V}$$

Example 3.10 :

Design an adjustable positive voltage regulator using LM 317 for an output voltage V_o varying from 4 to 12 V and an output current I_o of 1 A.

Solution :

Maximum I_{ADJ} for LM 317 = 100 μA

Assume a typical value of R_1 = 240 Ω. Here, V_{ref} = 1.25 V, we know that

$$V_o = V_{ref}\left(1 + \frac{R_2}{R_1}\right) + I_{ADJ} R_2$$

For output voltage, V_o = 4 V

$$4 = 1.25\left(1 + \frac{R_2}{240}\right) + 100 \times 10^{-6} \times R_2$$

∴ R_2 = 0.52 kΩ

Similarly, for V_o = 12 V.

$$12 = 1.25\left(1 + \frac{R_2}{240}\right) + 100 \times 10^{-6} \times R_2$$

∴ $R_2 = \dfrac{10.75}{5.3 \times 10^{-3}} = 2.01$ kΩ

3.4.7 LM 137/LM 337 Adjustable Negative Voltage Regulator

LM137/LM 337 series of adjustable negative voltage regulators are available for the corresponding types of LM 317 positive voltage regulators. Fig. 3.35 shows the circuit arrangement for negative voltage regulator.

Here R_1 is of value 120 Ω and the maximum input voltage V_i is 50 V compared to 60 V for LM 317.

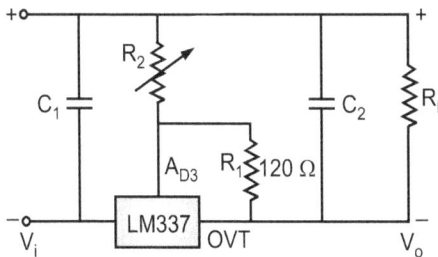

Fig. 3.35 : LM 337 adjustable negative voltage regulator

The output voltage V_o is given by

$$V_o = 1.2\left(1 + \frac{R_2}{R_1}\right) = 1.2\left(1 + \frac{R_2}{120}\right) = 1.2 \text{ V} + 10 \text{ mA} \times R_2$$

Table shows the package types and grade of LM337 regulators.

Device	Available V_o (V)	Output current (A)	$V_{i\,max}$ (V)	Ripple rejection (dB)	Package type
LM 337	−1.2 to −37	1.5	40	77	TO-39
LM337H	−1.2 to −37	0.5	40	77	TO-39
LM337HV	−1.2 to −37	1.5	50	77	TO-3
LM337HVH	−1.2 to −37	0.50	50	77	TO-39
LM337L	−1.2 to −37	0.10	40	65	TO-92
LM337M	−1.2 to −37	0.50	40	77	TO-202

Fig. 3.36 also shows the schematic symbols and package types of the positive and negative voltage regulators.

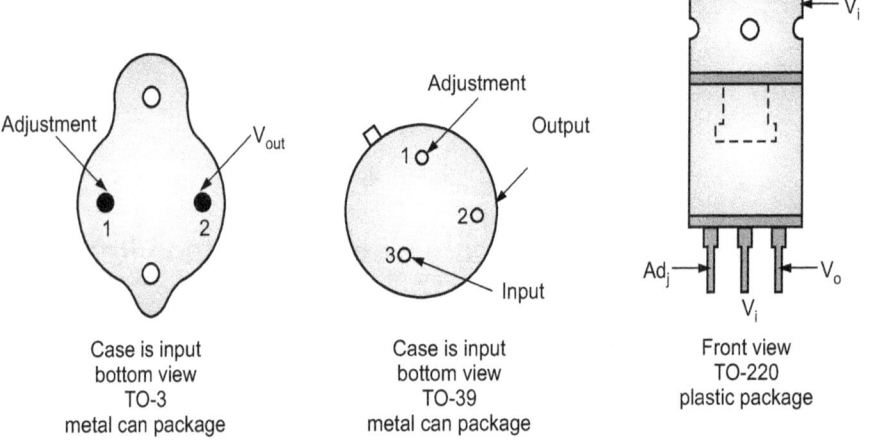

Fig. 3.36 : Schematic symbols and package types of LM317/LM337

3.4.8 Low Drop Out voltage Regulators

Standard voltage regulators require about 2V drop between V_{in} and V_{out} to ensure correct biasing of internal circuits. Regulation may suffer if the voltage drop is reduced below this figure. The limitations occurs because of the use of npn transistor. The output of the op-amp must be greater than 0.6V above V_{out} to overcome the base-emitter voltage drop.

Low drop out regulators overcome this limitations by using a pnp power transistor, instead of the npn type in standard regulators. The minimum voltage drop between V_{in} and V_{out} is the saturation voltage across the power transistor, which is about 0.2 V. Fig. 3.37 shows such type of low drop out voltage regulator.

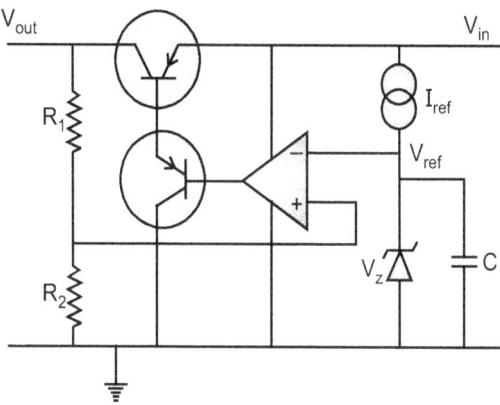

Fig. 3.37 : Low drop out voltage regulators

3.4.9 Output Current Boosting

The three terminal voltage regulator 7805 an be employed as a current source. To achieve this, a current setting resistor, R between gained and OUT terminals of the regulator I_C is connected. Since the output is always constant at 5V, the current through R is also maintained constant.

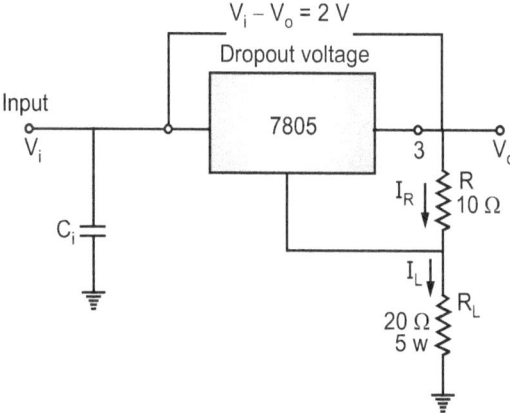

Fig. 3.38 : IC 7805 used a constant current source current

The output current of the regulator can be boosted or amplified by connecting an external pass-transistor Q_1 as shown in Fig. 3.38.

The voltage drop across resistor R_1 for low value of load currents is insufficient to make the transistor Q_1 ON and the regulator supplies the load current. When load current I_L increases beyond a certain limit, the drop across R_1 increases and when it reaches 0.7 V, the transistor Q_1 turns ON and supplies the additional current to the load.

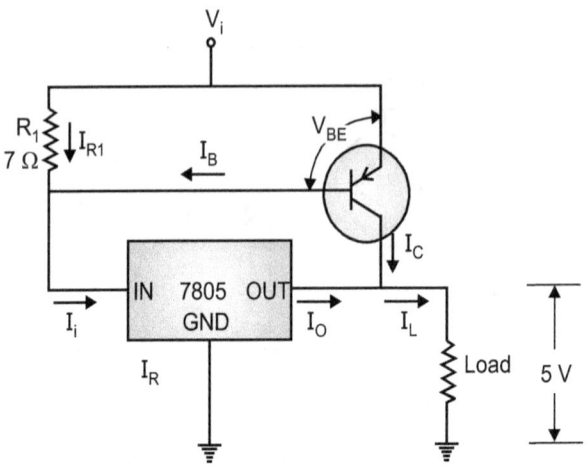

Fig. 3.39 : Boosting the output current of IC 7805

The additional current is β times the base current

$$I_L = I_C + I_o \quad \ldots (3.50)$$

$$I_C = \beta I_B$$

$$I_L = \beta I_B + I_o \quad \ldots (3.51)$$

The output current I_o is given by

$$I_o = I_i - I_Q \approx I_i \text{ since } I_Q \text{ is negligibly small}$$

$$I_B = I_i - I_{R1}$$

$$\approx I_o - \frac{V_{EB(ON)}}{R_1} \quad \ldots (3.52)$$

Substitute equation (3) in equation (2),

$$I_L = I_o(\beta + 1) - \beta \frac{V_{EB(ON)}}{R_1} \quad \ldots (3.53)$$

The maximum 1 A current can be obtained by using a 7805 regulator.

Assuming $V_{EB(ON)} = 0.7$ V and β = 12 for the transistor

$$I_L = 1(12+1) - 12 \times \frac{0.7}{7}$$

$$= 11.8 \text{ A}$$

Example 3.11 :

Assume $V_{EB(ON)} = 0.7$ V and β = 50. Determine the output current I_o and I_C for a load of (a) 100 Ω, (b) 2 Ω in IC 7805 regulator circuit.

Solution :

(a) Load current, $I_L = \dfrac{5\ V}{100\ \Omega} = 50\ mA$

Voltage across, $R_1 = 50\ mA \times 7\ \Omega = 350\ mV$

Since a minimum of 0.7 V is required to switch a transistor ON, Q_1 is OFF.

∴ $\quad I_L = I_o = I_i = 50\ mA$

(b) Load current, $I_L = \dfrac{5\ V}{2\ \Omega} = 2.5\ A$

The voltage drop across R_1 is $2.5\ A \times 7\ \Omega = 17.5\ V > 0.7\ V$.

Thus, Q_1 is ON.

Using equation (4), we get

$$2.5 = I_o \times (50 + 1) - 50 \times \dfrac{0.7\ V}{7\ \Omega}$$

$\quad I_o = 0.147\ A$

∴ $\quad I_C = I_L - I_o = 2.500 - 0.147 = 2.353\ A$

3.5 BASIC SWITCH REGULATOR

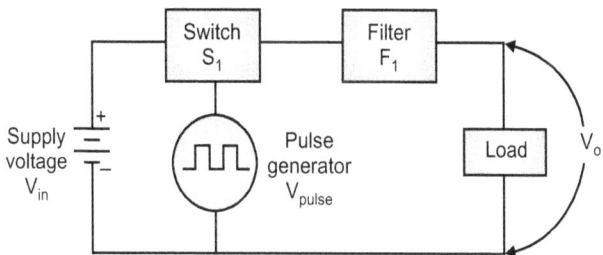

Fig. 3.40 : Basic switching regulator

A basic switching regulator consists of four major components :

1. Voltage source V_{in}
2. Switch S_1
3. Pulse generator V_{pulse}
4. Filter F_1.

1. Voltage source V_{in} :

It may be any DC supply, a battery or an unregulated or regulated voltage supply.

Requirements of voltage source :

1. It must supply the required output power and the losses associated with the switching regulator.

2. Must be large enough to supply sufficient dynamic range for line and load variations.

3. Must be sufficiently high to meet the minimum requirement of regulator system to be designed.

4. It may be required to store energy for a specified amount of time during power failures.

2. Switch S_1 :

Mostly a transistor or thyristor used as a power switch and is operated in the saturated mode. The pulse generator output alternately turns the switch ON and OFF.

3. Pulse Generator :

It produces an asymmetrical square wave which varies either in frequency or pulse width. The most effective frequency range for optimum efficiency and component size is around 20 kHz. It is within the switching speeds of most expensive transistors and diodes. The duty cycle is used to determine the relationship between input and output voltages.

$$\text{Duty cycle} = \frac{t_{ON}}{t_{ON} + t_{OFF}}$$

$$= \frac{t_{ON}}{T}$$

$$= t_{ON} \cdot f$$

Typical operating frequencies of switching regulators are from 10 to 50 kHz.

4. Filter F_1 :

Filter F_1 converts the pulse waveform from the output of the switch into a DC voltage. Due to this conversion mechanism it is often referred as DC transformer.

The output voltage V_o of the switching regulator is a function of duty cycle and the input voltage V_{in}.

$$V_o = \frac{t_{ON}}{T} \times V_{in}$$

The method of varying the output voltage by varying t_{ON} is called as pulse width modulation and if t_{ON} is held constant, the output voltage V_o, is inversely proportional to the period T or directly proportional to the frequency f of the pulse waveform. This method is called frequency modulation. The frequency modulated switching regulator is generally easier to design and built.

The basic filter types are RC, RL or RLC. The RLC filter is most commonly used in switching regulators.

3.5.1 IC 1723 Switching Regulator

Motorola's IC 1723 is a fixed positive or negative output voltage regulator, variable output voltage regulator or switching regulator.

It is designed to deliver load current upto 150 mA. The capacity can be increased by using one or more external pass transistors.

The regulator requires an external transistor and a 1 mH choke. The external transistor is a switching power transistor to minimize its power dissipation during switching. The 1 mH choke smooths out the current pulses delivered to the load, while capacitor C holds output voltage at a constant DC level.

To improve the efficiency of a regulator, the series-pass transistor is used as a switch.

Switching regulators come in various circuit configuration.

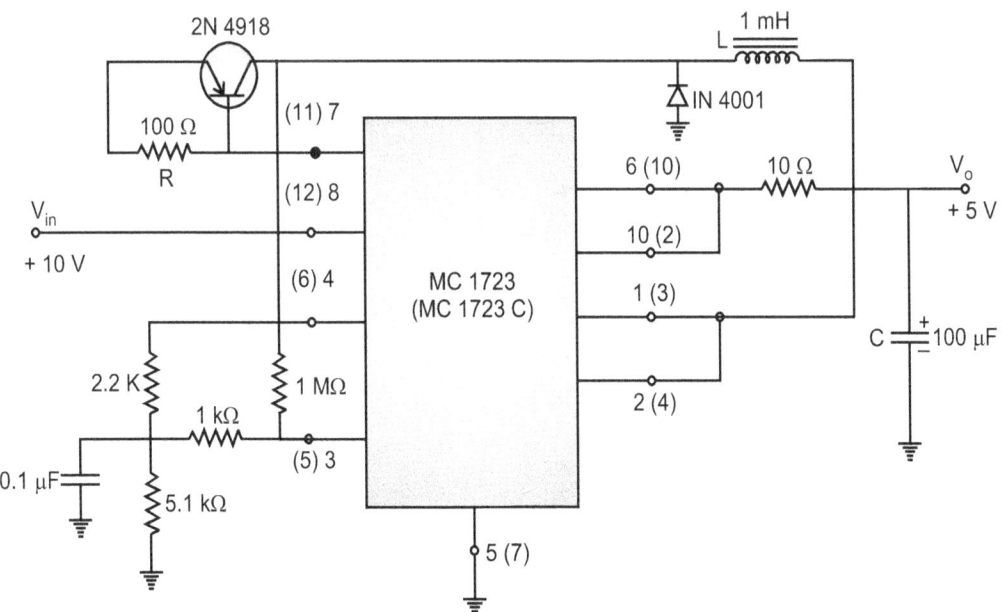

Fig. 3.41 : Motorola MC 1723 as a 5 V-1 A switching regulator

Various Configurations of Switching Regulators :

- Flyback,
- Feed-forward,
- Push-pull,
- Non-isolated single-ended or single polarity type.

Operating Modes of Switching Regulators :

1. Step-down,
2. Step-up,
3. Polarity inverting.

3.5.2 µA 78S40 Switching Regulator

The µA 78S40 consists of a temperature-compensated voltage reference, a duty-cycle controllable oscillator with an active current limit circuit, a high-gain comparator, a high current, high-voltage output switch, a power-switching diode, and an uncommitted operational amplifier.

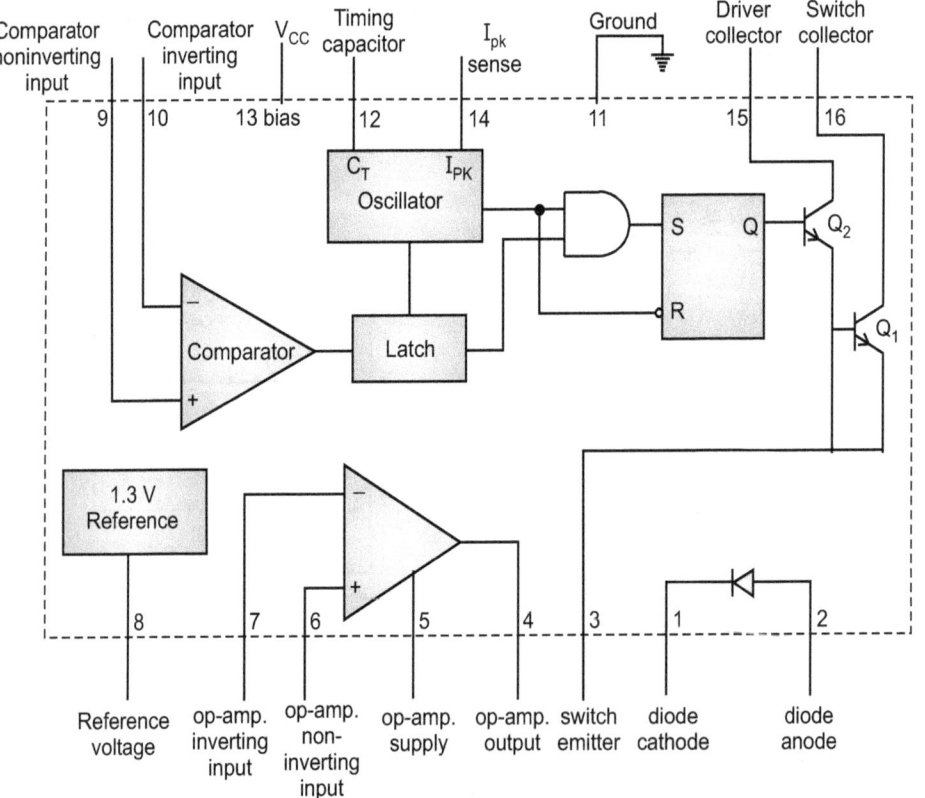

Fig. 3.42 : Block diagram of a µA 78S40 switching regulator

EXERCISE

1. What are the advantages of active filter over passive filters.
2. Design an active high pass filter to meet the following requirements.
   (a) Butterworth response
   (b) Cutoff frequency = 4kHz
   (c) Decay rate in the stop band = 40 dB/decade.
3. Write a short note on all pass filter.
4. Design a second order high pass filter for a cutoff frequency of 10 kHz and a pass band gain of 1.5. assume $C = C_3 = C_2 = 0.02$ µF and $R_f = 100$kΩ.
5. Design a second order low pass filter for a cutoff frequency of 200Hz and draw the circuit diagram. Assume C = 0.1 µF.
6. Design a wideband band pass filter to meet the following specifications:
   $F_1 = 5$kHz; $f_2 = 15$kHz. Pass band gain = 2
7. Design an active low=pass filter to meet the following specifications
   (a) Butterworth approximation response
   (b) Cutoff frequency $f_c = 1$kHz.
   (c) Decay rate in the stop band is 40dB/decade.
8. Design a notch filter to eliminate 50 Hz frequency signal.
9. Design a wide band reject filter having $f_H = 200$ Hz and $F_L = 1$ kHz
10. Discuss the feature of IC voltage regulator 723. Draw the schematic of a circuit which can provide a regulated output voltage of 5V.
11. What are the limitations of linear voltage regulators over switching regulators?
12. Write a short note on switching regulators?
13. Design an op-amp series voltage regulator to meet the following specifications:
    $V_1 = 18 \pm 3$v, $V_0 = 9$v at $I_0 = 10$ to 15 mA
    Zener available $V_z = 5.6$V, $P_z = 0.5$W
14. Design a regulator using IC 723 to meet the following specifications:
    $V_0 = 5$V; $I_0 = 100$ mA.
    $V_{in} = 15 \pm 20\%$
    $I_{sc} = 150$ mA; $V_{sense} = 0.7$V.

15. Explain the basic principle of a switching regulator.

16. Write a short note on :

    (a) Three terminal IC regulators

    (b) IC 78S40

17. Determine the regulated output voltage available from LM317 regulator if R_2 is set to 1.8 kΩ. assume R_1 = 240Ω and I_{adj} as 100μA

18. For a 7805 IC voltage regulator, a current boosting is provided with a transistor with V_{BE} = 0.7 v and β= 20. Assuming R_1 as 5Ω, calculate how much maximum current it can deliver to the load.

19. Explain how adjustable voltage regulator IC works. Derive the expression for the output voltage for LM317 adjustable voltage regulator.

20. How regulator output current can be boosted? Explain with neat circuit diagram.

Unit IV

COMPARATORS AND WAVEFORM GENERATION

4.1 COMPARATORS

A comparator is a circuit which compares a signal voltage which is applied to one of the terminal of op-amp with a known reference voltage at another terminal of the op-amp.

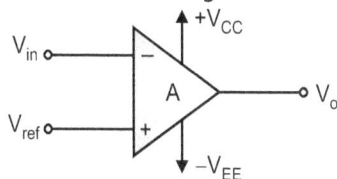

Fig. 4.1 : Basic comparator

The output is produced either high or low output voltage depending upon which input is greater. The comparator has two output levels high or low. It is not linear with input voltage. The two voltages are compared with each other and output V_o is either $+V_{sat}$ or $-V_{sat}$ as A_{OL} is very large.

Depending upon the application of the input to which terminal, the comparators are divided into two categories :

1. Inverting comparator
2. Non-inverting comparator

4.1.1 Basic Inverting Comparator

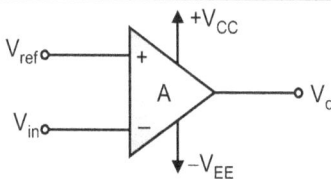

Fig. 4.2 (a) : Inverting Comparator

Fig. 4.2 (a) shows the inverting comparator in which the reference voltage V_{ref} is applied to the non-inverting input terminal of the op-amp and signal voltage V_{in} is applied to the inverting terminal of the op-amp. The V_{ref} can be set using a battery and potential divider.

When V_{in} is less than V_{ref}, the output voltage V_o is at $+V_{sat}$ ($\approx +V_{CC}$) because of the output at the inverting input (–) is less than that at the non-inverting input.

When V_{in} is greater than V_{ref}, the non-inverting (+) input becomes negative w.r.t. inverting input and V_o goes to $-V_{sat}$. The V_{ref} can be set positive and negative infinite values by using potential divider circuit.

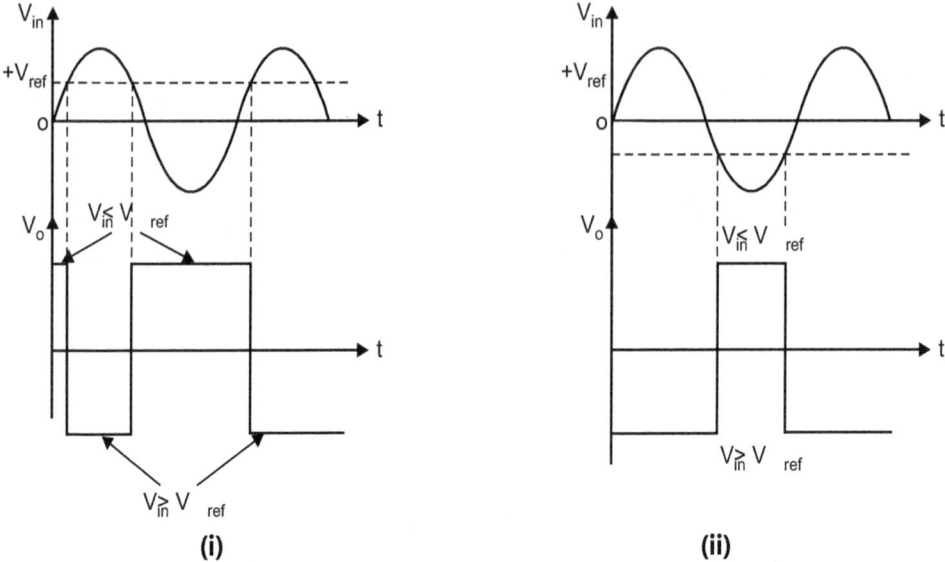

Fig. 4.2 (b) : Input and output waveforms when V_{ref} is (i) positive and (ii) negative

4.1.2 Non-Inverting Comparator

In a non-inverting comparator, a fixed reference voltage V_{ref} of 1 V is applied to the (–V) input and the other time-varying signal voltage V_{in} is applied to the (+) input.

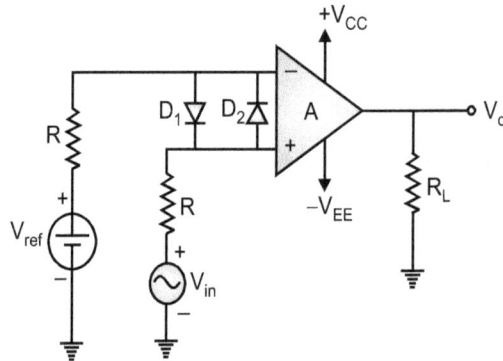

Fig. 4.3 : Practical non-inverting comparator

When V_{in} is less than V_{ref}, the output voltage V_o is at $-V_{sat}$ ($\approx -V_{EE}$) because the voltage at the (–) input is higher than that at the (+) input. On the other hand, when V_{in} is greater than V_{ref}, the (+) input becomes positive w.r.t. the (–) input, the V_o goes to $+V_{sat}$ ($\approx +V_{CC}$). The V_o changes from one saturation level to another whenever $V_{in} \approx V_{ref}$.

The comparator is a type of analog-to-digital converter. At any given time, the V_o waveform shows whether V_{in} is greater or less than V_{ref}. The comparator sometimes is also called as voltage level detector because for a desired value of V_{ref}, the voltage level of the input V_{in} can be detected.

In Fig. 4.4, diodes D_1 and D_2 are used to protect the op-amp from damage due to excessive input voltage V_{in}. The resistor R in series with V_{in} is used to limit the current through D_1 and D_2.

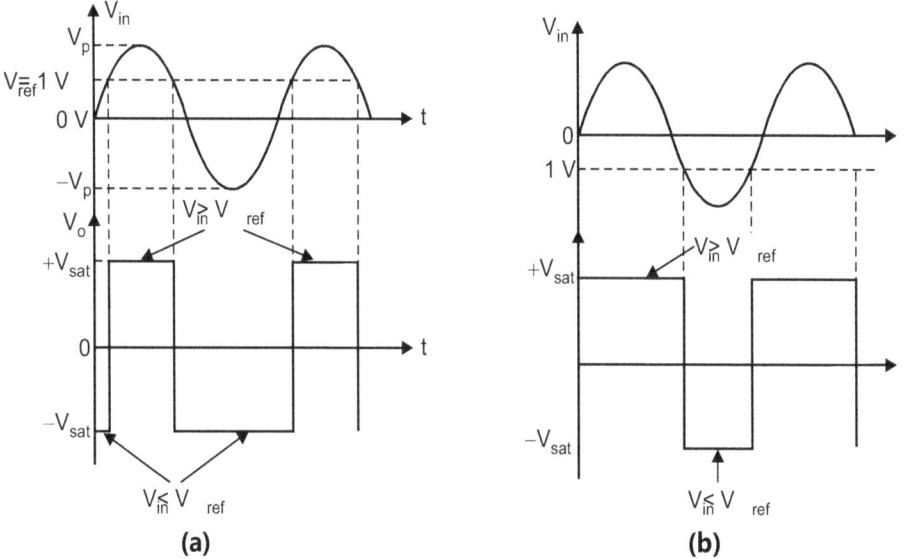

Fig. 4.4 : Input and output waveforms when V_{ref} is (a) positive , (b) negative

Fig. 4.4 shows the input and output waveforms for positive and negative reference voltage.

If the reference voltage V_{ref} is negative w.r.t. ground, with a sinusoidal signal applied to the (+) input, the output waveforms will be as shown in Fig. 4.4 (b). When $V_{in} > V_{ref}$, V_o is $+V_{sat}$.

On the other hand, when the $V_{in} < V_{ref}$, V_o is at $-V_{sat}$. Obviously, the amplitude of V_{in} must be large enough to pass through V_{ref} if the switching action is to take place.

4.1.3 Limitations of Op-amp as a Comparator

1. To obtain more accuracy of the comparator, a high CMRR, high gain and negligible input offset current and input offset voltage is required for the op-amp.
2. To obtain the better response time, the switching of the op-amp must be fast between two saturation levels and it should also respond quickly to any change of input conditions.

4.1.4 Applications of Comparators

1. Voltage level detector.
2. Zero crossing detector.
3. Window detector.
4. Pulse generator.
5. Duty cycle controller.

4.1.5 Comparator Characteristics

The important characteristics of the comparator are :
1. Speed of operation
2. Accuracy
3. Compatibility.

1. Speed of operation :

The output of the comparator must switch rapidly between saturation levels and also respond instantly to any changes of input conditions. This implies that the bandwidth of the op-amp comparator must be rather wide; in fact, the wider the bandwidth, the higher is the speed of operation. The speed of operation of the comparator is improved with positive feedback (hystresis).

2. Accuracy :

The accuracy of the comparator depends on its voltage gain, common-mode rejection ratio, input offsets and thermal drifts. High voltage gain requires a smaller difference voltage (hystresis voltage) to cause the comparator's output voltage to switch between saturation levels.

On the other hand, a high CMRR helps to reject the common-mode input voltages, such as noise at the input terminals. Finally, to minimize the offset problems, the input offset current and input offset voltage must be negligible, also the changes in these offsets due to temperature variations, should be very slight.

3. Compatibility of output :

Since, the comparator is a form of analog-to-digital converter, its output must swing between the two logic levels suitable for a certain logic family such as Transistor-Transistor Logic (TTL).

4.1.6 LM 710 Voltage Comparator

The LM 710 series are high-speed voltage comparators intended for use as an accurate, low-level digital level sensor or as a replacement for operational amplifiers in comparator applications where speed is of prime importance. The circuit has a differential input and a single-ended output, with saturated output levels compatible with practically all types of integrated logic.

The device is built on a single silicon chip which insures low offset and thermal drift. The use of a minimum number of stages along with minority-carrier lifetime control (gold doping) makes the circuit much faster than operational amplifiers in saturating comparator applications. In fact, the low stray and wiring capacitances that can be realized with monolithic construction make the device difficult to duplicate with discrete components operating at equivalent power levels.

The LM 710 series are useful as pulse height discriminators, voltage comparators in high-speed A/C converters or go, on-go detectors in automatic test equipment. They also have applications in digital system as an adjustable-threshold line receiver or an interface between logic types. In addition, the low cost of the units suggests them for applications replacing relatively simple discrete component circuitry.

4.1.6.1 Schematic and Connection Diagrams

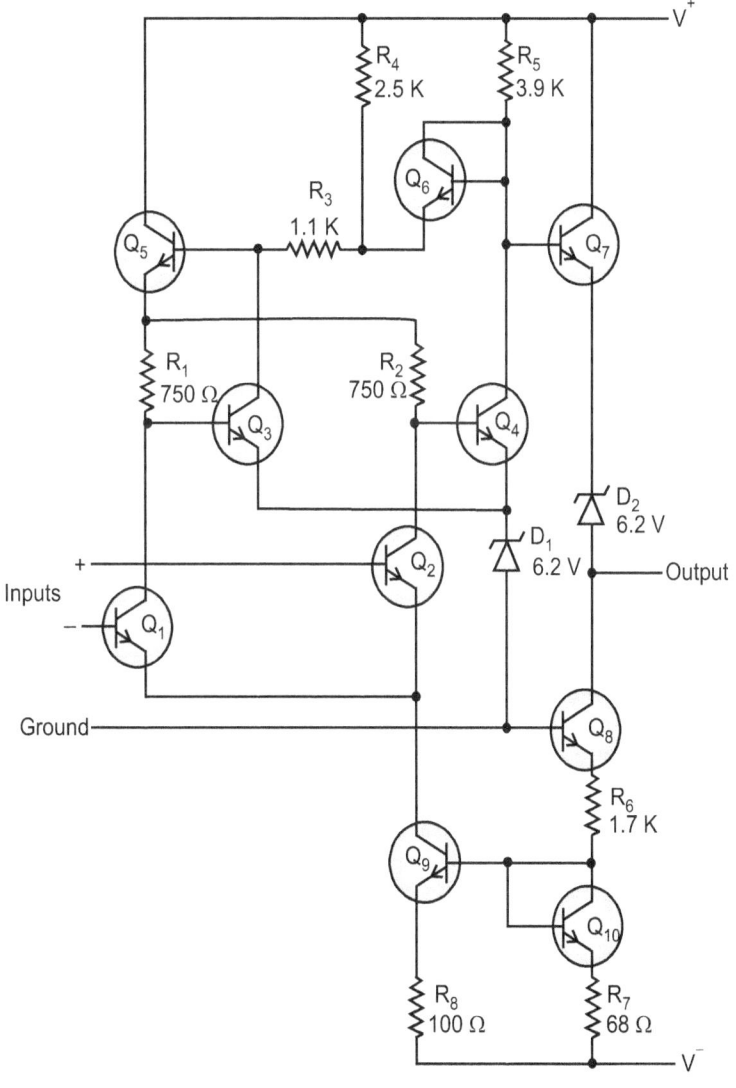

Fig. 4.5

4.1.6.2 Metal Can Package

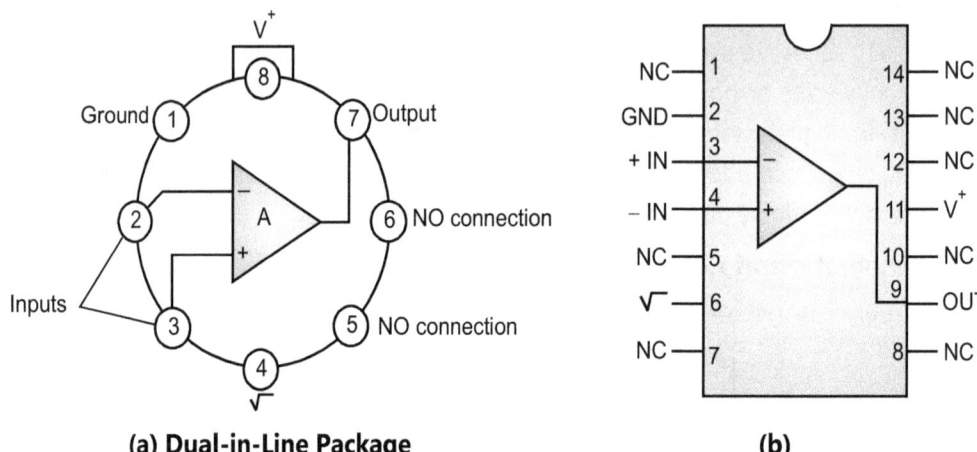

(a) Dual-in-Line Package (b)

Fig. 4.6

4.1.6.3 Absolute Maximum Ratings

Positive Supply Voltage	+ 14 V
Negative Supply Voltage	– 7 V
Peak Output Current	10 mA
Output Short Circuit Duration	10 seconds
Differential Input Voltage	± 5 V
Input Voltage	± 7 V
Power Dissipation	
TO-99 (Note 1)	700 mW
Plastic Dual-In-Line Package (Note 2)	950 mW
Operating Temperature Range	
LM 710	– 55° C to + 125° C
LM 710 C	0° C to + 17° C
Storage Temperature Range	– 65 ° C to + 150° C
Lead Temperature (Soldering, 10 seconds)	260° C

4.1.6.4 Electrical Characteristics

Parameter	Conditions	LM 710 Min.	LM 710 Type	LM 710 Max.	LM 710 C Min.	LM 710 C Type	LM 710 C Max.	Units
Input Offset Voltage	$R_S \leq 200\ \Omega$, $V_{CM} = 0\ V$, $T_A = 25°\ C$	–	0.6	2.0	–	1.6	5.0	mV
Input Offset Current	$V_{OUT} = 1.4\ V$, $T_A = 25°\ C$	–	0.75	3.0	–	1.8	5.0	µA
Input Bias Current	$T_A = 25°\ C$	–	13	20	–	16	25	µA
Voltage Gain	$T_A = 25°\ C$	1250	1700	–	1000	1500	–	–
Output Resistance	$T_A = 25°\ C$	–	200	–	–	200	–	Ω
Output Sink Current	$V_{OUT} = 0$, $T_A = 25°\ C$	–	–	–	–	–	–	–
	$\Delta V_{IN} \geq 5\ mV$	2.0	2.5	–	–	–	–	mA
	$\Delta V_{IN} \geq 10\ mV$	–	–	–	1.6	2.5	–	mA
Response Time	$T_A = 25°\ C$ (Note 4)	–	40	–	–	40	–	Ns
Input Offset Voltage	$R_S \leq 200\ \Omega$, $V_{CM} = 0\ V$	–	–	3.0	–	–	6.5	mV
Average Temperature Coefficient of Input Offset Voltage	$T_{MIN} \leq T_A \leq T_{MAX}$, $R_S \leq 50\ \Omega$	–	3.0	10	–	5.0	20	µV/°C
Input Offset Current	$T_A = T_{A\ MAX}$	–	0.25	3.0	–	–	7.5	µA
	$T_A = T_{A\ MIN}$	–	1.8	7.0	–	–	7.5	µA
Average Temperature Coefficient of Input Offset Current	$25°\ C \leq T_A \leq T_{MAX}$	–	5.0	25	–	15	50	nA/°C
	$T_{MIN} \leq T_A \leq 25°\ C$	–	15	75	–	24	100	nA/°C
Input Bias Current	$T_A = T_{MIN}$	–	27	45	–	25	40	µA
Input Voltage Range	$V^- = -7\ V$	± 5.0	–	–	± 5.0	–	–	V
Common-Mode Rejection Ratio	$R_S \geq 200\ \Omega$	80	100	–	70	98	–	dB
Differential Input Voltage Range	–	± 5.0	–	–	± 5.0	–	–	V
Voltage Gain	–	1000	–	–	800	–	–	V/V
Positive Output Level	$-5\ mA \leq I_{OUT} \leq 0$	–	–	–	–	–	–	–
	$V_{IN} \geq 5\ mV$	2.5	3.2	4.0	–	–	–	V
	$V_{IN} \geq 10\ mV$	–	–	–	2.5	3.2	4.0	V
Negative Output Level	$V_{IN} \geq 5\ mV$	– 1.0	– 0.5	0	–	–	–	V
	$V_{IN} \geq 10\ mV$	–	–	–	– 1.0	–0.5	0	V
Output Sink Current	$V_{IN} \geq 5\ mV$, $V_{OUT} = 0$	–	–	–	–	–	–	–
	$T_A = 125°\ C$	0.5	1.7	–	–	–	–	mA
	$T_A = -55\ C$	1.0	2.3	–	–	–	–	mA
	$V_{IN} \geq 10\ mV$, $V_{OUT} = 0$, $0°\ C \leq T_A \leq +70°\ C$	–	–	–	0.5	–	–	mA
Positive Supply Current	$V_{IN} \geq 5\ mV$	–	5.2	9.0	–	–	–	mA
	$V_{IN} \geq 10\ mV$	–	–	–	–	5.2	9.0	mA
Negative Supply Current	$V_{IN} \geq 5\ mV$	–	4.2	7.0	–	–	–	mA
	$V_{IN} \geq 10\ mV$	–	–	–	–	4.6	7.0	mA
Power Consumption	$V_{OUT} \geq 0$	–	–	–	–	–	–	–
	$V_{IN} \geq 5\ mV$	–	90	150	–	–	–	mW
	$V_{IN} \geq 10\ mV$	–	–	–	–	–	150	mW

4.1.7 Peak Detector

A conventional AC voltmeter cannot be used to measure non-sinusoidal waveforms because it is designed to measure the rms value of the pure sine wave. The solution to this problem is to measure the peak value of the non-sinusoidal waveforms.

Fig. 4.7 (a) shows a peak detector that measures the positive peak values of the square wave input.

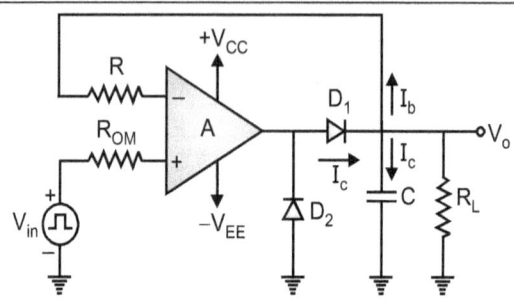

Fig. 4.7 (a) : Peak detector circuit

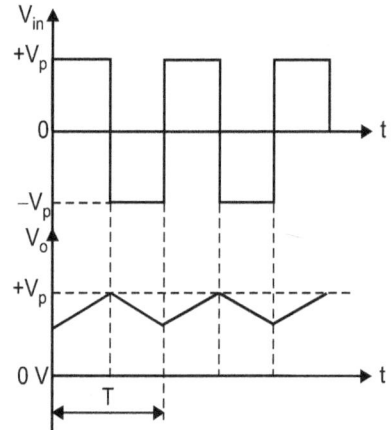

Fig. 4.7 (b) : Input and output waveforms

During the positive half cycle of V_{in}, the output of the op-amp drives D_1 ON, charging capacitor C to the positive peak value V_p of the input voltage V_{in}. Thus, when D_1 is forward biased, the op-amp operates as a voltage follower.

On the other hand, during the negative half cycle of V_{in}, diode D_1 is reverse biased and voltage across C is retained. The only discharge path for C is through R_L since the input bias current I_B is negligible for proper operation of the circuit, the charging time constant (CR_d) and discharging time constant (CR_L) must satisfy the following conditions :

$$CR_d \leq \frac{T}{10} \qquad \ldots (4.1)$$

where, R_d = Resistance of the forward diode, 100 Ω typically

T = Time period of the input waveform

and $CR_L \geq 10\,T$

where R_L is the load resistor.

If R_F is very small then to satisfy the condition above, use a buffer between capacitor C and load resistor R_L. The resistor R is used to protect the op-amp against the excessive discharge currents, especially when the power supply is switched OFF.

The resistor $R_{OM} = R$ minimizes the offset problems caused by input currents. In addition, diode D_2 conducts during the negative half cycle of V_{in} and hence prevents the op-amp from going into negative saturation. The negative peaks of input signal V_{in} can be detected simply by reversing diodes D_1 and D_2.

4.2 WAVEFORM GENERATION

4.2.1 Schmitt Trigger

Fig. 4.8 (a) shows the inverting comparator with positive feedback. The circuit has the ability to convert an irregular-shaped waveform to a square wave or pulse. The circuit is known as Schmitt trigger or Squaring circuit.

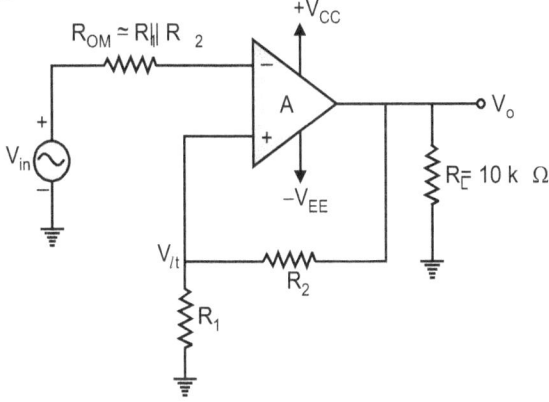

Fig. 4.8 (a) : Inverting comparator as a Schmitt trigger

The input voltage V_{in} triggers or changes the state of the output V_o every time it exceeds certain voltage levels called the upper threshold voltage V_{ut} and lower threshold voltage V_{lt} as shown in Fig. 4.8 (b) (waveforms).

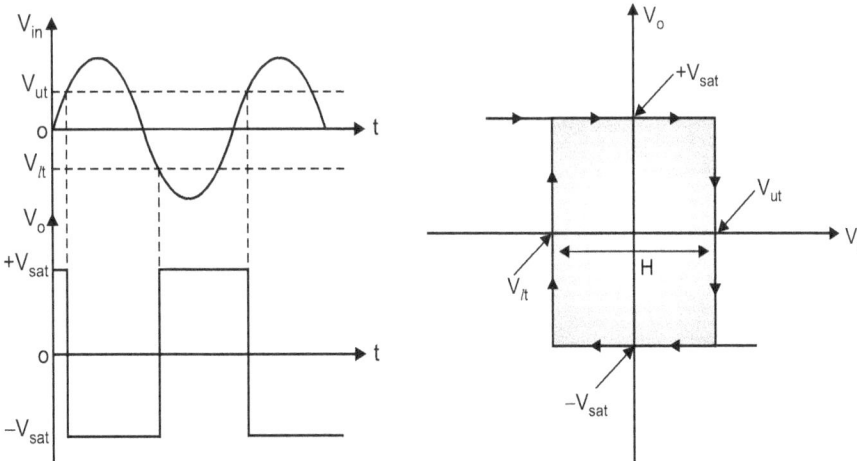

Fig. 4.8 (b) : Input and output waveforms of Schmitt trigger

Fig. 4.8 (c) : V_o versus V_{in} plot of the hysteresis voltage

$$H = V_{ut} - V_{lt} \qquad \ldots (4.2)$$

These threshold voltages are obtained by using the voltage divider $R_1 - R_2$ where the voltage across R_1 is fed back to the (+) input. The voltage across R_1 is a variable reference threshold voltage that depends on the value and polarity of the output voltage V_o.

When $V_o = +V_{sat}$, the voltage across R_1 is called the upper threshold voltage V_{ut}. The input voltage V_{in} must be slightly more positive than V_{ut} in order to cause the output V_o to switch from $+V_{sat}$ to $-V_{sat}$. As long as $V_{in} < V_{ut}$, V_o is at $+V_{sat}$. Using the voltage divider rule,

$$V_{ut} = \frac{R_1}{R_1 + R_2}(+V_{sat}) \qquad \ldots (4.3\ a)$$

On the other hand, when $V_o = -V_{sat}$, the voltage across R_1 is referred to as the lower threshold voltage V_{lt}. V_{in} must be slightly more negative than V_{lt} in order to switch from $-V_{sat}$ to $+V_{sat}$.

$$V_{lt} = \frac{R_1}{R_1 + R_2}(-V_{sat}) \qquad \ldots (4.3\ b)$$

Thus, if the threshold voltages V_{ut} and V_{lt} are made larger than the input noise voltages, the positive feedback will eliminate the false output transitions. Also, the positive feedback, because of its regenerative action, will make V_o switch faster between $+V_{sat}$ and $-V_{sat}$.

Fig. 4.8 (b) shows the output of the Schmitt trigger is a square wave when input is a sine wave.

The comparator with positive feedback is said to exhibit hystresis, a dead band condition means, when the input of the comparator exceeds V_{ut}, its output switches from $+V_{sat}$ to $-V_{sat}$, and reverts back to its original stage, $+V_{sat}$, when input goes below V_{lt}. The hysteresis voltage is equal to the difference between V_{ut} and V_{lt}.

$$V_H = V_{ut} - V_{lt}$$

$$= \frac{R_1}{R_1 + R_2}[+V_{sat} - (-V_{sat})] \qquad \ldots (4.4)$$

4.2.1.1 Non-Inverting Schmitt Trigger

When the input is applied to non-inverting terminal with positive feedback then the circuit is called as non-inverting Schmitt trigger. Fig. 4.9 (a) shows the circuit diagram of the non-inverting Schmitt trigger.

Fig. 4.9 (a) non-inverting Schmitt trigger.

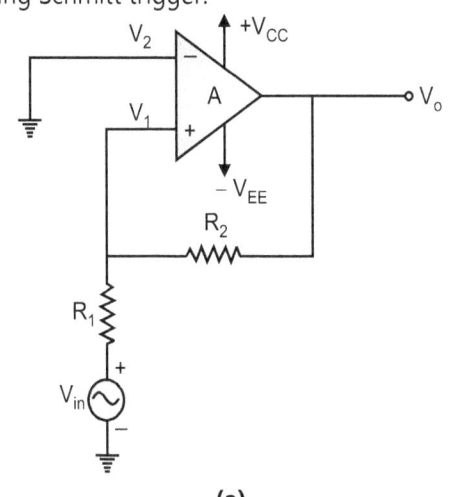

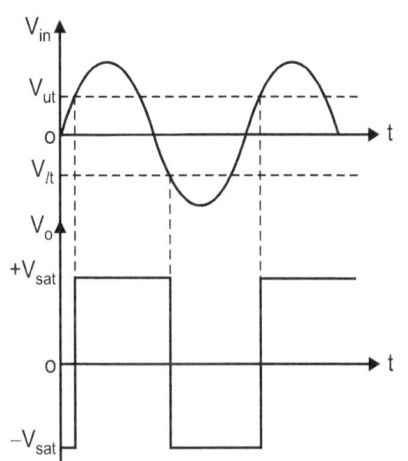

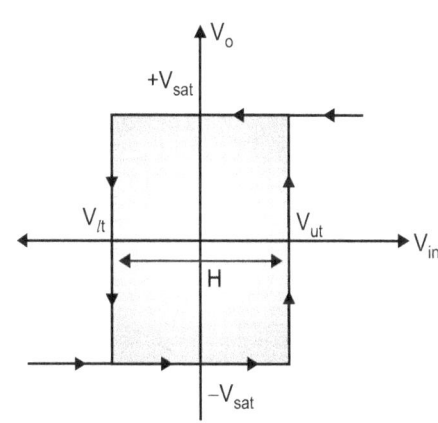

(b) Input and output waveforms of non-inverting Schmitt trigger

(c) V_o versus V_{in} plot the hystresis voltage

Fig. 4.9

When the input voltage V_{in} is more negative, the output voltage will be $-V_{sat}$ because the input is applied to non-inverting terminal of the op-amp. To change the state increase V_{in} such that $V_1 = 0$. This point when the output changes its state from $-V_{sat}$ to $+V_{sat}$ is called upper threshold level and the value of V_{in} such that $V_1 = 0$ forces the op-amp to change its output from $+V_{sat}$ to $-V_{sat}$ is called lower threshold level.

The value of V_1 can be obtained by applying superposition rule as :

$$V_1 = \frac{R_1}{R_1 + R_2} V_o + \frac{R_2}{R_1 + R_2} \times V_{in} \quad \ldots (4.5)$$

To obtain V_{ut} and V_{lt} point V_1 should be 0 V.

$$\therefore \quad 0 = \frac{R_1}{R_1 + R_2} V_o + \frac{R_2}{R_1 + R_2} V_{in}$$

$$\frac{-R_1}{R_1 + R_2} V_o = \frac{R_2}{R_1 + R_2} V_{in}$$

$$\therefore \quad V_{in} = \frac{-R_1}{R_2} V_o$$

$$\therefore \quad V_{ut} = \frac{-R_1}{R_2}(-V_{sat}) = \frac{R_1}{R_2} V_{sat}$$

$$\therefore \quad V_{lt} = \frac{-R_1}{R_2}(+V_{sat})$$

$$= \frac{-R_1}{R_2} V_{sat}$$

The hystersis voltage or hystersis width (H) is given by

$$H = V_{ut} - V_{lt} = \frac{R_1}{R_2} V_{sat} + \frac{R_1}{R_2} V_{sat} = \frac{2R_1}{R_2} V_{sat} \quad \ldots (4.6)$$

Comparison of Schmitt Trigger and Comparator :

Comparator	Schmitt trigger
1. It does not use feedback.	1. It uses feedback.
2. The op-amp is used in open loop configuration.	2. The op-amp is used in closed loop configuration.
3. False triggering is possible due to noise.	3. False triggering due to noise is not possible.
4. A single reference voltage is present i.e. V_{ref} to trigger.	4. The two different triggering voltages are present i.e. V_{ut} and V_{lt}.

Design of Schmitt trigger with different UTP and LTP :

Example 4.1 :

Design an op-amp Schmitt trigger for the following specifications :
$V_o = \pm 10$ V, $V_{ut} = 4$ V and $V_{lt} = -2$ V.

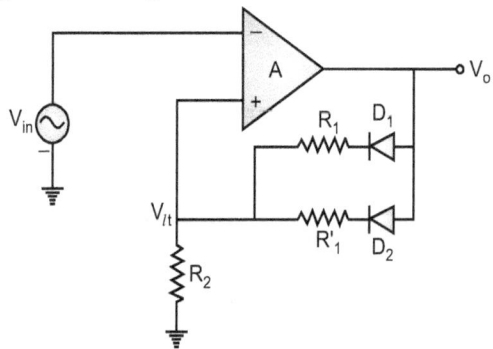

Fig. 4.10 : An inverting Schmitt trigger

Solution:

$$UTP = \frac{R_2}{R_1 + R_2} V_{sat} \qquad LTP = \frac{R_2}{R_1' R_2} \times (-V_{sat})$$

$$4 = \frac{R_2}{R_1 + R_2} \cdot 10 \qquad -2 = \frac{R_2}{R_1' + R_2} \times (-10)$$

$$\therefore \frac{R_2}{R_1 + R_2} = 0.4 \qquad -2 = \frac{10\,K}{R_1' + 10K} \times (-10)$$

Assume $\boxed{R_2 = 10\ k\Omega}$ $\qquad -2(R_1' + 10\ K) = -100\ K$

$$R_2 = 0.4\ (R_1 + R_2) \qquad R_1' + 10\ K = \frac{-100\ K}{20} = 50\ K$$

$$10\ K = 0.4\ (R_1 + 10\ K) \qquad R_1' = 50\ K - 10\ K$$

$$10\ K = 0.4 R_1 + 4K \qquad\qquad\qquad = 40\ K \quad \boxed{R_1' = 40\ K}$$

$$10\ K - 4\ K = 0.4\ R_1$$
$$6\ K = 0.4\ R_1$$
$$R_1 = \frac{6\ K}{0.4} \quad \boxed{R_1 = 15\ K}$$

Design of Schmitt:

Example 4.2:

Design inverting Schmitt trigger for $V_{ut} = 4$ V, $V_{lt} = -2$V.
Assume supply voltage = ± 12 V.

Solution:

For the given Schmitt trigger, $V_{ut} = 4$ V, $V_{lt} = -2$ V, $± V_{sat} = ± 12$ V

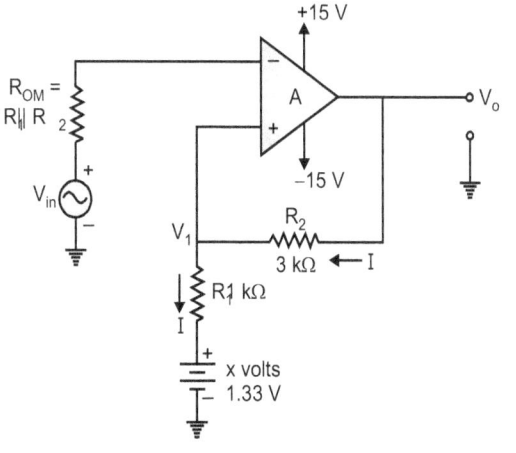

Fig. 4.11

The voltage V_1 decides upper threshold and lower threshold levels. Applying KVL to the output circuit and neglecting op-amp input current,

$$-IR_2 - IR_1 - x + V_o = 0$$

$$\therefore \quad I = \frac{V_o - x}{R_1 + R_2}$$

and

$$V_1 = IR_1 + x$$

$$= \frac{V_o - x}{R_1 + R_2} R_1 + x$$

For $+V_{sat} = +12$ V, $V_1 = V_{ut} = 4$ V, $V_o = +12$ V

$$\therefore \quad 4 = \frac{12 - x}{R_1 + R_2} R_1 + x \qquad \ldots (1)$$

For $-V_{sat} = -12$ V, $V_1 = V_{lt} = -2$V, $V_o = -12$ V.

$$\therefore \quad -2 = \frac{-12 - x}{R_1 + R_2} R_1 + x \qquad \ldots (2)$$

Subtracting equation (2) from equation (1),

$$4 - (-2) = \frac{R_1}{R_1 + R_2}(12 - x + 12 + x)$$

$$6 = \frac{24 R_1}{R_1 + R_2}$$

$$R_2 = 3R_1 \qquad \ldots (3)$$

Substituting equation (3) in equation (1),

$$4 = \frac{12 - x}{R_1 + 3R_1} R_1 + x$$

$$4 = \frac{12 - x}{4R_1} R_1 + x$$

$$4 = \frac{12 - x}{4} + x$$

$$16 = 12 - x + 4x$$

$$4 = 3x$$

$$\therefore \quad x = \frac{4}{3} = 1.333 \text{ V}$$

Choose $R_1 = 1$ kΩ, hence $R_2 = 3$ kΩ

$$R_{OM} = R_1 \| R_2 = \frac{R_1 R_2}{R_1 + R_2} = \frac{1 \times 3}{1 + 3} = \frac{3}{4} = 0.75 \text{ k}\Omega$$

Example 4.3 :

For the inverting Schmitt trigger given in Fig. 4.12, find V_{th}, V_{TL}, ΔV_T and draw the input/output waveforms.

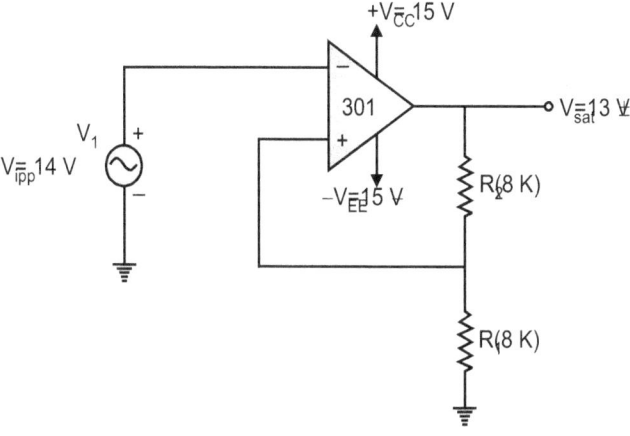

Fig. 4.12

Solution :

$$V_{sat} = \pm 13 \text{ V}$$

$$V_{ut} = V_{th} = \frac{(+13) \times 8 \times 10^3}{(8+8) \times 10^3} = 6.5 \text{ V}$$

$$V_{lt} = V_{TL} = \frac{(-13) \times 8 \times 10^3}{(8+8) \times 10^3} = -6.5 \text{ V}$$

$$\Delta V_T = V_{ut} - V_{lt}$$
$$= 6.5 - (-6.5) = 6.5 + 6.5 = 13 \text{ V}$$

Fig. 4.13

Example 4.4 :

For the Schmitt trigger shown in Fig. 4.14. Calculate the trip points and hysteresis if $V_{sat} = \pm 12.5$ V. If the resistances have a tolerance of ± 5%, what is the minimum hysteresis ?

Solution :

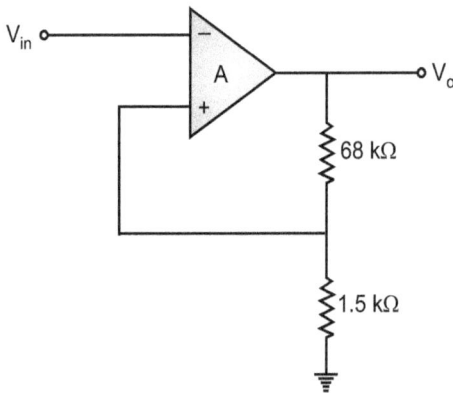

Fig. 4.14

Solution : From Fig. 4.14, $R_1 = 68$ kΩ, $R_2 = 1.5$ kΩ and $V_{sat} = \pm 12.5$ V.

$$V_{ut} = \frac{R_2}{R_1 + R_2} V_{sat}$$

$$= \frac{1.5}{68 + 1.5} \times 12.5 = 0.2697 \text{ V}$$

$$V_{lt} = -0.269 \text{ V}$$

$$H = V_{ut} - V_{lt}$$

$$= 0.269 - (-0.269) = 0.538 \text{ V}$$

Now, $$H = \frac{2R_2}{R_1 + R_2} \times V_{sat}$$

For minimum H, R_2 must be minimum and R_1 must be maximum.

$$R_{2\,min} = R_2 - 5\% \, R_2$$

$$= 1.5 \text{ k}\Omega - \frac{5}{100} \times 1.5 \times 10^3$$

$$= 1.425 \text{ k}\Omega$$

$$R_{1\,max} = R_1 + 5\% \text{ max. } R_1$$

$$= 68 \times 10^3 + \frac{5}{100} \times 68 \times 10^3 = 71.4 \text{ k}\Omega$$

$$H_{min} = \frac{2 \times 1.425 \times 10^3}{(1.425 + 71.4) \times 10^3} \times 12.5 = 0.489 \text{ V}$$

Example 4.5 :

A system is used as ON-OFF temperature controller. Temperature is to be maintained between 25°C to 30°C. The temperature transducer generates a voltage of +0.5 V at 25°C and 1.5 V at 30°C. Heater is operated through a relay of 12 V, 100 mA. Design a suitable circuit using op-amp and draw detailed circuit diagram.

Solution :

The upper threshold and lower threshold levels are corresponding to 25°C and 30°C are 0.5 V and 1.5 V.

$$V_{ut} = 1.5 \text{ V}, \quad V_{lt} = 0.5 \text{ V}$$

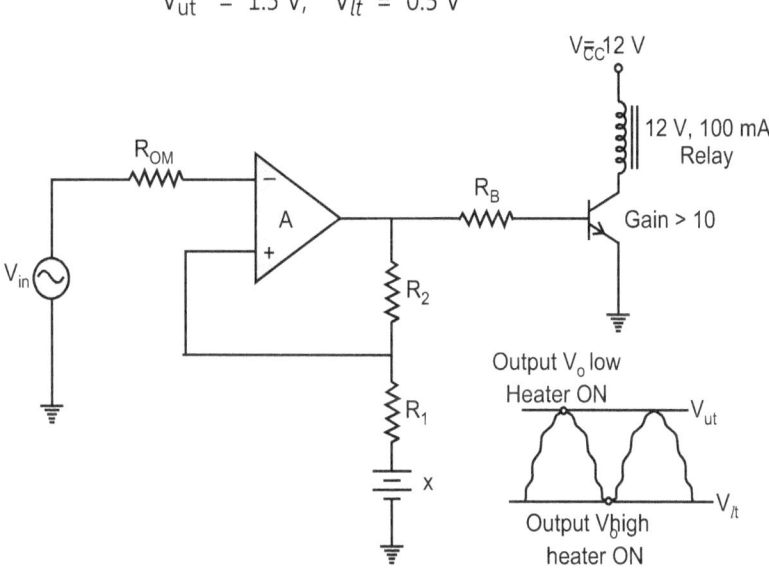

Fig. 4.15

$$V_1 = IR_1 + x$$

$$= \frac{(V_o - x) R_1}{R_1 + R_2} + x$$

$$V_o = +V_{sat} = +15 \text{ V}, \quad V_{ut} = 1.5 \text{ V}$$

$$\therefore \quad 1.5 = \frac{(15 - x) R_1}{R_1 + R_2} + x \qquad \ldots (1)$$

At $V_o = -V_{sat} = -15 \text{ V}, \quad V_{lt} = 0.5 \text{ V}$

$$0.5 = \frac{(-15 - x) R_1}{R_1 + R_2} + x \qquad \ldots (2)$$

Subtract equation (2) from equation (1),

$$1.5 - 0.5 = \frac{R_1}{R_1 + R_2}(15 - x + 15 + x)$$

$$1 = \frac{R_1}{R_1 + R_2} \times 30$$

$$\frac{1}{30} = \frac{R_1}{R_1 + R_2}$$

$$R_1 + R_2 = 30 R_1$$
$$R_2 = 30 R_1 - R_1$$
$$R_2 = 29 R_1$$

Choose $R_1 = 1 \text{ k}\Omega$
$R_2 = 29 \text{ k}\Omega$

$$R_{OM} = R_1 \parallel R_2 = \frac{R_1 R_2}{R_1 + R_2}$$

$$= \frac{29 \times 1 \times 10^3 \times 10^3}{(29 + 1) \times 10^3} = \frac{29 \times 10^3}{30} = 0.96 \text{ k}\Omega$$

4.2.2 A Square Wave Generator (Astable)

Square wave outputs are generated when the op-amp is forced to operate in the saturated region. That is, the output has to swing repetitively between positive saturation $+V_{sat}$ ($\cong +V_{CC}$) and negative saturation $-V_{sat}$ ($\cong -V_{EE}$), resulting in the square wave output. The square wave generator is also called as a free running or astable multivibrator. The output of the op-amp in this circuit will be in positive or negative saturation, depending on whether the differential voltage V_{id} is positive or negative respectively.

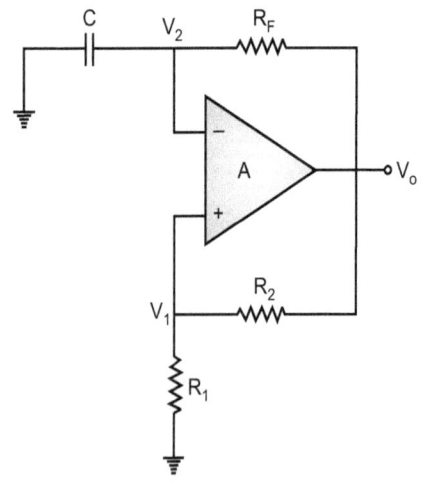
(a) Square wave generator

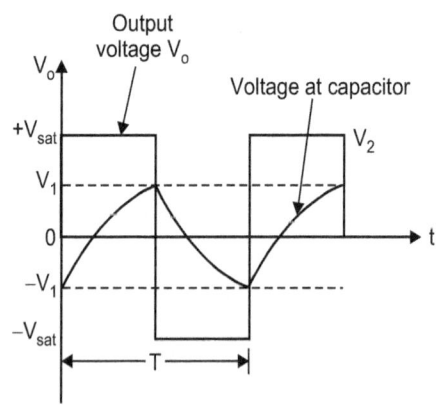
(b) Waveforms of output voltage

Fig. 4.16

Assume that voltage across capacitor C is zero voltage when the DC supply voltages $+V_{CC}$ and $-V_{EE}$ are applied. This means that the voltage at the input inverting terminal is initially zero. At the same time the voltage V_1 at the non-inverting terminal is a very small finite value due to output offset voltage V_{OOT} and the values of resistors R_1 and R_2. Thus, the differential voltage V_{id} is equal to V_1. The voltage V_1 drives the op-amp into saturation. The capacitor C starts charging towards $+V_{sat}$ through resistor R. When the voltage V_2 across capacitor C is slightly more positive than V_1, the output of op-amp is forced to switch to a negative saturation $-V_{sat}$. The voltage V_1 across R_1 is also negative.

$$V_1 = \frac{R_1}{R_1 + R_2}(-V_{sat}) \qquad \ldots (4.7)$$

Thus, the net differential voltage $V_{id} = V_1 - V_2$ is negative, which holds the op-amp in negative saturation. The output remains in negative saturation until the capacitor C discharges and then recharges to a negative voltage slightly higher than $-V_1$. As soon as the capacitor's voltage V_2 becomes more negative than $-V_1$, the net differential voltage V_{id} becomes positive and hence drives the op-amp back to positive saturation.

$$V_1 = \frac{R_1}{R_1 + R_2}(+V_{sat})$$

The time period T of the waveform is given by

$$T = 2RC \ln\left(\frac{2R_1 + R_2}{R_2}\right) \qquad \ldots (4.8)$$

or

$$f_o = \frac{1}{2RC \ln[(2R_1 + R_2)/R_2]} \qquad \ldots (4.9)$$

Example 4.6 :

Design a square wave oscillator so that $f_o = 1$ kHz. The op-amp is a 741 with DC supply voltages $= \pm 15$ V.

Solution :

Use $\quad R_2 = 1.16 R_1$

Let $\quad R_1 = 10$ kΩ

$\quad R_2 = (1.16) \times 10 = 11.6$ kΩ

Next, choose a value of C and calculate the value of R.

Hence, let C = 0.05 μF.

$$R = \frac{1}{(10)(10^{-8}) \times (10^3)}$$

$= 10 \text{ k}\Omega$

Thus, $R_1 = 10 \text{ k}\Omega$

$R_2 = 11.6 \text{ k}\Omega$

$R = 10 \text{ k}\Omega$

$C = 0.05 \text{ μF}$

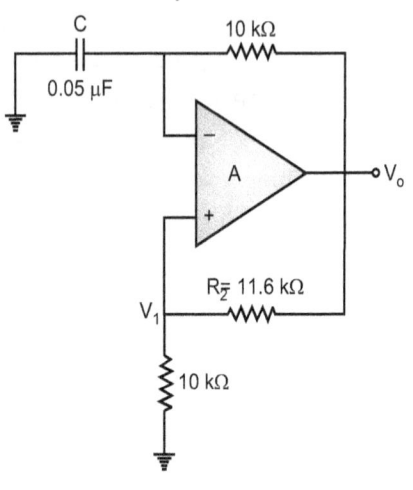

Fig. 4.17

4.2.2.1 Frequency of Oscillation

The instantaneous voltage across the capacitor is given as

$$V_C(t) = V_{max} + (V_{init} - V_{final}) e^{-t/T}$$

Let us consider the charging of capacitor from V_{lt} to V_{ut}.

V_{lt} = Initial voltage

V_{ut} = Instantaneous voltage

$+V_{sat}$ = Maximum voltage

At $t = T_1$, $\quad V_{ut} = +V_{sat} + [V_{lt} - (+V_{sat})] e^{-T_1/RC}$

$-[V_{lt} - (+V_{sat})] e^{-T_1/RC} = +V_{sat} - V_{ut}$

$$e^{-T_1/RC} = \frac{(+V_{sat} - V_{ut})}{(+V_{sat} - V_{lt})}$$

$$\frac{-T_1}{RC} = \ln\left[\frac{+V_{sat} - V_{ut}}{+V_{sat} - V_{lt}}\right]$$

$$T_1 = -RC \ln\left[\frac{+V_{sat} - V_{ut}}{+V_{sat} - V_{lt}}\right] = RC \ln\left[\frac{+V_{sat} - V_{lt}}{+V_{sat} - V_{ut}}\right]$$

Total time T = 2T$_1$

$$= 2RC \ln\left[\frac{+V_{sat} - V_{lt}}{+V_{sat} - V_{ut}}\right]$$

$$T = 2RC \ln\left[\frac{+V_{sat} - \left(\frac{-V_{sat} \cdot R_1}{R_1 + R_2}\right)}{+V_{sat} - \left(\frac{+V_{sat} \cdot R_1}{R_1 + R_2}\right)}\right]$$

$$= 2RC \ln\left[\frac{+V_{sat}(1 + R_1/(R_1 + R_2))}{+V_{sat}(1 - R_1/R_1 + R_2)}\right]$$

$$= 2RC \ln\left[1 + \frac{R_1}{R_1 + R_2} \times \frac{R_1 + R_2}{R_1 + R_2 - R_1}\right]$$

$$\boxed{T = 2RC \ln\left[\frac{2R_1 + R_2}{R_2}\right]} \quad \ldots (4.10)$$

Example 4.7 :

For the circuit shown in Fig. 4.18 if R_2 = 100 kΩ, R_1 = 86 kΩ, ± V_{sat} = ± 15 V, R_F = 100 kΩ and C = 0.1 µF, find (i) V_{ut} (ii) V_{lt} (iii) frequency of oscillation.

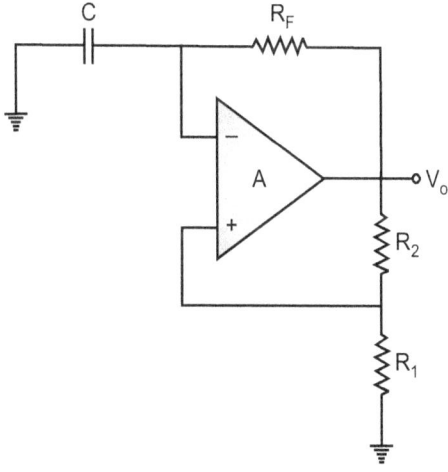

Fig. 4.18

Solution :

$$V_{ut} = \frac{R_1}{R_1 + R_2}(+V_{sat}) = \frac{86 K \times 15}{(86 + 100) K} = \frac{86 \times 15}{186} = 6.94 V$$

$$V_{lt} = -6.94 V$$

$$f_o = \cfrac{1}{2R_F\, C\, \ln\left[\dfrac{+V_{sat} - V_{lt}}{+V_{sat} - V_{ut}}\right]}$$

$$= \cfrac{1}{2\times 100 \times 10^3 \times 0.1 \times 10^{-6}\, \ln\left[\dfrac{15-(-6.94)}{15-6.94}\right]}$$

$$= \frac{1}{0.02} = 50\ \text{Hz}$$

Example 4.8 :

For the AMV show that $T = 2R_F C$ when $R_1 = 0.86\, R_2$.

Solution :

$$T = 2R_F\, C\, \ln\left[\cfrac{+V_{sat} - \left(\dfrac{-V_{sat}\, R_1}{R_1 + R_2}\right)}{+V_{sat} - \left(\dfrac{+V_{sat}\, R_1}{R_1 + R_2}\right)}\right]$$

$$= 2R_F\, C\, \ln\left[\dfrac{V_{sat}(1 + R_1/R_1 + R_2)}{V_{sat}(1 - R_1/R_1 + R_2)}\right]$$

$$= 2R_F\, C\, \ln\left[\dfrac{2R_1 + R_2}{R_1 + R_2}\, /\, \dfrac{R_2}{R_1 + R_2}\right]$$

$$= 2R_F\, C\, \ln\left[\dfrac{2R_1 + R_2}{R_2}\right] = 2R_F\, C\, \ln\left[\dfrac{2\times 0.86 R_2 + R_2}{R_2}\right]$$

$$= 2R_F\, C\, \ln\left[\dfrac{1.72 R_2 + R_2}{R_2}\right] = 2R_F\, C\, \ln\left[\dfrac{2.72 R_2}{R_2}\right]$$

$$= 2R_F\, C\, \ln(2.72) \quad \text{where } \ln(2.72) \cong 1$$

$$\therefore \quad T = 2R_F\, C$$

Example 4.9 :

For the square wave oscillator shown in Fig. 4.19, calculate the frequency of oscillations if $R_2 = 10\ \text{k}\Omega$, $R_1 = 8.6\ \text{k}\Omega$, $R_F = 100\ \text{k}\Omega$ and $C = 0.01\ \mu\text{F}$.

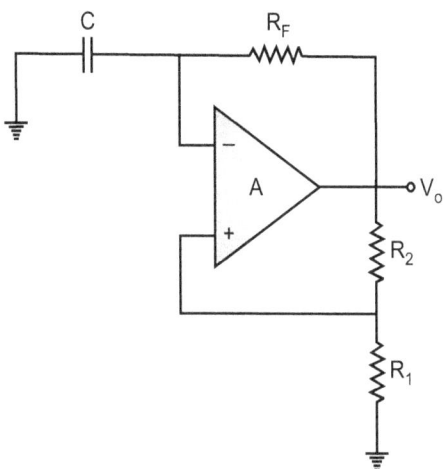

Fig. 4.19

Solution :

$$T = 2R_F C \ln\left[\frac{2R_1 + R_2}{R_2}\right]$$

$$= 2 \times 100 \times 10^3 \times 0.01 \times 10^{-6} \ln\left[\frac{2 \times 8.6\,K + 10\,K}{10\,K}\right]$$

$$= 2 \times 10^{-3}$$

$$f = \frac{1}{T} = \frac{1}{2 \times 10^{-3}} = 499.68\,Hz = 0.5\,kHz$$

4.2.3 Triangular Wave Generator Using OP-Amp

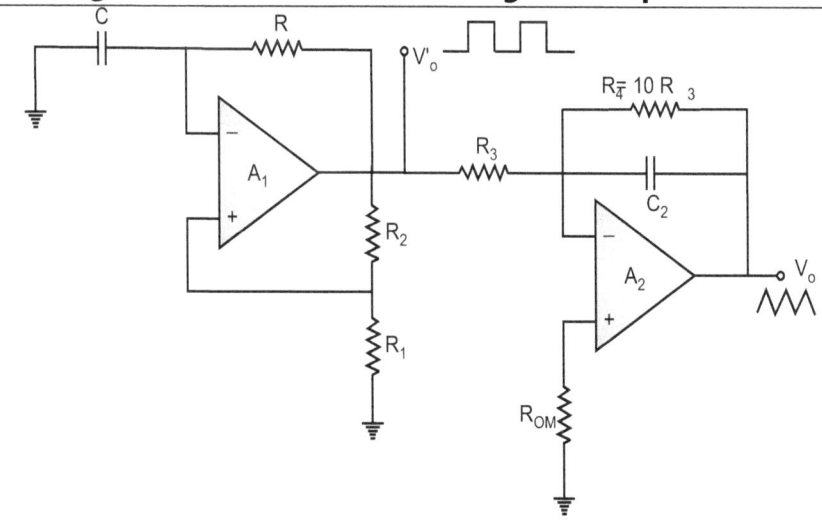

Fig. 4.20 (a) : Triangular wave generator using op-amp

A triangular wave generator can be formed by simply connecting an integrator to a square wave generator as the output of the integrator is triangular if its input is a square wave.

For fixed values of R_1, R_2 and C_1 the frequency of the square wave as well as the triangular wave depends on the resistance R. As R is increased or decreased, the frequency of the triangular wave will decrease or increase respectively. Since, the amplitude of the square wave is constant ($\pm V_{sat}$); the amplitude of the triangular wave decreases with an increase in its frequency and vice versa.

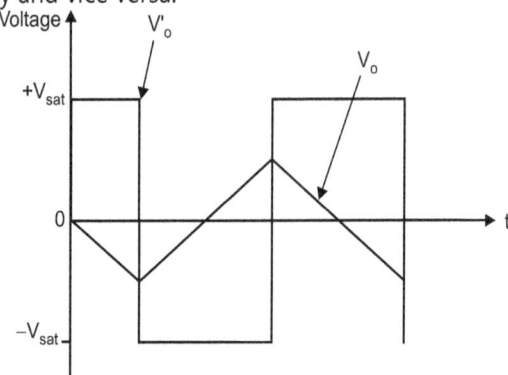

Fig. 4.20 (b) : Waveforms

The frequency of oscillation is given by

$$f_0 = \frac{R_3}{4R_1C_1R_2} \qquad \ldots (4.11)$$

4.2.4 Pulse Generation OR Monostable Multivibrator

Monostable multivibrator is called single shot multivibrator. The circuit produces a single pulse of fixed duration in response to each external trigger signal. For such circuits only one stable state exists. When an external trigger is applied, the output changes it's state. The new state is called quasistable state. The circuit remains in this state for a fixed interval of time. After some time if returns back to it's original state. Infact an internal trigger is generated which drives the circuit back to it's original stable state. Usually, the charging and discharging of a capacitor provides this internal trigger signal.

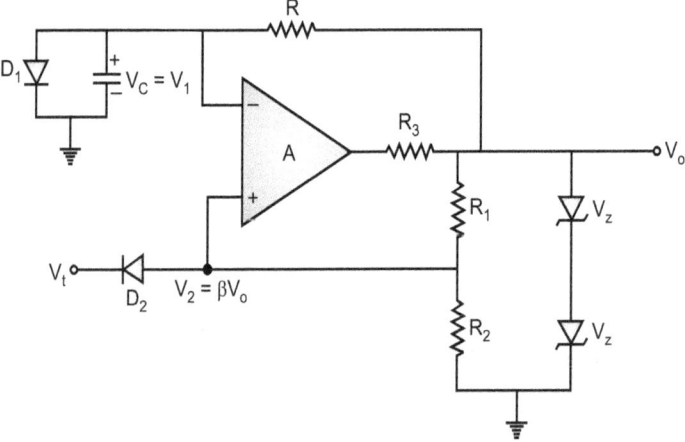

Fig. 4.21 : Monostable multivibrator using op-amp as a pulse generator

Operation :

Diode D_1 is a clamping diode connected across C. The diode clamps the capacitor voltage to 0.7 V when the output is at $+V_{sat}$. A narrow negative triggering pulse V_t is applied to the non-inverting input terminal through diode D_2.

To understand the operation of the circuit let us assume that the output V_o is at $+V_{sat}$ i.e. in it's stable state. The diode D_1 conducts and the voltage across the capacitor C i.e. V_C gets clamped to 0.7 V. The voltage at the non-inverting input terminal is controlled by potentiometric divider of R_1R_2 to βV_o i.e. $+\beta V_{sat}$ in the stable state.

Now if V_t, a negative trigger pulse is applied to the non-inverting terminal, so that the effective voltage at this terminal is less than 0.7 V $(+ \beta_{sat} - V_t)$. Then the output of the op-amp changes it's state from $+V_{sat}$ to $-V_{sat}$.

The diode is now reverse biased and capacitor starts charging exponentially to $-V_{sat}$ through resistance R.

The voltage at the non-inverting input terminal is now $-\beta V_{sat}$. When the capacitor voltage V_C becomes just slightly more $-ve$ than $-\beta V_{sat}$, the output of the op-amp changes it's state back to $+V_{sat}$.

The capacitor now starts charging towards $+V_{sat}$ through R until V_C reaches 0.7 V as capacitor gets clamped to the voltage.

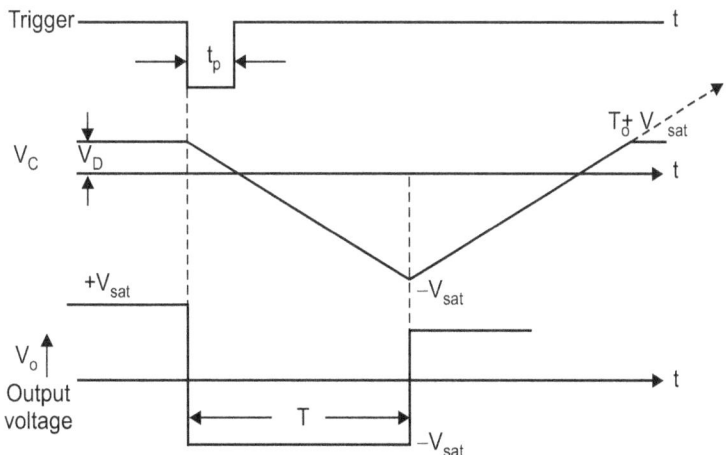

Fig. 4.22 : Waveforms of monostable multivibrator

The output voltage can be calculated as follows :

$$V_o = V_{final} + (V_{initial} - V_{final})\, e^{-t/RC}$$

Here
$$V_{final} = -V_{sat}, \quad V_{initial} = V_{D_1}$$

$$V_o = \text{Output} = \text{Capacitor voltage} = V_C$$

$$V_C = -V_{sat} + [(V_{D_1} - (-V_{sat})]\, e^{-t/RC}$$

At $t = T$.
$$V_C = -\beta V_{sat}$$

$$-\beta V_{sat} = [-V_{sat} + (V_{D_1} + V_{sat})]\, e^{-T/RC}$$

$$(V_{D_1} + V_{sat})\, e^{-T/RC} = V_{sat}(1-\beta)$$

$$e^{-T/RC} = \frac{V_{sat}(1-\beta)}{(V_{D_1} + V_{sat})}$$

$$T = RC \ln\left[\frac{1 + V_{D_1}/V_{sat}}{1-\beta}\right]$$

$$\therefore \quad \beta = \frac{R_2}{R_1 + R_2}$$

If $\quad V_{sat} >> V_{D_1}$

and $\quad R_1 = R_2 \;$ so that $\beta = 0.5$

then $\quad \boxed{T = 0.69\, RC}$

The diode D_2 is not essential but it is used to avoid multifunctioning if any +ve noise spikes are present in the triggering line.

4.3 TIMER IC 555 :

Signetics corporation introduced this device as the SE/NE 555 in the early 1970. The 555 is a monolithic timing circuit that can produce accurate and highly stable time delays. The device is available as 8-pin metal can, an 8-pin mini DIP, or a 14-pin DIP.

Fig. 4.23 shows block diagram and connection diagram of IC SE/NE 555 timer.

Features of IC 555 :
- It is a 8-pin metal can, an 8-pin mini DIP or a 14-pin DIP IC.
- It's operating temperature range is 0° to +70°C.
- It operates on +5 to +18 V supply voltage.
- It has an adjustable duty cycle.
- It generates timings from microseconds to hours.
- It has a high current output.
- It can source or sink 200 mA.
- The output can drive TTL.

- It provides the temperature stability 50 parts per million (ppm) per degree celsius change in temperature or 0.005% / °C.
- It is reliable easy to use and low cost.

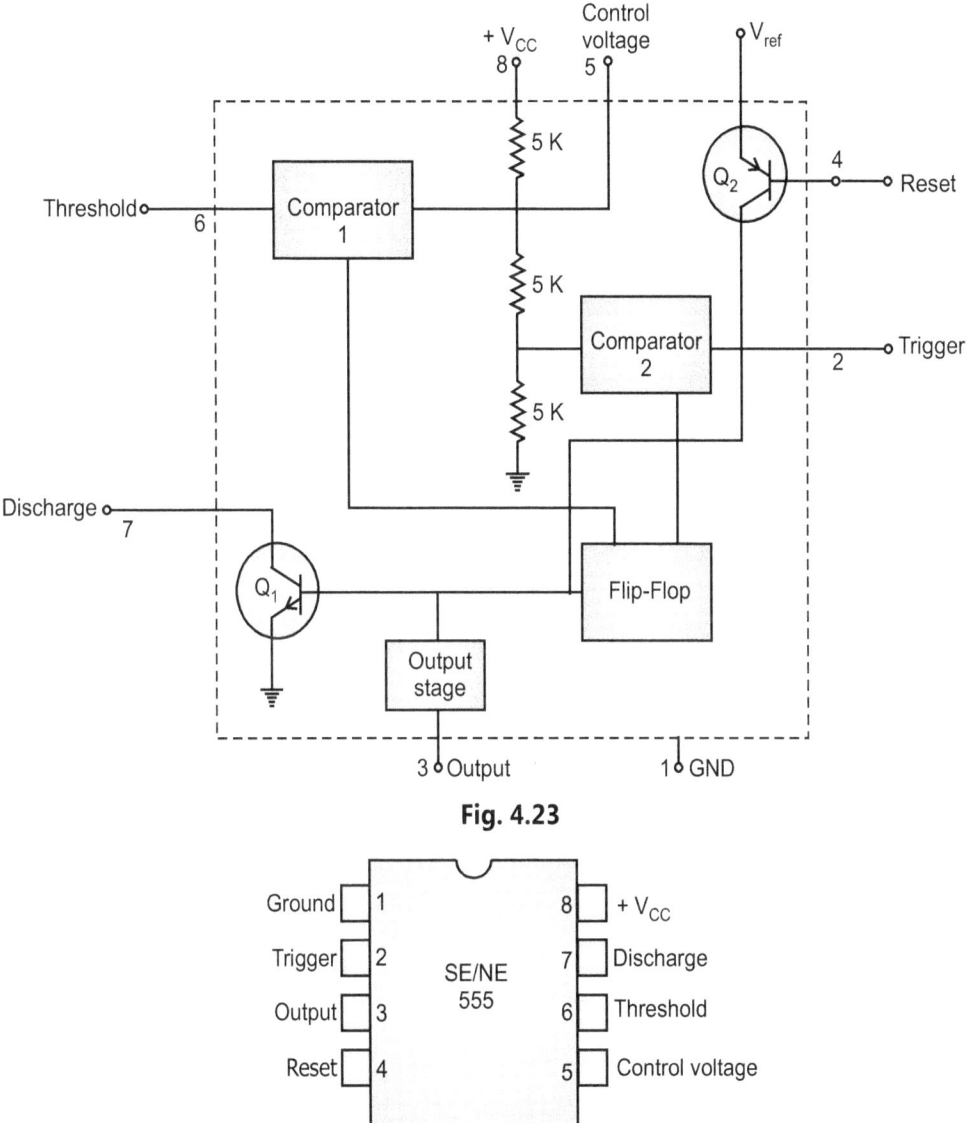

Fig. 4.23

Fig. 4.24 : 555 timer (a) Connection diagram (b) Pin diagram

Pin Description :

1. **Pin No. 1 Ground :** All the voltages are measured with respect to ground.

2. **Pin No. 2 Trigger :** The output of the timer depends on the amplitude of the external trigger pulse applied to this pin. If the voltage at this pin is grater than 2/3 V_{CC} then the output is low.

When a –ve going pulse of amplitude grater than 1/3 V_{CC} is applied at this pin, then the comparator 2 output goes low, which in turn 'switches the output of the timer high'. The output remains high as long as the trigger terminal is held at a low voltage.

3. Pin No. 3 Output : The load at the output can be connected in two ways between pin 3 and ground or between pin 3 and + V_{CC} supply voltage.

When the output is low, the load current flows through the load connected between pin 3 and +V_{CC} into the output terminal and is called the sink current is called as normally on load and when load is connected between pin 3 and ground. It is called as normally off load.

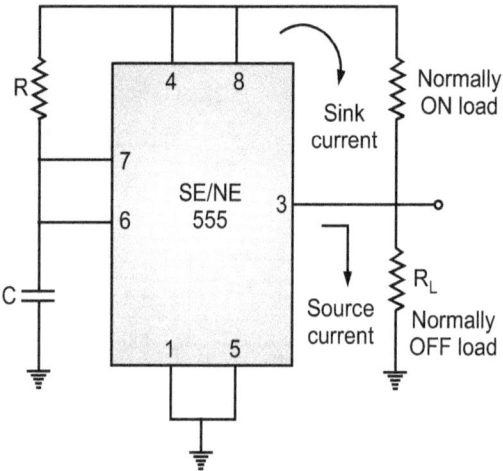

Fig. 4.25 : Normally off load

When the output is high, the current through the load connected between pin 3 and +V_{CC} is zero. Therefore, output terminal supplies current to the normally off load. This current is called as source current. The maximum value of source and sink current is 200 mA.

4. Pin No. 4 : Reset : The timer can be reset by applying a negative pulse to this pin. When the reset function is not in use, it is connected to +V_{CC} to avoid false triggering.

5. Pin No. 5 : Control Voltage : To change the threshold voltage or trigger voltage, an external voltage is applied to this terminal. The pulse width of the output waveform can be varied by giving some voltage on this pin or by connecting a potentiometer between this pin and ground. When this pin is not in use, it is connected to the ground through a 0.01 µf capacitor to avoid noise pick-ups.

6. Pin No. 6 : Threshold : This pin monitors the voltage across the external capacitor. When the voltage at this pin is ≥ threshold voltage 2/3 V_{CC}, the output of the comparator 1 goes high, to switch the output of the timer low.

7. **Pin No. 7 : Discharge :** This pin is internally connected to the collector of transistor Q_1. When output is high, Q_1 is off and acts as an open circuit to the external capacitor C connected across it.

When the output is low, Q_1 is saturated and acts a short circuit. Shorting out the external capacitor C to the ground.

8. **Pin No. 8 : +V$_{CC}$:** The supply voltage of + 5 V to + 18 V is applied to this pin with respect to ground.

4.3.1 IC 555 as a Monostable Multivibrator

Monostable multivibrator is also called as single-shot multivibrator. It generates a pulse of fixed duration which can be determined by the RC network connected externally to IC 555 timer. It has only one stable state (output low).

When an external pulse is applied, the output is forced to go high. The time period for which the output remain high is determined by the external RC circuit. At the end, the output automatically goes back to its original stage.

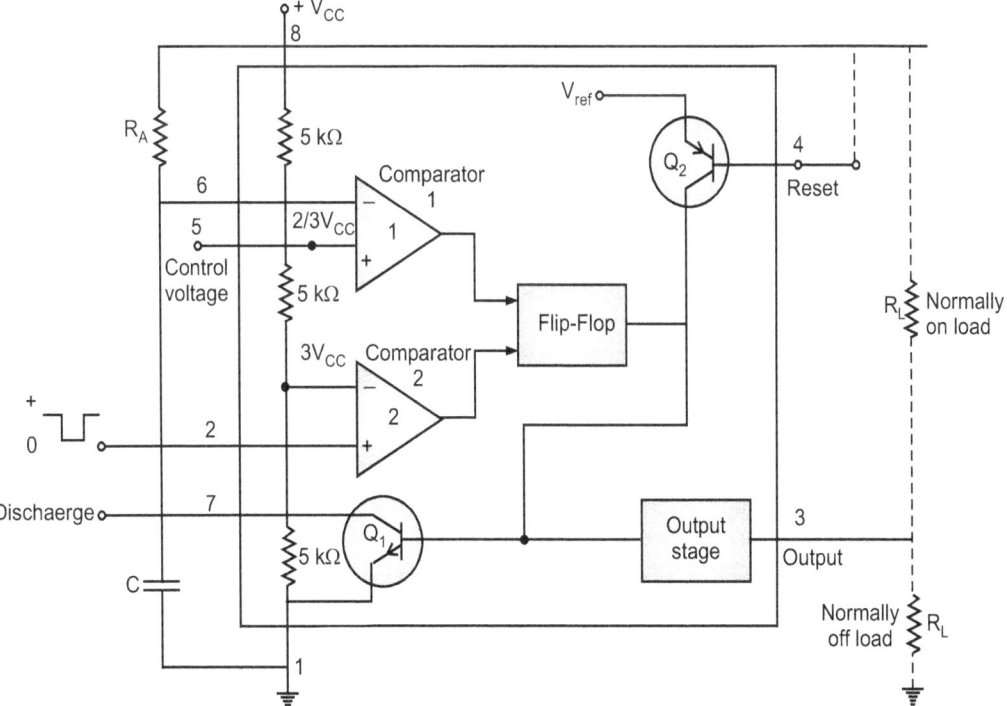

Fig. 4.26 (a) : Monostable multivibrator using IC 555 timer

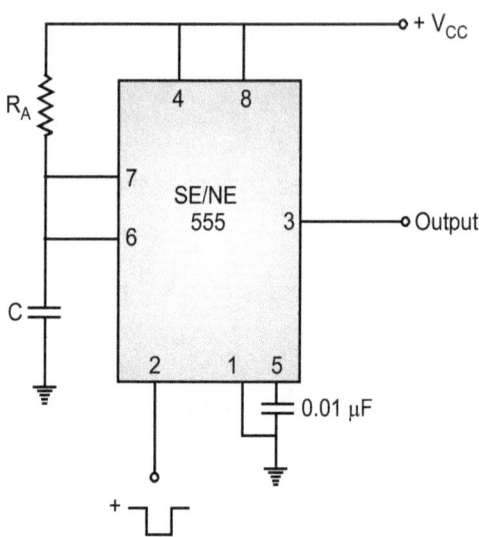

Fig. 4.26 (b) : Monostable multivibrator using IC 555 timer

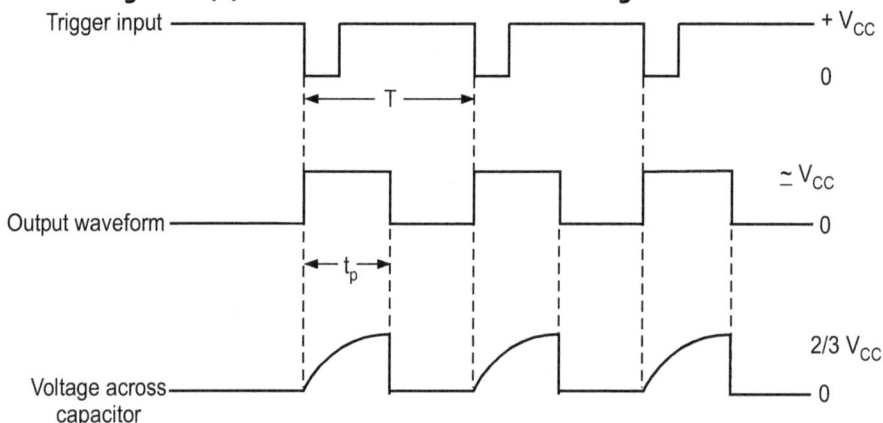

Fig. 4.26 (c) : Input and output waveforms

Operation :

When the output is low, the circuit is in stable state, transistor Q_1 is ON and capacitor C is shorted to ground.

When the negative trigger pulse is applied at pin No. 2, transistor Q_1 becomes OFF. Now the capacitor C starts charging towards V_{CC} through R_A. When the voltage across the capacitor equals 2/3 V_{CC}, comparator 1 output changes from low to high which drives the output to its low state through the flip-flop. At the same time the output of the flip-flop turns transistor Q_1 ON and hence capacitor C starts discharging. The output of the monostable remains low until a trigger pulse is applied again. Thus, the cycle repeats.

Fig. 4.26 (c) shows the input and output waveform. The width of the trigger pulse must be smaller than the expected pulse width of the output waveform. Also, the trigger pulse must be a negative going input signal with an amplitude larger than 1/3 V_{CC}.

4.3.1.1 Derivation of the Pulse Width

The instantaneous voltage across the capacitor is given by

$$V_C(t) = V_{max}(1 - e^{-t_p/T})$$

$$V_C(t) = 2/3 \, V_{CC}$$

$$V_{max} = V_{CC}$$

$$2/3 \, V_{CC} = V_{CC}(1 - e^{-t_p/RC})$$

$$\left(\frac{2}{3} - 1\right) = e^{-t_p/RC}$$

$$\frac{-t_p}{RC} = -1.0986$$

$$t_p = 1.0986 \, RC$$

$$\mathbf{t_p = 1.1 \, RC} \quad \ldots(4.12)$$

In practice, a decoupling capacitor (10 μf) is connected between +V_{CC} and ground to eliminate unwanted voltage spikes in the output waveform. Sometimes, a waveshaping circuit consisting of R, C_2 and diode D is connected between pin no. 2 and V_{CC} to prevent any possibility of mistriggering of the monostable multivibrator on positive pulse edges.

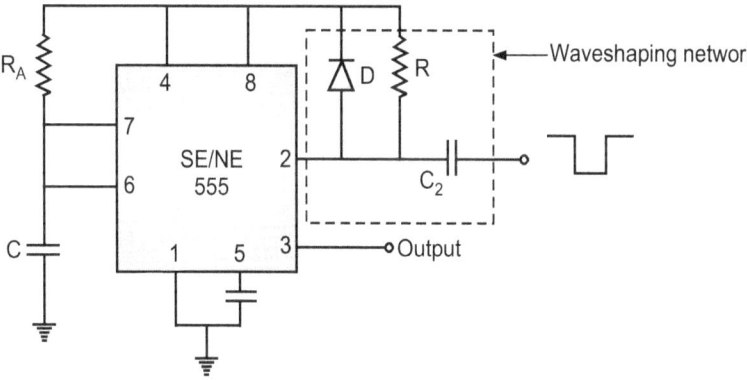

Fig. 4.27 : Monstable multivibrator with waveshaping network

4.3.2 Monostable Multivibrator Applications

(a) Frequency Divider : Monostable multivibrator can be used as a frequency divider by adjusting the length of the timing cycle t_p w.r.t. the time period T of the trigger input signal applied to pin no. 2.

To use the monstable multivibrator as a divide-by-2 circuit, the timing interval t_p must be slightly larger than the time period T of the trigger input signal.

Similarly to design divide-by-3 circuit, t_p must be slightly larger than twice the period of the input trigger signal and so on.

The frequency divider application is possible because the monostable multivibrator cannot be triggered during the timing cycle.

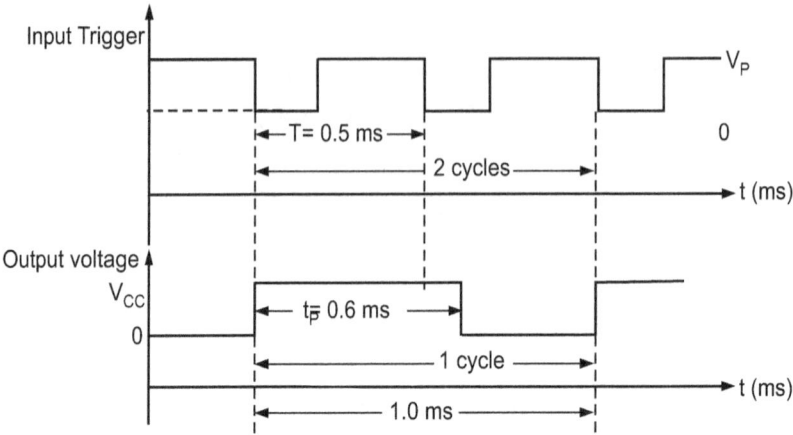

Fig. 4.28 : Input and output waveforms of monostable multivibrator as a divide-by-2 network

(b) Pulse Stretcher : This application makes the use of fact that output pulse width of the monostable multivibrator is of longer duration than the negative pulse width of the input trigger. The output pulse width of the monostable multivibrator can be viewed as a stretched version of the narrow input pulse, hence it is called as pulse stretcher. The pulse stretcher can be used to drive LED display. Fig. 4.29 shows the monostable multivibrator used as a pulse stretcher with an LED indicator at the output. The LED will be ON during timing interval $t_p = 1.1\, R_A\, C$ which can be varied by changing the value of R_A and /or C.

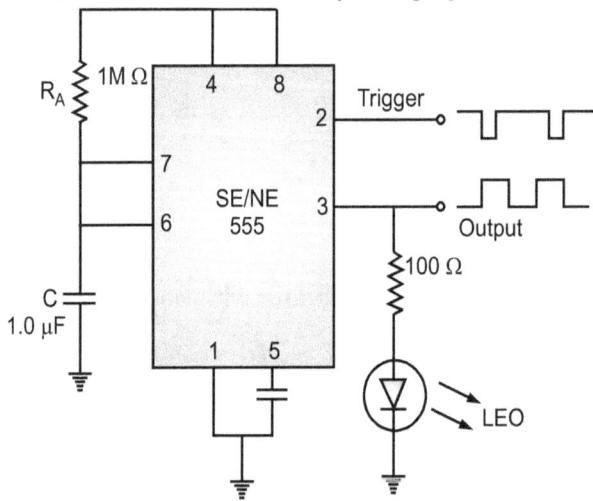

Fig. 4.29 : Monostable multivibrator as a pulse stretcher

4.3.3 IC 555 as an Astable Multivibrator

Astable multivibrator is also called as free running oscillator. The circuit does not require any external trigger to change the state of the output. Therefore, it is called as free running oscillator. The time period is determined by two resistors and a capacitor which are external to 555 timer Fig. 4.30 shows the IC 555 used as a Astable Multivibrator.

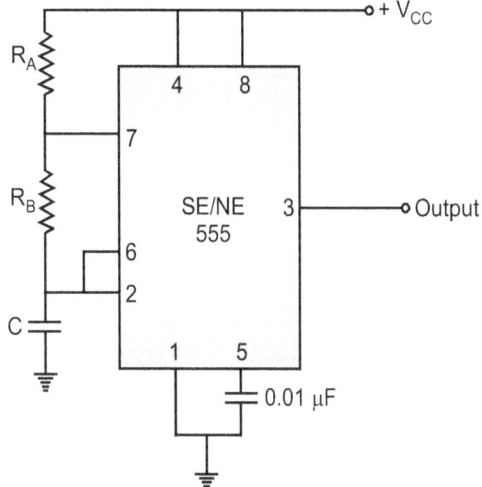

Fig. 4.30 (a) : Circuit diagram

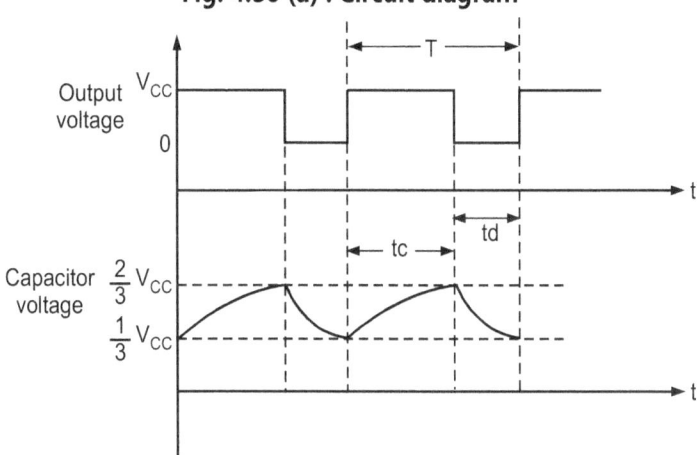

Fig. 4.30 (b) : Output and capacitor voltage waveforms

Circuit Operation : Assume that initially output is high, and capacitor C starts charging towards V_{CC} through R_A and R_B. When the voltage across the capacitor becomes 2/3 V_{CC} comparator 1 triggers the flip flop and the output becomes low. Now, the capacitor starts discharging through R_B and transistor Q_1, when voltage across C becomes 1/3 V_{CC}, comparator 2's output triggers the flip-flop and the output goes high. Thus, the cycle repeats. The output voltage and capacitor voltage waveforms are shown in Fig. 4.30 (b).

The time period during which the capacitor charges from 1/3 V_{CC} to 2/3 V_{CC} is equal to the time the output is high and is given by

$$t_c = 0.69 \, (R_A + R_B) \, C \qquad \ldots(4.13)$$

where R_A and R_B is in ohms and C is in farads.

The time during which the capacitor discharges from 2/3 V_{CC} to 1/3 V_{CC} is given by
$$t_d = 0.69\, R_B \cdot C$$
The total time period
$$T = t_c + t_d$$
$$T = 0.69\, (R_A + 2R_B)\, C$$

Thus, the frequency of oscillation is given as
$$f_o = \frac{1}{T} = \frac{1.45}{(R_A + 2R_B)\, C}$$

The % duty cycle is calculated as
$$\% \text{ Duty cycle} = \frac{t_c}{T} \times 100$$
$$= \frac{R_A + R_B}{R_A + 2R_B} \times 100 \qquad \ldots(4.14)$$

When R_A is much smaller than R_B the duty cycle approaches to 50% and the output waveform becomes square wave.

4.3.4 Applications of Astable Generator

1. As a square wave generator : In astable timer circuit it is not possible to achieve 50% duty cycle. Some modifications are done to obtain the square wave as shown in Fig. 4.31.

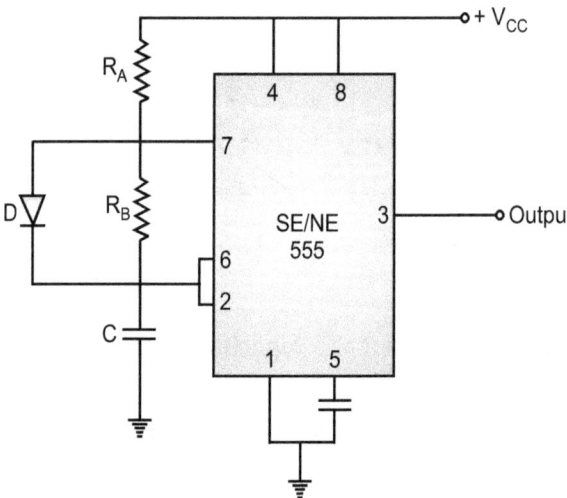

Fig. 4.31 : Square wave generator

Here capacitor C charges through R_A and diode D and discharges through R_B.

2. FSK Generator : Binary codes 1's and 0's can be transmitted by shifting a carrier frequency. Fixed frequency represents one and other represents zero. Such type of transmission is called frequency shift keying (FSK). IC 555 can be used to generate FSK. Fig. 4.32 shows the circuit for FSK generation.

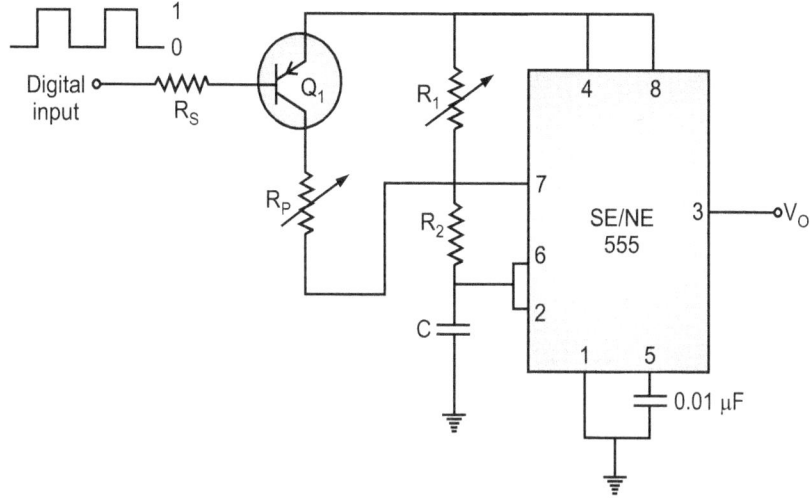

Fig. 4.32 : FSK generator

When digital input is High (or logic 1), transistor Q_1 is OFF and IC 555 works as a normal astable timer. The frequency of the output waveform can be given as

$$f_o = \frac{1.45}{(R_1 + 2R_2)C} \qquad ...(4.15)$$

When input is Low (logic 0), transistor Q_1 is ON and connects the resistance R_P in parallel with R_1. The frequency of output waveform is given by

$$f_o = \frac{1.45}{[(R_1 \parallel R_P) + 2R_2]C}$$

Example 4.10 :

Design an astable multivibrator for an output frequency of 1 kHz but a variable duty cycle of 30% to 70%. Assume V_{CC} = 12 V.

Solution :

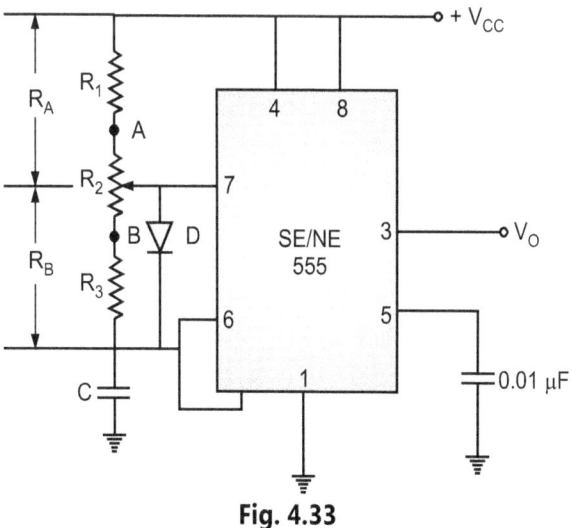

Fig. 4.33

$$f = \frac{1.44}{C(R_1 + R_2 + R_3)}$$

$$C = 0.1\ \mu f$$

$$1 \times 10^3 = \frac{1.44}{0.1 \times 10^{-6}(R_1 + R_2 + R_3)}$$

$$R_1 + R_2 + R_3 = 14400$$

$$\%\ D_{min} = \frac{R_1}{R_1 + R_2 + R_3} \times 100$$

$$30 = \frac{R_1}{R_1 + R_2 + R_3} \times 100$$

$$30 = \frac{R_1}{14400} \times 100$$

$$R_1 = 4.32\ k\Omega$$

$$\%\ D_{max} = \frac{R_1 + R_2}{R_1 + R_2 + R_3} \times 100$$

$$70 = \frac{R_1 + R_2}{R_1 + R_2 + R_3} \times 100$$

$$70 = \frac{4.32 \times 10^3 + R_2}{14400} \times 100$$

$$R_2 = 5.76\ k\Omega$$

$$R_3 = 4.32\ k\Omega$$

$$C = 0.1\ \mu f$$

4.4 ANALYSIS AND DESIGN OF R-C OSCILLATORS

4.4.1 Phase Shift Oscillator Using op-amp

Phase shift oscillator consists of an op-amp as the amplifying stage and three RC cascaded networks as the feedback circuit. Fig. 4.34 shows the phase shift oscillator. The feedback circuit provides feedback voltage from the output back to the input of the amplifier. The op-amp is used in the in the inverting mode.

The inverting terminal and the output has 180° phase shift, so any signal that appears at the inverting terminal is shifted by 180° at the output. An additional 180° phase shift required for oscillation is generated by the cascaded RC networks. Therefore, the total phase shift around the loop is 360° or 0°. The frequency of oscillator f_o is given by

$$f_o = \frac{1}{2\pi\sqrt{6}\ RC}$$

$$= \frac{0.065}{RC}$$

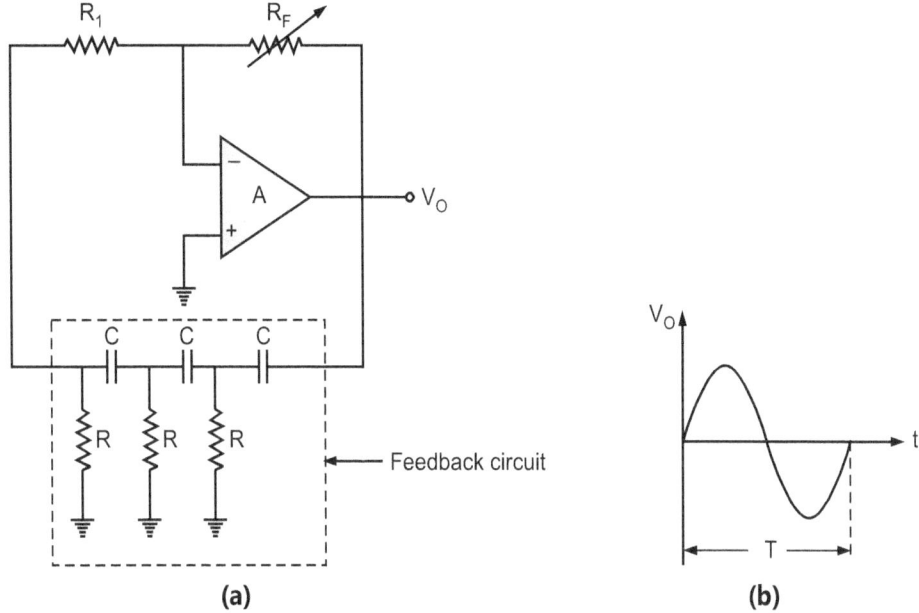

Fig. 4.34 : Phase shift oscillator and its output waveform

At this frequency, the gain A must be at least 29. i.e.

$$\left|\frac{R_F}{R_1}\right| = 29$$

$$R_F = 29\, R_1 \qquad \ldots(4.16)$$

Example 4.11 :

Design the phase shift oscillator for f_o = 200 Hz.

Solution :

Let
$$C = 0.1\ \mu f$$

$$R = \frac{0.065}{200 \times 10^{-7}}$$

$$= 3.25\ k\Omega$$

Use $\qquad R = 3.3\ k\Omega$

To avoid the loading effect of the amplifier because of RC networks, it is necessary that $R_1 \geq 10\ R$.

Let
$$R_1 = 10\ R$$
$$= 33\ k\Omega$$

$$R_F = 29 \times 33\ k\Omega$$
$$= 957\ k\Omega$$

Use $\qquad R_F = 1\ M\Omega$ pot

For selecting op-amp type IC 741 is selected for lower frequencies < 1 KHZ. For higher frequencies an op-amp such as LM 318 or LF 351 is recommended because of its increased slew rate.

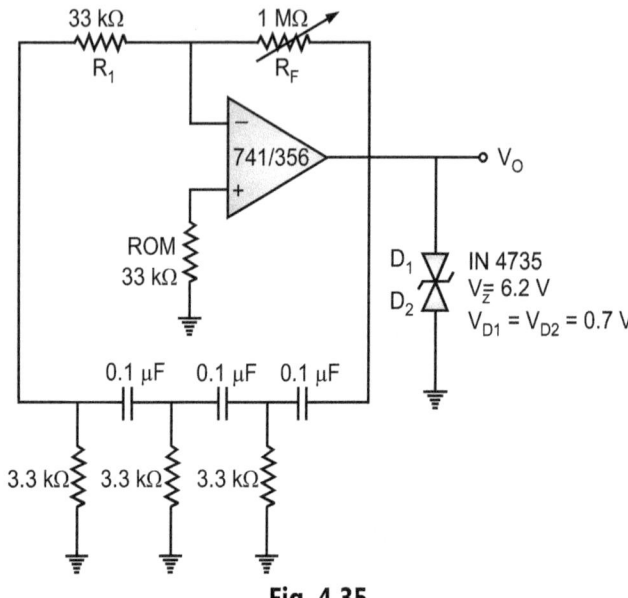

Fig. 4.35

4.4.2 Wien Bridge Oscillator

Wien bridge oscillator is the most commonly used audio frequency oscillator because of its simplicity and stability. Fig. 4.36 shows the wien bridge oscillator in which the wien bridge circuit is connected between the amplifier input terminals and the output terminal. The bridge has a series RC network in the adjoining arm. In the remaining two arms of the bridge, resistor R_1 and R_F are connected.

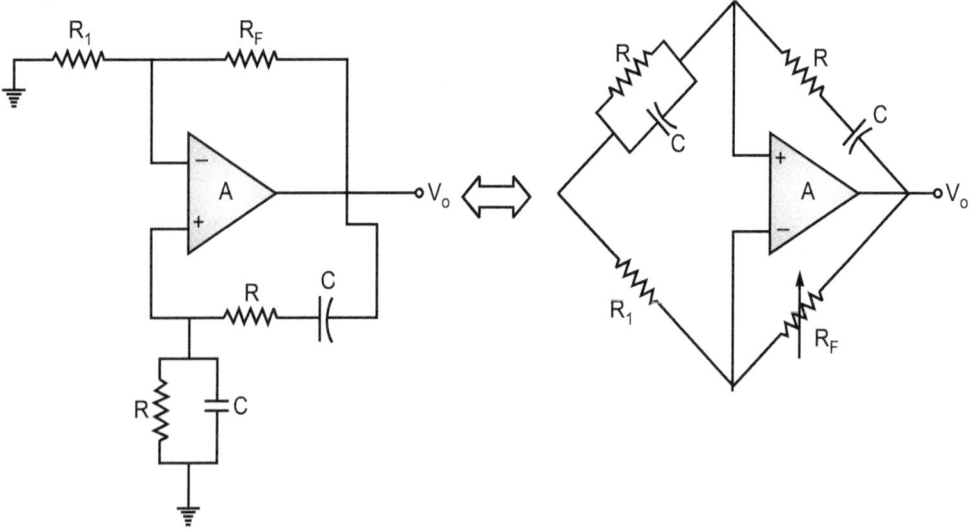

Fig. 4.36 : Wien bridge oscillator

When the bridge is balanced the condition is known as resonance. The frequency of oscillation f_o is exactly the resonant frequency of the balanced wien bridge and is given by

$$f_o = \frac{1}{2\pi RC} = \frac{0.159}{RC} \qquad \ldots(4.17)$$

Assuming that the resistors are equal in value and the capacitors are equal in the reactive leg of the wien bridge. At this frequency the gain required for sustained oscillation is given by

$$A = \frac{1}{\beta} = 3$$

$$1 + \frac{R_F}{R_1} = 3$$

$$R_F = 2 R_1$$

Example 4.12 :

Design the wien bridge oscillator for f_o = 965 Hz

Solution :

Let $\quad C = 0.05\ \mu f$

$$R = \frac{0.159}{5 \times 10^{-8} \times 965} = 3.3\ k\Omega$$

Let $\quad R_1 = 12\ k\Omega$

$\quad R_F = 2 \times 12\ k\Omega = 24\ k\Omega$

Use $\quad R_F = 50\ k\Omega$ potentiometer

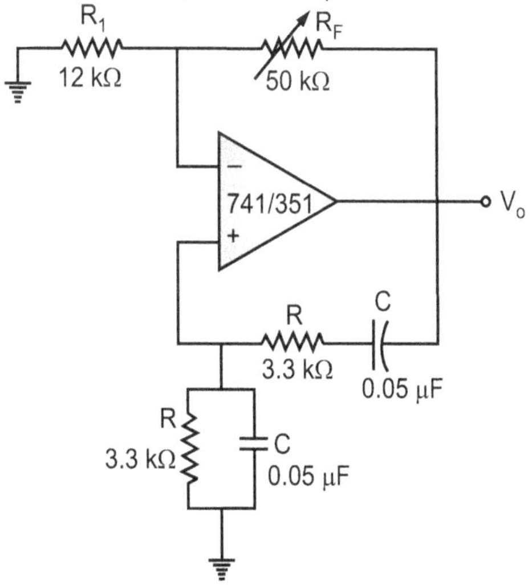

Fig. 4.37

4.5 VOLTAGE CONTROLLED OSCILLATOR IC SE/NE 566

The VCO generates an output frequency that is directly proportional to its input voltage. SE/NE 566 VCO is the typical example of VCO which provides simultaneous square wave and triangular wave outputs as a function of input voltage. Fig. 4.38 (a) shows the block diagram of SE/NE 566 VCO.

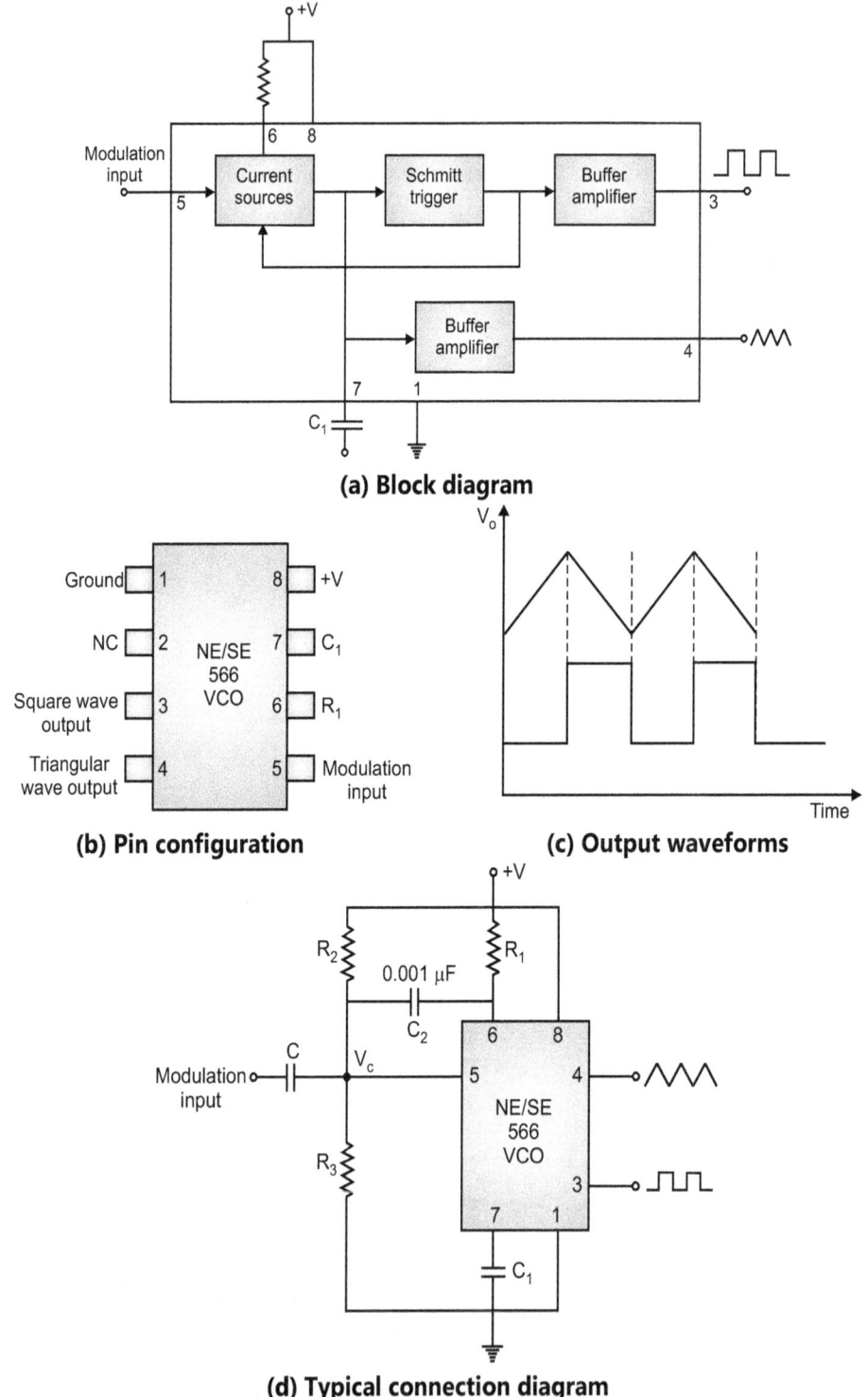

(a) Block diagram

(b) Pin configuration

(c) Output waveforms

(d) Typical connection diagram

Fig. 4.38 : Voltage controlled oscillator 566

The frequency of oscillation is determined by an external resistor R_1, capacitor C_1 and the voltage V_c applied to the control terminal 5. The triangular wave is generated by alternately charging the external capacitor C_1 by one current source and then linearly discharging it by another. The charge-discharge levels are determined by Schmitt trigger action. The Schmitt trigger also provides the square wave output. Both the waveforms are buffered so that the output impedance of each is 50 Ω. The typical amplitude of the triangular wave is 2.4 V_{PP} and that of the square wave is 5.4 V_{PP}.

Fig. 4.38 (d) shows a typical connection diagram. In this arrangement, the R_1C_2 combination determines the free running frequency and the control voltage V_c at terminal 5 is set by the voltage divider formed with R_2 and R_3. The initial voltage V_c at terminal 5 must be in the range

$$\frac{3}{4}(+V) \leq V_C \leq +V \qquad \ldots (4.18)$$

where, +V is the total supply voltage. The modulating signal is AC coupled with the capacitor C and must be < 3V_{PP}. The frequency of output waveform is given by

$$f_o = \frac{2(+V - V_C)}{R_1 C_1 (+V)} \qquad \ldots (4.19)$$

where R_1 should be in the range 2 kΩ < R_1 < 20 kΩ. The maximum output frequency of the SE/NE 566 is 500 kHz.

4.5.1. Applications of VCO

- Used to convert low-frequency signals, for example, electroencephalograms (EEG) or electrocardiograms (ECG) into an audio-frequency range.
- Used in phase locked loops.

4.6 FUNCTION GENERATOR IC LM 8038

The ICL 8038 waveform generator is a monolithic integrated circuit capable of producing high accuracy sine, square, triangular, sawtooth and pulse waveforms with a minimum of external components. The frequency (or repetition rate) can be selected externally from 0.001 Hz to more than 3000 kHz using either resistor or capacitors, and frequency modulation and sweeping can be accomplished with an external voltage. The ICL 8038 is fabricated with advanced monolithic technology, using schottky barrier diodes and thin film resistors, and the output is stable over a wide range of temperature and supply variations. These devices may be interfaced with phase locked loop circuitry to reduce temperature drift to less than 250 ppm/°C.

4.6.1 Features

- Low frequency drift with temperature .... 250 ppm/°C
- Low distortion .... 1 % (sine wave output)
- High linearity .... 0.1% (triangle wave output)
- Wide frequency range .... 0.001 Hz to 3000 kHz
- Variable duty cycle .... 2% to 98%
- High level outputs .... TTL to 28 V
- Simultaneous sine, square, and triangle wave outputs.
- Easy to use just a handful of external components required.

Ordering Information :

Part Number	Stability	Temperature Range (°C)	Package	Package No.
ICL8038CCPD	250 PPM/°C (Type)	0 to 70	14 Ld PDIP	E14.3
ICL8038CCJD	250 PPM/°C (Type)	0 to 70	14 Ld CERDIP	F14.3
ICL8038BCJD	180 PPM/°C (Type)	0 to 70	14 Ld CERDIP	F14.3
ICL8038ACJD	120 PPM/°C (Type)	0 to 70	14 Ld CERDIP	F14.3

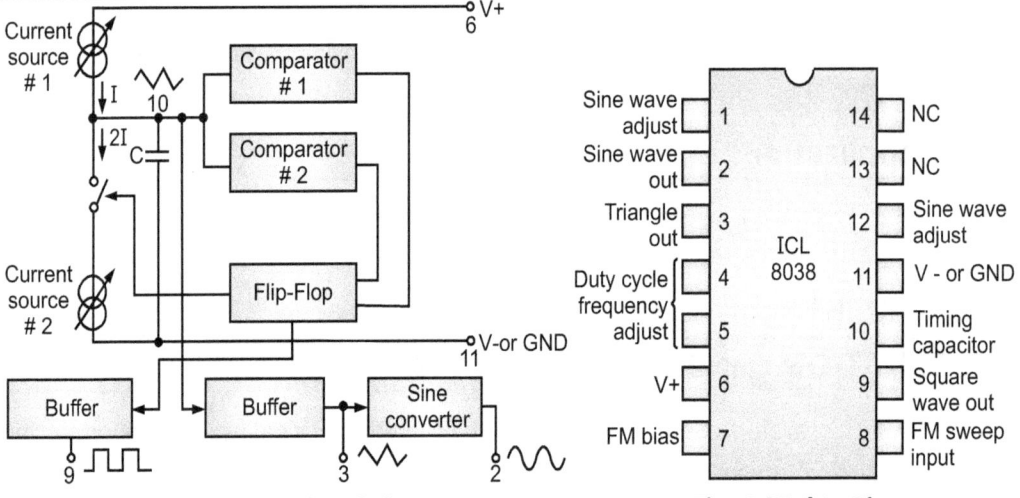

Fig. 4.39 (a) : Functional diagram   **Fig. 4.37 (b) : Pinout**

An external capacitor C is charged and discharged by two current sources. Current source #2 is switched on and off by a flip-flop, while current source #1 is on continuously. Assuming that the flip-flop is in a state such that current source #2 is off, and the capacitor is charged with a current I, the voltage across the capacitor rises linearly with time. When this voltage reaches the level of comparator #1 (set at 2/3 of the supply voltage), the flip-flop is triggered, changes states, and releases current source #2. This current source normally carries a current 2I, thus the capacitor is discharged with a net-current I and the voltage across it drops linearly with time. When it has reached the level of comparator #2 (set at 1/3 of the supply voltage), the flip-flop is triggered into its original state and the cycle starts again. Four waveforms are readily obtainable form this basic generator circuit. With the current sources set at I and 2I respectively, the charge and discharge times are equal. Thus a triangle waveform is created across the capacitor and the flip-flop produces a square wave. Both waveforms are fed to buffer stages and are available at pins 3 and 9.

The levels of the current sources can, however, be selected over a wide range with two external resistors. Therefore, with the two currents set at values different from I and 2I, an asymmetrical sawtooth appears at terminal 3 and pulses with a duty cycle from less than 1% to greater than 99% are available at terminal 9.

The sine wave is created by feeding the triangle wave into a nonlinear network (sine converter). This network provides a decreasing shunt impedance as the potential of the triangle moves toward the two extremes.

4.6.2 Waveform Timing

The symmetry of all waveforms can be adjusted with the external timing resistors. Two possible ways to accomplish this are shown in Fig. 4.38. Best results are obtained by keeping the timing resistors R_A and R_B separate (A). R_A controls the rising portion of the sine wave and the 1 state of the square wave. The magnitude of the triangle waveform is set at 1/3 V_{SUPPLY}; therefore the rising portion of the triangle is,

$$t_1 = \frac{C \times V}{1}$$

$$= \frac{C \times 1/3 \times V_{SUPPLY} \times R_A}{0.22 \times V_{SUPPLY}}$$

$$= \frac{R_A \times C}{0.66} \qquad \text{...(4.20)}$$

The falling portion of the triangle and sine wave and the 0 state of the square wave is :

$$T_2 = \frac{C \times V}{1}$$

$$= \frac{C \times 1/3 \times V_{SUPPLY}}{2(0.22)\frac{V_{SUPPLY}}{R_B} - 0.22\frac{V_{SUPPLY}}{R_A}}$$

$$= \frac{R_A R_B C}{0.66 (2R_A - R_B)} \qquad \text{...(4.21)}$$

Thus, a 50% duty cycle is achieved when $R_A = R_B$.

If the duty cycle is to be varied over a smaller range about 50% only, the connection shown in Fig. 4.40 (b) is slightly more convenient. A 1 kΩ potentiometer may not allow the duty cycle to be adjusted through 50% on all devices. If a 50% duty cycle is required, a 2kΩ or 5 kΩ potentiometer should be used.

With two separate timing resistors, the frequency is given by :

$$t = \frac{1}{t_1 + t_2}$$

$$= \frac{1}{\frac{R_A C}{0.66}\left(1 + \frac{R_B}{2R_A - R_B}\right)}$$

or, if $R_A = R_B = R$

$$t = \frac{0.33}{RC} \text{ [for Fig. 4.40 (a)]} \qquad ...(4.22)$$

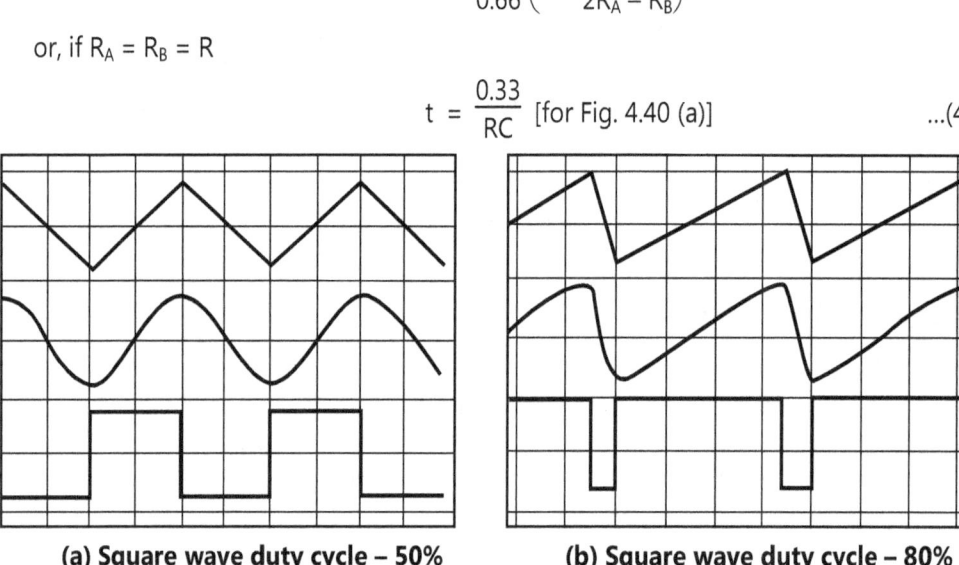

(a) Square wave duty cycle – 50%   (b) Square wave duty cycle – 80%

Fig. 4.40 : Phase relationship of waveforms

Neither time nor frequency are dependent on supply voltage, even through none of the voltage are regulated inside the integrated circuit. This is due to the fact that both currents and thresholds are direct, linear functions of the supply voltage and thus their effects cancel.

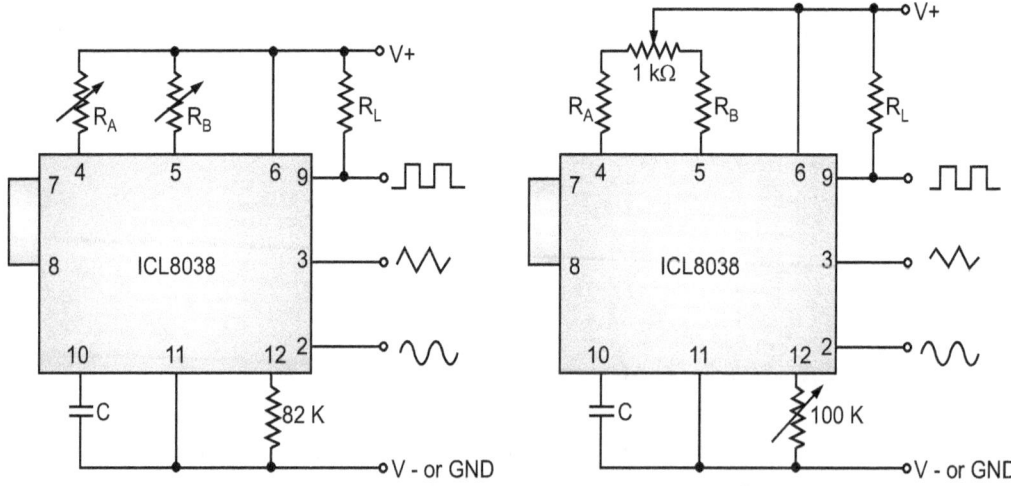

Fig. 4.41 : Possible connections for the external timing resistors

4.6.2.1 Absolute Maximum Ratings

- Supply Voltage (V− to V+) .... 36 V
- Input Voltage (Any Pin) .... V − to V+
- Input Current (Pins 4 and 5) .... 25 mA
- Output Sink Current (Pins 3 and 9) .... 25 mA

4.6.2.2 Operating Conditions

- Temperature Range
- ICL8038AC, ICL8038BC, ICL8038CC .... 0°C to 70°C

4.6.2.3 Thermal Information

- Thermal Resistance (Typical, Note 1) θ_{JA} (oC/W) θ_{JC} (°C/W)
- CERDIP Package 75 20
- PDIP Package .... 115 N/A
- Maximum Junction Temperature (Ceramic Package) .... 175° C
- Maximum Junction Temperature (Plastic Package) .... 150° C
- Maximum Storage Temperature Range .... −65° C to 150° C
- Maximum Lead Temperature (Soldering 10s) .... 300° C

4.6.2.4 Die Characteristics

- Back Side Potential V

4.6.3 Electrical Specifications $V_{SUPPLY} = \pm 10$ V or +20 V, $T_A = 25°$ C, $R_L = 10$ kΩ, Test Circuit Unless Otherwise Specified

Parameter	Symbol	Test conditions	ICL 8038CC			ICL8038BC			ICL8038AC			Units
			Min.	Typ	Max	Min	Typ	Max	Min	Typ	Max	
Supply voltage operating range	V_{supply} V+	Single supply	+10	-	+30	+10	-	+30	+10	-	+30	V
	V+, V−	Dual supplies	±5	-	±15	±5	-	±15	±5	-	±15	V
Supply current	I_{supply}	V_{supply} = ±10V (Note 2)		12	20	-	12	20	-	12	20	mA

Frequency Characteristics (All Waveforms)

Parameter	Symbol	Test conditions	ICL8038CC Min	ICL8038CC Typ	ICL8038CC Max	ICL8038BC Min	ICL8038BC Typ	ICL8038BC Max	ICL8038AC Min	ICL8038AC Typ	ICL8038AC Max	Units
Max. frequency of oscillation	f_{max}		100	-	-	100	-	-	100	-	-	kHz
Sweep frequency of FM input	f_{sweep}		-	10	0	0	10	0	0	10	0	kHz
Sweep FM range		(Note 3)	-	35.1	-	-	35.1	-	-	35.1	-	-
FM linearity		10.1 ratio	-	0.5	-	-	0.2	-	-	0.2	-	%
Frequency drift with temperature (Note 5)	$\Delta f/\Delta V$	Over supply voltage range	-	0.05	-	-	0.05	-	-	0.05	-	%/V

Output Characteristics

Parameter	Symbol	Test conditions	ICL8038CC Min	ICL8038CC Typ	ICL8038CC Max	ICL8038BC Min	ICL8038BC Typ	ICL8038BC Max	ICL8038AC Min	ICL8038AC Typ	ICL8038AC Max	Units
Square wave Leakage current	$I_{O\Lambda K}$	$V_g = 30$ V	-	-	1	-	-	1	-	-	1	µA
Saturation voltage	$V_{\Sigma AT}$	$I_{SINK} = 2$ mA	-	0.2	0.5	-	0.2	0.4	-	0.2	0.4	V
Rise time	t_P	$R_L = 4.7$ kΩ	-	180	-	-	180	-	-	180	-	ns
Fall time	t_F	$R_L = 4.7$ kΩ	-	40	-	-	4-	-	-	40	-	ns
Typical duty cycle adjust (Note 6)	ΔD		2		98	2	-	98	2	-	98	%
Triangle / Sawtooth / Ramp aplitude	$V_{TRIANGLE}$	$R_{TRI} = 100$ kΩ	0.30	0.30	=	0.30	0.33	-	0.30	0.30	-	xV_{Supply}
Linearity			-	0.1	-	-	0.05	-	-	0.05	-	%
Output impedance	Z_{OUT}	$I_{OUT} = 5$ mA	-	200	-	-	200	-	-	200	-	Ω

4.6.4 Electrical Specification $V_{SUPPLY} = \pm 10$ V or + 20 V, TA = 25°C, RL = 10 kΩ, Test Circuit Unless Otherwise Specified

Parameter	Symbol	Test conditions	ICL 8038CC Min.	ICL 8038CC Typ	ICL 8038CC Max	ICL8038BC Min	ICL8038BC Typ	ICL8038BC Max	ICL8038AC Min	ICL8038AC Typ	ICL8038AC Max	Units
Sine wave amplitude	V_{SINE}	$R_{SINE} = 100$ kΩ	0.2	0.22	-	0.2	0.22	-	0.2	0.22	-	xV_{Supply}
THD	THD	$R_S = 1$ MΩ (Note 4)	-	2.0	5	-	1.5	3	-	1.0	1.5	%
THD adjusted	THD	Use Fig. 4.40	-	1.5	-	-	1.0	-	0	-.8	-	%

4.6.5 Detailed Schematic

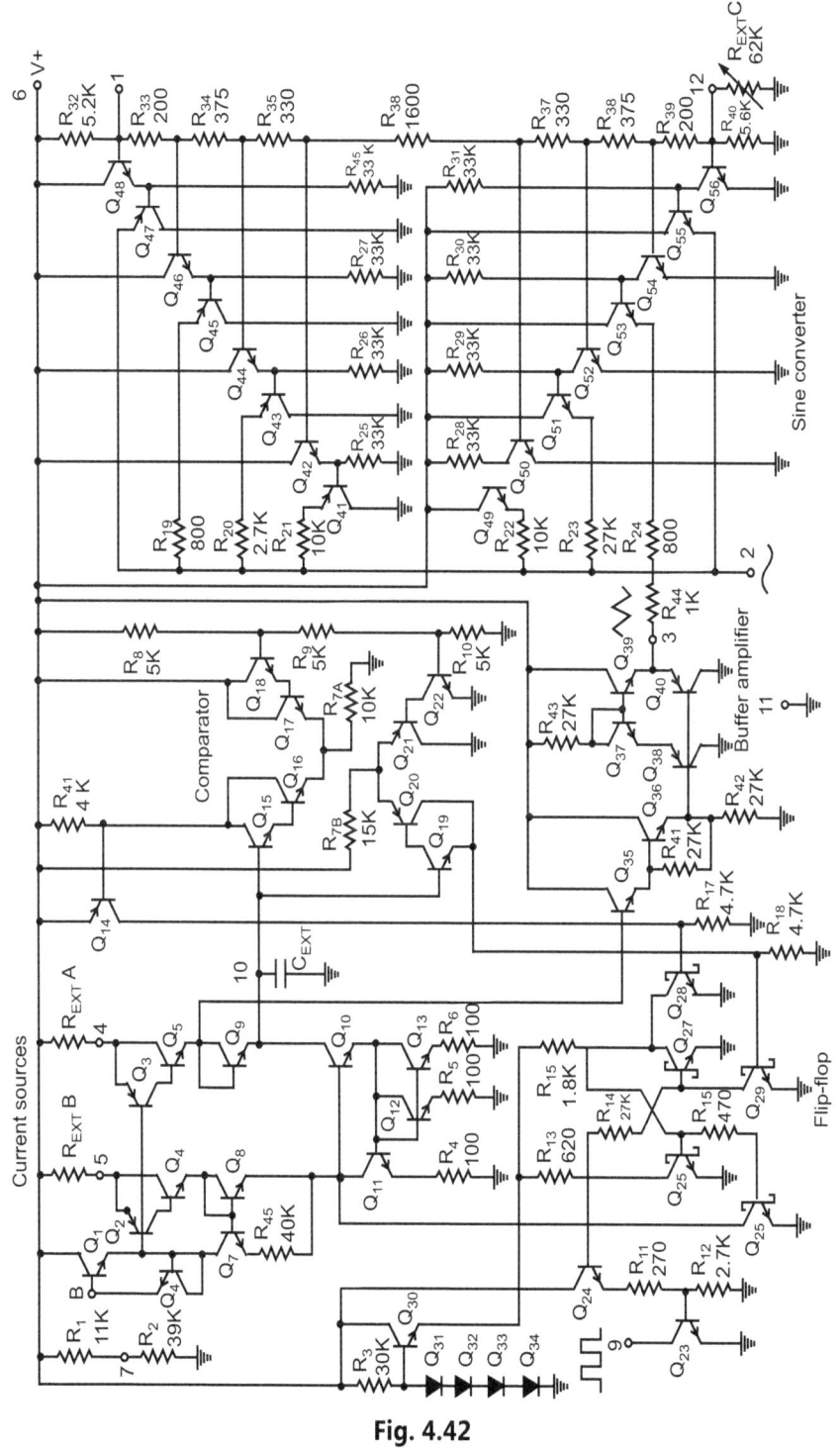

Fig. 4.42

4.6.6 Definition of Terms

1. **Supply voltage (V_{Supply})** : The total supply voltage from V+ to V−.

2. **Supply current** : The supply current required from the power supply to operate the device, excluding load currents and the currents through R_A and R_B.

3. **Frequency range** : The frequency range at the square wave output through which circuit operation is guaranteed.

4. **Sweep FM range** : The ratio of maximum frequency to minimum frequency which can be obtained by applying a sweep voltage to pin 8. For correct operation, the sweep voltage should be within the range : $(2/3\ V_{Supply} + 2V) < V_{Sweep} < V_{supply}$.

5. **FM linearity** : The percentage deviation from the best fit straight line on the control voltage versus output frequency curve.

6. **Output amplitude** : The peak-to-peak signal amplitude appearing at the outputs.

7. **Saturation voltage** : The output voltage at the collector of Q23 when this transistor is turned on. It is measured for a sink current of 2 mA.

8. **Rise and Fall times** : The time required for the square wave output to change from 10% to 90% or 90% to 10%, of its final value.

9. **Triangle waveform linearity** : The percentage deviation from the best fit straight line on the rising and falling triangle waveform.

10. **Total harmonic distortion** : The total harmonic distortion at the sine wave output.

4.6.7 Applications of ICL 8038

1. **Frequency modulation and sweeping** : The frequency of the waveform generator is a direct function of the DC voltage at terminal 8 (measured from V+). By alternating this voltage, frequency modulation is performed. For small deviations (e.g. ± 10%) the modulating signal can be applied directly to pin 8, merely providing DC decoupling with a capacitor as shown in Fig. 4.43. An external resistor between pins 7 and 8 is not necessary, but it can be used to increase input impedance from about 8 kΩ (pins 7 and 8 connected together), to about (R + 8 kΩ). For larger FM deviations or for frequency sweeping, the modulating signal is applied between the positive voltage and pin 8 (Fig. 4.43 b). In this way the entire bias for the current sources is created by the modulating signal and a very large (e.g. 1000 : 1) sweep range is created (f = Minimum at V_{Sweep} = 0, i.e., pin 8 = V+). Care must be taken, however, to regulate the supply voltage, in this configuration the charge current is not longer a function of the supply voltage (yet the trigger thresholds still are) and thus the frequency becomes dependent on the supply voltage.

The potential on pin 8 may be sweep down from V+ by (1/3 V_supply − 2V).

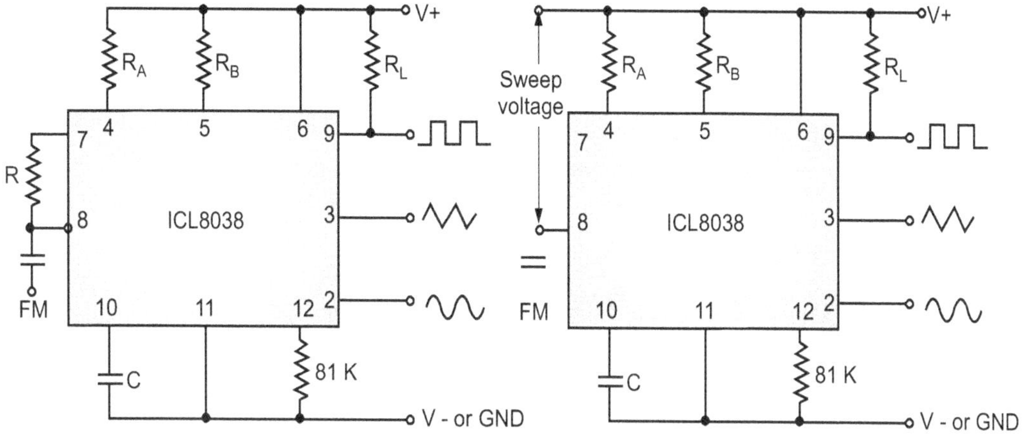

(a) Connections for frequency modulation **(b)** Connections for frequency sweep

Fig. 4.43

2. **Use in Phase Locked Loops :** Its high frequency stability makes the ICL8038 an ideal building block for a phase locked loop as shown in Fig. 4.44. In this application the remaining functional blocks, the phase detector and the amplifier, can be formed by a number of available ICs (e.g., MC4344, NE562).

In order to match these building blocks to each other, two steps must be taken. First, two different supply voltages are used and the square wave output is returned to the supply of the phase detector.

This assures that VCO input voltage will not exceed the capabilities of the phase detector. If a smaller VCO signal is required, a simple resistive voltage divider is connected between pin 9 of the waveform generator and the VCO input of the phase detector.

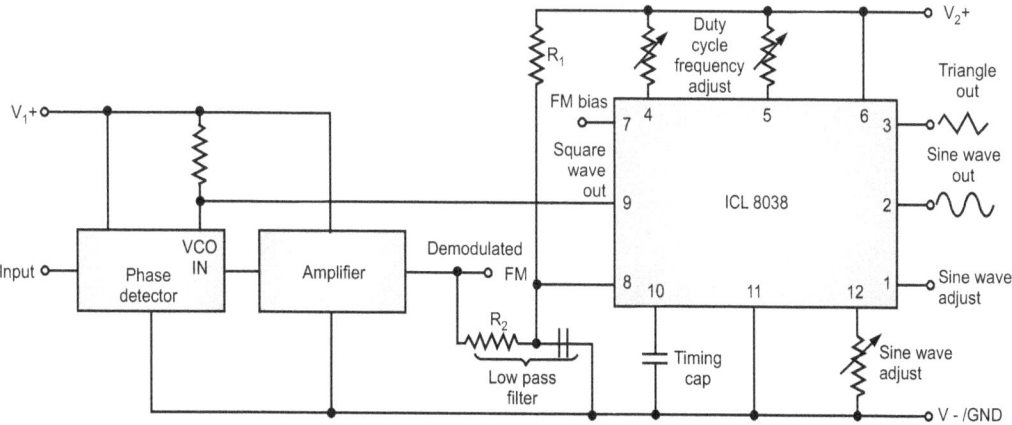

Fig. 4.44 : Waveform generator used as stable VCO in a Phase-Locked Loop

Second, the DC output voltage of the amplifier must be compatible to the DC level required at the FM input of the waveform generator (pin 8, 0.8V+). The simplest solution here is to provide a voltage divider to V+ (R_1, R_2 as shown) if the amplifier has a lower output level, or to ground if its level is higher. The divider can be made part of the low-pass filter. This application not only provides for a free-running frequency with very low temperature drift, but is also has the unique feature of producing a large reconstituted sine wave signal with a frequency identical to that at the input.

4.7 CLIPPERS AND CLAMPERS

4.7.1 Clipper

Waveshaping circuits are mostly used in digital computers and communications such as TV and FM receiviers.

Waveshaping techniques consists of limiting, clipping and clamping.

A rectifier diode can be used to clip off a certain portion of the input signal to obtain a desired output waveshape. There are two types of clipper circuits :

(a) Positive clipper (b) Negative clipper

4.7.1.1 Positive Clipper

A positive clipper is a circuit which removes the positive part of the input signal while the negative clipper removes the –ve part of the clipper.

Fig. 4.45 shows the positive clipper using op-amp.

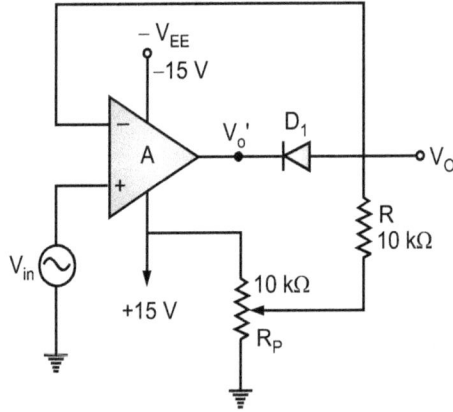

Fig. 4.45 : Positive clipper circuit

Here the op-amp acts as a voltage follower with a diode in the feedback path. The clipping level is determined by the reference voltage V_{ref}, which should be less than the input voltage range of the op-amp. V_{ref} is derived from the positive supply voltage (+V_{CC}). Above V_{ref} the output is clipped off.

During the positive half cycle of the input the diode D_1 conducts only until $V_{in} = V_{ref}$ because when $V_{in} < V_{ref}$, the voltage (V_{ref}) at the (–) input is higher than that at the (+) input; hence the output voltage V'_o of the op-amp, becomes –ve to drive D_1 into conduction. When diode D_1 conducts, it closes the feedback loop and op-amp acts as a voltage follower i.e. V_o follows the V_{in} until $V_{in} = V_{ref}$. When $V_{in} > V_{ref}$ the output of the op-amp becomes positive. So diode D becomes off. Therefore $V'_o = +V_{CC}$ and $V_o = V_{ref}$. Fig. 4.46 shows the input and output waveforms with $V_{ref} = 1$ V and $V_{ref} = -1$ V.

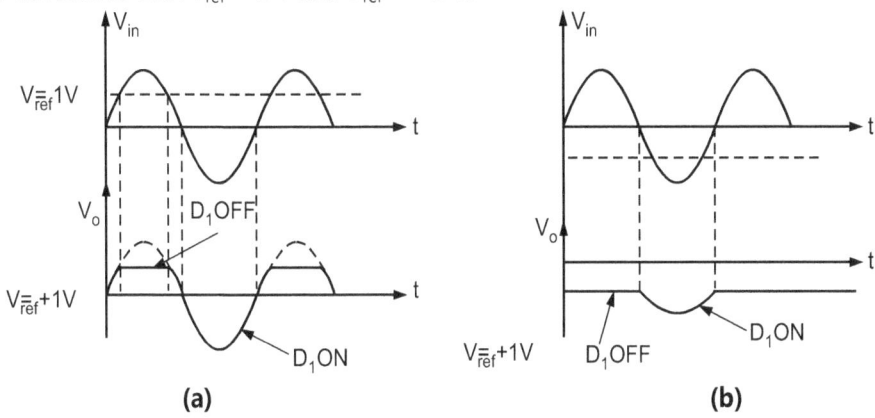

Fig. 4.46 : Input and output waveforms with $+V_{ref} = 1$ and $-V_{ref} = -1$ V

In Fig. 4.46 if pot R_p is connected to the negative supply – V_{EE} instead of $+V_{CC}$, the reference voltage V_{ref} will be negative. The output follows the input only when $V_{in} < -V_{ref}$.

4.7.1.2 Negative Clipper

The positive clipper is converted into a negative clipper by simply reversing diode D_1 and changing the polarity of reference voltage V_{ref}.

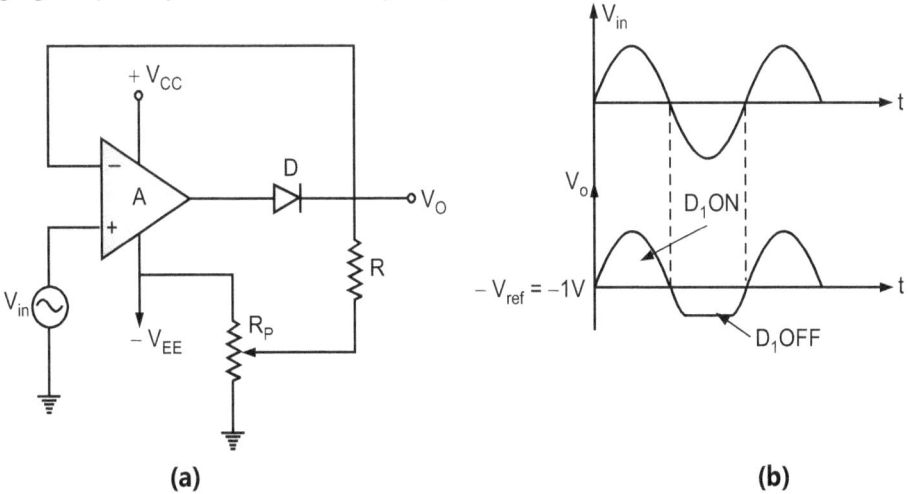

Fig. 4.47 : Negative clipper circuit and input and output waveforms with $-V_{ref} = -1$ V and $+V_{ref} = +1$ V

The negative clipper clips off the negative parts of the input signal below the reference voltage.

Diode D_1 conducts when $V_{in} > -V_{ref}$ and therefore during this period output V_o follows the input V_{in}. When $V_{in} < -V_{ref}$, diode D_1 remains off and the negative portion of the output voltage below $-V_{ref}$ is clipped off.

If $-V_{ref}$ is changed to $+V_{ref}$ by connecting the potentiometer R_p to the $+V_{CC}$, the output voltage below $+V_{ref}$ will be clipped off. The diode remains ON. For $V_{in} > V_{ref}$ and OFF for $V_{in} < +V_{ref}$.

4.7.2 Clampers

A clamper circuit is used to add a fixed voltage level to the minimum or maximum value of an input signal. The output is clamped to a desired level by either shifting up or shifting down on input signal, depending on whether a positive or negative clamping action is required.

4.7.2.1 Positive Clamper

Fig. 4.48 shows the positive clamping circuit. The input signal V_{in} is applied to the negative input terminal through a capacitor C.

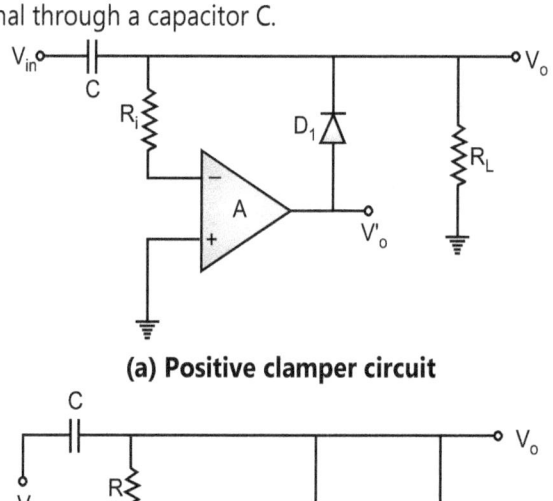

(a) Positive clamper circuit

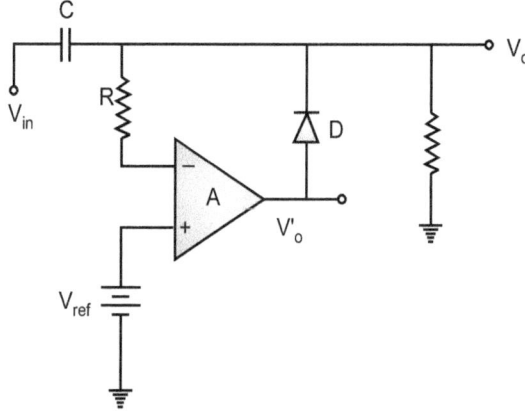

(b) Positive clamper circuit with V_{ref}

Fig. 4.48

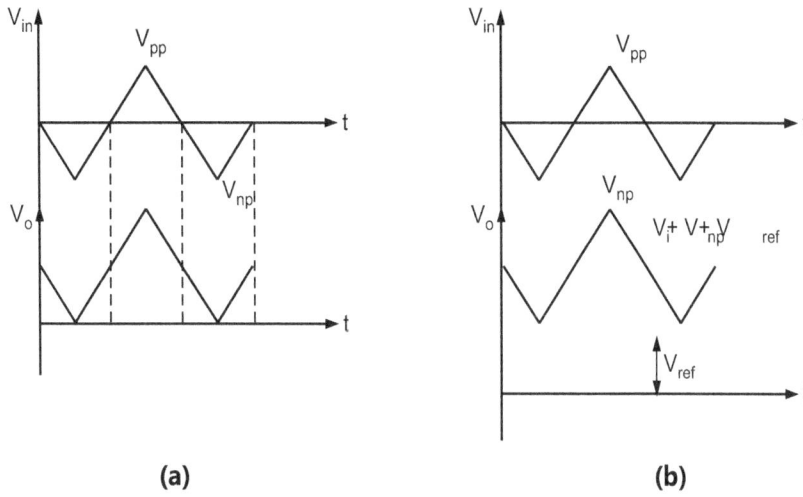

Fig. 4.49 : Positive clamper with and without V_{ref} and input and output waveforms

During the –ve half cycle of V_{in}, the output of op-amp becomes positive. The diode D_1 becomes forward biased and capacitor starts charging. The charging continues until the inverting input terminal of the op-amp attains virtual ground conditions. At the same instant, the voltage across capacitor becomes equal to the negative peak V_{np} of the input signal.

$$V_c = V_{np}$$

When the V_{in} is +ve, diode D_1 becomes reverse biased. The capacitor retains the previous voltage V_c. The output voltage is thus given by

$$V_o = V_{in} + V_c$$

Thus the voltage V_{in} is shifted by the voltage across capacitor.

If a reference voltage V_{ref} is connected to the non-inverting input terminal of op-amp then the capacitor charges to a value V_c such that $V_c = V_{np} + V_{ref}$. The total output is thus given by

$$V_o = V_{in} + V_{np} + V_{ref}$$

The negative clamping can be achieved by reversing the diode connection and with the use of negative reference voltage – V_{ref}.

4.7.2.2 Negative Clamper

During +ve half cycle of V_{in}, the output of the op-amp becomes negative and diode D_1 turns ON and the capacitor starts charging to peak value.

During the –ve half cycle of V_{in} the output of op-amp becomes positive, so the diode gets reverse biased therefore the output is the sum of input and capacitor voltage.

$$V_o = V_{in} - V_{np} \qquad \text{... (4.23)}$$

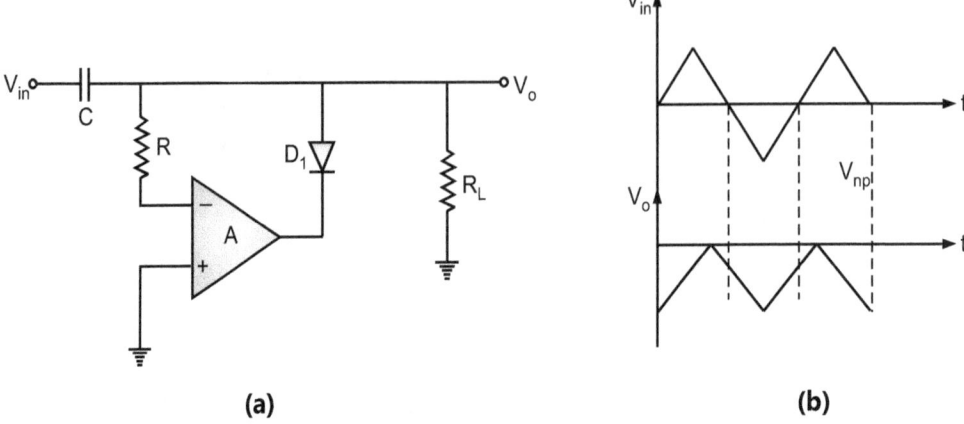

Fig. 4.50 : Negative clamper circuit and input output waveforms

Thus, a negative dc level of $-V_{np}$ is added to the output therefore it is called as negative clamper circuit.

4.7.2.3 Applications of Clamper

It is mainly used in television circuit as d.c. resistor to resistor the d.c. level for the video signal. It is also called as d.c. inserter.

4.8 PRECISION RECTIFIERS

4.8.1 Necessity of Precision Rectifiers

In conventional rectifier circuit,

$$V_o = V_{in} - V_D \text{(ON) V} \quad \text{for } V_i \geq V_D \text{(ON)}$$
$$V_o = 0 \text{ V} \quad \text{for } V_i < V_D \text{(ON)} \quad \ldots (4.24)$$

To keep V_o equal to $V_i > 0$ V, an op-amp is used along with diodes called as precision rectifiers. Thus, this circuit can rectify voltages when $V_i < 0.7$ V.

There are two types of precision rectifiers :

1. Precision half wave rectifier
2. Precision full wave rectifier

4.8.2 Precision Half Wave Rectifier

These are of two types :

 (i) Positive half wave rectifier,

 (ii) Negative half wave rectifier.

(i) Positive half wave rectifier :

Here the cut-in-voltage is divided by the open loop gain of the op-amp so that cut-in-voltage is virtually eliminated.

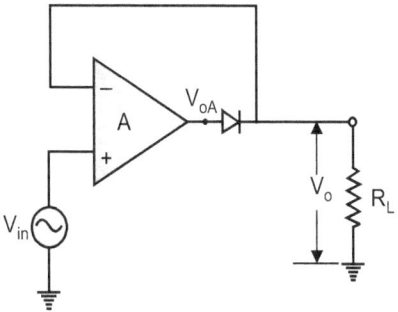

Fig. 4.51 (a)

When the input voltage $V_i > V_\lambda/A_{OL}$, then V_{OA}, the output of the op-amp exceeds V_λ and the diode D conducts.

Thus, the circuit acts as a voltage follower for input $V_i > V_\lambda/A_{OL}$.

When V_i is negative or less than V_λ/A_{OL}, the diode D is OFF and no current flows to the R_L load.

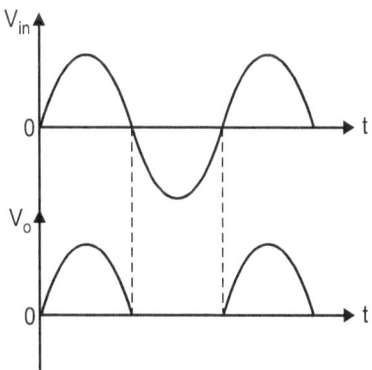

Fig. 4.51 (b) : Waveforms

(ii) Negative half wave rectifier :

Fig. 4.52 (a) shows a negative small-signal half wave rectifier. In this, during the positive half cycle of input voltage V_{in}, D_1 is reverse biased, therefore, $V_o = 0$ V. On the other hand, during the negative half cycle, D_1 is forward biased, hence V_o follows V_{in}.

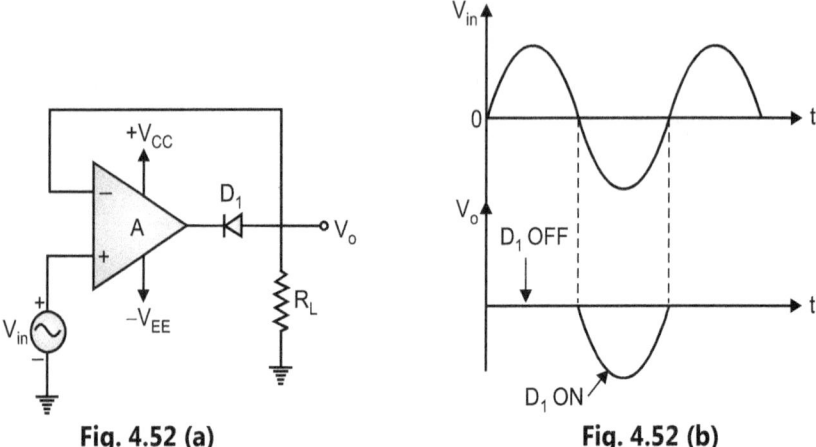

Fig. 4.52 (a)　　　　　　　　　　　Fig. 4.52 (b)

Yet another negative half wave rectifier is shown in Fig. 4.52 (a). In this circuit, two diodes are used so that the output V_o' of the op-amp does not saturate. This minimizes the response time and increases the operating frequency range of the op-amp.

Here the op-amp is used in the inverting mode and the output is measured at the anode of diode D_1 w.r.t. ground. Also, the output resistance is non-uniform since it depends on the state of diode D_1. In other words, the output impedance is low when D_1 is ON and high when D_1 is OFF.

During the positive half cycle of V_{in}, output V_o' is negative, which forward biases diode D_1 and closes the feedback loop through R_F. Since, $R_1 = R_F$, $V_o = V_{in}$.

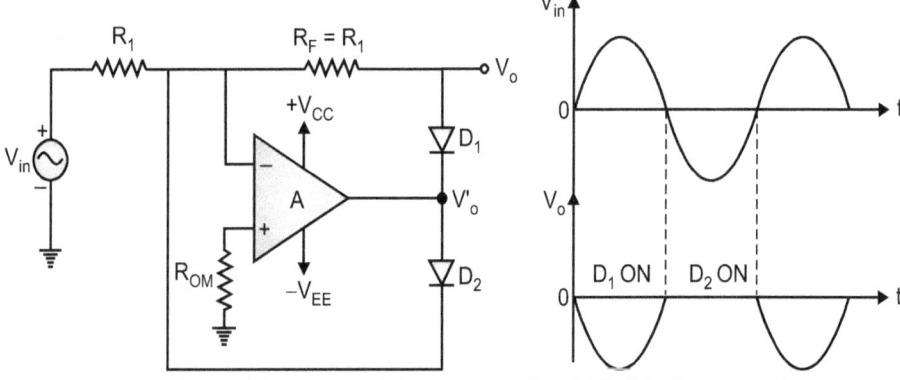

Fig. 4.53 (a) : Negative half wave rectifier　　　Fig. 4.53 (b) : Input and output waveforms

During the negative half cycle of V_{in}, output V_o' is positive; hence diode D_2 is forward biased. In fact, it is this diode that prevents the op-amp from going into positive saturation. Since, diode D_1 is OFF, output $V_o = 0$ V.

4.8.3 Full Wave Precision Rectifiers

Here the circuit accepts an AC input and inverts either positive or negative half and delivers both inverted and non-inverted halves at the output. Fig. 4.54 shows the precision full wave rectifier. When $V_i > 0$, diode D_1 is forward biased i.e. D_1 is ON and D_2 is reverse biased i.e. D_2 is OFF. Both the op-amps A_1 and A_2 acts as inverter.

$$V_o = \left(-\frac{R}{R}\right) \cdot \left(-\frac{R}{R}\right) = V_i$$

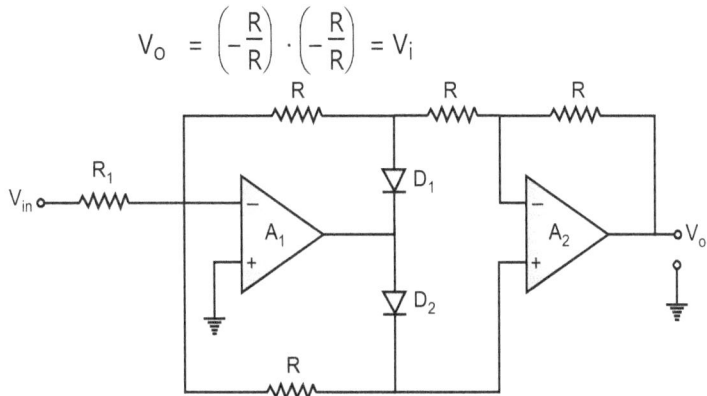

Fig. 4.54 : Precision full wave rectifiers

When $V_i < 0$, the output voltage of A_1 swings to positive making diode D_2 forward biased and D_1 reverse biased. It can be shown that $V_o = -V_i$.

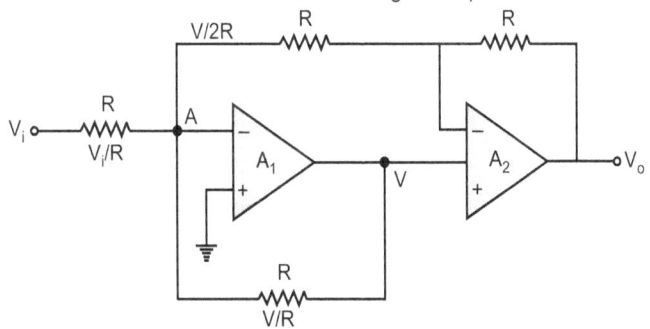

Fig. 4.55

Apply KCL at node A,

$$\frac{V_i}{R} + \frac{V}{2R} + \frac{V}{R} = 0$$

$$\frac{V_i}{R} + \frac{V + 2V}{2R} = 0$$

$$\frac{V_i}{R} + \frac{3V}{2R} = 0$$

$$\frac{V_i}{R} = -\frac{3}{2}\frac{V}{R}$$

$$V = -\frac{2}{3}V_i$$

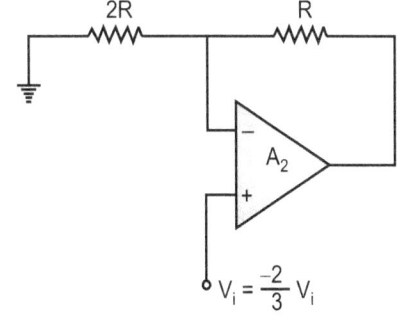

$$V_i = -\frac{2}{3}V_i$$

Fig. 4.56 (a)

$$V_O = \left(1 + \frac{R_F}{R_1}\right) V_i$$

$$= \left(1 + \frac{R}{2R}\right)\left(-\frac{2}{3} V_i\right)$$

$$= \left(\frac{3R}{2R}\right) \times -\frac{2}{3} V_i$$

$$\therefore V_O = -V_i$$

The input and output waveforms are as shown in Fig. 4.56 (b).

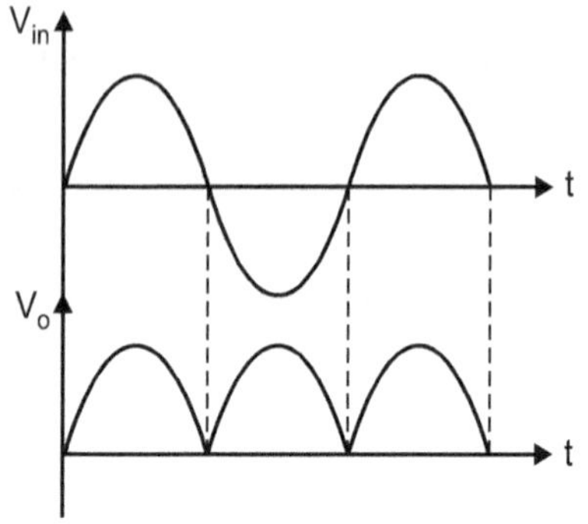

Fig. 4.56 (b)

EXERCISE

1. Draw the circuit diagram of asstable multivibrator using op-amp. Explain its operation with neat waveforms. Obtain the expression for frequency of oscillations.
2. Draw the circuit diagram of monostable multivibrator using op-amp. Explain its operation with neat waveforms. Obtain the expression for output pulse width.
3. Design an op-amp Schmitt trigger for the following specifications:
   $V_0 = \pm 10V$, tripping voltages are 4V and –2V
4. With the help of circuit diagrams, explain the working of the following circuits.
   (i) half wave precision rectifier. (ii) sample and hold circuit
   (iii) Mention its area of application
5. Design an op-amp Schmitt trigger circuit with UTP = 2V, LTP = 1V, supply voltage = $\pm 15V$, $V_{sat} = \pm 12V$
6. Write a short note on peak detector.
7. Draw the internal architecture of 555 timer. Explain how 555 timer can be used as monostable multivibrator. Obtain the expression for width of the pulse.
8. Design an asstable multivibrator using 555 timer to generate a clock of 1 kHz with 40% duty cycle.
9. Design a 555 based square wave generator to produce a symmetrical square wave of 2kHz. If $V_{CC} = 12V$, draw the voltage across timing capacitor and the output?
10. What do you understand by precision rectifiers? How do they differ from conventional rectifiers?
11. With help of neat diagram and waveform explain the full wave precision rectifier circuit.
12. Discuss comparator applications: a) zero crossing detector b) window detector.
13. Design a wien bridge oscillator for cutoff frequency $f_H = 500Hz$
14. Explain with neat waveform, a positive clipper circuit.
15. Explain with neat waveforms, a negative clipper circuit.
16. What is a clamper circuit? How they are classified?
17. Explain the functional block diagram of IC 8038 function generator.
18. Explain the application of IC8038 for frequency modulation and sweeping.

Unit V

A/D INTERFACE CIRCUIT AND PLL

5.1 A/D INTERFACE CIRCUITS

5.1.1 A/D Converters (Analog to Digital Converter)

A/D converters convert an analog voltage to the digital output.

There are many types of A/D converters

- Single-ramp integrating.
- Dual-ramp intergrating.
- Single counter.
- Tracking.
- Successive approximation.

5.1.1.1 Successive Approximation A/D Converter

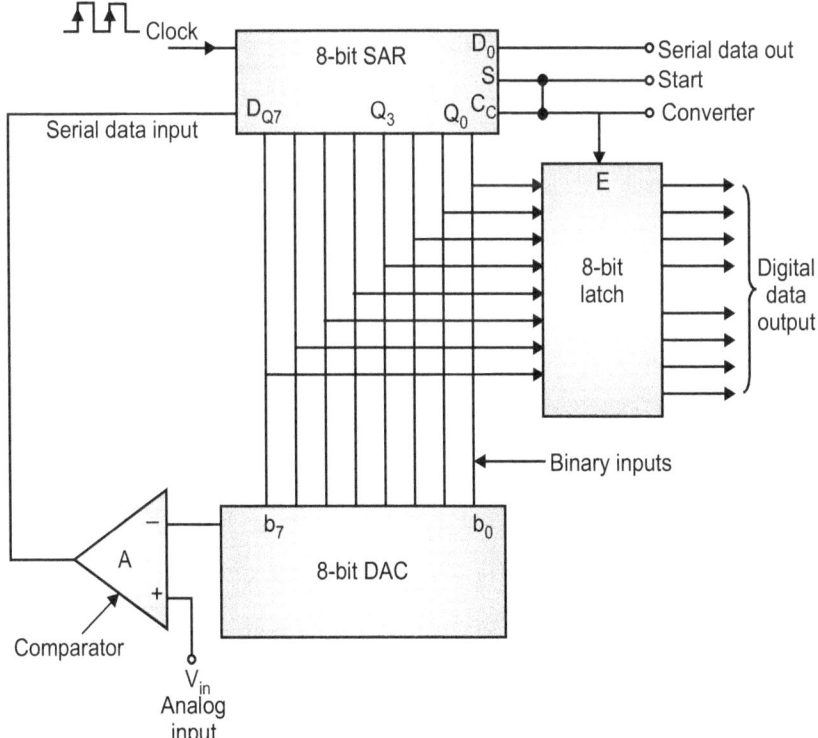

Fig. 5.1 : Successive approximation type A/D converter

Fig. 5.1 shows the successive approximation type of A/D converter. The heart of the circuit is an 8-bit successive approximation register (SAR), whose output is applied to an 8-bit D/A converter. The analog output (V_a) of the D/A converter is then compared to an analog input signal V_{in} by the comparator. The output of the comparator is a serial data input to the SAR. The SAR adjusts its digital output until it is equivalent to analog input V_{in}. The 8-bit latch at the end of conversion holds onto the resultant digital data output.

Working :

At the start of conversion cycle, the SAR is reset by holding the start (S) signal high. At the low to high transition of the first clock pulse, the most significant output bit Q_7 of the SAR is set. The D/A converter then generates an analog equivalent to the Q_7 bit, which is compared with the analog input V_{in}.

If the comparator output is low, the D/A output > V_{in} and the SAR will clear its MSB and the SAR will keep the MSB Q_7 set. On the next clock pulse low to high transition, the SAR will set the next MSB Q_6.

Depending on the output of the comparator the SAR will then either keep or reset the bit Q_6. This process is continued until the SAR tries all the bits. When the LSB Q_0 is tried, the SAR forces the conversion complete (CC) signal high to indicate that the parallel output lines contain valid data. The CC signal in turn enables the latch and digital data appears at the output of the latch.

Advantages :

- High speed
- Excellent resolution.

5.1.1.2 Dual Slope A/D converter

Dual slope conversion is an indirect method for A/D conversion where an analog voltage and a reference voltage are converted into time periods by an integrator and then measured by a counter. The speed of this converter is slow but accuracy is high.

Fig. 5.2 (a) shows a typical dual slope converter circuit. It consists of an integrator, comparator binary counter, output latch and reference voltage.

The ramp generator input is switched between the analog input voltage V_i and a negative reference voltage – V_{ref}.

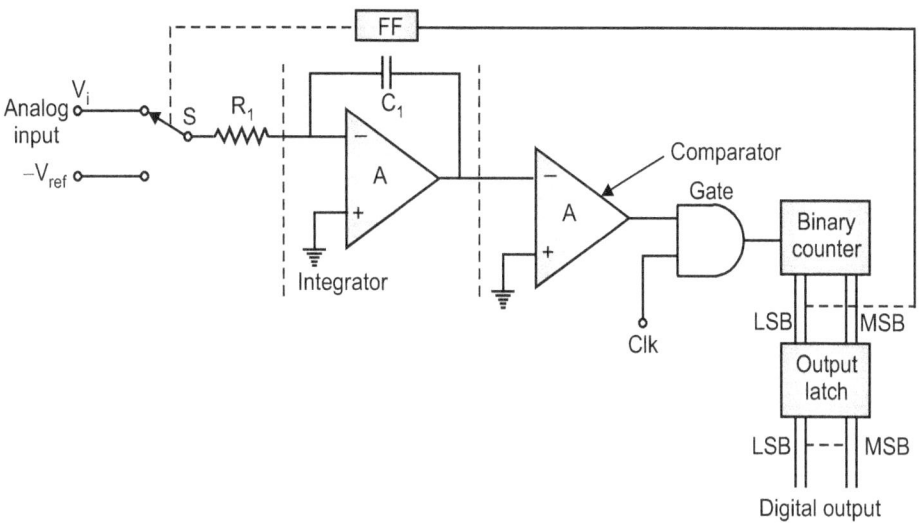

(a) Dual slope A/D converter

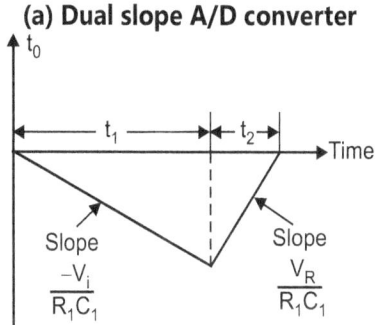

(b) Integrator output

Fig. 5.2

The analog switch is controlled by the MSB of the counter when MSB is a logic 0, the voltage being measured is connected to the ramp generator input. When MSB is logic 1, the negative reference voltage is connected to the ramp generator.

At time t = 0, analog switches is connected to the analog input voltage V_i, so that the analog input voltage integration begins. The output of the integrator is

$$V_o' = \frac{-1}{R_1 C_1} \int_0^t V_i \, dt$$

$$= \frac{-V_i t}{R_1 C_1}$$

Where, $R_1 C_1$ is the time constant of the integrator and V_i is assumed constant over the integration time period. At the end of 2^N clock periods MSB of the counter goes high. As a result the output of the flip-flop goes high which causes analog switch S to be switched from V_i to $-V_R$. At the same time the binary counter which has gone, through its entire count sequence is reset.

The negative input voltage $(-V_R)$ connected to the input of integrator causes the integrator output to ramp positive. When the integrator output reaches zero the comparator output voltage goes low which disables the clock AND gate. This stops the clock pulses reaching the counter, so that the counter will be stopped at a count corresponding to the number of clock pulses in time t_2.

The integrator output ramp down to a voltage V and get back upto 0. Therefore, the charge voltage is equal to discharge voltage.

$$\frac{V_i t_1}{R_1 C_1} = \frac{V_R t_2}{R_1 C_1}$$

$$V_i t_1 = V_R t_2$$

$$t_2 = \frac{V_i t_1}{V_R}$$

The above equation shows that t_2 is directly proportional only to V_i since V_R and t_1 are constants. The binary digital output of a counter gives corresponding digital value for the time period t_2 and hence it is also directly proportional to input signal V_i.

The actual conversion of analog voltage V_{in} into a digital count occurs during t_2. The control circuit connects the clock to the counter at the beginning of t_2. The clock is disconnected at the end of t_2. Thus, the counter content is digital output. Hence, we can write,

$$\text{Digital output} = \left(\frac{\text{Counts}}{\text{Second}}\right) t_2$$

$$\text{Digital output} = \left(\frac{\text{Counts}}{\text{Second}}\right) t_1 \left(\frac{V_i}{V_R}\right)$$

Advantages :
- Highly accurate.
- Cost is low.
- Immune to temperature variations in R_1 and C_1.

5.1.1.3 Flash Type A/D Converter (Parallel Comparator)

Flash type A/D converters are mainly used where the system requires high speed. They are also called as parallel comparators conversion speed is provided by the comparators. Here the input signal is compared with unique reference levels which are spaced 1 LSB apart.

Fig. 5.3 shows 3-bit flash A/D converter to obtain 3-bit flash converter seven $(2^3 - 1)$ comparators are required.

One of the inputs of comparator is connected to input signal and another terminal is connected to the reference voltage level generated by the voltage divider networks.

The comparators produces output 1 or 0 state depending upon the comparison of input voltage with reference voltage whether it is above or below the reference level. When comparator input voltage is greater than the reference voltage then the output of the comparator is 1. When it is below the input signal level then the op-amp output is zero.

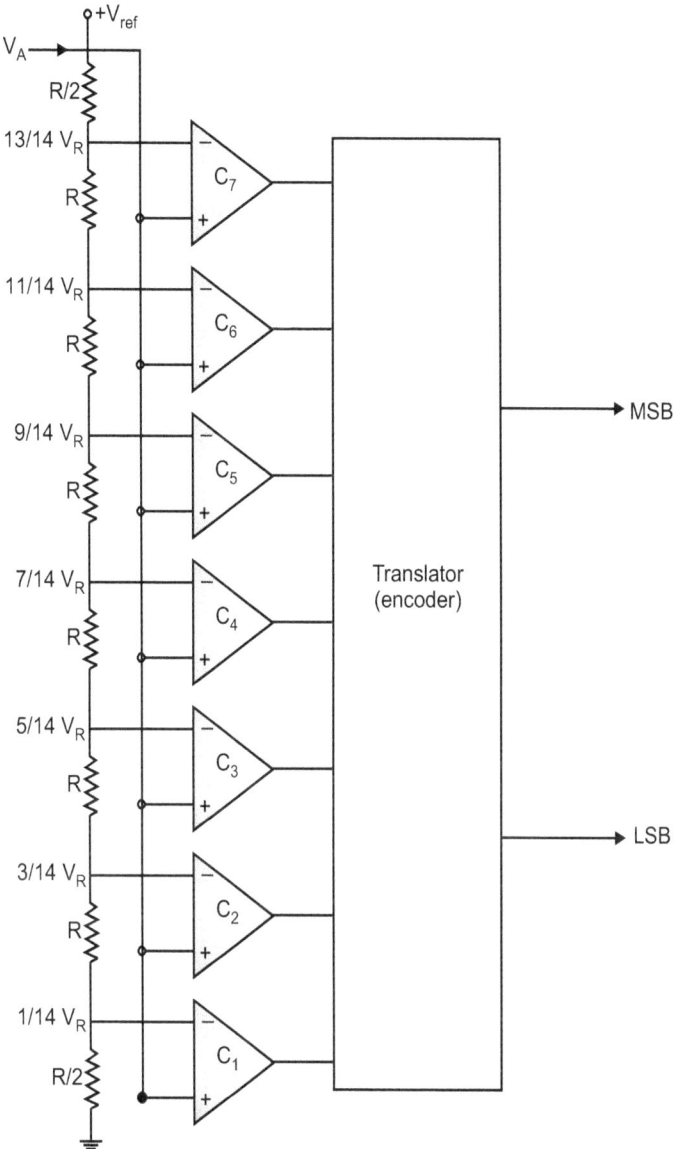

Fig. 5.3 : 3-bit flash converter

To obtain n-bit resolution, the number of comparators required are

Number of Comparators = $2^n - 1$

The maximum frequency for the input within the accuracy of $\pm 1/2$ LSB is given as :

$$F_{max} = \frac{1}{2\pi T_C 2^n}$$

where, F_{max} = Maximum input frequency
T_C = Conversion time
n = Cumber of bits

5.1.2 Specifications of A/D Converter

1. **Resolution :** It is the ratio of a change in value of input voltage V_i needed to change the digital output by 1 LSB.

If the full scale input voltage is V_{ifs} to cause a digital output of all 1's then resolution can be given as

$$R = \frac{V_{ifs}}{2^n - 1}$$

2. **Quantization Error :** There is an unavoidable uncertainty about the exact value of V_i when the output is 011. The binary output is 011 for all values of V_i between $\frac{1}{4}$ and $\frac{1}{2}$ V. This uncertainty is specified as quantization error. Its value is $\pm\frac{1}{2}$ LSB.

$$Q_e = \frac{V_{ifs}}{(2^n - 1)^2}$$

3. **Conversion time :** It is defined as the total time required to convert an analog signal into its digital output. It depends on the conversion technique used and propagation delay of the circuit components.

5.1.3 Comparison of A/D Converters

Parameter	Flash Type	Successive Approximation	Dual slope
Conversion time	Very less	Less	More
Accuracy	Less	Medium	More
Resolution	upto 2^8	Upto 2^{16}	2^{16} or more
Cost	High	Medium	Less
Application Area	Digital Storage Oscilloscope Where high speed is required	Used where high resolution is required	Used where high accuracy and resolution is required

5.1.4 Digital to Analog Converters

For data processing in digital system where inputs are available as zero or one. The data which is processed by the microcomputer must be converted from analog form to digital form. The circuit which converts analog form into digital form are called Analog to Digital Converter (ADC). On the other hand, a Digital to Analog Converter (DAC) is used when a binary output from a digital system must be converted to some equivalent analog voltage or current. The function of a D/A converter is exactly opposite that of an A/D converter.

Two types of digital to analog converters are available :

- Binary weighted resistors
- R/2R ladder network.

5.1.4.1 Binary Weighted Resistor D/A Converter

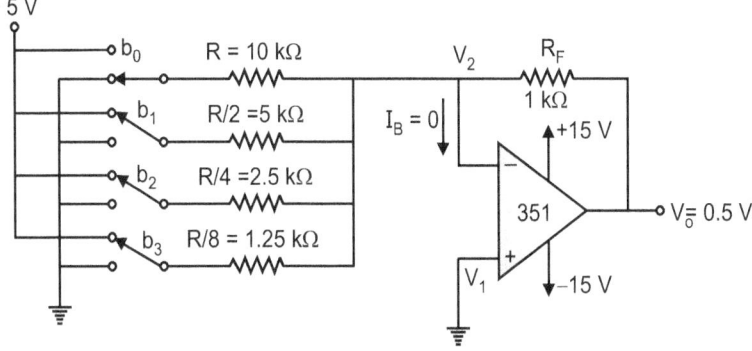

(a) D/A converter with binary-weighted resistors

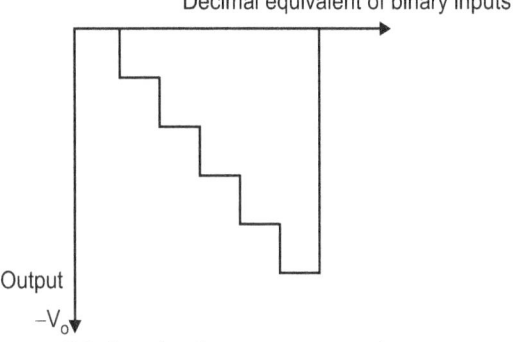

(b) Graph of output versus inputs

Fig. 5.4

Fig. 5.4 (a) shows the D/A converter using an op-amp and binary-weighted resistors. Here the op-amp is connected in inverting mode since the number of binary inputs is four, the converter is called a 4-bit (binary digit) converter for 16 combinations of binary inputs, an analog output should have 16 possible corresponding values. Four switches are used (b_0 - b_3) to give the binary inputs.

When switch b_0 is closed, the voltage across R is 5 V because $V_2 = V_1 = 0$ V, so the current through R is 5 V/10 kΩ = 5 mA. The bias current for op-amp is negligible, so the current through feedback resistor R_F is also 0.5 mA, which in turn produces the output voltage of $-$ (1 kΩ) (0.5 mA) = $-$ 0.5 V.

Here the op-amp acts as a voltage to current converter.

When b_1 is closed and b_0 is open it connects R/2 to the positive supply of + 5 V, causes twice of the current to flow through R_F, which in turn doubles the output voltage.

Depending upon whether switches b_0 to b_3 are open or closed, the binary weighted currents will be set up in input resistors. The sum of these currents is equal to the current through R_F, which in turns is converted as a output voltage. When all the switches are closed, the output will be maximum.

$$V_0 = -R_F \left(\frac{b_0}{R} + \frac{b_1}{R/2} + \frac{b_2}{R/4} + \frac{b_3}{R/8} \right)$$

Fig. 5.4 (b) shows the analog outputs versus possible input combinations. The output is a negative going staircase waveform with 15 steps of – 0.5 V each. The steps may not be the same size of all steps depending upon the value of R_F. We can select a step size by selecting proper R_F.

For accurate operation of the D/A converter precision metal film resistors are recommended.

Disadvantages :

It requires binary weighted resistors which are not readily available in practice.

5.1.4.2 R/2R Ladder D/A Converter

Fig. 5.5 (a) shows a D/A converter with R and 2R resistors. The inputs are given through switches b_0 to b_3 and the proportional output is taken at the output terminal.

Assume that the most significant bit (MSB) switch b_3 is connected to + 5 V and other switches are connected to ground.

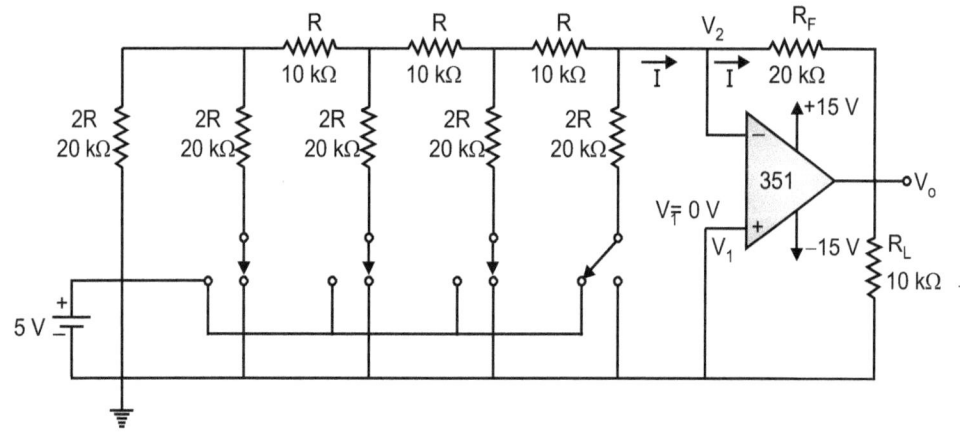

(a) D/A converter with R/2R resistors

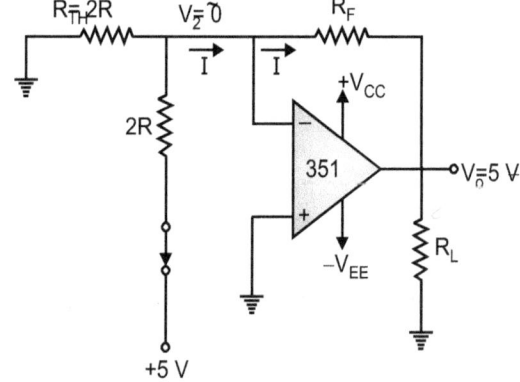

(b) Equivalent circuit when b_3 is high and b_0, b_1, b_2 are low

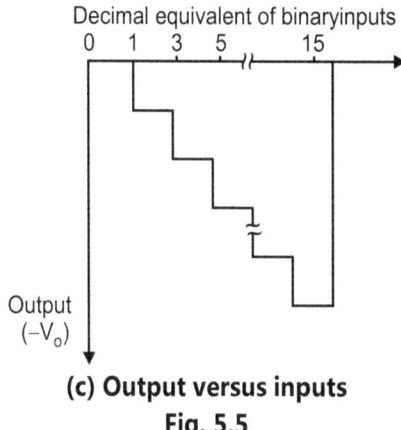

(c) Output versus inputs

Fig. 5.5

Obtain the Thevenin's equivalent circuit to the left of switch b_3.

$$R_{TH} = \left[\left\{\left[(2R \| 2R + R) \| 2R\right] + R\right\} \| 2R\right] + R = 2R$$

The resultant circuit is shown in Fig. 5.5 (b). Here the (–ve) terminal is virtually grounded i.e. $V_2 \cong 0$ therefore the current through R_{TH} (= 2R) is zero. Therefore, the current through 2R connected to +5 V is 5 V/20 kΩ = 0.25 mA. The same current flows through R_F and in turn produces the output voltage.

$$V_0 = -(20 \text{ k}\Omega)(0.25 \text{ mA}) = -5 \text{ V}$$

Using the same analysis, the output voltage corresponding to all possible combinations of binary inputs can be calculated as follows :

Decimal equivalent of input binary	Input (V) $b_3b_2b_1b_0$	Output Voltage
0	0000	0
1	0001	– 0.625
2	0010	– 1.25
3	0011	– 1.875
4	0100	– 2.50
5	0101	– 3.125
6	0110	– 3.750
7	0111	– 4.375
8	1000	– 5.0
9	1001	– 5.625
10	1010	– 6.25
11	1011	– 6.875
12	1100	– 7.50
13	1101	– 8.125
14	1110	– 8.875
15	1111	– 9.375

The maximum or full scale output of –9.375 V is obtained when all the inputs are 1111. The output votage equation can be written as

$$V_o = -R_F \left[\frac{b_3}{2R} + \frac{b_2}{4R} + \frac{b_1}{8R} + \frac{b_0}{16R} \right]$$

Advantages of R/2R ladder D/A Converter

- It requires only two sets of precision resistance values.
- More accurate than weighted registers.

Disadvantages

It requires more resistors. It is more difficult to analyze than the binary weighted resistor type. As the number of binary inputs is increased beyond 4 both the D/A converters gets complex and their accuracy degenerates.

Therefore, in critical applications an integrated circuit specially designed as a D/A converter should be used.

5.1.5 MC1408 Monolithic D/A converter

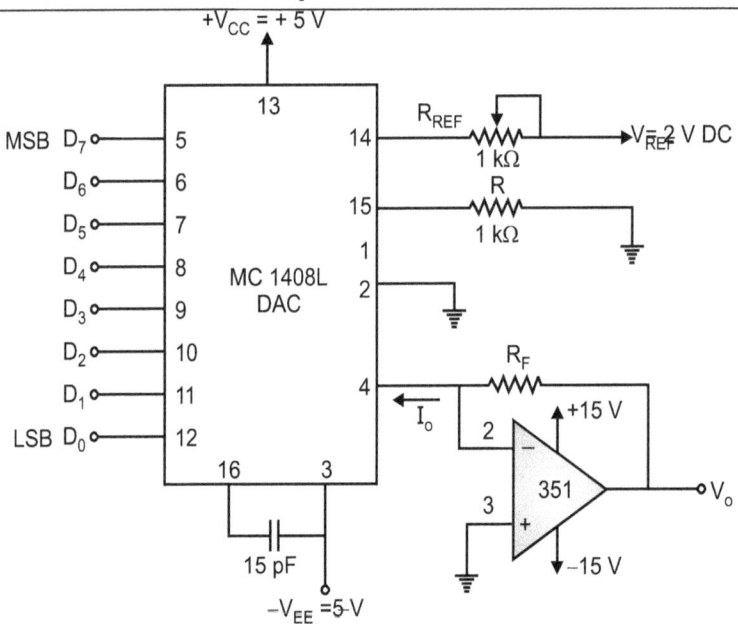

Fig. 5.6 : MC1408 monolithic D/A converter

$$V_o = \frac{V_{ref}}{R_{ref}} (R_F) \left\{ \frac{D_7}{2} + \frac{D_6}{4} + \frac{D_5}{8} + \frac{D_4}{16} + \frac{D_3}{32} + \frac{D_2}{64} + \frac{D_1}{128} + \frac{D_0}{256} \right\}$$

The MC 1408 is a common 8-bit monolithic D/A converter with a current output that can be converted to a voltage type by using an I to V converter op-amp.

5.1.6 SE/NE 5018

SE/NE 5018 is a typical 8-bit D/A converter with voltage output. Fig. 5.7 shows the SE/NE 5018 configured for unipolar output (0 to 10 V). For 12 bits of resolution as well as current and voltage outputs, hybrid D/A converters such as DATEL DAC - HZ series are an excellent choice.

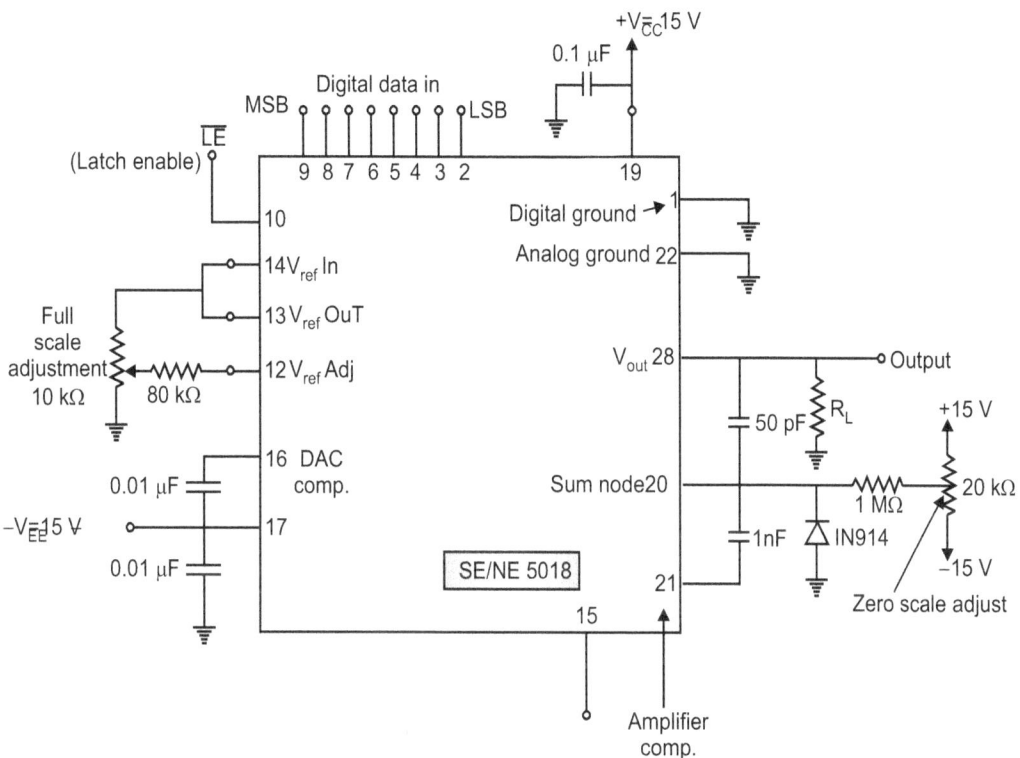

Fig. 5.7 : SE/NE 5018 D/A converter with voltage output

5.1.7 Key Specifications of D/A Converters

To make the excellent selection of D/A converters from a variety to suit a given application.

(1) Resolution :

Resolution is determined by the number of input bits i.e. 2^n where n is the number of input bits. For example, an 8 bit converter has $2^8 = 256$ possible output levels. Resolution is the value of LSB.

(2) Non-linearity or Non-linearity Error :

This is the difference between the actual output of the DAC and its ideal straight-line output. The error is normally expressed as a percentage of the full-scale range.

(3) Gain Error and Offset Error :

Gain error is usually caused by the deviations in the feedback resistor on the I to V converter. When the binary inputs are all zero, the output of the DAC is not i.e. the offset error. This error is due to input offset current and input offset voltage.

(4) Settling Time :

This is the time for the output to settle to within ± 1/2 LSB of the final value for a given digital input i.e. zero for full scale.

Applications of D/A Converter

- Micro computer interfacing.
- CRT graphics generation.
- Programmable power supplies.
- Digitally controlled gain circuits.
- Digital filters.

5.2 SAMPLE AND HOLD CIRCUIT

5.2.1 Need of Sample and Hold Circuit

For accurate analog to digital conversion the analog input voltage should be held constant in the conversion cycle. If the input analog voltage changes by more $\pm \frac{1}{2}$ LSB an error may occur in the digital output. The sample and hold circuit samples the value of the input signal in response to a sampling command and holds it at the output until arrival of the next command. This minimizes the error.

5.2.2 Circuit Diagram

The sample and hold circuit, as its name implies, samples an input signal and holds on to its last sampled value until the input is sampled again. Fig. 5.8 (a) shows a sample and hold circuit using an op-amp with an E-MOSFET.

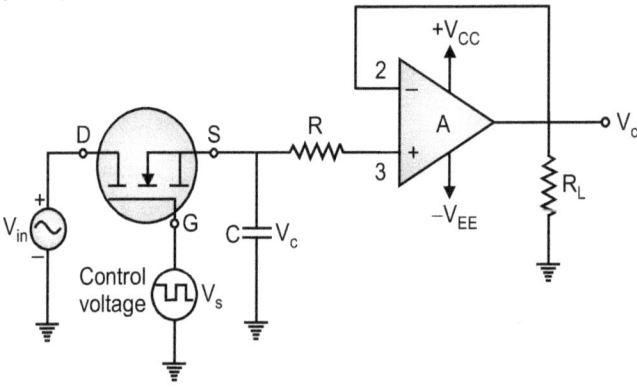

Fig. 5.8 (a) : Sample and hold circuit

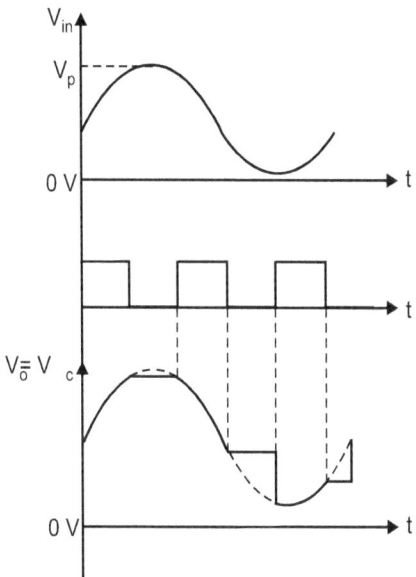

Fig. 5.8 (b) : Input and output waveforms of sample and hold circuit

Here E-MOSFET acts as a switch which is controlled by the sample and hold control voltage. V_S and the capacitor C serves as a storage element. The analog signal V_{in} to be sampled is applied to the drain and sample-and-hold control voltage V_S is applied to the gate of the E-MOSFET.

During the positive portion of V_S, the E-MOSFET conducts and acts as a closed switch. This charges the capacitor C.

On the other hand, when V_S is zero, the E-MOSFET is OFF (non-conductive) and acts as an open switch. The only discharge path for C is through the op-amp. However, the input resistance of the op-amp voltage follower is very high; hence the voltage across capacitor C is retained. The time periods T_S of the sample and hold control voltage V_S during which the voltage across the capacitor is equal to the input voltage are called sample periods.

The time period T_H during which the voltage across the capacitor is constant are called hold periods.

The improved performance can be achieved by a specially designed sample-and-hold I_C such as LF 398.

5.2.3 Applications of Sample and Hold Circuits

1. Used in digital interfacing and communications.
2. Analog to digital interfacing.
3. Pulse modulation systems.

5.3 PHASE LOCKED LOOPS

Phase locked loop circuit is basically a closed loop system used to lock the output frequency and phase with that of input signal's frequency and phase. Evolution of the phase locked loop began in the early 1930's but with the rapid development of integrated-circuit technology, the phase locked loop has emerged as one of the fundamental building blocks in electronics technology. The phase locked loop principle is used in number of applications such as FM stereo decoders, motor speed controls, tracking filters, frequency synthesized transmitters and receivers, FM demodulators, frequency shift keying (FSK) decoders and a generation of local oscillator frequencies in TV and in FM tuners.

5.3.1 Basic Principle of Operation

Fig. 5.9 shows the Phase Locked Loop (PLL) in its basic form.

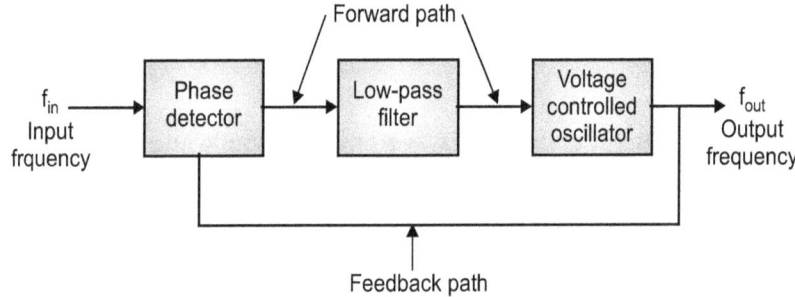

Fig. 5.9 : Block diagram of a phase locked loop

As shown in Fig. 5.9, the phase locked loop consists of (1) a phase detector, (2) a low pass filter, (3) a voltage controlled oscillator.

The phase detector or comparator compares the input frequency f_{IN} with the feedback frequency f_{OUT}. The output of the phase detector is proportional to the phase difference between f_{IN} and f_{OUT}. The output of phase detector is a DC voltage and therefore, it is called as **error voltage.** The output of the phase detector is then applied to the low-pass filter, which removes the high frequency noise and produces a DC level. This DC level is the input to the voltage-controlled oscillator (VCO). The filter also helps in establishing the dynamic characteristics of the PLL system. The output frequency of VCO is directly proportional to the input DC level.

The output frequency is compared with the input frequency and adjusted until it is equal to the input frequency.

The phase locked loop goes through the three states : free-running, capture and phase lock.

(1) Lock Range :

The range of frequencies over which the PLL can maintain lock with the incoming signal is called the lock range or tracking range of the PLL. It is usually expressed as a percentage of f_O, the VCO frequency.

(2) Capture Range :

The range of frequencies over which the PLL can acquire lock with an input signal is called the capture range. It is also expressed as a percentage of f_o.

(3) Pull-in-time :

The capture of the input signal does not take place as soon as the signal is applied, but it takes finite time. The total time taken by the PLL to establish a lock is called pull-in-time. This depends on the initial phase and frequency difference between the two signals as well as on the overall loop gain again and bandwidth of the low-pass filter.

5.3.2 Phase Detector

The phase detector compares the input frequency and the VCO frequency and generates a DC voltage that is proportional to the phase difference between the two frequencies. There are two types of phase detectors : (1) Analog phase detector, (2) Digital phase detector.

A double-balanced mixer is a classical example of an analog phase detector.

(1) Balanced Modulator Type Phase Detector :

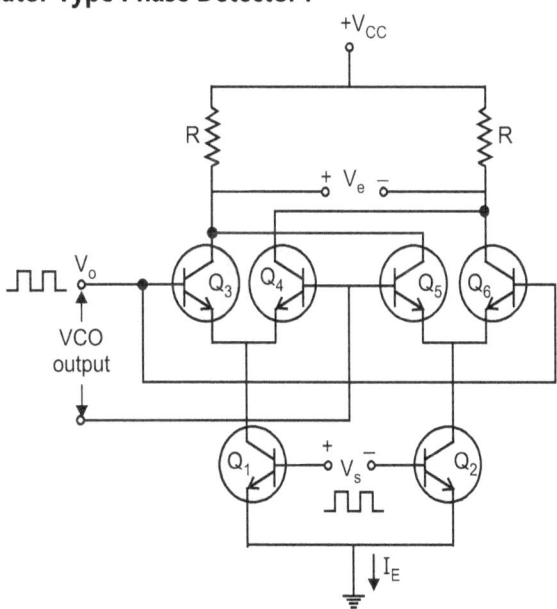

Fig. 5.10 (a) : Balanced modulator type phase detector

V_S	V_O	Q_1	Q_2	Q_3 Q_6	Q_4 Q_5	V_e
+ve	+ve	ON	OFF	ON	OFF	–ve
+ve	–ve	ON	OFF	OFF	ON	+ve
–ve	+ve	OFF	ON	ON	OFF	+ve
–ve	–ve	OFF	ON	OFF	ON	–ve

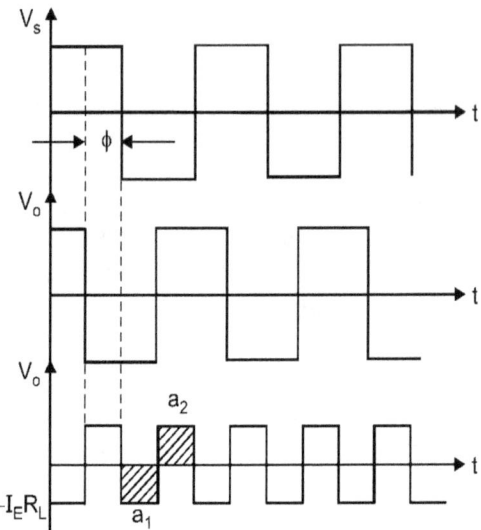

Fig. 5.10 (b) : Input-output waveforms

Fig. 5.10 (a) shows the circuit diagram for the balanced modulator used as a full wave switching phase detector. Here, the input signal is applied to the differential pair Q_1 and Q_2. The transistor pairs Q_3 - Q_4 and Q_5 - Q_6 act as a SPDT switches. These switches are controlled by the output signal from VCO. The amplitudes of VCO signal and input signal are kept such that transistors are driven into saturation and cut-off, so that they can act as a closed switch and open switch respectively.

When V_s is +ve, Q_1 is ON and Q_2 is OFF. When V_o is positive, Q_3 and Q_6 are ON and Q_4 and Q_5 are OFF. Obviously, when V_s is negative, Q_1 is OFF and Q_2 is ON. Similarly when V_o is negative, Q_3 and Q_6 are OFF and Q_4 and Q_5 are ON.

The output error voltage is given by

$$V_e = I_E R_L$$

The average value of the output voltage of the phase detector, V_e can be obtained as :

$$V_{e\ (average)} = \frac{1}{\pi}(a_1 + a_2)$$

$$V_{e\ (average)} = \frac{1}{\pi}\left[-I_E R_L (\pi - \phi) + I_E R_L (\phi)\right]$$

$$= \frac{I_E R_L}{\pi}\left[-\pi + \phi + \phi\right] = \frac{I_E R_L}{\pi}\left[-\pi + 2\phi\right]$$

$$= \frac{2 I_E R_L}{\pi}\left[\phi - \frac{\pi}{2}\right]$$

$$V_{e\ (average)} = \frac{4I_L R_L}{\pi}[\phi - \pi/2] \qquad \because I_E = 2I_L$$

$$V_{e\ (average)} = k\phi\ [\phi - \pi/2] \qquad \ldots (5.1)$$

where,
$$k\phi = \frac{4I_L R_L}{\pi}$$

where $k\phi$ is the phase angle to voltage transfer coefficient. It is the conversion ratio of the phase detector.

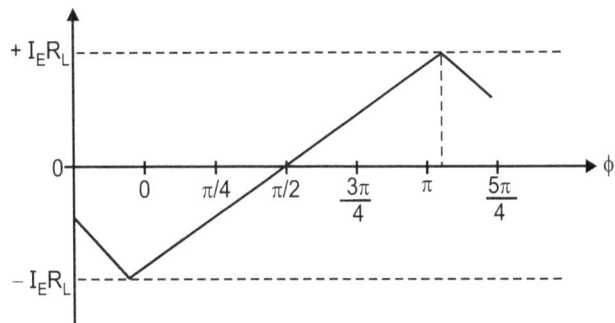

Fig. 5.10 (c) : Average output voltage versus phase difference

(2) On the other hand, examples of digital phase detectors are :
1. Exclusive-OR phase detector,
2. Edge-triggered phase detector,
3. Monolithic phase detector (such as type 4044).

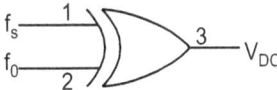

Fig. 5.11 : (a) Ex-OR gate phase detector

The Exclusive-OR gate can be used as a digital phase detector when both signals f_s and f_o are square waves. We know that the output of Exclusive-OR gate is high only when one of the input signal is high. Fig. 5.11 (b) shows the input and output waveforms for digital phase detector. Here f_s is leading f_o by ϕ degrees.

From Fig. 5.11 (c), when $\phi = 0$, $V_{dc} = 0$ and when $\phi = \pi$, $V_{dc} \approx V_{CC}$. The relationship between V_{dc} and phase difference ϕ is plotted. The slope of the curve gives the conversion ratio $k\phi$ of the phase detector. It is given by

$$k\phi = \frac{V_{CC}}{\pi} \qquad \ldots (5.2)$$

For $V_{CC} = 5$ V, $\quad k\phi = \dfrac{5}{\pi} = 1.591$ V/rad.

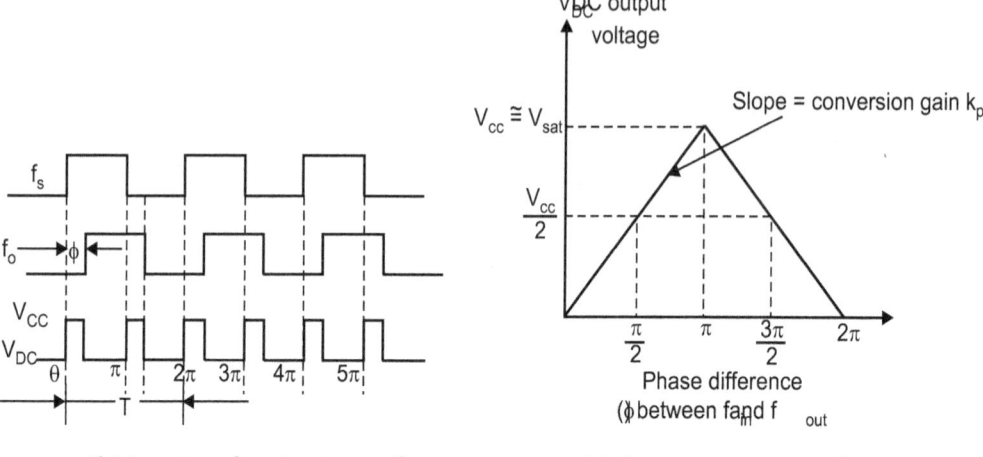

(b) Input and output waveforms

(c) Average output voltage versus phase difference between f_{IN} and f_{OUT} curve

Fig. 5.11

Phase Detector using RS Flip-Flop :

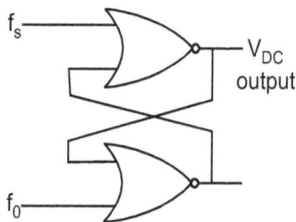

(a) NOR gate R-S flip-flop connection diagram

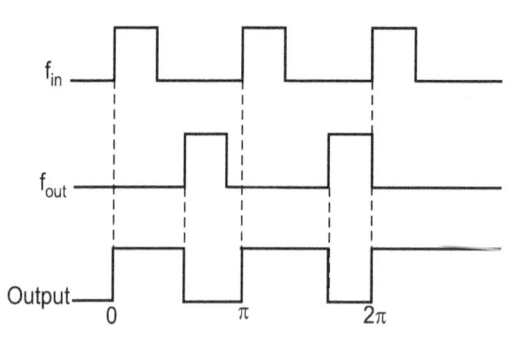

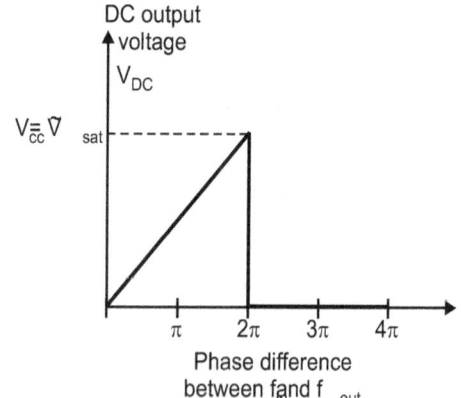

(b) Input and output waveforms

(c) DC output voltage versus phase difference between f_{IN} and f_{OUT}

Fig. 5.12 : Edge-triggered type of phase detector

Fig. 5.12 shows the digital phase detector using edge triggered flip-flop. This phase detector is used when f_s and f_o are both pulse waveforms with duty cycle less than 50%. The flip-flop consists of NOR gates and it changes its state at the positive going edge. The input signal f_s is connected to S input of the RS flip-flop and the output of VCO, f_o is connected to R input of RS flip-flop, therefore, at the rising edge of the input signal, output goes high and at the rising edge of the VCO output signal, output goes low.

Since, the duty cycle is less than 50%, the maximum ϕ can approach upto 360°. As a result, the DC output voltage is linear upto 360° compared to 180° in the case of Ex-OR gate detector. Thus, the phase detector using RS flip-flop has better capture tracking and locking characteristics than Ex-OR gate.

5.3.3 Transfer Characteristics of PLL

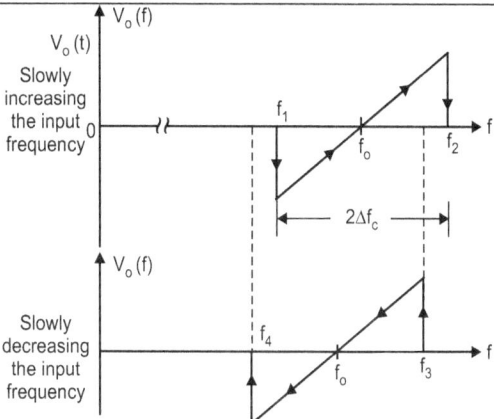

Fig. 5.13 : Transfer characteristics of PLL

As shown in Fig. 5.13, the vertical axis corresponds to loop error voltage V_o (t) and horizontal axis corresponds to frequency swift over a broad frequency range. From Fig. 6.36, we can observe that the input frequency is slowly increased. However, the PLL does not respond to the input frequency till it reaches a frequency f_1. The f_1 is the lower edge of the capture range. After this the PLL locks the input frequency. This causes the negative jump of the error voltage V_o (t) to shift the output frequency of VCO. At $f_s = f_o$, error voltage is zero. If the input frequency is increased still further the loop tracks the input until the input frequency reaches f_2 which corresponds to the upper edge of the lock range. After this frequency, the PLL loses the lock and the error voltage drops to zero and the V_{CO} frequency returns to its centre frequency or free running frequency. If the input frequency is reduced slowly back, the cycle repeats itself. This time the PLL recaptures the signal frequency at f_3 and tracks it down upto a frequency f_4. Thus, frequency f_3 corresponds to the upper edge of the capture range and frequency f_4 is the lower edge of lock range.

The frequency range between f_3 and f_1 is called capture range and frequency range between f_2 and f_4 is called lock range. The capture range is as large as lock range, but in general capture range is less than the lock range.

5.4 IC 565 PLL

Monolithic phase locked loops are introduced by signetics as SE/NE 560 series. The SE/NE 560, 561, 562, 564, 565 and 567 differ mainly in operating frequency range, power supply requirements and frequency and bandwidth adjustment ranges. SE/NE 565 is the most popular and commonly used phase locked loop IC in 560 series.

Fig. 5.15 shows the block diagram and connection diagram of the 565 PLL. It is available in 14-pin DIP package and as a 10-pin metal can package.

5.4.1 Electrical Characteristics of IC 565 PLL

1. Operating range : 0.001 Hz to 500 kHz.
2. Operating voltage range : ± 6 V to ± 12 V.
3. Input level required for tracking : 10 mV rms minimum to 3 V peak-to-peak maximum.
4. Input impedance : 10 kΩ typically.
5. Output sink current : – 1 mA typically.
6. Output source current : – 10 mA typically.
7. Drift in VCO centre frequency (f_{OUT}) with temperature : 300 ppm/°C typically.
8. Drift in VCO centre frequency with supply voltage : 1.5%/V maximum.
9. Triangular wave amplitude : Typically 2.4 V_{PP} at ± 6 V.
10. Square wave amplitude : Typically 5.4 V_{PP} at ± 6 V.
11. Bandwidth adjustment range : < ± 1 to > ± 60%.

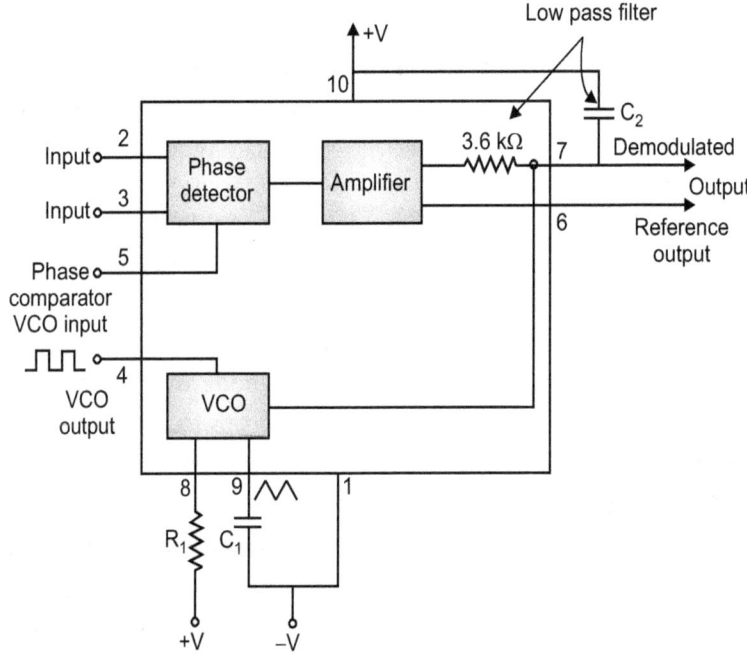

(a) NE/SE 565 PLL block diagram

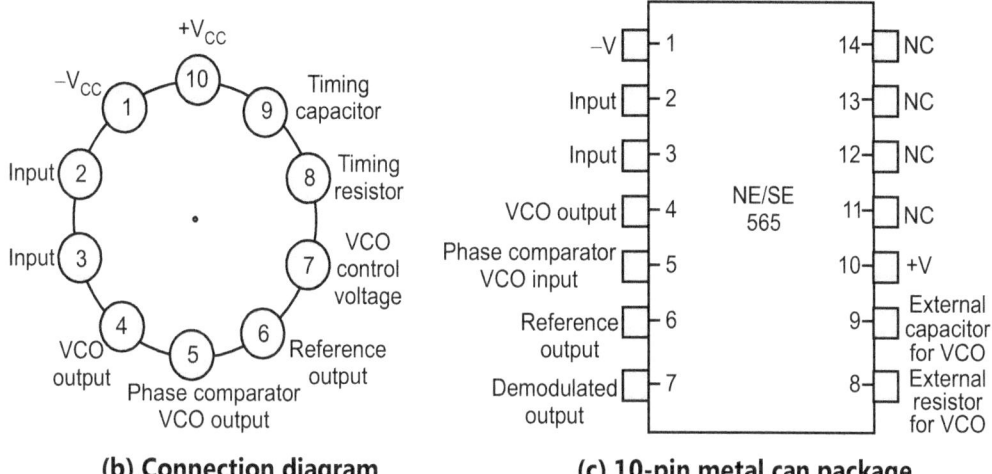

(b) Connection diagram   **(c) 10-pin metal can package**

Fig. 5.14

The centre frequency of the PLL is determined by the free-running frequency of the VCO, which is given by the equation

$$f_{OUT} \cong \frac{1.2}{4R_1 C_1} \text{ Hz}$$

where R_1 and C_1 are an external resistor and a capacitor connected to pins 8 and 9 respectively. A capacitor C_2 connected between pin 7 and the positive supply forms a first order low-pass filter with an internal resistance of 3.6 kΩ. The filter capacitor C_2 should be large enough to eliminate variations in the demodulated output voltage at pin 7 in order to stabilize the VCO frequency.

The 565 PLL can lock to and track an input signal over typically ± 60% bandwidth w.r.t. f_{OUT} as the centre frequency. The lock range f_L and capture range f_C of the PLL are given by the equations :

$$f_L = \pm \frac{8 f_{OUT}}{V} \text{ Hz} \qquad \text{... (5.3)}$$

where, f_{OUT} = Free running frequency of VCO (Hz)

$$V = (+V) - (-V) \text{ volts}$$

and

$$f_C = \pm \left[\frac{f_L}{(2\pi)(3.6)(10^3)(C_2)} \right]^{1/2} \qquad \text{... (5.4)}$$

The lock range usually increases with an increase in input voltage but decreases with an increase in supply voltages.

Example 5.1 :

For the circuit diagram as shown in Fig. 5.15 (a) determine the free running frequency f_{OUT}, the lock range f_L and the capture range f_C.

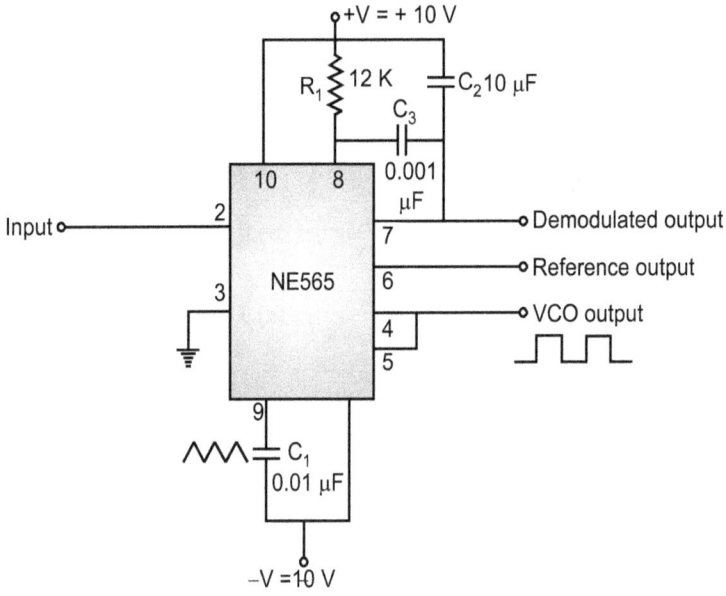

(a) Circuit diagram for example

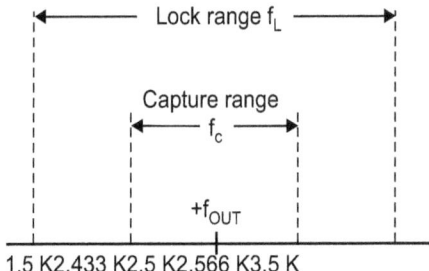

(b) Relation between f_{OUT}, f_L and f_C

Fig. 5.15

$$f_{OUT} = \frac{1.2}{4R_1C_1}$$

$$= \frac{1.2}{4 \times 12 \times 10^3 \times 0.01 \times 10^{-6}} = 2.5 \text{ kHz}$$

$$f_L = \pm \frac{8 f_o}{V}$$

$$V = (+V) - (-V)$$

$$= 10 - (-10) = 20 \text{ V}$$

$$f_L = \frac{\pm 8\,(2.5) \times 10^3}{20} = \pm 1 \text{ kHz}$$

$$f_C = \pm \left[\frac{f_L}{2\pi \times 3.6 \times 10^3 \times C_2} \right]^{1/2}$$

$$= \pm \left[\frac{1 \times 10^3}{2\pi \times 3.6 \times 10^3 \times 10 \times 10^{-6}} \right]$$

$$= \pm 66.49 \text{ Hz}$$

Example 5.2 :

Design a PLL circuit using 565 IC to get free running frequency = 4.5 kHz.

Lock range = 2 kHz

Capture range = 100 Hz

Assume supply voltages of ± 10 V are available.

Solution :

$$f_{OUT} = \frac{1.2}{4R_1C_1}$$

Assume $C_1 = 0.01\,\mu F$ and $f_{OUT} = 4.5 \text{ kHz}$

$$R_1 = \frac{1.2}{4 \times 0.01 \times 10^{-6} \times 4.5 \times 10^3}$$

$$R_1 = 6.67 \text{ k}\Omega$$

Capture range is given as

$$f_C = \pm \left[\frac{f_L}{2\pi \times 3.6 \times 10^3 \times C_2} \right]^{1/2}$$

$$100 \text{ Hz} = \pm \left[\frac{2 \times 10^3}{2\pi \times 3.6 \times 10^3 \times C_2} \right]^{1/2}$$

Squaring both sides,

$$(100)^2 = \pm \left[\frac{2 \times 10^3}{2\pi \times 3.6 \times 10^3 \times C_2} \right]$$

$$C_2 = \pm \left[\frac{2 \times 10^3}{2\pi \times 3.6 \times 10^3 \times 100 \times 100} \right]$$

$$C_2 = \pm 8.84 \,\mu F$$

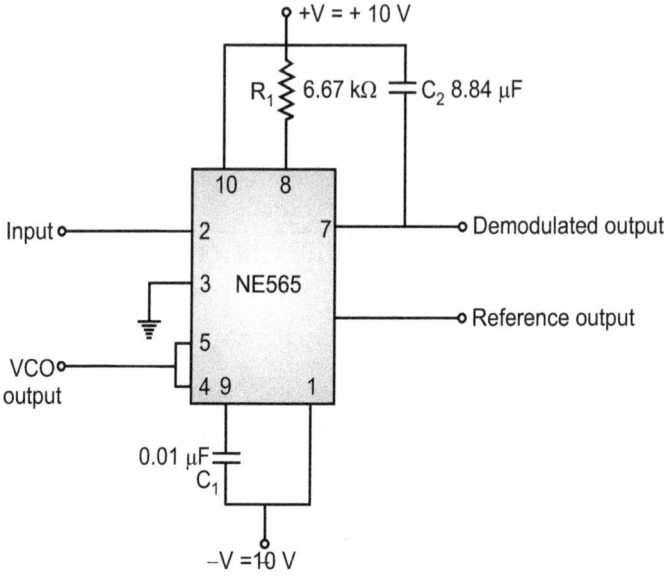

Fig. 5.16

5.6 APPLICATIONS OF IC 565 PLL

1. Frequency Multiplier :

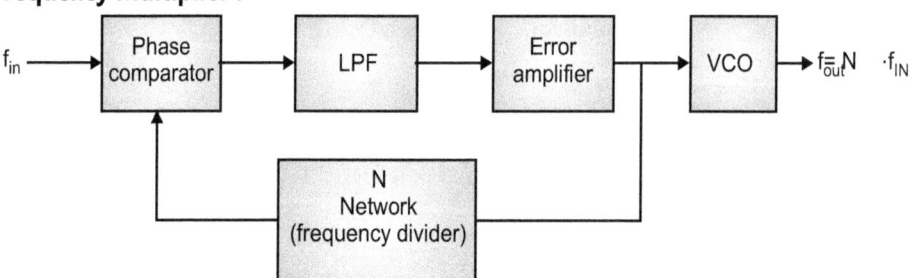

Fig. 5.17 : Block diagram of frequency multiplier using IC 565 PLL

Fig. 5.17 shows the block diagram for a frequency multiplier using PLL 565. Here a divided by N network is inserted between the VCO output (pin 4) and the phase comparator input (pin 5). Since, the output of the divider is locked to the input frequency f_{IN}, the VCO is actually running at a multiple of the input frequency. Therefore, in the locked state, the VCO output frequency f_O is given by

$$f_{OUT} = N \cdot f_{IN} \qquad \ldots (5.5)$$

By selecting proper divided by N network, we can obtain the desired amount of multiplication.

2. PLL as a Frequency Synthesizer :

The PLL can be used as a frequency synthesizer which produces a series of frequencies derived from a stable crystal oscillator. Fig. 5.19 shows the block diagram of a frequency synthesizer.

It is similar to the frequency multiplier with a additional divided by M network that is added at the input of phase locked loop. The frequency of crystal oscillator is divided by an integer M to produce a frequency f_{osc}/M, where f_{osc} is the frequency of the crystal oscillator.

Similarly the VCO frequency is divided by a factor N to give frequency equal to f_{VCO}/N.

When the PLL is in lock condition, the input frequency which is f_{osc}/M and the output frequency i.e. f_{VCO}/N must be equal.

i.e. $\qquad f_{osc}/M = f_{VCO}/N$

So, $\qquad f_{VCO} = \left(\dfrac{N}{M}\right) f_{osc}$

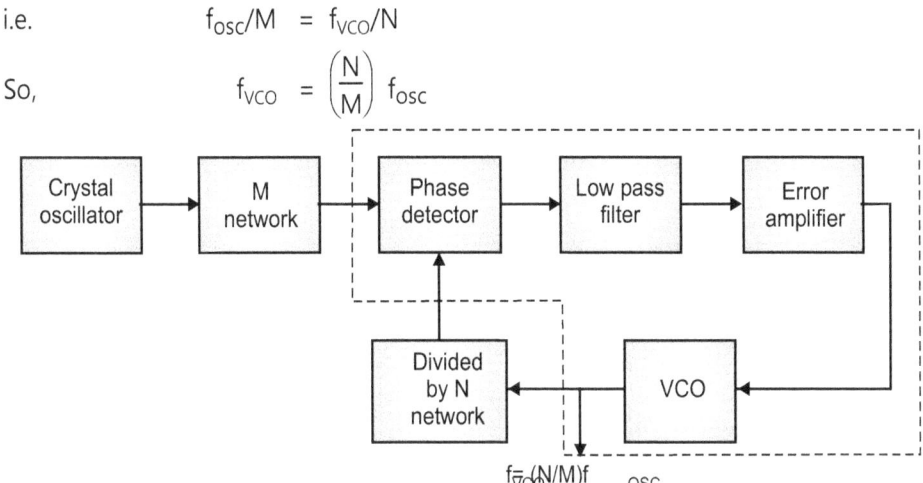

Fig. 5.18 : Block diagram of frequency synthesizer

By selecting the counter values to desired value, a number of frequencies can be generated from a single crystal oscillator.

3. PLL as a FM Demodulator :

Another application of PLL is in FM demodulation. PLL can be used as a FM demodulator. Fig. 5.19 shows the block diagram of PLL used as a FM demodulator.

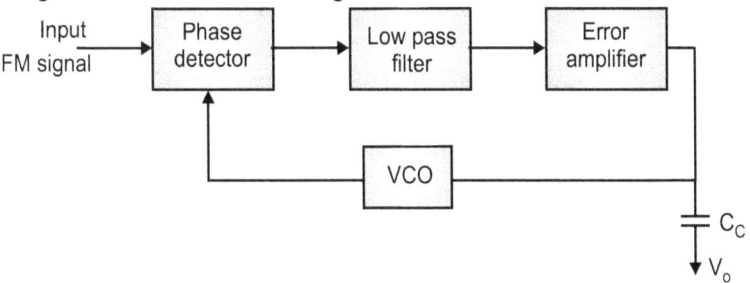

Fig. 5.19 : PLL used as FM demodulator

When the PLL is locked to input FM signal, then the VCO frequency follows the instantaneous frequency of the FM signal and the error voltage or VCO control voltage is proportional to the deviation of the input frequency from the centre frequency. Therefore, the AC component of error signal is the true replica of the modulating signal voltage. The faithfulness of the modulating signal voltage depends upon the linearity between the instantaneous frequency deviation and the control voltage of VCO. To obtain faithfulness of the modulating signal the FM frequency deviation and the modulation frequency must be in the lock range of the PLL. If the product of the modulation frequency f_m and the frequency deviation exceeds the $(\Delta f_c)^2$, the VCO will not be able to follow the instantaneous frequency variations of the FM signal.

4. Coherent Demodulation by a PLL

The noise performance of coherent demodulators is much better than that of their non-coherent counterparts. A circuit configuration which is suitable for coherent PM, FM, and AM demodulation is shown in Fig. 5.20.

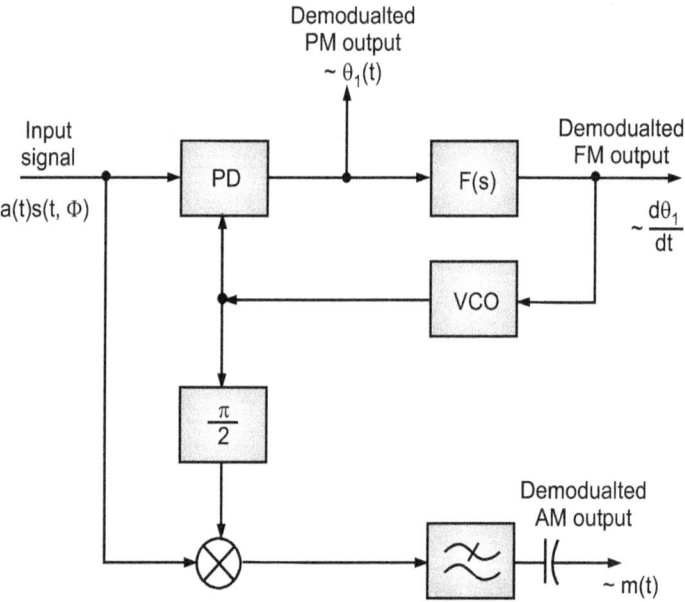

Fig. 5.20 : Coherent PM, FM and AM demodulation by APLL

PM Demodulator :

Assume first that the input signal s (t, ϕ) is phase modulated and a(t) = A = constant. The demodulated PM signal appears at the output of the phase detector.

$$V_d(s) = [1 - H(s)] AD_d \Theta_i(s)$$

where £i(s) denotes the input PM and AKd is the gain of the PM demodulator. The demodulated PM signal is multiplied by the closed-loop error function which has a high-pass characteristic. Distortion is avoided if the closed-loop bandwidth is less than the lowest modulation frequency. The other source of distortion is the PD non-linearity. This type of distortion does not appear if the total variance of the phase error given by remains small enough, that is, if the phase error remains in the close neighbourhood of its steady-state value during the operation.

FM Demodulator :

Assume that a frequency modulated input signal is applied to the PLL input. Due to the phase-locked condition, the CVO frequency follows the income frequency. Since the instantaneous VCO frequency is voltage. By means of the transfer function concept, the demodulated signal is obtained

$$V_e(s) = H(s)\frac{1}{K_v}s\Theta_i(s)$$

where $1/K_v$ is the gain of FM demodulator. This equation shows that the FM demodulator output that is, the VCO control voltage, is proportional to the input FM if the closed-loop bandwidth exceeds the highest modulation frequency.

The distortion caused by the PD non-linearity is reduced by feedback, consequently, the PD distortion is not critical. However, the VCO transfer function must be linear in order to get and FM demodulator with low distortion.

AM Demodulator :

Let the input signal be amplitude modulated

$$x(t) = [1 + m(t)]\sqrt{2}A \sin(\omega_I + \theta_{i0}) \qquad ...(5.6)$$

where m(t) carries the information, and A, ω_I and θ_{i0} are constants. The PLL demodulator contains a carrier recovery circuit (see the PLL in Fig. 5.14) and an AM demodulator (see the analog multiplier and low-pass filter in Fig. 5.14. Since the PLL needs an input signal to be tracked continuously, the spectrum of the AM signal must contain a carrier component.

The carrier is recovered by the PLL, its VCO output is

$$R(t, \Phi) = \sqrt{2}V_o \cos(\omega_I t + \theta_{i0}) \qquad ...(5.7)$$

This signal is multiplied by the AM input signal. The low-pass filter selects the difference frequency output of multiplier and the DC blocking capacitor removes its DC component. The demodulated signal is obtained from equations (5.6) and (5.7)

$$AV_o m(t)$$

where AV_o is the gain of the AM demodulator.

EXERCISE

1. Explain the following with reference to DAC :
   (i) Resolution
   (ii) Linearity
   (iii) Accuracy
   (iv) Settling time.
2. Write a note on R-2R ladder network.
3. Explain the binary weighted resistor technique of D/A conversion.
4. For the R-2R ladder 4 bit type DAC, find the output voltage and resolution if digital input is 1111. Assume V_R 10 V and $R = R_F = 10$ K.
5. Explain the working of successive approximation ADC.
6. With a neat circuit diagram explain the working of a dual slope analog to digital converter mentioning its uses.
7. Write an explanatory note on flash type A/D converter.
8. Sketch the sample and cold circuit and explain the principle of working.
9. Describe the principle of operation of PLL and show how this can be used for frequency multiplication. Sketch the diagram.
10. Describe a method of demodulating an FM signal using PLL.
11. Explain the working of PLL with block diagram. Mention its applications.

www.ingramcontent.com/pod-product-compliance
Lightning Source LLC
Chambersburg PA
CBHW080422230426
43662CB00015B/2180